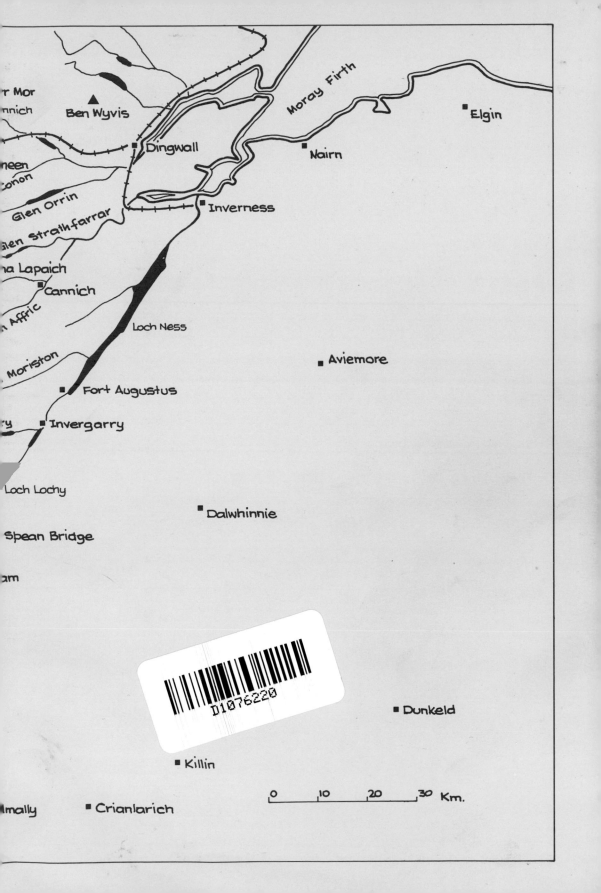

Scottish Mountaineering Club
District Guidebooks

THE NORTHWEST HIGHLANDS

Series Editor : D J BENNET

Non fiction Gift Aid
£

0 031140 024830

Published by
The Scottish Mountaineering Trust

THE
NORTHWEST HIGHLANDS

Donald Bennet
Tom Strang

Scottish Mountaineering Club District Guidebook

PUBLISHED BY THE SCOTTISH MOUNTAINEERING TRUST: 1990
© THE SCOTTISH MOUNTAINEERING TRUST

British Library Cataloguing in Publication Data
Bennet, Donald J. (Donald John) *1928–*
    The Northwest Highlands.
    1. Scotland. Northern Highland Region. Mountaineering
    I. Title II. Strang, Tom III. Scottish Mountaineering Trust
    796.522094115

    ISBN 0–907521–28–2

Front cover: The Five Sisters of Kintail. *D. J. Bennet*
Back cover: Suilven. *T. Strang*

Book design by Donald Bennet
Maps drawn by Jim Renny
Production by Peter Hodgkiss
Typeset by Newtext, Glasgow
Graphic work by Capital Scanning Studios, Edinburgh
Printed by Ivanhoe Printing, Musselburgh
Bound by Hunter and Foulis, Edinburgh

CONTENTS

MORVERN TO GLEN CARRON
Donald Bennet

APPLECROSS TO CAITHNESS
Tom Strang

ILLUSTRATIONS

Uncredited illustrations by D.J.Bennet

ACKNOWLEDGEMENTS

In writing this guidebook the authors have been assisted by many fellow climbers. In particular, thanks are due to Bill Murray and Peter Hodgkiss for their help in reading manuscripts and making corrections and suggestions for improvements, and to Scott Johnstone for making available his unrivalled knowledge of the Highlands. Jim Renny's maps are an invaluable feature of the book, and Noel Williams has contributed a description of the geology of the Northwest Highlands. Finally, the contributions of the many photographers who have made their pictures available for inclusion, and who are named elsewhere, is acknowledged with thanks.

THE CLIMBER AND THE MOUNTAIN ENVIRONMENT

With increasing numbers of walkers and climbers going to the Scottish hills, it is important that all of us who do so should recognise our responsibilities to those who live and work among the hills and glens, to our fellow climbers and to the mountain environment in which we find our pleasure and recreation.

The Scottish Mountaineering Club and Trust, who jointly produce this and other guidebooks, wish to impress on all who avail themselves of the information in these books that it is essential at all times to consider the sporting and proprietory rights of landowners and farmers. The description of a climbing, walking or skiing route in any of these books does not imply that a right of way exists, and it is the responsibility of all climbers to ascertain the position before setting out. In cases of doubt it is always best to enquire locally.

During the stalking and shooting seasons in particular, much harm can be done in deer forests and on grouse moors by people walking through them. Normally, the deer stalking season is from 1st July to 20th October, when stag shooting ends. Hinds may continue to be culled until 15th February. The grouse shooting season is from 12th August until 10th December. These are not merely sporting activities, but essential for the economy of many Highland estates. During these seasons, therefore, especial care should be taken to consult the local landowner, factor or keeper before taking to the hills.

Climbers and hillwalkers are recommended to consult the book HEADING FOR THE SCOTTISH HILLS, published by the Scottish Mountaineering Trust on behalf of the Mountaineering Council of Scotland and the Scottish Landowners Federation,which gives the names and addresses of factors and keepers who may be contacted for information regarding access to the hills.

It is also important to avoid disturbance to sheep, particularly during the lambing season between March and May. Dogs should not be taken onto the hills at this season, and at all times should be kept under close control.

Always try to follow a path or track through cultivated land and forests, and avoid causing damage to fences, dykes and gates by climbing over them carelessly. Do not leave litter anywhere except in your rucksack.

The increasing number of walkers and climbers on the hills is leading to increased, and in some cases very serious and unsightly erosion of footpaths and hillsides. Some of the revenue from the sale of this and other SMC guidebooks is used by the Trust to assist financially the work being carried out to repair and maintain hill paths in Scotland. However, it is important for all of us to recognise our responsibility to minimise the erosive effect of our passage over the hills so that the enjoyment of future climbers shall not be spoiled by landscape damage caused by ourselves.

As a general rule, where a path exists walkers should follow it and even where it is is wet and muddy should avoid walking along its edges, thereby extending erosion sideways. Do not take short-cuts at the corners of zig-zag paths. Remember that the worst effects of erosion are likely to be caused during or soon after prolonged wet weather when the ground is soft and waterlogged. A route on a stony or rocky hillside is likely to cause less erosion than on a grassy one at such times.

The proliferation of cairns on ths hills detracts from the feeling of wildness, and may be confusing rather than helpful as regards route-finding. The indiscriminate building of cairns on the hills is therefore to be discouraged.

Climbers are reminded that they should not drive along private estate roads without permission, and when parking their cars should avoid blocking access to private roads and land, and should avoid causing any hazard to other road users.

Finally, the Scottish Mountaineering Club and Trust can accept no liability for damage to property nor for personal injury resulting from the use of any route described in their publications.

The Scottish Mountaineering Trust will donate £1 from the proceeds of the sale of each copy of this guidebook to grant aid for repair and maintenance of mountain footpaths in Scotland.

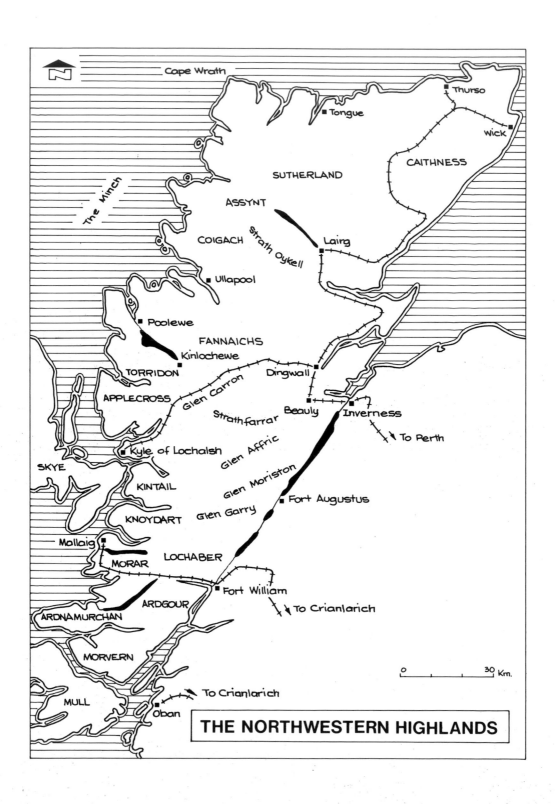

THE NORTHWESTERN HIGHLANDS

Introduction

The area described in this guidebook under the title The Northwest Highlands is the entire Scottish mainland to the west and north of the Great Glen, thereby combining the contents of the two former District Guidebooks, *The Western Highlands* and *The Northern Highlands*.

This is a massive part of the Scottish Highlands. It extends from the southern tip of Morvern, Rubha an Ridire, to the far northern points of Cape Wrath and Dunnet Head, and includes almost the entire western seaboard of the Highlands. This combination of mountains and sea gives to the Northwest Highlands (and to some of the nearby Hebridean islands) a character which is quite distinct from the mountains of the Central, Southern or Eastern Highlands. Quite apart from the climatic influence of the sea and the mild Gulf Stream which produces much more rain and a milder climate in the west than further east, the sea and the long, narrow sea-lochs which penetrate far into the mountains are important geographical features. The combination of mountain and glen, sea and loch, produce in the Northwest Highlands a landscape which is unique in Britain, and with the exception of the west coast of Norway, with which this area has much in common, it is unique in Europe.

The Northwest is also the wildest and most rugged part of the Highlands; vast tracts of it are remote from roads and human habitation and the walker and climber in these mountains can experience a sense of solitude and isolation as in few other parts of the country. This north-west part of Scotland has gained the reputation of containing in its remotest areas the last remaining wilderness in Western Europe. This comment may well be an exaggeration, but it certainly conveys the character and quality of the land as we see it today.

However, the landscape that we see today is not the same as the landscape of three or four centuries ago. Then the clan system still flourished, men and women lived in the glens and had their summer shielings high in the mountain corries. The great Caledonian Forest still covered much of the Highlands, although it was already being destroyed to provide wood and charcoal for the iron-smelting industries of the south. The break-up of the clan system followed the abortive Jacobite Rising of 1745. The harassment of the Highlanders by Hanoverian troops started the mass exodus from the glens that half a century later gained momentum in the Clearances that drove tens of thousands of Highland people from their homes and glens to make way for sheep. Famine in the following decades accelerated the emigration from the Highlands; the destruction of the Caledonian Forest was all but complete, and the shoals of herring disappeared from the western seas and sea-lochs. The 19th century was a succession of disasters for the people of north-west Scotland; only the sheep and their owners prospered.

We who now look on this land and landscape see the aftermath of these centuries of exploitation and neglect. The hills are bare of their native pine forests; the remote glens are empty, their cottages ruined and the high shielings no more than piles of stones in the heather. It is a sobering thought to look at the remains of the houses at Carnoch at the head of Loch Nevis and reflect that once several families lived there with enough able-bodied men (so it is said) to field a shinty team. Now the fields, once dug and drained, are overgrown by rank grass and reeds, and the little walled gardens beside the ruined houses are smothered by nettles. We may take pride in the accolade given to the Northwest Highlands as one of the finest wilderness areas of Europe, worthy of conservation, but we must also regret that this wilderness has been created as a result of the hardship and cruelty which forced many Highlanders away from their native land, leaving it to be taken over by sheep and red deer.

Recent decades have seen the emergence of new industries in the Northwest Highlands to supplement traditional crofting and inshore fishing. The generation of hydro-electric power has transformed many of the glens and brought a better standard of living to remote communities. Forestry seems to have covered the hillsides with great expanses of dark coniferous trees, and most recently the fish farming industry has taken up residence in nearly every sea-loch along the western coast, and many an inland loch as well. For a few years the oil construction industry flourished in Loch Kishorn, but its stay was short-lived. Unfortunately, although these industries have been important employers and have helped to stem the tide of depopulation, they have been the target of opposition from conservationists and environmentalists: hydro-electric power schemes have ruined the glens, forests cover the hills with dark geometric masses of impenetrable trees and fish farming pollutes the lochs; so say the critics. Tourism remains the mainstay of the West Highland economy, and for many the mountains are the magnet that draws them back to this land year after year.

THE LAND AND THE MOUNTAINS

A glance at the map shows the principal geographical features of the Northwest Highlands. It is a great wedge of land shaped like an arrowhead pointing south-west at Mull. The southern half of the area, from Morvern northwards to the latitude of Inverness is bounded on the east by the Great Glen and on the west by the much indented western seaboard. Between these bounds there is a series of parallel glens and lochs running from east to west, with well-defined ranges of mountains between them. The watershed which separates the eastward from the westward flowing rivers is in most cases quite close to the west coast, in some cases as close as five or six kilometres, so that there are many long straths draining to the Great Glen, and short steep glens dropping to the western seaboard.

To the north of a line from Inverness to Applecross this east-west orientation of the main glens is not so prominent. The main straths which carry the roads from Dingwall to points west and north seem to radiate outwards from the Cromarty and Dornoch firths: Strath Bran towards Kinlochewe, the Dirrie More towards Ullapool, Strath Oykel to Lochinver and Loch Shin towards Kinlochbervie.

The orientation of the main glens and straths is emphasised along the west coast where many long and narrow sea-lochs penetrate into the mountainous interior of the land. Loch Sunart, Loch Nevis, Loch Hourn, Loch Duich and Loch Torridon are surrounded by steep mountains, and they are the grandest examples in Scotland of the classic combination of sea, loch and mountain landscape.

Far to the north, in the north-east corner of Scotland, is the low-lying country of east Sutherland and Caithness. This is not mountainous land, rather it is a vast tract of moorland, largely uninhabited except along the north and east coast. At its heart is the Flow Country, a great expanse of waterlogged peat bog studded with lochans forming the home for many birds, some of them rare and important among British and European species. This unique wilderness of wetland and wild birds has recently been threatened by the expansion of commercial forestry across its face.

With the exception of Caithness, east Sutherland and a narrow coastal strip along the eastern seaboard of Ross-shire, nearly the entire area of the Northwest Highlands is mountainous. In this large expanse of mountains it is possible to pick out some individual peaks and some groups which are of particular importance. In Ardgour, Garbh Bheinn is the outstanding mountain, not for its height but for its shape and position. For many it is the first of the north-western mountains to be met on the northward journey and it is a fine introduction to the greater peaks to come. Knoydart is one of the remotest and wildest parts of the Northwest Highlands, and its great mountains Sgurr na Ciche and Ladhar Bheinn have few equals. A short distance further north, Kintail is an area of classic mountain grandeur. The Five Sisters of Kintail and The Saddle are the principal peaks, and with the main road to Skye passing between them, they are both accessible and popular.

The highest mountains in the Northwest Highlands are situated around the upper reaches of Glen Affric and Glen Cannich. They are more massive and less starkly rocky than their western neighbours, having some of the character of the highest of the Grampians further south. Torridon is for many the epitome of Northwest Highland landscape and mountain character. Liathach, Beinn Eighe, Slioch and An Teallach are the peaks that give this district its great reputation among mountaineers. Further north in the north-west corner of Ross-shire and in

Liathach, the classic example of Torridonian mountain architecture

west Sutherland there is a unique landscape of isolated peaks, not high but of great character. From south to north, Morvern to Caithness, there is a wonderful variety of hills and mountains in this north-western part of Scotland.

MOUNTAINEERING

The splendid variety of hills and mountains in the Northwest Highlands is matched by the variety of hillwalking, cross-country walking, rock climbing, winter climbing and even ski-mountaineering that is possible within their bounds.

There is an almost unlimited selection of hills, mountains and cross-country paths for hillwalkers and backpackers. Many old drove roads and rights of way go through the glens and over passes, and in addition there are stalker's paths leading up many of the hills and corries. At the same time as some of these old paths are deteriorating due to lack of maintenance, new roads have been bulldozed up the glens and onto the hills in the interests of forestry, agriculture and stalking.

Once the paths and tracks are left behind, the climber is likely to find that the terrain of the Northwest Highlands is fairly rough; rocky in some places and boggy in others. It is quite an effort to keep up with Naismith's time-honoured formula which (in metric terms) is about four and a half kilometres per hour on the level, plus six hundred metres per hour (or ten metres per minute) going uphill.

There are many fine areas for rock and ice climbing, of which mention may be made of a few. Garbh Bheinn of Ardgour is well known for its excellent rock and fine climbs, and Ladhar Bheinn in Knoydart, though not noted for summer climbing, has good possibilities when its cliffs are ice-bound in winter. Much further north, the Applecross and Torridon mountains have a wealth of good rock climbing on Torridonian sandstone and Cambrian quartzite, and in recent years the winter potential of these mountains, such as Beinn Bhan, Fuar Tholl, Liathach and Beinn Eighe, has come to be realised. North of Loch Maree the wilderness of the Letterewe and Fisherfield forests gives possibly the best rock climbing in the Northwest Highlands on the cliffs of Carnmore Crag and Beinn Lair. The Fannaichs and the Beinn Dearg group on opposite sides of the Dirrie More have revealed some excellent winter mountaineering, and far to the north Foinaven and its subsidiary peaks have some fine crags. Finally, mention must be made of the great extent of sea-cliffs round the north-west coast, and in particular two sea-stacks, the Old Man of Stoer and Am Buachaille. However, this guidebook contains only brief information about the most noteworthy climbs, and detailed information should be sought from the Scottish Mountaineering Club's *Climbers Guide to The Northern Highlands* edited by G.Cohen, to be published in 1991.

SKI-MOUNTAINEERING

In general the mountains of the Northwest Highlands are too steep and rocky, and their climate is too mild, for them to be considered ideal for ski-mountaineering, but there are exceptions. The high rounded mountains of Glen Affric, Glen Cannich and Strath Farrar give excellent skiing, although the distances to them are rather long for short winter days. The mountains on the north side of Loch Cluanie are excellent for skiing when well snow-covered, and they have the advantage of accessibility. Moruisg, Fionn Bheinn and Ben Wyvis give good short tours, and the Fannaichs and Beinn Dearg groups can provide splendid long tours of a more serious nature. The vast tract of the Easter Ross hills, though lower, have some good ski mountains among the glens that converge into Strath Carron, but the driving distance to them from the south is rather long. Details of these and other ski-mountaineering tours can be found in the Scottish Mountaineering Club's guidebook *Ski Mountaineering in Scotland*, edited by D.J.Bennet and W.Wallace.

TRANSPORT

Most climbers rely on their own cars to get to and from the mountains, but for those without cars the rather tenuous public transport services of north-west Scotland will have to suffice. These include rail, bus, postbus and ferry services, and an attempt has been made in this guidebook to indicate those services which are at present available. Inevitably these services and their timetables will change, and the information in this book will become out of date. The comprehensive guide published by the Highlands and Islands Development Board entitled *Getting Around the Highlands and Islands* contains timetables for all services in the area covered by this guidebook and is published each year. This guide is absolutely invaluable to anyone using public transport in the north-west of Scotland. It is available at stores, bookshops and tourist offices in the Highlands and can also be obtained from the Highlands and Islands Development Board, Bridge House, 27 Bank Street, Inverness IV1 1QR. (The price of the 1989-90 edition is £2.25).

ACCOMMODATION

With the continuing growth in the tourist business in the Highlands there is a wide choice of accommodation throughout the area covered by this guidebook, whether it be hotels, caravans cottages and hostels, or the simpler joys of wild camping and bothy dwelling. However, it should be borne in mind that many of the hostels and caravan sites and even some hotels are closed during winter. An indication is given in each chapter of this book of the accommodation available in each area, but detailed information is not possible. The publications of the Scottish Tourist Board give a comprehensive listing of different types of holiday accommodation under the title *Where to Stay in Scotland.* There are four such booklets describing hotels and guest houses, self-catering accommodation, camp and caravan sites and bed and breakfast accommodation. These books are available in bookshops and tourist information offices, or from the Scottish Tourist Board, 23 Ravelston Terrace, Edinburgh EH4 3EU. They may also be ordered by telephone, using a credit card, on Freephone 0800 833 993

The Scottish Youth Hostels Association has several hostels in the north-west of Scotland, and the relevant ones are noted in each chapter. There are also a few independent hostels (no membership required), and these are also mentioned. Wild camping is possible widely in the glens and on the mountains, but campers should bear in mind the law regarding camping and should seek permission if camping in the vicinity of farms, crofts and other habitation. (The relevant law is that it is an offence to camp or light a fire on private land without the landowner's permission).

There are in the Highlands many remote cottages, once occupied by shepherds and stalkers, but long since abandoned and fallen into disrepair. Many of these cottages have been renovated by, among others, the Mountain Bothies Association and with the landowners' permission these bothies are now available as simple shelters for climbers and walkers. These bothies are usually no more than four walls and a roof with the bare minimum of furniture inside, but they do provide dry spartan accommodation. They are not suitable for large parties, and during the stalking season they should not be used without the owners' permission. The cardinal bothy rule is that no damage should be caused to the building, nor any litter left in or near it.

Camban bothy at the head of Glen Affric

MAPS

No mountaineering guidebook can be used by itself, and it is assumed that the readers of this book will also have and be able to read suitable maps for hillwalking. The recommended maps are the Ordnance Survey 1:50,000 maps, of which the most recent edition is the Landranger Series. These maps have sufficient detail for the needs of hillwalkers except possibly on a few peaks, such as those in Torridon, where very careful navigation is needed on steep and rocky mountains. There is a very useful 1:25,000 Outdoor Leisure map for the Torridon Hills (with the Cuillin on the reverse side) published by the Ordnance Survey. There are 1:25,000 maps for all the Highlands which show very fine detail, but each one covers only a relatively small area of 20 x 10 kilometres.

The Bartholomew 1:100,000 maps are much less detailed than the 1:50,000 maps, and they are not particularly suitable for hillwalking, but they are quite adequate for those who walk in the glens and valleys, and their colour contouring enables them to give a good impression of the nature of the country at a glance.

The names and spellings used in this book are taken from the 1:50,000 maps except where the authors are convinced that an error has been made. Mountain and other heights are taken from Ordnance Survey 1:10,000 and 1:25,000 maps which are more up-to-date than the 1:50,000 maps in this respect. Thus there are many instances where heights quoted in this book do not agree with the 1:50,000 Landranger Series maps. In order to distinguish in the text between distances horizontally along the ground and heights of mountains, crags or climbs, the word *metres* is spelt in full to denote distances, and is abbreviated to *m* to denote heights.

The Landranger Series has been quite recently revised and most maps are up-to-date in their showing of features such as forests, tracks, paths and footbridges. There are, however, a few instances where newly planted forests are not shown, and walkers should be aware of this. There are also a few cases where the Ordnance Survey has not been able to keep up with changes in paths and tracks; the appearance of some and disappearance of others. Finally, there are instances where the existence of footbridges is incorrectly shown. For example, at the head of Loch Nevis two existing footbridges, which are vital if the streams are in spate, are not shown over the River Carnach and the Allt Coire na Ciche.

HYDRO-ELECTRIC POWER

Everyone travelling in the Northwest Highlands must be aware of the works of the North of Scotland Hydro-Electric Board, and no other part of Scotland has been so affected scenically by the hydro-electric developments of the last 50 years. The high rainfall of much of the area is one good reason for these developments, and most of the major glens have been tapped for their power. While these schemes may have their critics on the grounds of their spoiling the natural features and beauty of the glens, and some of the big dams when seen from below are certainly rather stark, on the whole the developments have been carried out with respect for the environment. With the passage of time the scars of former years have mellowed, and the benefits that have come to the local population have been considerable.

The Quoich-Garry scheme has involved the enlargement of the two major lochs in Glen Garry. The level of Loch Quoich has been raised to such an extent that a small cut-off dam has also been built at its western end to prevent the waters flooding westwards to Lochan nam Breac and the Carnach River. The Quoich Power Station has a power of 22MW, and the water flows from it into the enlarged Loch Garry, which now floods much of the glen and supplies Invergarry Power Station (20MW) which is situated near the outflow of the River Garry into Loch Oich.

To the north, the Great Glen scheme has its major reservoir in Loch Cluanie, which is topped up by water from Loch Loyne just to its south. Water from Loch Cluanie flows to the Ceannacroc Power Station (20MW), and thirteen kilometres down Glen Moriston it is used again. The River Moriston is dammed below Dundreggan Lodge to form the small and narrow Dundreggan Reservoir, and deep underground below its dam is the Glenmoriston Power Station (36MW), from

Hydro-electric power; Loch Quoich benefits from Scotland's highest rainfall

which the water flows in a long underground tailrace to Loch Ness near Invermoriston. Livishie is another small scheme (15MW) which takes its supply from the hills north of Glen Moriston and tops up the Dundreggan Reservoir.

The Affric-Beauly scheme has as one of its main reservoirs the greatly enlarged Loch Mullardoch, whose waters flow to Loch Beinn a' Mheadhoin to keep that loch at a more or less constant level, thus avoiding an unsightly 'tide-mark' in beautiful Glen Affric. From Loch Beinn a' Mheadhoin the waters flow to the Fasnakyle Power Station (66MW) and join the River Glass. The other major reservoir of this scheme is Loch Monar at the head of Glen Strath Farrar, which is impounded just below Monar Lodge by a fine double-curvature dam. Deanie (38MW) and Culligran (24MW) power stations in Strath Farrar make use of the Loch Monar waters before they join the River Glass at Struy. Lower down Strath Glass two run-of-the-river power stations at Aigas (20MW) and Kilmorack (20MW) extract the last of the potential energy of the Affric and Strath Farrar waters before they reach the Beauly Firth.

Another large scheme further north is the Conon scheme which takes its waters from as far afield as Loch Vaich, Loch Glascarnoch, Loch Fannich and the Orrin Reservoir. There are three power stations at the west end of Loch Luichart: Achanalt (2.4MW) takes its water from the River Bran, Grudie Bridge (24MW) from Loch

Fannich and Mossford (24MW) from Loch Glascarnoch. The combined flow passes through the Luichart Power Station (34MW) and enters the River Conon at Scatwell. The waters from the Orrin Reservoir flow north to the Orrin Power Station (18MW) on the side of Loch Achonachie in Strath Conon. The combined flow from all these reservoirs finally pass from this loch through the Tor Achilty Power Station (15MW) to augment the River Conon.

The northernmost hydro-electric scheme is the Shin Scheme. A small power station high up Glen Cassley generates 10MW. At Lairg the low head Lairg Power Station (3.5MW) is situated just below the dam at the south end of Loch Shin, and several kilometres down the river the Shin Power Station generates 24MW.

Other very small schemes are at Loch Morar, where the large rainfall and catchment area compensate for the very low head, a mere 5m, to produce 750kW, Nostie Bridge (Lochalsh) where the high head and small catchment area produce 1.25MW, Kerry Falls near Gairloch (1.25MW) and Loch Dubh near Ullapool (1.2MW).

NATIONAL NATURE RESERVES

Within the Northwest Highlands there is a wide range of natural habitats containing a wealth of specimens covering the whole range of indigenous flora and fauna. Many of these which are of particular importance have been designated as National Nature Reserves. These reserves are considered to be of national or international importance for nature conservation, and the best examples in Britain of their particular features of interest. They represent an important part of our natural heritage. Visitors to Nature Reserves should familiarise themselves with local regulations as regards access.

The following is a list of Reserves in the Northwest Highlands:

Loch Sunart Woodlands. A natural oakwood at Ariundle in the Strontian Glen, and an ashwood at Glencripesdale on the south shore of Loch Sunart reached by a long walk from Liddesdale. (See paths and walks section in Chapter 1).

Claish Moss. A raised mire on the south side of Loch Shiel between Acharacle and Ben Resipol.

Allt nan Carnan. A one and a half kilometre stretch of thickly wooded gorge situated in bare moorland north-west of Lochcarron village. There is a considerable mixture of deciduous trees and a wealth of flora.

Rassal Ashwood. This reserve, situated near the head of Loch Kishorn,is one of the very few natural ashwoods in Scotland, and the most northerly in Britain.

Strathfarrar. The pinewoods in Glen Strath Farrar are the largest surviving fragment in the central group of native pinewoods of Scotland, and carry the largest area of mature fully stocked forest in Scotland after Abernethy and Ballochbuie.

Beinn Eighe. This reserve is situated a few kilometres north-west of Kinlochewe. It was the first National Nature Reserve to be declared in Britain, and was acquired primarily for the preservation and study of the fairly large remnant of the Caledonian pinewood. The slopes of Beinn Eighe are of great geological, physiographical and floristic interest. Pine martens are among the animals protected, and ptarmigan, Scottish crossbill and golden eagle breed on the reserve. The Coille na Glas-leitre Nature Trail on the hillside above Loch Maree gives an opportunity to see many of the features of this reserve.

Loch Maree Islands. This reserve comprises three major islands and about forty small islets. The chief interest is the native Scots pinewood which has an abundant shrub layer of well-grown juniper. A boat and a permit are required for access.

Ben Wyvis. The size, altitude and location of Ben Wyvis give it a distinctive ecological character, and it is also an outstanding locality for periglacial landforms created under severe frost conditions, both during and since the last Ice Age.

Corrieshalloch. This gorge on the south side of the Garve to Ullapool road near Braemore is a magnificent example of a box-canyon, formed by the cutting back of the Abhainn Droma through hard, horizontally disposed rocks. The plant communities are of interest.

Inverpolly. A wild, remote and uninhabited area of Coigach on whose eastern boundary is the classic geological locality of Knockan Cliff, which exposes a section of the Moine Thrust zone. Among the animals of the reserve are wildcats and pine martens.

Inchnadamph. The famous Allt nan Uamh Bone Caves contain Palaeolithic cave earths with a fauna of Pleistocene mammals and traces of occupation by early man.

Loch a' Mhuilin. This reserve is situated on the wild and isolated north-west coast, and the main interest lies in its woodland. The oak is of particular interest, being near its northern limit in Britain.

Gualin. This reserve in north-west Sutherland has outstanding examples of northern montane and bog plant communities. It extends from the quartzite ridges and spurs of Foinaven to Strath Dionard.

Invernaver. This reserve is situated at the mouth of the River Naver. It contains a wide variety of habitats including those on blown sand, and has the finest assemblage of boreal plant communities in the north of Scotland.

Strathy Bogs. This is one of the most interesting peatland sites in northern Scotland. Four areas of blanket bog form the best example of valley side flowes yet identified.

Blar nam Faoileag. This reserve in Caithness contains the largest area of least disturbed blanket bog in Britain, which is of major importance for breeding moorland birds, especially several species of wader and wildfowl.

The Nature Conservancy Council publish a *Directory of National Nature Reserves in Scotland.* The address of the North-west Region of the Council is Fraser Darling House, 9 Culduthel Road, Inverness IV2 4AG.

The eastern peaks of Beinn Eighe, part of the National Nature Reserve

WEATHER

The weather of the Northwest Highlands is even less reliable than that in other parts of the Scottish Highlands. The rainfall can vary considerably between the western seaboard where the annual average is about 125cm, and the mountainous interior where the annual average is about 300 to 400cm. Along the Great Glen the figure is about 125cm, and the east coast of Ross-shire and Sutherland is quite dry with a mere 60cm per year. Within the mountains themselves, the rainfall tends to decrease the further north one goes.

The wettest part of the Northwest Highlands is around Sgurr na Ciche in the area between Loch Nevis and Loch Quoich. There the average annual rainfall is about 400cm, and in 1961 the year's rainfall at the west end of Loch Quoich was 520cm.

As in most parts of the Highlands, May and June are the best months as regards the weather. They are also good months insofar that neither lambing nor stalking are in progress, and there are not likely to be any restrictions on going onto the hills. On the other hand, July and August , particularly the latter, have the reputation of being wet months.

The River Carnach near its outflow into Loch Nevis was a notoriously difficult and dangerous crossing in wet weather. The footbridge, swept away by the river in spate, was rebuilt in 1981

The foregoing remarks about rainfall should be coupled with a warning about river-crossing. After a spell of wet weather, possibly only a few hours of heavy rain, rivers and burns can rise alarmingly and a stream that in normal circumstances is easy and safe to cross by stepping stones or wading can become impossible, and any attempt to cross may be extremely dangerous. It must therefore be borne in mind that any route through the mountains involving a river-crossing where there is no bridge may be foiled by wet weather, and it may be necessary to make a long detour upstream to find a possible crossing place, or one may even have to retreat and wait for the floods to subside.

MOUNTAIN RESCUE

There are several mountain rescue posts and teams in the Northwest Highlands. However, the standard advice to anyone seeking assistance in the rescue of an injured climber , or the search for a missing one, is to contact the Police (telephone 999) who will set in motion a rescue or search operation and liase with mountain rescue teams.

DROVE ROADS AND RIGHTS OF WAY

Cattle droving was for three centuries an important part of Highland life and commerce. Every year, as summer drew towards its end, great herds of cattle fattened by long days of grazing on lush pastures started their long journey to the markets of the south. There was a great demand for cattle in southern Scotland and England, and the animals provided their own transport to the markets; thus droving was a natural way to export this valuable product of the Highlands. For the Highland drovers, also, it was a natural activity, relying on their ability to endure hardship in the open for day after day.

Thus it was that the drove roads came into existence as the trade routes along which flowed the endless herds of cattle each year. The northernmost routes started in Caithness and the Hebrides, and the cattle were driven to their first market at Muir of Ord where they were joined by the herds from Wester Ross coming through Strath Bran, Glen Cannich and Glen Affric. Further south the Skye cattle were forced to swim the narrows at Kyle Rhea before their journey through Glen Garry to reach the Great Glen and the crossing of the Corrieyairack Pass. Eventually all streams merged as the drove neared its destination at the Crieff tryst, or (after the middle of the 18th century) the Falkirk market. The trade reached its climax about the middle of the 19th century, but with the advent of steamer services and railways droving was finished by the end of that century.

Although droving has long since ended, the drove roads remain as rights of way and a valuable part of the social heritage of the Highlands. Other rights of way have come into existence for other reasons. They may have been traditional routes for Highlanders to and from their churches and burial grounds, and many rights of way are known as coffin routes. The cairns along them may mark the spots where the carriers rested from their heavy labour. Other rights of way came into existence simply as the usual route on foot between one village and the next. Had our Highland forebears been keen climbers, we might have had rights of way to the summits of our hills, but that is not the case.

The network of rights of way in the Highlands remain as a most valuable heritage. These are ways along which everyone has the right to walk, without obstruction, at any time of the year.

In many cases the original path or drove road may have disappeared through lack of use, but the right remains so long as once every 20 years (the prescriptive period) someone walks along it.

A public right of way is defined as a right of passage, open to the public, over private property by a route which is more or less well defined. Rights of way can be of three types: vehicular routes, drove roads and footpaths. Only the two latter categories are of much relevance in the rough terrain of the Northwest Highlands, and both confer right of passage for walkers. A drove road also confers a right of way on horseback, or leading a horse. It is generally considered that a pedal cyclist has the same rights as a pedestrian, but this has not been definitely established in law.

The essential elements of a right of way are that it should at some time in the past have been in continuous use for a period of not less than 20 years; that its use is a matter of right and not due to tolerance on the part of a landowner; that the right of way must connect two public places, or places to which the public habitually and legitimately resorts; and that it must follow a more or less well-defined route. It is not (at present) considered that mountain tops can be regarded as public places, and this would seem to be an important point, because if they were then many of our mountains could be considered to have rights of way to their summits. As regards the definition of a well-defined route, it is not necessary that there should be a visible track, rather that it should be established that the public has followed a more or less consistent line during the period in question. Minor deviations such as might be required following the raising of the level of a loch do not invalidate a right of way.

It is to be hoped, however, that walkers along rights of way will have regard for the legitimate interests of those who live in the country and earn their livelihood there.

For further information the reader is referred to the booklet *Rights of Way, A Guide to the Law in Scotland* published by the Scottish Rights of Way Society Limited, 1 Lutton Place, Edinburgh EH8 9PD.

The use of mountain bicycles is on the increase, both as a sport in itself and as a means of enabling hillwalkers and climbers to reach remote mountains more easily. There is also increasing evidence that the use of mountain bicycles causes quite considerable erosion of footpaths, particularly those which are wet and muddy. It is therefore the policy of the authors of this guidebook to recommend the use of bicycles only on 'hard' tracks such as forest roads and private estate roads following rights of way, where their use can cause only negligible damage. It should be borne in mind, however, that the legal position about cycling along a right of way is not clear. As stated earlier in this section, it is considered that a cyclist has the same right as a pedestrian, but this is not absolutely certain. It may be diplomatic, therefore, to seek permission before cycling along a private road.

CAVE EXPLORATION

Opportunities for this sport occur in three main areas, all in Sutherland.

Around Durness on the north coast the Smoo Cave is the largest and best-known. It figures in several local legends concerned with the supernatural. Further exploration has been done in the sea-caves at Balnakeil and further inland at Ach a' Chorrain.

At the east end of Loch Assynt the strip of Cambrian dolomite near Inchnadamph offers greater scope for investigation. The main area is along the course of the River Traligill and its tributaries, which are easily reached from Inchnadamph Hotel by a track up Gleann Dubh. The main cave, Cnoch nan Uamh at grid reference 276 206, forms part of a master cave system for the streams which flow underground from the Breabag plateau at the head of the glen. It is the largest of the Traligill caves, with three main entrances and 1400 metres of recorded passages.

Just over three kilometres to the south the course of the Allt nan Uamh has also been the site of worthwhile investigation, and further cave complexes have been discovered. It was there that the famous Bone Caves (grid reference 268 170) were found. They were first excavated in 1889 by Peach and Horne, and later in 1927 by Cree, Callander and Ritchie. They have long been regarded as the most northerly habitation of Palaeolithic Man in Britain and were found to contain relics of now extinct fauna. They are one of the most important Palaeolithic sites in the country. This area is now part of the Inchnadamph Nature Reserve, and comes under its regulations. Permission is required to visit the reserve in late summer and autumn, and should be sought from the Assynt Estates Office, Lochinver. (Telephone 05714 203).

The most southerly of the three main cave systems is at Knockan. The limestone area to the south of the villages of Knockan and Elphin is largely drained by the Abhainn a' Chnocain which flows underground at Uamh an Tartair (grid reference 217 092) above a dry watercourse. Two other pots, Uamh Poll Eoghainn (grid reference 205 094) and Tobhar na Glaise (grid reference 210 105), have also been investigated.

The Grampian Speliological Group are very active in the area of Knockan and Elphin, and are responsible for much of the current exploration there. For those seeking further information on the subject, their updated publication *The Caves of Assynt* is well worth reading. It gives details and maps of all caves in the area. The club has a field-hut at Knockan which is also a cave rescue post. Enquiries can be made to Mr A L Jeffries, 8 Scone Gardens, Edinburgh EH8 7DQ.

The Geology of the Northwest Highlands
by Noel Williams

The Northwest Highlands lie north and west of a major trough-like depression which cuts right across the Scottish mainland from Fort William to Inverness – the Great Glen. This remarkable physical feature has been formed by erosion along the line of an important geological structure, the Great Glen fault. The latter is a fundamental dislocation in the earth's crust which has been active intermittently over many hundreds of millions of years.

The Great Glen fault has a very complex history, and movement along it has probably occurred in different directions at different times. It was particularly active about 400-350 million years ago, during which time it is thought to have behaved as a tear fault i.e. with lateral displacement of the rocks on either side. Numerous comparatively small movements, each of which would have been associated with an earthquake, over time resulted in the Northwest Highlands slipping sideways many tens of kilometres relative to the rest of the country. Whether this was in a north-easterly or a south-westerly direction cannot be determined with any certainty. Similar movements take place at the present day along the San Andreas fault in California.

The huge forces associated with this fault activity pulverized the rocks along the plane of the fault, and shattered the rocks for a kilometre or so on either side. As a consequence the rocks along the fault have eroded preferentially to produce the Great Glen.

The Great Glen fault is the most important member of a set of south-west to north-east trending faults which fracture the rocks of the Highlands. Other members of this set which lie within the Northwest Highlands area include the Strathconon and Strath Glass faults. A lesser set of north-west to south-east trending faults includes one which passes through Kinloch Hourn and another which marks the hollow of Loch Maree.

The Moine Thrust

One of the fascinating aspects of the geology of the Northwest Highlands is the extraordinary contrast in the character of the mountains in the far north-west with those in the remainder of the area. The boundary between these two regions is marked by another major geological structure, the Moine Thrust, which extends in a south-south-westerly direction (i.e. roughly parallel to the western seaboard) from Whiten Head on the north coast, through Kinlochewe down to Loch Alsh on the west coast. From there it leaves the mainland and continues onto the Sleat peninsula of Skye.

A thrust is in effect a fault which is orientated at a low angle to the horizontal. The plane of the Moine Thrust slopes up gently towards the west-north-west. In fact the Moine Thrust itself is the highest and possibly oldest of a series of parallel thrusts which lie within a narrow belt of dislocated rocks known as the Moine Thrust zone. Movement took place along this zone towards the end of a major mountain building episode known as the Caledonian orogeny about 430 million years ago.

As a result of this movement, metamorphic rocks belonging to the Moine Series (see below) were pushed several tens of kilometres west-north-westwards up onto a varied sequence of Lewisian, Torridonian and Cambro-ordovician rocks which formed a more stable north-western 'foreland.' This resulted in older metamorphic rocks (Moine schists) being superimposed on younger sedimentary rocks (Cambro-ordovician quartzites and limestones). The thrust zone is very complex and numerous slices of the foreland rocks are present within it.

The discovery of the Moine Thrust in 1883 had a profound influence on geological thinking. The Assynt district was one of the first localities in the world where convincing evidence was found for large scale horizontal translation of huge sheets of rock. The Geological Survey memoir to the region, which was published in 1907, is widely regarded as one of the most important memoirs ever produced, though sadly it is now out of print.

The rocks south-east of the Moine Thrust suffered intense deformation and metamorphism during the Caledonian orogeny about 520-440 million years ago, but the rocks north-west of the Moine Thrust behaved as a stable block and were not affected by these events. The three distinctive rock groups which make up this foreland area are now described.

The Lewisian Complex

Rocks belonging to the Lewisian Complex formed the foundation or 'basement' upon which later rocks of the foreland were laid. The complex consists mainly of extremely old, metamorphic rocks generally referred to as banded gneisses. These are permeated by countless basic dykes, granite sheets and pegmatite veins which themselves have been metamorphosed to varying degrees. Two ancient metamorphic episodes can be recognised in these gneisses (Scourian 2900-2300 and Laxfordian 2300-1700 million years ago). The Outer Isles, which formed part of the foreland area, are themselves built almost entirely from rocks belonging to the Lewisian complex – hence the name.

Lewisian gneiss is widely distributed throughout the far north-west Highlands. Being crystalline and impervious it tends to form rugged, lochan-peppered moorland. It seldom forms much of the high ground, although Ben More Assynt and Ben Stack in Sutherland, and the hills around Carnmore by Fionn Loch, are notable exceptions. The rock is extremely rough and generally sound, and where it forms crags there is some superb climbing. A particularly fine crag is situated above the lodge at Carnmore. Lesser but more accessible crags occur by Diabeg in Torridon, near the western end of Loch Maree (the Tollie crags) and at Gruinard Bay.

The rocks of the Lewisian complex were deeply eroded before the next sequence of rocks was deposited.

Torridonian Sandstone

At least seven kilometres of sandstones and conglomerates, with lesser amounts of mudstone, were subsequently deposited on the very irregular land surface of Lewisian gneiss. Hills and valleys cut into the original land surface are still preserved where the mantle of Torridonian sandstone has remained intact. This buried relief (or 'fossil' land surface) is well revealed on the slopes of Slioch above Loch Maree.

The sedimentary deposits belonging to the Torridonian sandstone group were laid down some 1000-800 million years ago, probably under semi-arid conditions as extensive alluvial fans. Exotic pebbles found within these deposits suggest that some of the material at least was derived from south-eastern Greenland, which at that time lay along the Scottish area and formed part of an upland region. The rocks are too old to contain readily recognisable fossils, but microscopic fossils of primitive life forms have been extracted from some of the beds.

The extensive outcrops of Torridonian sandstone which occur throughout the foreland area are largely responsible for its unique character. The Torridonian sequence is the best exposed sedimentary formation in Britain, and being red in colour and evenly stratified it contrasts starkly with the contorted crystalline gneiss on which it rests. The extraordinary difference in character between these two rock types has been emphasised by erosion, and has produced some of the most dramatic mountain scenery in the country. The rock strata are mainly gently inclined or horizontal, and are cut by numerous vertical joints. They weather to produce terraced cliffs with steep chimneys and gullies, as well as rounded bastions and pinnacled ridges.

Suilven, though by no means the highest, is perhaps the best known and certainly one of the most spectacular of the peaks in the foreland area. It consists of an isolated remnant of flat-lying Torridonian sandstone resting on a platform of Lewisian gneiss. Among the other peaks of Torridonian sandstone situated north of Ullapool are Cul Beag, Stac Pollaidh and Ben Mor Coigach. Several other peaks in that area (notably Quinag, Canisp and Cul Mor), consist chiefly of Torridonian strata but have a capping of Cambrian quartzite (see below).

Further south near Dundonnell, mighty An Teallach is built largely of Torridonian sandstone. Around Torridon itself, Beinn Alligin is one of the many peaks built entirely from this rock, whilst Liathach and Beinn Eighe have minor and major caps of quartzite respectively. The Applecross hills are also carved from rocks of Torridonian age. There are not as many opportunities for long rock climbs on Torridonian sandstone as the quantity of exposed rock might suggest, some of the bigger faces tending to be broken up too frequently by terraces. Nevertheless some excellent climbing can be had on the more continuous buttresses. Care has to be exercised with loose blocks which lie on some of the ledges, and belays can sometimes be surprisingly scarce.

The Cioch Nose is a classic route on A'Chioch of Sgurr a'Chaorachain in Applecross, and in good winter conditions some fine ice routes can be found on the stupendous corrie walls of neighbouring Beinn Bhan. Good quality rock climbs have been put up on the Mainreachan Buttress of Fuar Tholl, and on other mountains such as Stac Pollaidh, Suilven and the Barrel Buttress of Quinag. Dozens of short routes have been pioneered recently on small crags at Ardmair near Ullapool.

Sea-stacks of Torridonian sandstone, such as the Old Man of Stoer, the Great Stack of Handa and Am Buachaille by Sandwood Bay, make unusual and adventurous climbs, whilst hundreds of short climbs have been recorded on the sea cliffs near Reiff.

Stac Pollaidh, a sandstone mountain in the last stages of erosion

Cambro-ordovician Sediments

Prior to the deposition of Cambro-ordovician sediments, considerable erosion and gentle folding affected the older rocks. Then about 570 million years ago the sea began to transgress across the land, and some 1500m of marine sandstones and limestones were laid down on an almost level platform of Lewisian and Torridonian rocks. The earlier Cambrian deposits consist mainly of siliceous sandstones called quartzites, including a distinctive type known as Pipe Rock. This is characterised by numerous vertical tubes or pipes up to a metre in length. The pipes are thought to represent the sand-filled burrows of organisms which lived in the sediment.

As time went by the sandy sediments gave way to limestones and dolomites of the Durness Group. These contain a very remarkable fossil fauna entirely unlike any other found in Britain. The dominant fossils are gastropods, though bivalves, brachiopods and a few trilobites are also found. These fossils can best be matched in North America, notably with the Beekmantown Limestone in Canada and north-west Newfoundland.

This is but one of many lines of evidence which now lead geologists to believe that the foreland area, which lies north-west of the Moine Thrust, must once have formed part of the large North American 'plate.' The head on collision between this plate and the remainder of Britain (which formed part of the European 'plate') resulted in the formation of the Caledonian Mountain Chain about 450 million years ago.

The Triple Buttress of Coire Mhic Fhearchair, Beinn Eighe, showing clearly the pale Cambrian Quartzite overlying dark Torridonian Sandstone

The base of the Cambrian strata dips to the south-east, which indicates that the present horizontal orientation of the Torridonian sandstone is fortuitous. The whole sequence must have been tilted south-eastwards after the deposition of the Cambro-ordovician sediments.

Only in a few cases is the greater part of a mountain composed of Cambrian quartzite, Foinaven and Arkle in the north of Sutherland being the best examples. There the quartzite rests directly on Lewisian gneiss. However, for the most part the quartzite forms a cap or top tier to what are largely Torridonian sandstone mountains.

The contrast between the light-coloured quartzite and the red-brown Torridonian strata is every bit as spectacular as that between the Torridonian and the underlying Lewisian gneiss. Even the untrained eye cannot fail to notice contacts between such distinctive rocks. One clear example of the junction between Torridonian sandstone and quartzite occurs on the Triple Buttress of Coire Mhic Fhearchair, Beinn Eighe.

Cambrian quartzite is a hard, well-jointed rock which breaks up readily into sharp-edged blocks. These rocks remain angular even after prolonged weathering and consequently are awkward to walk on. The rock is often badly shattered and some impressive scree slopes flank the ridges of Foinaven for example, but where crags of sounder rock occur there is very fine climbing, notably on Creag Urbhard (Foinaven) and Beinn Eighe.

The limestone and dolomite beds of the Durness group do not form any high ground of note, but in the far north around Durness village they contain some massive sea-caves. Further south in the Assynt district around Inchnadamph numerous stream caves offer sport for speleologists.

The Moine Series

The greater part of the Northwestern Highlands, which lies south-east of the Moine Thrust, consists of a broad belt of metamorphic rocks belonging to the Moine Series. These rocks originally accumulated as water laid sediments about 1200–1000 million years ago, but they were subsequently changed and deformed by more than one period of metamorphism. The final phase of metamorphism took place some 520–440 million years ago when two major plates (see above) collided with each other and formed the Caledonian mountains.

Prior to being eroded and fragmented, the Caledonian mountain chain ran along the eastern side of North America, across Ireland and Scotland, and up the western side of Scandinavia to Spitsbergen. The rocks belonging to the Moine series that we see today represent the exposed root of part of this enormous mountain chain.

The Moine rocks are structurally very complex, and it is extremely difficult to unravel the various episodes of deformation they have suffered. However, it is clear that they have been overturned into gigantic flat-lying folds called 'nappes', and dislocated by major thrusts and slides. In places this intense squeezing has also exposed the underlying Lewisian basement.

Two main types of metamorphic rocks can be recognised. The first type known as 'quartz-granulites' (or psammites), were originally sandy sediments, whilst the second type, called 'mica schists' (or pelites), were originally shales. Where the two types alternate rapidly they are described as 'striped schists.' In many places where the mica schists are permeated by granite-like material they have produced a rock known as 'gneiss.' Also intruded into the mica schists are broad white and pink veins of coarsely crystalline granite known as 'pegmatite.' Sizeable plates of flaky mica are sometimes conspicuous within these veins. Countless dykes and sheets, composed of various igneous rocks, have been injected throughout the area.

Larger igneous masses are also present within the Moine rocks, and although there are fewer of these than in the rocks of the Central Highlands and Cairngorms, they are more varied in character. Some of the older intrusions appear to predate, and hence were metamorphosed by, the Caledonian orogeny (e.g. the Carn Chuinneag granite), whilst others were formed after the main period of metamorphism had waned (e.g. the Strontian and Cluanie granites). Of particular interest is the Ben Loyal syenite – a more alkaline igneous rock than granite – which has weathered in the form of slabby buttresses and tors.

Mica schist is a notoriously vegetatious rock, and consequently it offers few worthwhile opportunities for rock climbing. Where Moine rocks have been altered to gneiss, or widely injected with pegmatite, or where bands of sounder quartzite occur, some good climbing can be found – such as on Garbh Bheinn of Ardgour.

Vegetatious cliffs often prove more interesting in winter, and this is certainly the case with Ladhar Bheinn for example, which has some fine snow and ice routes.

Old Red Sandstone

Of the deposits which were laid down following the Caledonian orogeny, the only ones well represented in the area are the conglomerates and flagstones of Old Red Sandstone age, which outcrop in the north-west. These rocks are only of minor mountaineering interest, since on the whole they form fairly featureless lowland – Morven in Caithness being the most significant summit.

However, the northern coastline between Holborn Head and Duncansby Head is extremely scenic, a number of climbs have been put up on the stacks and sea-cliffs there. Fossil fish are found at many localities from John O' Groats to the Black Isle, suggesting that these are freshwater deposits.

A narrow strip of much younger sedimentary rocks (of Jurassic age) outcrops between Brora and Helmsdale. A metre-thick seam of coal was worked at Brora for many years. Much further south around Lochaline, Jurassic rocks are overlain by an unusually pure sandstone (99.7 per cent silica) which is mined and crushed to make glass sand.

Tertiary

A spectacular episode of volcanic activity broke out along the west coast of Scotland in Tertiary times about 60 million years ago, when Greenland began to drift away from Britain and Europe. Much of this activity took place in the Inner Hebrides rather than the Northwest Highlands, but lavas from an enormous volcano on Mull poured over onto Morvern. A great volcanic centre also developed around the western end of the Ardnamurchan peninsula. The centre has since been deeply eroded, but its outline can readily be picked out from aerial photographs. It is built mainly of gabbro. Several small outcrops of this rock have produced quite a number of short climbs.

Quaternary

The final moulding of the Northwest Highlands was brought about mainly by the action of ice within the last million years or so. Tremendous quantities of rock were scooped out of the glens and corries. At times of maximum glaciation most of the country was covered by ice, but at other times the ice built up principally where precipitation was greatest i.e. over the western hills. Then large glaciers flowed eastwards towards the hollow of the Great Glen. Glacial moraines generally increase in thickness in an eastwards direction as a consequence.

Shorter glaciers spilled westwards to the coast, and gouged out deep fjords, including the deepest sea-loch in Europe – Loch Nevis. Nearby Loch Morar is the deepest freshwater loch in Britain, its floor being more than 300m below sea level at its deepest point. Only glacial debris blocks off its previous link with the sea at its south-west corner.

CHAPTER 1

Morvern, Sunart and Ardnamurchan

MAPS: Ordnance Survey   1:50,000   Sheets 40, 47 and 49
           Bartholomew   1:100,000   Sheets 47 and 50

PRINCIPAL HILLS

Sidhean na Raplaich	551m	636 517
Beinn na h-Uamha	464m	682 535
Beinn Iadain	571m	692 561
Beinn Mheadhoin	739m	799 514
Fuar Bheinn	766m	853 563
Creach Bheinn	853m	871 577
Beinn Resipol	845m	767 655
Ben Laga	512m	645 621
Ben Hiant	528m	537 632
Beinn na Seilg	342m	456 642

The southernmost district of mainland Scotland west of the Great Glen is Morvern. It is almost entirely surrounded by the sea, being joined to Ardgour only at its north-east corner where Glen Tarbert slices through the hills between Loch Linnhe and the head of Loch Sunart. The name Morvern is derived from *A'Mhorbhairn,* which means *the sea-gap,* and refers to the Sound of Mull which, with Loch Sunart and Loch Linnhe, forms the coastal perimeter of Morvern.

With the exception of its north-east corner, Morvern is not a mountainous land. For the most part it is high undulating moorland and rounded hills. The Forestry Commission own several large areas, and there are some extensive forests. Some of these, such as the Fiunary Forest north of Lochaline, are now mature and have been partly felled, and second rotation planting has started. Elsewhere, for example on the moors east of Gleann Geal, the plantings are more recent.

The principal village of Morvern is Lochaline on the Sound of Mull. The main road there (A884) leaves the A861 road at the head of Loch Sunart and more or less bisects Morvern on its way south-west through Gleann Geal. A minor road continues north-west from the village along the Sound of Mull to Drimnin. Another minor road leaves the A884 near Claggan and goes north-west along Loch Arienas to Kinloch at the head of Loch Teacuis, where a rough private road continues to Rahoy. The road along the north side of Morvern from Laudale to Glencripesdale is also private. Finally, there is the narrow B8043 road from Inversanda in the north-east corner of Morvern which goes south-west to Kingairloch and then west to join the A884. At one point along the side of Loch Linnhe this road is quite spectacular, with the hillside rising very steeply in red cliffs on one side and providing the home for a herd of wild goats, and the sea pounding against the retaining wall on the other. This road gives access to the most mountainous corner of Morvern.

Lochaline is just about the only place in Morvern where visitors is are likely to find accommodation and refreshment. It is not a particularly attractive village, but a car ferry to Mull sails from there so at times it is quite a busy place. Lochaline's main claim to fame is the sand mine whose tunnels run for a considerable distance underground, beneath the village. The sand is of a very pure quality, suitable for optical glass. It was first mined in 1939, and the deposits have been worked ever since then, providing Morvern with one of its main sources of employment, others being forestry and fish farming.

On the Loch Linnhe shore of Morvern, facing Lismore, there is a huge granite quarry at the foot of Glen Sanda. This spot is very remote, with no road access (the granite is shipped out in large bulk carriers), and the great scar on the hillside is only seen from Appin and Lismore.

Among several points of interest in Morvern that might be visited on an off-day, mention may be made of a few. Ardtornish Castle on a peninsula south-east of Loch Aline was the stronghold of the Lords of the Isles in the 14th and 15th centuries, and later of MacLean of Duart. Now little remains of this dark fortress. It can be reached by a private road along the east side of Loch Aline, or possibly by boat across the narrows at the mouth of the loch. Ardtornish Point, on which the castle stands, commands a fine view in both directions along the Sound of Mull. At the head of Loch Aline stands Kinlochaline Castle on a crag above the loch. This square keep was once the seat of the chiefs of Clan MacInnes, but it was stormed and burned by Cromwellian troops in the 17th century. It was restored in 1890, and anyone wishing to look inside the castle should enquire at the nearby cottage where the key is kept.

Not far up the River Aline are the cottages of Larachbeg where the folk from St Kilda were settled in 1930 after they left their native island. Some of the men worked in the Fiunary Forest nearby. The road from Claggan (one kilometre north of Larachbeg) to Kinloch is pleasantly quiet, and gives some good views of the north side of Sidhean na Raplaich. Just beyond the end of the public road one comes to the experimental deer farm at Kinloch funded by the Highlands and Islands Development Board. Three kilometres further along a private road, just beyond Rahoy, there is the dun of Rahoy, a vitrified fort on a wooded knoll overlooking the entrance to Loch Teacuis. The name Rahoy is derived from *rath thuaith,* meaning *north fort,* and the dun was excavated by Professor Childe in 1936-7. It is now rather overgrown, but perfectly recognisable.

On the opposite side of Loch Sunart from Morvern is the small district of Sunart. It is little more than a westward extension of Ardgour, and it is dominated by a single hill, Beinn Resipol. Despite its modest height, this hill is the most conspicuous landmark in this corner of the Highlands by virtue of its isolated position, surrounded on three sides by lochs and low-lying country. Strontian is the biggest village on the border between Ardgour and Sunart, and from there the A861 road goes west along the shore of Loch Sunart to Salen, and then north to Acharacle. A minor road goes north from Strontian over a high pass (342m) and descends to Loch Doilet and the small forestry village of Polloch in a very isolated situation near Loch Shiel.

Strontian is probably best known for the mines in the glen north of the village, and the road to Loch Doilet passes the largest of these mines which has recently been reopened, and there are now extensive workings. The mines originally dated from 1722 and were worked for lead until 1904, when they ceased production until the recent revival. In 1764 the mineral strontianite was first found in these mines, and from it the element strontium was discovered for the first time.

Elsewhere in Sunart there are fairly extensive forests in the north round Loch Doilet, in the south along Loch Sunart and in the west near Salen.

Ardnamurchan is the long peninsula which extends 28 kilometres west from Salen and Acharacle to the Point of Ardnamurchan, the westernmost tip of the British mainland. It is not a mountainous district, being for the most part rough undulating moorland which only in a few places rises high and steeply enough to form recognisable hills. The charm of Ardnamurchan lies in its remoteness (for it is reached by a narrow and twisting road) and in its fine coastline which in some places shows wild and rocky cliffs and in others placid sandy bays.

The eastern half of Ardnamurchan is composed of metamorphic rock, and the hills and moors are typical of the Highlands, rough and craggy. Further west, beyond Loch Mudle, the geology is quite different and so is the scenery. The rock is principally gabbro, the region having once been the site of a great volcano. The last vent of this volcano can be identified as a rather insignificant little knoll midway between Achnaha and Glendrian, six kilometres north-north-west of Kilchoan. This knoll is at the centre of a plain about four kilometres in diameter, and surrounded on all sides except one by low gabbro hills, the only gap in this ring being the valley of the Allt Sanna on the north-west. There is a good deal of bare rock in the western half of Ardnamurchan, and the hills, which are mostly grassy on their lower slopes, have gabbro outcrops on their crests and one or two of them have crags which are big enough to give some climbing.

Mingary Castle, one and a half kilometres south-east of Kilchoan, is a fine ruined keep on the cliff-edge above the Sound of Mull. Its origins in the 13th century are obscure, but for two or three centuries it was occupied by the MacIains of Ardnamurchan, close relatives of the Lords of the Isles. At the end of the 15th century King James IV visited the castle twice to receive the allegiance of the island chiefs, and a hundred years later the castle withstood a siege by Spanish soldiers, hence the name Port nam Spainteach for the little bay below the castle. In 1644 Colkitto MacDonald, in support of King Charles I and Montrose, took the castle from the Campbells who were then in occupation, and withstood a siege by Argyll's army. However, the Campbells regained possession and were in Mingary at the time of the 1745 rising.

ACCESS

The main route of access to the districts described in this chapter is by the Corran Ferry across Loch Linnhe, and from there along the A861 road to Strontian, Salen and Acharacle. These villages can also be reached from the north by the A861 road from Lochailort. The A884 road branches off the A861 at the head of Loch Sunart and goes to Lochaline, and the B8007 road branches off the A861 at Salen and goes to Portuairk at the western tip of Ardnamurchan.

PUBLIC TRANSPORT

Ferries: Corran Ferry (Highland Regional Council). Daily.
Lochaline to Fishnish (Caledonian MacBrayne). Mondays to Saturdays, and Sundays in summer only.
Tobermory to Kilchoan (Foot Passengers only). (Caledonian MacBrayne).Mondays to Saturdays.

Bus: Salen – Acharacle – Lochailort – Fort William. (Shiel Buses, Acharacle). Mondays to Fridays.
Ardgour – Strontian – Lochaline. (Shiel Buses, Acharacle). Mondays to Fridays.
Ardgour – Strontian – Kilchoan. (Shiel Buses, Acharacle). Mondays to Saturdays.

ACCOMMODATION

Hotels at Corran, Strontian, Salen, Acharacle, Kilchoan and Lochaline. Numerous bed and breakfasts, cottages and caravans to let. Camping and caravan sites at Strontian and Resipole (three kilometres east of Salen).

THE HILLS

Sidhean na Raplaich *(fairy hill of the screes)* (551m)

This is a very extensive hill, occupying many square kilometres of high moorland and forest to the north-west of Lochaline. The best view of it is from the north, from Loch Arienas or Kinlochteacuis, from where the size of the hill and the long basaltic escarpment that extends for several kilometres along its north-east side are obvious. There are extensive forests over the hill, some of which have been felled and some replanted,so access in the future may depend on the state of felling and planting.   The Landranger edition of the 1;50,000 Ordnance Survey map is at present misleading in its showing of some of the forested areas.

One route to Sidhean na Raplaich which is possible at present starts at a parking place beside the road a short distance east of the east end of Loch Doire nam Mart. Go south-west across a very rickety bridge and through a clearing towards a stone dyke, turn right and continue through a clearing across very rough ground with many hidden ditches. In a few hundred metres cross the Allt an Aoinidh Mhoir and climb west beside a fence along the north side of a block of forest to reach the open hillside one kilometre north-east of Sidhean na Raplaich. Grassy slopes lead easily to the top.

Beinn na h-Uamha *(hill of the cave)* (464m)

Despite its modest altitude, this hill is well worth climbing. It displays its volcanic origins by the horiontal strata of basaltic rock which are exposed along its flanks. The north face forms a very steep and impressive escarpment. The ascent starts from the road just east of Loch Doire nam Mart and goes north-east up a broad shoulder towards the west end of the summit table. Climb the steeper escarpment near its west end and traverse east along the nearly level ridge to the summit.

Beinn Iadain (571m)

This hill is rather inaccessible as there is an extensive area of hillside on the east of the Kinloch River which is fenced off for the experimental deer farm, and the ascent from the south-west is officially discouraged. It might be possible, however, to get permission to climb the hill from Kinloch. Alternatively, a much longer approach is necessary. For example, cycle up the track in Gleann Dubh as far as possible and climb the hill from the south-east.

Beinn Mheadhoin *(middle hill)* (739m)

This hill is much further north-east, overlooking Loch Linnhe opposite the north end of the island of Lismore. It has some fine corries on its north-east side overlooking Loch a' Choire and the policies of Kingairloch House, but on the south-west side there is featureless moorland above Gleann Geal.

The most direct ascent of Beinn Mheadhoin is up the prominent ridge rising to the south-west of the Old Mill in Corry. This leads directly to the summit. If the weather is fine, one should continue the traverse south-east along the ridge to the col at Lag a' Mhaim and descend to the head of Loch a' Choire by one of the spurs

Looking across the Lynn of Morvern from Lismore to the hills of Morvern. Creach Bheinn is the most prominent hill on the left

bounding Coire Reidh. (In view of the fact that the approach just described goes through the grounds of Kingairloch House, discretion is required and permission should be sought. The road along the north side of Loch a' Choire to Kingairloch House is private).

An alternative route starts from the B8043 road about one kilometre east of the outflow of Loch Uisge and goes up Coire Shalachain. Continue over the twin knolls of Meall na Greine and down slightly to the Bealach a' Choire Bhain to approach Beinn Mheadhoin up a broad ridge from the north-west, crossing a false summit and passing a tiny lochan a few hundred metres before reaching the summit.

Fuar Bheinn *(cold hill)* (766m)
Creach Bheinn *(bare windswept hill)* (853m)

These two hills are the highest points of a big horseshoe-shaped ridge which encloses Glen Galmadale to the north-east of Loch a' Choire. Other high points on the ridge are Beinn na Cille (652m) and Maol Odhar (794m). The complete traverse of the horseshoe is the best day's hillwalking in Morvern, and Camasnacroise at the foot of Glen Galmadale is the best starting and finishing point.

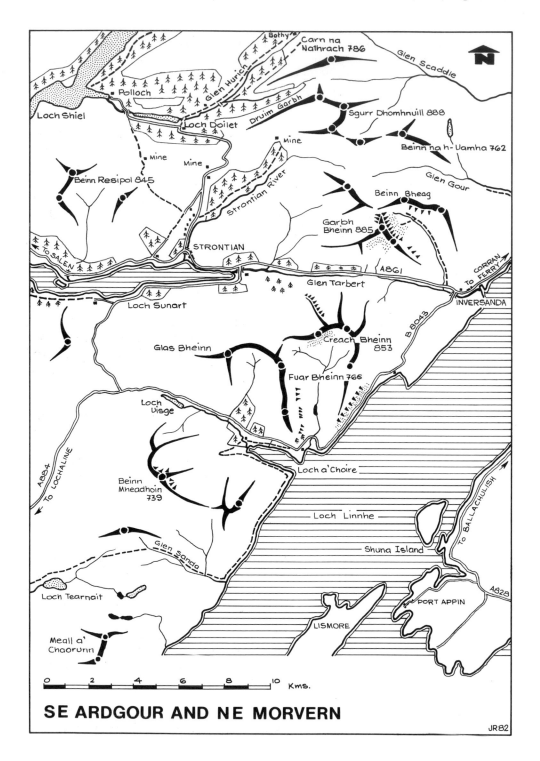

SE ARDGOUR AND NE MORVERN

Going in a clockwise direction, leave the road just south of Camasnacroise and climb the south ridge of Beinn na Cille, which is grassy with outcropping granite. The map indicates a number of steep little corries on the east side of the ridge leading to Fuar Bheinn, but they are not particularly impressive and the ridge itself is broad as it rises to Fuar Bheinn.

Continue due north on a descending traverse to the broad featureless col, the Cul Mham, and climb the steepening ridge to Creach Bheinn. There is a fairly large cairn on this bouldery summit, which commands a fine view, particularly towards the Firth of Lorn. A short distance north of the summit, at a slight dip in the ridge, there is a substantial dry-stone walled enclosure, rather like a primitive fortification, but probably a look-out post which is reputed to have been built on the mountain at the time of the Napoleonic wars. It is marked on the 1:50,000 Landranger map as 'camp'; it must have been a very cold one.

Continuing north-east, the ridge becomes narrower with steep corries on both sides as it drops towards the next col. Bear east across this col, then south-east to reach the rounded top of Maol Odhar. There the ridge turns south and continues undulating over Meall nan Each and down the Druim na Maodalaich. The east side of the ridge drops precipitously into Loch Linnhe in broken cliffs of red granite cut by many basalt dykes which form gullies and chimneys lined with trees and bushes, but useless for climbing. The descent of the ridge brings one back to the foot of Glen Galmadale barely one kilometre from the day's starting point.

The shortest route of ascent of Creach Bheinn alone is by its north-west ridge. Cross the Carnoch River in Glen Tarbert about four and a half kilometres east of Strontian, climb through a birch wood to gain the broad north-west ridge which is most pleasantly climbed along its eastern edge overlooking Coire Duibh. This leads to the north-east ridge of Creach Bheinn half a kilometre from the summit.

Beinn Resipol (845m)

This mountain stands in solitary splendour in the centre of Sunart, surrounded on all sides by rough moorland from which the summit rises in steep and in places rocky slopes. Being totally isolated, it commands a very extensive panorama, particularly westwards to the seaboard from Mull north to Skye. It is for its views that Beinn Resipol is renowned, and it is a mountain that should if possible be climbed on a fine day.

The ascent is probably best made from some point on the road along Loch Sunart. Resipole (where there is a camp and caravan site) is one possible starting point, from where there is a path up the Allt Mhic Chiarain. This very pleasant path leads through oak and birch trees high on the south side of the stream, which flows through a deep wooded gorge. Higher up, as open country is reached, the path continues some distance further towards Beinn Resipol and the final ascent is up the west ridge.

Looking across Loch Sunart from Morvern to Beinn Resipol

Another slightly shorter route is from Ardery, an isolated house above the tree-covered hillside on the north shore of Loch Sunart three kilometres south-south-west of Beinn Resipol. Walk up the steep track to Ardery and continue north round the west side of Beinn an Albannaich to reach Lochan Bac an Lochain and the rocky summit slopes of Beinn Resipol.

The 'traditional' route of ascent is from Strontian, following the old miners' track north-west to the now disused mines in Coire an t-Suidhe. Climb (with due regard for private property) through fields on the west side of the road up the Strontian River to reach the start of this track at (813 633). Three kilometres further, just past the cairn marking the pass, leave the track and bear west to Beinn Resipol, which is climbed by its east ridge. This route is rather longer than the two described above.

Ben Laga (512m)

The highest point in the eastern half of Ardnamurchan is Ben Laga, a rugged little hill which rises very steeply above Loch Sunart five kilometres south-west of Salen. There is a path on the west side of the hill which can be used to gain height above the B8007 road before climbing north-east to the summit.

Ben Hiant *(holy mountain)* (528m)

This is the highest hill in Ardnamurchan, and it is the one which must be climbed for the view, if nothing else. The southern side rises steeply from the Sound of Mull, the lowest precipitous slopes forming the bold headland called Maclean's Nose. To the north of the summit there is a steep basalt buttress below which grassy corries drop towards flatter moorland which has been afforested in recent years.

The shortest and most pleasant ascent of Ben Hiant is from the road about one and a half kilometres north-east of the summit. After the first short steep climb one reaches a grassy ridge which forms a fine escarpment on its south-east side. The walk up this undulating ridge is delightful, with a final short steeper climb to the summit.

If coming from Kilchoan, it is possible to climb the hill from the north-west, but this involves crossing cattle-graing land east of the Allt Choire Mhuilinn. There is a track which leads towards the north side of Beinn na h-Urchrach, and from it one can climb the north-west shoulder of Ben Hiant.

As a viewpoint, the summit of Ben Hiant has no equal in Ardnamurchan. To the east there are fine views up Loch Sunart and into the lonely recesses of Loch Teacuis backed by the hills of Morvern. In the other direction there is a panorama of the western seaboard from the Sound of Mull to the Sound of Sleat, with the islands of the Hebrides along the horion.

Beinn na Seilg *(hill of hunting)* (342m)

The westernmost 300m hill in Ardnamurchan is Beinn na Seilg, which rises above rough moorland three kilometres west of Kilchoan. There is a lot of bare gabbro on this little hill, and the north peak has a fine crag on its west side where some rock climbing has been done.

The ascent of Beinn na Seilg can be made from almost any point around its eastern perimeter. For example, one can start from Ormsaig, leaving the road about one kilometre beyond its junction on the west side of Kilchoan, walk up past the east end of Lochain Ghleann Locha and climb the east ridge.

The moorland to the north and north-east is rough going over heather and peat bog, but it does give the shortest approach to the crags on the west face of the north peak.

The view from the summit is very fine, some might say finer than that from Ben Hiant. Certainly the outlook westwards is uninterrupted by any other hills.

PATHS AND WALKS

Kinloch to Liddesdale. This long walk starts at Kinloch at the head of Loch Teacuis and goes for most of its length along the south shore of Loch Sunart. Start at

Kinloch and walk for one and a half kilometres along the private road towards Rahoy. At the first cottage strike uphill along a path north-eastwards for one kilometre, then north across the Bealach Sloc an Eich on the west side of Beinn Ghormaig. Descend through the forest to Glencripesdale and continue along the private road beside Loch Sunart to Liddesdale. (21 kilometres).

Strontian to Loch Doilet. This route follows the old miners' track from Strontian north-west over the shoulder of Beinn Resipol and down into Coire an t-Suidhe, where there are remains of an old lead mine. Below this the path descends through forest to the road at the west end of Loch Doilet. (8 kilometres).

North coast of Ardnamurchan. There is a continuous Landrover track from Arivegaig at the head of Kentra Bay (two kilometres west of Acharacle) westwards to Ockle, linking with the road from there to Kilmory. It is thus possible to walk along much of the north side of the Ardnamurchan peninsula.

CLIMBING

There are two small gabbro-topped hills in west Ardnamurchan on which rock climbing has been reported. One crag is on the west face of the small north top of Beinn na Seilg, and is best approached from the B8007 road near Lochan na Crannaig. The other crag is on the west face of Meall nan Con (grid reference 504 682), which is approached from the B8007 near the junction of the minor road to Kilmory. Both crags give middle grade climbs up to about 40m length.

CHAPTER 2

Ardgour and Moidart

MAPS: Ordnance Survey   1:50,000   Sheets 40 and 41
          Bartholomew   1:100,000   Sheet 40

PRINCIPAL HILLS

Garbh Bheinn	885m	903 622
Sgurr Dhomhnuill	888m	890 679
Beinn na h–Uamha	762m	917 664
Sgurr na h–Eanchainne	730m	997 659
Carn na Nathrach	786m	887 699
Druim Tarsuinn	770m	875 727
Stob Coire a' Chearcaill	771m	017 727
Sgurr Ghiubhsachain	849m	876 751
Sgorr Craobh a' Chaorainn	775m	895 758
Beinn Odhar Bheag	882m	846 778
Beinn Mhic Cedidh	783m	828 788
Rois-Bheinn	882m	756 778
Sgurr na Ba Glaise	874m	770 777
Druim Fiaclach	869m	792 792
An Stac	814m	763 793

Ardgour may well be the first part of Scotland west of the Great Glen that greets the traveller as he comes north through Glen Coe towards Fort William. The view westwards from the bridge across the narrows of Loch Leven is dominated by the jagged skyline of the mountains of Ardgour, and in particular Garbh Bheinn which is an impressive sight.

With its neighbouring district of Sunart which was described in the preceding chapter, Ardgour is surrounded by four lochs – Linnhe, Eil, Shiel and Sunart – and the low lying glens which connect them. So low is the watershed between Loch Eil and Loch Shiel, less than 20m above sea-level, that Ardgour, Sunart, Ardnamurchan and Morvern almost form a large offshore island of complex shape. These districts seem to have as many of the characteristics of the Scottish islands as of the mainland.

It is in Ardgour that we first see the typical east-west 'grain' of the western Highlands. Glen Tarbert, Glen Gour, Glen Scaddle, the Cona Glen and Loch Eil all show this characteristic feature, and other glens and lochs further north are similar in this respect. In Ardgour these glens are separated by some very rugged ridges which culminate in three outstanding mountains – Garbh Bheinn, Sgurr Dhomhnuill and Sgurr Ghiubhsachain. Ardgour as a whole is a very wild and mountainous part of the Highlands, and only at the village of Strontian and around the shore-line of Loch Linnhe and Loch Eil are there signs of human habitation,with the exception of the very remote community of forestry workers at Polloch near Loch Shiel.

Moidart is the district which faces Ardgour across the long and narrow Loch Shiel. On its north it is bounded by Loch Eilt, and on its western seaboard by Loch Ailort. It is a land of striking contrast between the extreme south-west corner which shares with Ardnamurchan the village of Acharacle as its centre of population, and is in places beautifully wooded and cultivated, and the rest of the district which resembles Ardgour – wild, mountainous and almost totally uninhabited except at a few places round its perimeter. The highest mountains of Moidart are in the north: Rois-bheinn overlooking Loch Ailort and Beinn Odhar Bheag, with its twin Beinn Odhar Mhor, standing above the head of Loch Shiel. The heart of the district, where the headwaters of the Moidart and Glenaladale rivers rise on the steep sides of Croit Bheinn, is very remote.

In the south-west corner of Moidart there is some attractive wooded country where the River Shiel flows for a few kilometres into Loch Moidart. At the head of that loch stands Castle Tioram on a rocky knoll which at high tide becomes a little island, but at low tide can be reached across the sandy shore.

Moidart is closely associated with Prince Charles Edward Stuart and the ill-fated rising of 1745. After the Prince's landing at Loch nan Uamh at the end of July he moved south and stayed at Kinlochmoidart House for several days. From there he crossed to Dalelia on Loch Shiel and was rowed up the loch to Glenaladale by MacDonald men. Next day he continued by boat to Glenfinnan at the head of the loch where his standard was unfurled on 19th August.

ACCESS

The main route of access to Ardgour is across the Corran Ferry, from where the A861 road goes south and west along the southern edge of Ardgour to Strontian. The continuation of this road west to Salen and then north to Acharacle, Glenuig and Lochailort gives access to Moidart and connects with the A830, the main road from Fort William to Mallaig. The A861 road also goes north-east from Corran Ferry along the shore of Loch Linnhe and Loch Eil to join the A830 road near Glenfinnan, so these two roads completely encircle Ardgour, Sunart and Moidart.

The only other public road which penetrates more than two or three kilometres into the 'interior' is the narrow road from Strontian northwards over a 342m pass to Loch Doilet and the remote forestry village at Polloch. It is possible to continue by bicycle from Polloch for many kilometres along the rough private road on the south-east side of Loch Shiel to reach the A830 at Glenfinnan.

There is a ferry for foot passengers only from Fort William to Camusnagaul at the north-east tip of Ardgour.

PUBLIC TRANSPORT

Ferries: Corran Ferry. (Highland Regional Council).Daily.
Fort William to Camusnagaul. Foot passengers only. (Highland Regional Council). Daily.

Bus: Fort William – Glenfinnan – Lochailort – Mallaig. (West Highland Motor Services, Mallaig). Daily.
Fort William – Lochailort – Acharacle – Salen. (Shiel Buses, Acharacle). Mondays to Fridays.
Ardgour (Corran Ferry) – Strontian. (Shiel Buses, Acharacle). Mondays to Saturdays.

Train: Fort William to Mallaig. Stations at Locheilside, Glenfinnan and Lochailort.

ACCOMMODATION

Hotels around the perimeter of the area at Ardgour, Strontian, Salen, Acharacle, Glenuig, Lochailort and Glenfinnan. Bed and breakfast, self-catering cottages and chalets and caravans to let at many of these places. (Useful tourist information at Strontian for local accommodation). Camp and caravan sites at Strontian and Resipole (three kilometres south-east of Salen). Bothies at Resourie in Glen Hurich and Essan on the south side of Loch Eilt.

THE HILLS

Most of the high hills in Ardgour and Moidart are near the perimeter of these districts, and are both clearly seen and readily accessible from the roads that encircle this area. The interior is very rugged and mountainous, although the mountains themselves are lower and less conspicuous than, say, Garbh Bheinn, Sgurr Dhomhnuill or Rois-Bheinn. The general impression of the interior of Ardgour is one of a tangled land of peaks and glens which demands some very long walks to reach its heart. Moidart is hardly less wild.

Garbh Bheinn *(rough mountain)* (885m)

Situated in the south-east corner of Ardgour, Garbh Bheinn is the grandest mountain in the district. Its fine outline when seen from the east has already been mentioned, and this distant impression of bold rock ridges, buttresses and gullies is confirmed at close quarters. The chief glory of the mountain is its rocky east face rising above the head of Coire an Iubhair, but this is not visible from the road in Glen Tarbert. One has to walk three kilometres up the corrie by quite a good stalker's path before the face is revealed, and it is a great sight. On the left, rising directly to the summit, is the 300m high Great Ridge, with the dark gash of Great Gully on its right; further right are the towers of Pinnacle Ridge, and to the right again the slabby rocks of the North-east and North buttresses.

Garbh Bheinn is well named the rough mountain, for it has a lot of rough bare rock, a grey quartzo-felspathic gneiss, not only on its east face, but on all its flanks. There is a subsidiary top (862m) a few hundred metres west of the summit, and half a kilometre south-east is the top of Sron a' Gharbh Choire Bhig (823m) from which a long ridge continues south-eastwards, its slabby north-east face overlooking Coire an Iubhair. Northwards from the summit of Garbh Bheinn a broad rocky ridge goes over the top of the Pinnacle Ridge and the North-east Buttress (marked by a small quartzite cairn) to the top of the north face. This drops steeply to the Bealach Feith 'n Amean (536m) in which lies Lochan Coire an Iubhair.

There are four possible routes of ascent, all from the south or south-east, and of very varying lengths. The shortest and least aesthetic, and one that cannot be recommended except for its shortness, is the direct ascent up Coire a' Chothruim (unnamed on the 1;50,000 map). Start from the road in Glen Tarbert near its highest point and climb steeply due north up the corrie, bearing north-east near its head to reach the col (748m) south of the summit of Garbh Bheinn.

For the next three routes the starting point is at the foot of Coire an Iubhair, and cars can be parked off the road near the old bridge. There are good camp sites just up the corrie, and climbers are asked to request camping permission at Inversanda House. A fine route is up the long Sron a' Gharbh Choire Bhig ridge. There is a faint path for most of the way, starting about 100 metres west of the bridge just mentioned. From the Sron there is a grand view across the intervening corrie to the summit of Garbh Bheinn, with the tremendous south face of the Great Ridge immediately below it. Descend a short distance to the 748m col and climb easy rocky slopes to the summit of Garbh Bheinn, which is perched right on the edge of the steep south face.

The third route goes up Coire an Iubhair by the well-worn and often very muddy path on the east side of the stream. This is the rock climbers' trade route, and leads to the foot of the great east face. At the junction of the two main streams, follow the southern one uphill by a faint path among huge boulders below the slabby lower rocks of the Great Ridge to reach the 748m col where the preceding routes are joined.

The circuit of Coire an Iubhair is a very fine expedition, which gives magnificent views of Garbh Bheinn as well as the interesting ascent of its north ridge. Start up the Druim an Iubhair to Sgorr Mhic Eacharna (650m) and continue to Beinn Bheag (736m). One kilometre further west, after crossing the lower west top (696m) of Beinn Bheag, one reaches the top of a steep grass and scree gully which leads down to Lochan Coire an Iubhair, beautifully situated in the Bealach Feith 'n

The east face of Garbh Bheinn seen across Coire an Iubhair

The summit of Garbh Bheinn above the south face of Great Ridge

Amean. From the lochan the north ridge of Garbh Bheinn rises very steeply, the rocky North Face on the left and a straight gully on the right. In between there is a steep slope of mixed rock and grass which is an easy scramble in summer. In winter conditions the gully may be a better route as it is then a straightforward steep snow slope. Above this, scramble up superbly rough and easy-angled rock to reach the little quartzite cairn on top of North-east Buttress, and up another rise at the top of Pinnacle Ridge to reach the summit. The descent by the Sron a' Gharbh Choire Bhig ridge completes a superb traverse.

Sgurr Dhomhnuill *(Donald's peak)* (888m)

By a few metres Sgurr Dhomhnuill is the highest mountain in Ardgour. Situated as it is in the centre of the district, it is very remote, yet it is a prominent landmark which is clearly visible from many points. From the east, as one travels up the side of Loch Linnhe, the peak is clearly seen at the head of Glen Scaddle; from the west end of Loch Eil the steep summit cone appears above the hills at the head of Glen Garvan, and the view from Acharacle up Loch Shiel includes a distant glimpse of the peak. It is from Strontian, however, that one gets the closest view of the mountain, ten kilometres distant at the head of the Strontian River.

There are three principal ridges: the north-east one dropping into Glen Scaddle, the south ridge linking with the subsidiary top Sgurr na h-Ighinn (766m) and then

Sgurr Dhomhnuill from Strontian Glen, Druim Garbh on the left

turning west to drop towards the Strontian Glen, and the north-west ridge which drops to the Glas Bhealach, rises to the 803m top of Druim Garbh and continues west as a broad featureless shoulder for several kilometres.

Strontian is the best starting point for the ascent of Sgurr Dhomhnuill. One can drive up the Strontian Glen to a car park just inside the Ariundle Nature Reserve, at which point one is seven and a half kilometres (as the crow flies) from the peak. The continuation up the glen through the beautiful pine and oak woods of the Reserve is an excellent start to the day, and gradually the forest road climbs high above the Strontian River to give a fine view of the mountain. In four kilometres, at the abandoned Feith Dhomhnuill lead mines, cross the stream and climb easy grassy slopes to the Druim Leac a' Sgiathain, the narrow ridge leading to Sgurr na h-Ighinn. This top can be bypassed if one wishes by a rising traverse along a broad terrace on its north-west face, and the 682m col south of Sgurr Dhomhnuill is reached. The final ascent goes up the south ridge in two steps, with a short level section at mid-height.

An alternative route from Strontian is to drive to the highest point of the road to Loch Doilet and traverse the long broad ridge, studded with little lochans, to Druim Garbh and across the Glas Bhealach to Sgurr Dhomhnuill by its north-west ridge. This route may be shorter and involve less climbing than the previous one, but it lacks the delightful approach through the woods of the Ariundle Nature Reserve.

The ascent from the east, by Glen Scaddle, is very long, the round trip from the foot of the glen to Sgurr Dhomhnuill and back being about 30 kilometres. The path up Glen Scaddle gives the impression of going on for ever, and at the point where the glen divides in three, climb the ridge between Gleann Mhic Phail and Gleann Cloiche Sgoilte direct to the summit.

Beinn na h-Uamha *(hill of the caves)* (762m)

This hill is a few kilometres north of Garbh Bheinn, and seven kilometres up Glen Gour from Sallachan. It is seen very prominently up the glen from the A861 road where it crosses the River Gour, and the extent of bare rock on the hill is obvious. There is a path on the south side of the glen past the ruined cottage at Tigh Ghlinnegabhar, ending one and a half kilometres further. Cross the river above the confluence with the Allt an t-Sluichd and climb the long rocky south-east ridge of Beinn na h-Uamha, traversing a prominent knoll at mid-height.

The twin west peak Sgurr a' Chaorainn (761m) rises due north of the watershed at the head of Glen Gour. It is a long way up the glen to reach it, and a shorter approach is from the Strontian Glen.

Sgurr na h-Eanchainne *(peak of the brains)* (730m)

Despite its modest height, this pointed hill, rising directly behind Ardgour village, is very prominent in views up and down the Great Glen between Spean Bridge and Lismore, and it in turn commands very fine views. In wet weather the cascading falls of Maclean's Towel just above Ardgour House are a fine sight.

The ascent is best made from a point on the A861 road at the Clan Maclean burial ground, which is two kilometres north of the jetty on the Ardgour side of

NW ARDGOUR AND MOIDART

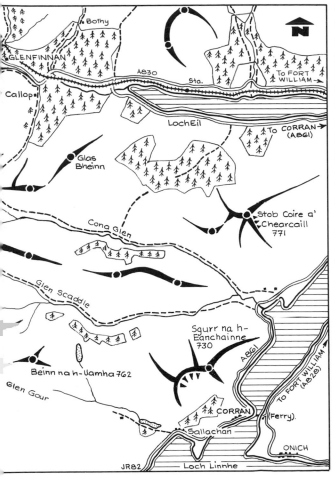

Corran Ferry. Climb west directly up the steep grassy ridge towards the col between Beinn na Cille and Sgurr na h-Eanchainne, and just before reaching it bear south and climb to the sharp summit of Sgurr na h-Eanchainne. There is quite an extensive area of high ground two kilometres west of this peak, and the flat top of Meall Dearg Choire nam Muc, with its two little lochans, is only a few metres lower.

Carn na Nathrach *(cairn of the adders)* (786m)

The centre of Ardgour is a tangle of rugged hills around the upper reaches of Glen Hurich, Glen Scaddle and the Cona Glen. Glen Hurich offers the shortest and easiest approach to these hills as one can drive from Strontian over the steep pass to Kinlochan near the east end of Loch Doilet. From there either walk or cycle (or possibly get permission to drive) up the forest road in Glen Hurich. One road on the north side of the glen goes for six kilometres to end above Resourie bothy; another road which crosses to the south side of the glen goes further (beyond the point shown on the 1:50,000 map). Resourie bothy is a good, but very remote, base for exploring the hills in the heart of Ardgour. There is a lot of recent tree planting round the bothy; the access path to it starts from the forest road at a gate in the fence directly above the bothy. There has also been, and continues to be, a lot of tree-felling in Glen Hurich, so access routes to the hills may be affected.

Carn na Nathrach is the highest point of the ridge on the south side of Glen Hurich which extends east to the head of Glen Scaddle. If approaching from Kinlochan, follow the road on the south side of Glen Hurich to a point north-north-west of the 602m top of Beinn Mheadhoin. From there climb south up the ridge on the west side of a prominent deep gully to reach the 602m top. Traverse east along the Beinn Mheadhoin ridge to Carn na Nathrach; at one point the crest is narrow and rocky for a short distance.

Druim Tarsuinn *(transverse ridge)* (770m)

This is the highest point of the long ridge on the south side of the Cona Glen. The name Druim Tarsuinn seems to apply to the whole ridge, and the highest point may have the name Stob a' Bhealach an Sgriodain. If approaching from Kinlochan, take the road on the north side of Glen Hurich past Resourie to its easternmost end at the edge of the forest. Climb steeply north below Teanga Chorrach and across the head of Coire an t-Searraich, crossing a forest fence, to the Bealach an Sgriodain overlooking the head of the Cona Glen. (The bealach is easily identified by one of the characteristically incongruous features of the Highlands: an iron gate standing in the middle of nowhere). From there climb half a kilometre south-east to the highest point of Druim Tarsuinn.

An alternative, but rather longer route starts from the A830 road a few kilometres east of Glenfinnan. Take the track past a locked gate to Callop and continue south along a good path up the glen of the Allt na Cruaiche which leads over a pass into the head of the Cona Glen. Cross the river and climb to the Bealach an Sgriodain where the preceding route is joined.

Stob Coire a' Chearcaill *(peak of the circular corrie)* (770m)

To the north of the Cona Glen and south of Loch Eil there is a range of smooth rounded hills with some extensive forested areas on their northern slopes. All these hills are featureless with the exception of Stob Coire a' Chearcaill, which has a prominent corrie just below the summit facing east across Loch Linnhe towards Fort William. The ascent can be most easily made by starting from the A861 road on the south side of Loch Eil just east of Duisky at the track on the east side of the Dubh Uisge, and climbing due south up a long and featureless hillside.

An alternative route, slightly longer but more attractive, is up the Gleann Sron a' Chreagain from Stronchreggan on the side of Loch Linnhe. A track leads up the north side of the glen for almost two kilometres, and from its end one can bear uphill to reach the ridge of Braigh Bhlaich which is followed to the summit.

Sgurr Ghiubhsachain *(peak of the fir wood)* (849m)
Sgorr Craobh a' Chaorainn *(rowantree peak)* (775m)

The north-west corner of Ardgour is dominated by a very fine mountain, Sgurr Ghiubhsachain, a steep and rocky peak between Loch Shiel and the head of the Cona Glen. It is well seen from Glenfinnan, and with Beinn Odhar Bheag it makes a superb mountainous setting for the head of Loch Shiel. Its north-west side and the slabby faces of its lower north-eastern peaks drop steeply to the lochside.

A good traverse of the mountain, together with its lower neighbour Sgorr Craobh a' Chaorainn, can be made by its east and north ridges, and the best starting point is the bridge over the Callop River at the foot of the Allt na Cruaiche (grid reference 924 793). There is a good path up the glen past Callop cottage. After three kilometres leave the path and climb south-west over Meall na Cuartaige to

Looking south-west down Loch Shiel to Sgurr Ghiubhsachain (left) and Beinn Odhar Bheag (right)

Sgorr Craobh a' Chaorainn. The descent south-westwards from this peak is quite steep and rocky for a short distance below the summit, and one should keep to the east, i.e.left if descending, to find an easy route down to the grassy continuation of the ridge to the col and then west to Sgurr Ghiubhsachain. The last part of this ascent is steep, and one has to pick a route upwards by slabs and grassy ledges to finish suddenly at a large cairn.

The descent down the north ridge is steep and rocky in places, but with good route-finding there need be no difficulty. The not insignificant knoll of Meall a' Choire Chruin (634m) has to be crossed. Towards the foot of the ridge there is a steep drop over a rocky crag, and it is best to traverse east onto the Coire Ghiubhsachain side of the ridge to avoid it. From Geusachan cottage at the foot of the ridge there is a five kilometre walk along the Forestry Commission road back to the day's starting point. (Note that the Callop River cannot be crossed at its outflow into Loch Shiel).

The traverse described above can be made longer and a good deal more strenuous by leaving the path near Callop cottage and traversing the two lower hills Meall a' Bhainne (559m) and Sgorr nan Cearc (668m) on the way to Sgorr Craobh a'Chaorainn.

To the west of the mountains just described is the long, narrow extent of Loch Shiel, which is the boundary between Ardgour and Moidart. All the high hills in Moidart lie near the northern edge of the district and are accessible from various points along the A830 and A861 roads. Despite their accessibility, these mountains have a fine wild character, and their southern slopes dropping down towards the heart of Moidart are remote and seldom visited.

Beinn Odhar Bheag *(little dun-coloured mountain)* (882m)

This mountain, with its twin peak Beinn Odhar Mhor (870m), stands at the head of Loch Shiel opposite Sgurr Ghiubhsachain. It is well seen from the east as one approaches along the road from Fort William, but from Glenfinnan the view towards the mountain is dominated by the lower buttresses, beyond which the tip of the summit is just visible.

The ascent is usually made from Glenfinnan, or a point on the A830 road three kilometres further west. From the Stage Coach Hotel, descend a few metres on the south side of the main road and cross the Abhainn Shlatach. (In spate this may not be possible, in which case see below for an alternative route). On the south side of this stream climb beside the Allt na h-Aire and its tributary leading to Lochan nan Sleubhaich, and go west from its head to a little col holding two tiny lochans. From there either climb south-west over Pt 529m and the knolly ridge to Sgurr na Boinaid and up the east ridge of Beinn Odhar Mhor, or go west-south-west for a short distance to reach a stream which is followed south-west up a narrow corrie between crags to reach the upper part of the east ridge of Beinn Odhar Mhor.

The ridge leading to Beinn Odhar Bheag drops to about 750m, the east side being very precipitous. The ridge is quite rocky, but there are no difficulties on the way to the pointed summit of Beinn Odhar Bheag, which has a commanding position above the long drop to Loch Shiel.

If it is not possible to cross the Abhainn Shlatach at Glenfinnan, start three kilometres west along the A830 road and after crossing the Allt a' Ghiubhais climb due south up the rather rough corrie to join the route described above west of Lochan nan Sleubhaich. In thick weather the route following the stream is easier to follow as it leads fairly directly towards the summit of Beinn Odhar Mhor.

Beinn Mhic Cedidh *(McCedidh's hill)* (783m)

This hill is separated from its neighbours by quite low cols, Bealach a' Choire Bhuidhe (c 490m) to its east and an unnamed col (c 350m) to its west. The most prominent feature of the hill is its north ridge, which is narrow and rocky and gives Beinn Mhic Cedidh a steep and rugged appearance when seen from the A830 road along the north side of Loch Eilt.

The most straightforward ascent of the hill is from the east end of Loch Eilt. The Allt Lon a' Mhuidhe which flows into this end of the loch is surprisingly awkward to cross if the weather is wet or the level of the loch high. Normally, however, it should be possible to cross about two hundred metres east of the head of the loch at some stepping stones. From there bear west through scattered birch trees beside the West Highland Railway, cross the Allt a' Choire Bhuidhe near the railway bridge and climb grassy slopes south-west to gain the foot of the north ridge. This ridge leads directly to the summit of Beinn Mhic Cedidh.

It is perfectly feasible to combine the ascent of Beinn Mhic Cedidh with Beinn Odhar Bheag and Beinn Odhar Mhor. The best starting and finishing point for such a circular trip is at the stepping stones over the Allt Lon a' Mhuidhe (see above), and the north ridge of Beinn Mhic Cedidh gives the most pleasant ascent. At the end of the traverse the descent from Beinn Odhar Mhor is best made down its north-west ridge to the Allt a' Choire Bhuidhe to rejoin the uphill route at the foot of this corrie.

Rois-Bheinn *(hill of showers)* (882m)
Sgurr na Ba Glaise *(peak of the grey cow)* (874m)
Druim Fiaclach *(toothed ridge)* (869m)
An Stac *(the stack)* (814m)

The most important group of mountains in Moidart is Rois-Bheinn and its neighbours, which stand near the head of Loch Ailort. Rois-Bheinn in particular is an outstanding mountain which, rising directly from the western seaboard, commands an uninterrupted view across the Sea of the Hebrides. By itself it is a fine, but quite easy climb. Taken with its four neighbouring peaks, it is one of the finest mountain traverses in the western Highlands.

The topography of the group is as follows:- Rois-Bheinn, the highest peak, rises directly above the narrow entrance to Loch Ailort, and from its twin summit a long ridge extends for several kilometres eastwards and then north-east over the peaks of Sgurr na Ba Glaise, An t-Slat-bheinn and Druim Fiaclach. The northern side of this ridge encloses the big grassy Coire a' Bhuiridh, while the south side (as far as An t-Slat-bheinn) overlooks the head of Glen Moidart. The very prominent conical peak of An Stac stands by itself to the north of the main ridge between Loch Ailort and Coire a' Bhuiridh.

There are two easy routes of ascent of Rois-Bheinn. One is the long, easy-angled west ridge which starts on the south side of the A861 road opposite Roshven Farm and leads directly to the top. One feature of this route is that it is rather lacking in interest and variety. However, the excellent views westwards from the ridge make it a good descent route.

The other way is by the Alisary Burn, leaving the A861 road at the track to Alisary cottage and following a narrow and in places rather overgrown path high on the south bank of the burn to the top of the forest. Continue south-east up a tributary into Coire na Cnamha where a drystone dyke leads right to the head of the corrie and onto the ridge north-east of Rois-Bheinn. Of the two tops, the eastern one which is the trig point is the higher, but the western one, only four

Looking west from Druim Fiaclach to Sgurr na Ba Glaise (left), Rois-Bheinn and An Stac (right)

metres lower, is the point with the view, having on a clear day a quite unexcelled panorama of the western seas and islands.

The Alisary Burn is also a convenient approach to An Stac. The final ascent is quite steep, but one can pick a route almost anywhere up the west or north side of the peak with plenty of optional scrambling on the many small rock outcrops.

The complete traverse of the four or five peaks of this group is best done (if the day is fine) from north-east to south-west, for going in that direction the seaward views are always in front. The first peak to be climbed in Druim Fiaclach, and the most convenient starting point is at Inverailort, near the Lochailort Salmon Hatchery. A track leads east past some old ruined buildings (relics of the Second World War) towards the wooded knoll Tom Odhar. On the south side of this knoll a path leads through a little pass and contours above the Allt a' Bhuiridh for a few hundred metres before disappearing. Continue up the corrie, crossing the main stream, and follow the tributary which has its source in the tiny lochan half a kilometre north of Druim Fiaclach. The going is very easy up the grassy corrie, but the last hundred metres of climbing directly up to the summit is rather steeper and rockier.

The name Druim Fiaclach refers to the east ridge of this mountain, which has some little rocky towers on its crest, but it is not part of this traverse. The summit of the peak and the south-west ridge leading to its lower top have a precipitous face overlooking Coire Reidh, the highest recess of Glen Aladale, and the walk along this ridge is delightful. The same can be said for the continuation along the undulating crest of An t-Slat-bheinn, where the long steep slopes on one's left plunge down to Glen Moidart, and in front the north face of Sgurr na Ba Glaise looms up. This peak is in some respects the finest of the group, having a very precipitous north face cleft by a long gully. The descent north-west from it to the Bealach an Fhiona is easy, as is the final climb to Rois-Bheinn, the culminating point of the traverse.

An Stac can be included at the end of the day by returning almost to the Bealach an Fhiona and then descending north to a lower col from which An Stac is climbed by its south ridge. From its summit the return to the day's starting point can be made northwards and then north-east over Seann Chruach to reach the path on the south side of Tom Odhar.

To mention briefly two of the other lower hills in Moidart, Croit Bheinn (663m) stands at the head of Glen Moidart, and is so remote as to be rarely climbed. It is steep on all sides, particularly on the north side which is quite rocky. The only other hill of note is Sgurr Dhomhuill Mhor (713m), which is the highest point south-west of Rois-Bheinn. The hill can be climbed easily from Roshven Farm up the ridge on the south side of Gleann Dubh. To its west is an extensive tract of lochan-studded moorland stretching towards Glen Uig and the western tip of Moidart.

PATHS AND WALKS

There are several long cross-country walks through Ardgour and Moidart; most of them involve rough going which is typical of this part of the Highlands.

Strontian to Sallachan by Glen Gour. Take the forest road through the Ariundle Nature Reserve, and follow the lower road out of the forest past the ruined cottages at Ceann a' Chreagain. Continue along the bare and pathless upper reaches of the Strontian River and over the narrow pass to Glen Gour where a path eventually materialises on the south side of the river and leads past the ruined cottage at Tigh Ghlinnegabhar to Sallachan. (19 kilometres).

Strontian to Glenfinnan. This is a splendid long walk, full of variety, which takes one through the heart of wildest Ardgour. Public transport is available to both ends of this walk. It may be taken in two stages, staying overnight in Resourie bothy. From Strontian the hill road past the mines is taken as far as Kinlochan near the head of Loch Doilet, and then the forest road on the north side of Glen Hurich is followed to its easternmost end just above Resourie. The next objective is to cross the Bealach an Sgriodain, two kilometres north-north-east. The most direct route is to climb steeply north, go either side of Pt 607m and continue across the head of Coire an t-Searraich to the bealach. From there descend north-east, cross the headwaters of the Cona River and make for the pass on the north side of the glen which leads north-east to the Allt na Cruaiche. At the pass a good path is joined

On the Great Ridge of Garbh Bheinn

and followed down past Callop cottage to the A830 road two kilometres east of Glen-finnan. (27 kilometres).

Strontian to Conaglen House (Loch Linnhe). Follow the route described above from Strontian to Glen Hurich, but take the forest road on the south side of the glen to its end. Continue past Lochan Dubh and down the interminably long path in Glen Scaddle. (32 kilometres).

Conaglen House to Glenfinnan. Walk up the Cona Glen, which is pleasantly wooded for the first few kilometres, and follow the track on the north side of the river to within two kilometres of the pass leading north to Callop cottage. Cross the pass and continue down this glen to the A830 road two kilometres east of Glenfinnan. (21 kilometres).

Ardmolich (Loch Moidart) to Lochailort. This is a fine cross-country walk through Moidart which shows the pastoral as well as the mountainous aspects of this district. Follow the road from Ardmolich past Brunery to Glenmoidart House. Continue along the west side of the River Moidart to the ruins at Assary, and from there climb north up steep grassy slopes to the Bealach an Fhiona. This is the line of an old track, possibly a coffin route, as is indicated by occasional cairns and the traces of a path near the bealach. On the north side of the pass descend steeply into Coire a' Bhuiridh and three kilometres further down take the path through the Tom Odhar col to reach Lochailort. (16 kilometres).

A very pleasant low-level walk can be made at the western tip of Moidart. Start from Shiel Bridge and walk down the road on the east side of the river to Doirlinn and Castle Tioram. Continue north then east along a path through trees on the steep side of Loch Moidart as far as Port a' Bhata. The return to Shiel Bridge can be varied by taking the path below the west face of Beinn Bhreac and past Loch Blain. (10 kilometres).

CLIMBING

Garbh Bheinn ranks high among Scottish mountains for the superb rock climbing
on its east face above Coire an Iubhair. The classic climb is *Great Ridge* (300m,
Difficult), the tapering ridge which rises from the corrie directly to the summit. On
the south face of Great Ridge there are several excellent climbs on steep and
perfect rock; the *South Wall* of Great Ridge is without doubt the rock climbers'
mecca in Ardgour. Immediately to the north of Great Ridge is the prominent dark
slash of *Great Gully,* which has been climbed in both summer (270m, Very Difficult)
and winter (Grade IV).

The next feature northwards is *Pinnacle Ridge,* an easy scramble up its crest, but
the south-east faces of the two pinnacles have given steep climbs. Further north,
beyond a slanting grassy gully, is the broad mass of *North-east Buttress.* The finest
route on this buttress is *Route II* (330m, Very Difficult or Severe according to
finish). This is a splendid route which goes up the *Leac Mhor,* the great smooth
slab at the centre of the buttress. Finally, there is the *North Face,* a slabby buttress
overlooking the Bealach Feith 'n Amean, which gives an indeterminate climb (200m,
Difficult).

The steep hillsides overlooking the head of Loch Shiel have given some rock
climbs. On the south-east side of the loch the west face of Meall Doire na Mnatha
(near grid reference 895 768) has given several climbs on a 100m high crag, and on
the opposite side of the loch at a height of about 400m on the spur of Sgurr an
Iubhair (at grid reference 859 780) two routes of just over 100m length have been
recorded on *Shiel Buttress.*

CHAPTER 3

Locheil, Glen Finnan and Morar

MAPS: Ordnance Survey   1:50,000   Sheets 33,34,40 and 41
Bartholomew   1:100,000   Sheet 50

PRINCIPAL HILLS

Beinn Bhan	796m	141 857
Stob a' Ghrianain	744m	087 823
Meall a' Phubuill	774m	030 854
Gulvain	987m	002 876
Braigh nan Uamhachan	765m	975 867
Beinn an Tuim	810m	929 835
Streap	909m	946 863
Sgurr Thuilm	963m	939 879
Sgurr nan Coireachan	956m	903 880
Sgurr an Utha	796m	885 839
Carn Mor	829m	903 910
Sgurr na h-Aide	867m	889 931

The well-defined valley which stretches westwards from the head of Loch Linnhe to the sea at Loch Ailort is one of the most obvious dividing lines in the western Highlands. It is also one of the most important lines of communication, for it carries the main road (A830) and the railway from Fort William to Mallaig. It also marks the beginning, as one goes from south to north, of the 'high' mountains, and although Munro baggers might think that the northwestern Highlands only start north of the Road to the Isles, this does little justice to the fine peaks of Ardgour and Moidart. About twelve kilometres further north, another east-west valley is formed by Loch Arkaig, Glen Dessarry and Loch Nevis, and between these two valleys are the western part of Lochaber, Morar and Arisaig, which together form the subject of this chapter.

This area can itself be divided into three regions of quite different characteristics. To the east, between Loch Eil and Loch Arkaig, there is an area of rather low rounded hills with smooth forested slopes and few features of mountaineering interest. Three long glens – Glen Loy, Glen Mallie and Gleann Suileag – penetrate into this area, and Beinn Bhan in its north-east corner, overlooking the Great Glen above Gairlochy, is the highest hill.

On the Road to the Isles, looking east along Loch Eil to Ben Nevis

Further west, beyond Gleann Fionnlighe, the mountains become much higher and steeper, and the head of Glen Finnan is surrounded by high and craggy peaks which are the centre of mountaineering interest in the area described in this chapter. North of Glen Finnan, between the west end of Loch Arkaig and Loch Morar, one comes to the southern fringe of Knoydart, and the peaks there have very much the wild and rugged character of Knoydart although they are within the district of Morar.

To the west of these high mountains, beyond Loch Beoraid, the terrain becomes less mountainous, though certainly no less rugged. This district, North and South Morar (with Loch Morar dividing it) is remarkably wild, uninhabited and rarely penetrated by walkers and climbers. It is a tangle of rocky hillocks of 500 to 600m rising above rough undulating moorland. In other parts of the Highlands these hills would probably be thoroughly explored by climbers, for there are innumerable crags, large and small, most of them protected by miles of rough heather; here, however, in this remote corner of the Highlands they pass almost unnoticed and unknown.

Finally, in the south-western corner of the area described in this chapter, there is Arisaig, a charming little peninsula of beautiful woodland, rocky headlands and sandy bays. The silver sands which extend northwards from Arisaig village to the

River Morar are renowned and justifiably popular in summer, when this corner of the Highlands takes on the appearance of a seaside holiday resort.

The districts of Morar and Locheil are, like Moidart, closely associated with Prince Charles Edward Stuart and the Jacobite rising of 1745. It was at Loch nan Uamh on the Arisaig coast that the Prince landed on 25th July that year, and he finally left Scotland from there on 19th September 1746. The early days of his campaign saw him march along the north shore of Loch Eil after the raising of his standard at Glenfinnan. The following year, after the Battle of Culloden, his flight from Hanoverian troops took him through Morar and over the hills between Glen Finnan and Loch Arkaig three times as he eluded his pursuers. Not surprisingly, there are several 'Prince Charlie's Caves' in the area, some of which (for example, the one near Druimindarroch on the shore of Loch nan Uamh) are authentic. Those who nowadays walk and climb among the rugged mountains of Glen Finnan, Morar and Knoydart can only admire the fortitude of the Prince and the loyalty of his followers during their weeks of travel and hiding in that wild country.

ACCESS

The main routes of access to the mountains described in this chapter are by road. In the south the A830 from Fort William goes along the north side of Loch Eil to Glenfinnan and Lochailort, Further north the B8004 road from Banavie goes along the Caledonian Canal to Gairlochy, and beyond the B8005 continues to the east end of Loch Arkaig. The public road continues along the north side of Loch Arkaig almost to its west end, and there seems to be no objection to cars being driven one kilometre further and parked near Strathan.

PUBLIC TRANSPORT

Bus: Fort William to Mallaig. (West Highland Motor Service, Mallaig). Daily.

Train: Fort William to Mallaig (The West Highland Line). Stations at Locheilside, Glenfinnan, Lochailort, Arisaig, Morar.

ACCOMMODATION

In the area immediately adjacent to the mountains, there are hotels at Glenfinnan and houses offering bed and breakfast along the roadside on the north of Loch Eil and at Achnacarry. Further from the mountains there is an abundance of accommodation of all types at Fort William and Spean Bridge.

There are camp sites and a youth hostel at Fort William. Permission to camp along the north side of Loch Arkaig should be sought from the West Highland Estates office in Fort William.

In addition to the accommodation noted above, there are several bothies which provide good, but spartan shelter. These include Corriehully (Glen Finnan), Dubh

Lighe bothy (Gleann Dubh Lighe), Glensulaig cottage (Gleann Sulaig), Inver Mallie (Glen Mallie), A'Chuil (Glen Dessarry), Pean (Glen Pean) and Oban (Loch Morar).

THE HILLS

The country between Loch Eil and Loch Arkaig has few features of interest until one reaches westwards as far as Gulvain, the first of the Munros. It is an area of rounded hills with smooth contours, and there is much forestry along the lower slopes above Loch Eil and in Gleann Suileag, Glen Loy and Glen Mallie. Although the hills themselves are not very interesting, some of them are very fine viewpoints for they stand just across the Great Glen from Ben Nevis and its high neighbours.

Beinn Bhan *(white mountain)* (796m)

This hill rises between Glen Loy and Glen Mallie a few kilometres west of Gairlochy at the south-west end of Loch Lochy. On a clear day it commands a superb view of the Lochaber mountains on the south side of Glen Spean beyond the Leanachan Forest. The quickest ascent is from the deserted farm at Inverskilavulin in Glen Loy, climbing up the steep grassy slope on the east side of stream flowing from Coire Mhuilinn to reach the summit. A fairly level crescent-shaped ridge extends west for two kilometres over two minor tops, both 771m, and this ridge can be traversed, following a line of fence posts, before descending the hillside west of the Coire Mhuilinn stream.

The north side of Beinn Bhan overlooking the foot of Glen Mallie is forested along the lower slopes. It is possible, however, to cross the River Mallie by the footbridge three kilometres upstream from Inver Mallie bothy and climb upwards across rough ground to reach the ridge on the west side of Coire Bhotrais two kilometres west of the summit.

Stob a' Ghrianain (744m)

This summit is the highest point of the long level hill Druim Fada which rises above the east end of Loch Eil. It too is a fine viewpoint. The ascent from any point along the A830 road beside Loch Eil tends to be featureless and uninteresting. A shorter route starts in Glen Loy at Puiteachan, where there is a fine stand of Scots pines in the Coille Phuiteachan, a remnant of the old Caledonian Forest. The route goes due south through the west edge of the forest and up the ridge between Coire Dubh and Coire Odhar.

Meall a' Phubuill *(hill of the tent)* (774m)

This rounded grassy hill rises due north of Glensulaig cottage, and is best approached from Fassfern on Loch Eil-side. Follow the forest road up the east side of Gleann Suileag to reach the open glen and, one and a half kilometres further, the cottage. From there climb more or less due north up the rounded grassy dome of Meall a' Phubuill. It is quite possible to use a mountain bike for the first three or possibly four kilometres up Gleann Suileag.

The boundary between the low hills just described and the higher ones further west is Gleann Fionnlighe. A very rough private road goes up the glen from the west end of Loch Eil for two and a half kilometres to the cottage at Wauchan. The west side of the lower glen is densely forested, while the east side is more open birch woodland. Above Wauchan a track continues for a further four kilometres to the confluence of the Fionn Lighe and the Allt a' Choire Reidh where there is a footbridge over the latter stream. It is quite possible to reach this point on a mountain bike. There is a good deal of new forest planting on the north-west side of the glen along the flank of Na h-Uamhachan which is not shown on the present edition of the Ordnance Survey 1:50,000 map.

Gulvain (alternatively, *Gaor Bheinn*) (987m)

The mountainous central part of the area described in this chapter starts with Gulvain, a massive mountain consisting of an isolated ridge running roughly from south to north on the west side of the watershed between Glen Mallie and Gleann Fionnlighe. Its two tops are connected by a high ridge which dips only slightly between them. The ascent is almost invariably made from the south, up Gleann Fionnlighe, as alternatives from the north and east are much longer.

From the footbridge over the Allt a' Choire Reidh (see above) climb the steepening grassy slope north-eastwards which leads relentlessly to a small knoll (855m) and then north along a more level ridge to the trig point (961m) which is the south-west top of Gulvain. The summit ridge continues north-east, broad at first, but beyond the col it becomes quite narrow and one is aware of the long steep drops on

Map labels: Sgurr na Ciche 1040; Garbh Chioch Mhor 1013; Sgurr nan Coireachan 953; Bothy; Loch Nevis; Mam na Cloich Airde; Sgurr na h'Aide 867; Glen Dessarry; Bothy; Loch Morar; Carn Mor 829; Bothy; Stra...; Bothy; Glen Pean; Sgurr Thuilm 963; Gleann Camgha...; Sgurr nan Coireachan 956; Streap 909; Bra... nc Uamh 765; Loch Beoraid; Bothy; Sgurr an Utha 796; Glen Finnan; Beinn an Tuim 810; Bothy; Gleann Fionn...; To MALLAIG; Sta.; Loch Shiel; GLENFINNAN; Callop; Beinn Odhar Mhor 870; Beinn Odhar Bheag 882; Loch...

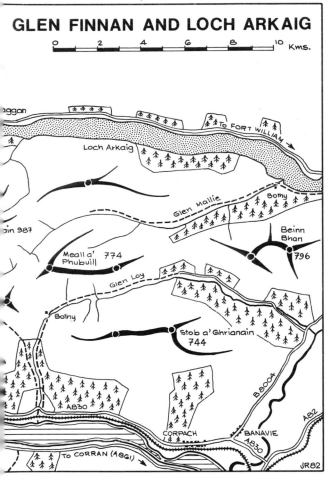

GLEN FINNAN AND LOCH ARKAIG

both sides. The higher north-east top, which is the true summit, has a large cairn. The rocks of Gulvain are largely a banded granite or 'granite-gneiss', and on the west side of the mountain this forms steep slabs which are no use for climbing, and are best avoided. So steep is that side of Gulvain that stags shot there are said to fall right down the mountainside.

It is also possible to climb Gulvain from the north and east. Three possibilities suggest themselves. First, from Kinloch-arkaig one can cross the steep-sided ridge of Leac na Carnaich and descend into Gleann Camgharaidh from where a steep ascent of the north-west face leads to the summit. (A detour further north to reach the north ridge lower down gives a less steep climb to the summit). Secondly, if one has a canoe in which to cross Loch Arkaig, a very fine approach to Gulvain can be made up Gleann Camgharaidh and the north ridge, whose flank above the glen is quite slabby. The third possibility is to approach Gulvain from the east end of Loch Arkaig by Glen Mallie. This is a very long way, and a mountain bike is more or less essential.

Braigh nan Uamhachan *(slope of the caves)* (765m)

This summit is the highest point of a long undulating ridge between Gleann Fionnlighe and Gleann Dubh Lighe, and being at the north-east end of the ridge, it is quite a long way from the nearest road. There is rather a lot of recent forestry planting, not shown on the present edition of the 1:50,000 Ordnance Survey map, on the flanks of Na h-Uamhachan, and a forest road has been made between Wauchan and the Dubh Lighe bothy.

With a mountain bike, the quickest way to Braigh nan Uamhachan is to cycle up Gleann Fionnlighe to the bridge over the Allt a' Choire Reidh and then make an ascending traverse across the east side of Sron Liath to reach the col (683m) half a kilometre south of Braigh nan Uamhachan. An alternative route from Gleann Fionnlighe is to take the forest road westwards above Wauchan to the crest of the ridge and then follow this ridge over many minor tops, large and small, for six kilometres. For about one kilometre along the crest of the ridge at Sron Liath there is a remarkably well built dry stone dyke. This is a fine traverse, which can equally well be approached from the Dubh Lighe bothy (see below).

Gleann Dubh Lighe is forested in its lower part, and the track on the west side of the stream is the easiest route up this part of the glen. For much of its first two kilometres this track goes alongside the tumbling waterfalls and dark pools of the Dubh Lighe. The path through the forest on the east side of the glen tends to be wet and darkly enclosed by trees. There is a bridge over the Dubh Lighe (at grid reference 945 817), and the forest road continues past the Dubh Lighe bothy (grid reference 945 820) to end about a kilometre further up the glen. This point can be reached on a mountain bike if one is prepared to lift it over two high stiles. The view up Gleann Dubh Lighe from the bothy towards the peaks of Streap and Streap Comhlaidh is fine, but this view will change when recently planted trees in the glen above the bothy become fully grown.

Glen Finnan is the next glen to the west, and it is the best known of these three glens. The River Finnan flows under the great concrete viaduct of the West Highland Railway and enters Loch Shiel near the Glenfinnan Monument and the National Trust for Scotland Visitor Centre, both of which are popular attractions for car-borne tourists. The monument commemorates the 1745 Rising, and the figure at its top is a bearded Highland soldier, not the Jacobite Prince as is commonly supposed.

There is a private road up the west side of the glen to Glenfinnan Lodge (an incongruously suburban looking house) and Corryhully bothy. Beyond the bothy this road deteriorates to a steep and rough track for a further three kilometres. There are recently built bridges over the Allt a' Choire Charnaig and the Allt Coire a' Bheithe, and also across the River Finnan above Corryhully. None of these are shown on the present edition of the 1:50,000 map. The east side of Glen Finnan is forested along the steep slopes of Beinn an Tuim northwards towards Streap, and the appearance of the glen will change considerably as this forest becomes mature.

Beinn an Tuim (810m)
Streap *(climbing hill)* (909m)

These two peaks are at opposite ends of the long undulating ridge between Gleann Dubh Lighe and Glen Finnan, and they can be climbed equally well from either glen. The southernmost point of this ridge is Beinn an Tuim, situated four kilometres north-east of Glenfinnan. North-eastwards along the ridge the peaks are Meall an Uillt Chaoil (844m), Stob Coire nan Cearc (887m), Streap and finally turning a short distance south-east, Streap Comhlaidh (898m). Beyond this summit the main ridge continues north-eastwards, gradually dropping towards the head of Loch Arkaig.

Streap is not only the highest, but also the finest peak of this group, and it is possibly the finest peak in the area described in this chapter. Seen from the north-east it looks very fine, with the steep north ridge   crowned by its pointed summit. It also has a very narrow south-west ridge, fine corries to the north-east and south, and the north-west face drops with remarkable steepness to the pass at the head of Glen Finnan. The south corrie, Coire Chuirn, contains the remains of an immense landslip which has detached from the headwall along a fault line, and some of the rocks high up in the corrie are still unstable, as signs of recent rockfall show. One should be very careful if scrambling up or down the corrie. The line of the fault crosses the south-west ridge and forms an easy-angled rake on the Glen Finnan side sloping down the steep hillside towards Corryhully.

The Gleann Dubh Lighe approach is probably the better of the two alternatives. Follow the track on the west side of the glen past the turning down to the bridge over the river, and a short distance further (near the upper limit of the more mature trees) leave the forest and gain the open hillside of Beinn an Tuim. Climb north-west to reach this hill, and then continue with quite a lot of up and downhill work along the undulating ridge to Streap. Just before reaching this summit the ridge becomes very narrow and exposed for a short distance, its crest little more than a sharp edge of rock. Turning south-east, another narrow ridge leads to Streap Comhlaidh. From there the descent can be made southwards along a grassy ridge which, beyond a minor top, plunges down to Gleann Dubh Lighe. A path on the east side of the stream leads down the glen to the end of the new forest road which can be followed past the Dubh Lighe bothy back to the A830 road.

If the Glen Finnan approach is preferred, Beinn an Tuim can be easily reached by crossing the River Finnan just below the railway viaduct and climbing up the easy-angled ridge on the south side of the Allt an Tuim. Alternatively, continue up the glen for half a kilometre beyond the viaduct, cross the river by a bridge and follow the forest road uphill onto the south-west ridge of Beinn an Tuim, which is climbed direct to the summit. The Allt an Tuim is not a good route as it forms a deep, crag-girt gorge high up. At the end of the traverse the descent from Streap to Glen Finnan can best be made by returning down the south-west ridge to the col one kilometre from the summit and then making a descending traverse along the rake mentioned above, still in a south-westerly direction, to reach the glen and cross the river by a footbridge near Corryhully bothy.

Streap can also be climbed from Strathan at the head of Loch Arkaig. Cross the River Pean by the bridge at the foot of Gleann a' Chaorainn and climb due south onto the crest of the Leac na Carnaich ridge. Follow this ridge over several knolls

Streap (left) and Sgurr Thuilm from Strathan

to Streap Comhlaidh and Streap. The descent is probably best made by the same route as the north ridge of Streap dropping to the head of Gleann a' Chaorainn is very steep.

Sgurr Thuilm *(peak of the rounded hillock)* (963m)
Sgurr nan Coireachan *(peak of the corries)* (956m)

Two kilometres north-east of Corryhully, Glen Finnan divides into two parts. The eastern branch is a narrow, steep-sided glen which rises to a pass at 471m, beyond which Gleann a' Chaorainn drops to Glen Pean and Loch Arkaig. The western branch is Coire Thollaidh, a great grassy hollow surrounded by a horseshoe of high peaks and ridges. Between Sgurr Thuilm at the east end and Sgurr nan Coireachan at the west end of this horseshoe are two lower tops, Meall an Tarmachain (826m) and Beinn Gharbh (825m), and to the south of Sgurr nan Coireachan is the narrow, rocky ridge of Sgurr a' Choire Riabhaich (852m). The traverse of these peaks is a very fine expedition, usually done from Glenfinnan. The road up the glen is private, but the use of a bicycle as far as Corryhully bothy saves some time.

The traverse can be done in either direction, however by going clockwise, the only part of the traverse which involves any scrambling is done in ascent. One kilometre beyond Corryhully bothy a stalker's path leads up to the south-east ridge

Looking up Glen Finnan from Corryhully bothy to Sgurr Thuilm

of Sgurr a' Choire Riabhaich. The ascent of this ridge is perfectly straightforward, but it is steep in places with some very easy scrambling, and the ridge itself is quite narrow, with steep rocky flanks. Coire Carnaig to the south-west is a grand rocky corrie, showing a fine expanse of glaciated slabs. Once the summit of Sgurr a' Choire Riabhaich is passed, the ridge broadens and leads easily to Sgurr nan Coireachan.

The continuation eastwards over Meall nan Tarmachain and Beinn Gharbh is easy. Old fence posts show the way in thick weather, and beyond the unnamed Pt 858m bear north-east to the top of Sgurr Thuilm, where the cairn is near the north of the flat summit area. Descend the long grassy ridge of Druim Coire a' Bheithe, which steepens near its foot, and cross the Allt Coire a' Bheithe by a bridge built in 1986. (Previously this was a hazardous crossing in spate conditions).

The north side of the ridge between Sgurr Thuilm and Sgurr nan Coireachan forms some wild corries overlooking Glen Pean, and the ascent from this glen is a steep, rough scramble. The Pean bothy is a good base, but if the River Pean is in spate it will be impossible to cross at the bothy, and the crossing should be made by the footbridge at the foot of Gleann a' Chaorainn. However, this leaves the Allt a' Chaorainn to be crossed before the north-east ridge of Sgurr Thuilm can be reached, so this northern approach is probably best avoided in wet weather.

To the west of Glen Finnan the district of South Morar is an extremely wild tract of country between the A830 road and Loch Morar. It is a land of rocky hills, rough undulating moorland and innumerable crags and lochans dotted high up on the moors. Few climbers and walkers go there for there are no high hills to attract attention, and the country is too rough for any but the hardiest of cross-country walkers. Near the centre of this district a path crosses the moorland north from Arieniskill at the west end of Loch Eilt to reach the west end of Loch Beoraid. In the woods above Loch Beoraid there is another of Prince Charlie's caves under a large fallen boulder. Continuing northwards, a track goes down the River Meoble to reach a jetty on the south shore of Loch Morar.There is a small dam and private hydro-electric plant at the outflow of Loch Beoraid, and a path eastwards along the north shore of the loch leads to the locked cottage at Kinlochbeoraid. (An outhouse is so ruined as to provide virtually no shelter). It is possible to continue east from Kinlochbeoraid up Gleann Donn (on the north side of the stream) and down the Allt a' Chaol-ghlinne to reach Glen Finnan.

Sgurr an Utha *(peak of the udder)* (796m)

Sgurr an Utha and its neighbouring top Fraoch-bheinn (790m) are about three kilometres north-west of Glenfinnan, and are close enough to the road to give a pleasant half-day climb. One line of ascent is from Glenfinnan, leaving the road just east of the hotel and climbing the Tom na h-Aire ridge over a few knolls before traversing Fraoch-bheinn on the way to Sgurr an Utha. The descent can be made down the Allt a' Choire Dhuibh. Another possible route is from a point just over two kilometres west of Glenfinnan along the A830 road (marked Cross on the 1:50,000 map). Follow a steep forest track onto the Druim na Brein-choille and then bear north across the Allt an Utha to reach Sgurr an Utha.

North Morar is the long peninsula between Loch Morar and Loch Nevis. At its eastern end between Glen Pean and Glen Dessarry it is very mountainous and rugged, having something of the character of the Rough Bounds of Knoydart immediately to the north. Further west along the peninsula the terrain is lower, but no less rough, and this applies to the low lying ground at loch-level as well as the high ground. The shoreline of Loch Morar (with the exception of that part between Morar and Swordland where there is a track) is extremely rough and precipitous, and the traverse along the lochside is not recommended.

Access to Glen Pean, Glen Dessarry and points further west is by the road along Loch Arkaig, and cars can, at present, be taken as far as Strathan and parked near the bridge over the River Dessarry. From that point private roads go up Glen Pean and Glen Dessarry. Both glens are now forested. The road up Glen Pean goes to within about one kilometre of the Pean bothy, beyond which a path continues up the glen and over to the head of Loch Morar. (See section on Paths and Walks). In Glen Dessarry one private road on the north side of the river goes to Glendessarry Lodge, and a track (deteriorating to a path) continues west past Upper Glendessarry.

On the south side of the river a forest road six kilometres long goes past A'Chuil bothy to end at the point where the Allt Coire nan Uth enters the River Dessarry. At that point, which can be reached by bicycle, there is a narrow bridge (one plank, no handrail) over the Dessarry and a path through newly planted trees connects with the main path on the north side of the river. There is quite extensive forestation on the south side of the River Dessarry as far west as the foot of Meall na Sroine.

Carn Mor *(big hill)* (829m)

This extensive hill lies between Glen Pean and Glen Dessarry, with an eight kilometre long ridge running east from the summit between these two glens. To the west the hill is much rockier, and its lowest buttresses drop steeply into the head of Loch Morar. Coming from the east, the ascent can most easily be made from Glen Dessarry, leaving the forest road one kilometre west of A'Chuil bothy and climbing the ridge over Meall nan Spardan which leads directly to the summit of Carn Mor. The southern slopes of the hill between the summit and Lochan Leum an t-Sagairt have been fissured by a great landslip, so this part of the hill should be avoided, particularly if there is snow on the ground.

Sgurr na h-Aide *(peak of the hat)* (867m)

This is a very fine sharp-topped mountain which is clearly seen from the side of Loch Arkaig to the east, and is sometimes mistaken for its higher and equally pointed neighbour, Sgurr na Ciche. It is formed by a long undulating ridge which starts near the head of Glen Dessarry, rises westwards to the summit and continues in the same direction for many kilometres over a succession of lower hills, forming the spine of the peninsula between Loch Morar and Loch Nevis.

The ascent is usually made from the head of Glen Dessarry, and for those with bicycles, or staying at A'Chuil bothy, the best approach as far as the Allt Coire nan Uth is along the road on the south side of the glen. Otherwise the road and path by Glendessarry Lodge and Upper Glendessarry is a slightly shorter way to the crossing of this burn. Continue north-west along the Glen Dessarry path for about one kilometre, and once past the forest leave the path and bear west up the lower slopes of Meall na Sroine. Traverse the undulating ridge over rocky knolls and past two lochans on the crest of the Druim Coire nan Laogh to the final steep peak, where some easy scrambling may be needed if one climbs directly to the top. The slightly lower west peak (859m) is less than one kilometre away along a pleasant ridge.

Both the north and south sides of Sgurr na h-Aide are very steep. On the north side boiler-plate slabs drop from the summit ridge towards Finiskaig and the Mam na Cloich' Airde; the ascent of this face of the mountain from the head of Loch Nevis is a good steep scramble, but it is not a recommended descent route. On the south side of the summit the drop to Gleann an Lochain Eanaiche is even steeper; 700m at an average angle of 45 degrees. There are no hillwalkers' routes there.

Looking west from the summit of Sgurr na h-Aide to the west peak and the distant islands of Eigg and Rhum

Far to the west, in the north-west corner of the peninsula, there are three small, rocky hills that can be approached from Mallaig by the path from Glasnacardoch to Loch Eireagoraidh. They are Sron an Eilein Ghiubhais (522m) and Carn a' Ghobhair (548m) to the north of the loch, and Sgurr Bhuidhe (436m) to its south. These hills give splendid views on a clear day, westwards to Skye and the Small Isles and east up Loch Nevis to Sgurr na Ciche.

PATHS AND WALKS

In addition to those walks already mentioned, there are several other fine cross-country routes through western Lochaber, leading to Morar and Knoydart. The route from Glenfinnan northwards to Strathan at the west end of Loch Arkaig,and from there westwards through Glen Dessarry to Loch Nevis, Inverie and Barrisdale is one the the great long distance walks in the western Highlands. Brief details of some of these walks are as follows:-

Fassfern to Glen Loy. From the right of way sign at the bridge over An t-Suileag at Fassfern follow the forest road and track to Glensulaig cottage. For the next two kilometres to the watershed the path is not well defined. Once in Glen Loy the path is well up on the north side of the river as far as the deserted cottage at Achnanellan where the road down the glen begins. (18 kilometres from Fassfern to Glen Loy Lodge).

Loch Beoraid in the wilds of Morar

Loch Eil to Loch Arkaig. This route follows the well-defined way through Gleann Fionnlighe and Glen Mallie. The track up Gleann Fionnlighe is followed to the foot of Gulvain as described above. Thereafter the going up the Fionn Lighe and over the watershed to the head of Glen Mallie is pathless for several kilometres. Eventually the track in Glen Mallie is reached, but the ruined house at (079 873) provides no shelter, and it is a long way to the excellent bothy at Inver Mallie. From there it is a relatively short distance to the east end of Loch Arkaig and the public road. (27 kilometres)

Fassfern to Strathan. This is the line of a very old route, part of it marked on the 1875 edition of the Ordnance Survey map, but seldom used nowadays, so that the paths which once existed have now largely disappeared. From Fassfern take the right of way up Gleann Suileag and cross the river at the first possible point after leaving the forest. Cross the col between Aodann Chleireig and Meall Onfhaidh and descend into Gleann Fionnlighe. Continue north up the east side of the Allt a' Choire Reidh, over the pass at its head into Gleann Camgharaidh and, still heading north, cross the ridge east of Leac na Carnaich and descend north-west to the bridge over the River Pean near Strathan. (15 kilometres).

Glenfinnan to Strathan. Follow the private road up Glen Finnan to Corryhully bothy, and continue along the rough track over the Allt Coire a' Bheithe (recently bridged) and a further kilometre towards the 471m pass. Cross this pass, which is a deep gash between Streap and Sgurr Thuilm, and descend the east side of the Allt a' Chaorainn to the bridge over the River Pean one kilometre south-west of Strathan. (14 kilometres).

Gleann Dubh Lighe to Strathan. This is an alternative to the more usual Glen Finnan route described above. Follow the forest road on the west side of the Dubh Lighe, cross the bridge and continue past the Dubh Lighe bothy. One kilometre further the road ends. Continue along a good path for a kilometre and cross the burn. The way northwards is indicated intermittently by posts towards the head of the glen. Once past Lochan a' Chomhlain make a rising traverse to cross the ridge south-west of Leac na Carnaich at its lowest point, and finally descend to the bridge over the River Pean near the foot of the Allt a' Chaorainn. (14 kilometres from the A830 to Strathan).

Strathan to Loch Morar by Glen Pean. This is a superb walk through a narrow glen enclosed by steep and rocky mountains. Take the forest road from Strathan westwards, and when the road ends before reaching the Pean bothy continue along the path, past the bothy towards Lochan Leum an t-Sagairt. Before reaching the lochan cross the River Pean and follow either of two paths along the precipitous south side of the lochan, not the north side as shown on the 1:50,000 map. Continue along the south side of the narrow glen to reach the head of Loch Morar near Oban bothy. This cottage is in a dilapidated state, but does provide rough shelter. (12 kilometres).

Strathan to Loch Morar by Gleann an Lochain Eanaiche. This route to Loch Morar is just as fine as the one described above, but slightly longer. The two routes can be combined in a single long day starting and finishing at Strathan. Follow the forest road on the south side of Glen Dessarry to its end in 6 kilometres at the bridge over the River Dessarry. Continue up the south bank of the river for half a kilometre, then west for a few hundred metres up the Allt Coire an t-Searraich to emerge from the forest. Continue west-south-west through the very obvious pass between Carn Mor and Meall na Sroine and descend on the north side of the burn to Lochan Eanaiche and on down the path in Gleann an Lochain Eanaiche to Kinlochmorar. There is a faint path round the head of Loch Morar which gives the best route across the steep lochside crags and enables one to reach the end of the path through Glen Pean. (15 kilometres).

Strathan to Loch Nevis. This right of way is the trade route westwards from the head of Loch Arkaig to Knoydart. In Glen Dessarry there is a choice of routes, either north or south of the river as described previously. Continuing north-west from the Allt Coire nan Uth, the path is quite good for two and a half kilometres to the cairn marking the pass, named the Bealach an Lagain Duibh on the 1:25,000 OS map. The next two kilometres past Lochan a' Mhaim and through the Mam na Cloich' Airde are rough going, but it is a wild and beautiful place, enclosed by steep craggy hills and huge fallen boulders. The path improves as it drops towards

Loch Nevis, showing in places signs of having once been well constructed. There is now a footbridge over the Allt Coire na Ciche, previously a notoriously dangerous crossing when in spate, and the path ends across grassy flats at the head of Loch Nevis to reach Sourlies bothy. (14 kilometres). It has been suggested by A.E. Robertson that this path may date from the days of herring fishing in Loch Nevis, the path being used for carrying the fish to markets in the south. This would explain its good construction, for example at the hairpins above Loch Nevis.

CLIMBING

Strange as it may seem, particularly when one considers the very steep and rocky character of many of the hills, very little climbing has been recorded on the

Mam na Cloich' Airde, the pass from Glen Dessarry to Loch Nevis

mountains and crags of western Lochaber and Morar. The only recorded rock climbing in this area is on some of the small, but very rocky hills a few kilometres east of Mallaig. Routes have been done on Carn Mhic a' Ghille-chaim and Sgurr Bhuidhe on the south side of Loch Eireagoraidh, which can be reached by a path starting one kilometre south of Mallaig. The climbing on Sgurr Bhuidhe is on its south face and is best approached from Bracora on Loch Morar. Some climbing has also been recorded on Creag Mhor Bhrinicoire two kilometres east of Bracorina.

CHAPTER 4

Loch Arkaig to Glen Garry

MAPS: Ordnance Survey   1:50,000   Sheets 33 and 34
           Bartholomew   1:100,000   Sheets 50 and 51

PRINCIPAL HILLS

Meall na Teanga	917m	220 924
Meall Coire Lochain	900m	215 920
Sron a' Choire Ghairbh	935m	223 945
Ben Tee	901m	241 972
Meall na h-Eilde	838m	185 946
Geal Charn	804m	156 943
Sgurr Mhurlagain	880m	012 944
Fraoch Bheinn	858m	986 940
Sgurr Cos na Breachd-laoigh	835m	948 947
Gairich	919m	025 996
Sgurr an Fhuarain	901m	987 980
Sgurr Mor	1003m	965 980
Sgurr nan Coireachan	953m	933 958
Garbh Chioch Mhor	1013m	909 961
Sgurr na Ciche	1040m	902 966
Ben Aden	887m	899 986

This slice of the western Highlands is just as well defined by long east-west valleys as are its neighbours to the south and north. Its southern boundary is Loch Arkaig and Glen Dessarry, and its northern boundary is Glen Garry, Loch Quoich and the pass at the west end of that loch which leads to the head of Loch Nevis. On the east the area is bounded by Loch Lochy, one of the long narrow lochs of the Great Glen.

At the eastern edge of this area the mountains rise abruptly from Loch Lochy, their lower slopes forested along the lochside. (Recent felling of parts of the South Laggan Forest has left the hillside looking rather bare).These mountains, Ben Tee, Sron a' Choire Ghairbh and Meall na Teanga, form a very prominent group, well seen in views up and down the Great Glen. Although Ben Tee lies well back from Loch Lochy, the other hills rise so steeply above it as to give an appearance of inaccessibility, their lower forested hillsides leading up to steep craggy slopes.

Further west the hills become progressively lower, and there is an extensive tract of country between Loch Arkaig and the forests in Glen Garry and Glen Kingie which is rather featureless, consisting of rounded hills and some very boggy terrain of no great interest to climbers and walkers. Further west still, approaching the head of Glen Kingie, the country becomes much more mountainous, and it is in the westernmost part of the area described in this chapter that we find its highest and finest peaks. There, round the desolate upper reaches of Glen Kingie and westwards to Glen Dessarry and the head of Loch Nevis, is a wild and rugged group of mountains which culminates in Sgurr na Ciche, one of the great landmarks of the north-western Highlands.

Apart from these high mountains, which in character at least are part of the Rough Bounds of Knoydart, the other remarkable feature of this area is Glen Kingie. Lying between Loch Arkaig and Loch Quoich, it is utterly desolate and devoid of human habitation in its seventeen kilometre length, with the possible exception of the bothy beside the ruined lodge at Kinbreack which offers spartan shelter to passing climbers and walkers. The River Kingie flows sluggishly in long curves through the boggy grassland of the glen, and only near its lower reaches are there any signs of human activity, and they not surprisingly are the plantings of the Forestry Commission. This sense of desolation is heightened when the rains come and the little mountain burns become cascading torrents; the River Kingie overflows its banks and crossing it is impossible, for there are no bridges upstream of the forest near the foot of the glen. Few other glens in this part of the Highlands epitomise so well the desolate wilderness that is so much a part of that land.

Like Loch Eil and Morar to the south, Loch Arkaig has many historical associations with the 1745 Jacobite Rising and its aftermath. On the day after the Battle of Culloden, Prince Charles fled down the west side of Loch Lochy and westwards through the Mile Dorcha (*the Dark Mile*) to reach the east end of Loch Arkaig. He continued along the loch and through Glen Pean on his way to the west coast. Two months later he was back on the mainland after his sojourn in the Hebrides, this time crossing the mountains northwards from Glen Dessarry to Loch Quoich. Later, in August that year, the Prince spent two weeks hiding in 'sundry fast places' near the east end of Loch Arkaig. One of these was a big tree, another a cave in Gleann Cia-aig above the Mile Dorcha. Finally, in September that year he passed again through the Mile Dorcha and along Loch Arkaig on his last flight to the west coast to board a ship for France.

ACCESS

The approach to these hills from the south is by the B8005 road from Gairlochy along the fine tree-lined avenue of the Mile Dorcha and right out westwards along Loch Arkaig to its far end as described in the last chapter. This is the most convenient access to the hills as all of them except Gairich and Ben Tee can be climbed from some point along this road. At the west end of the Mile Dorcha there is a car park at the fine waterfall, the Eas Chia-aig, and a path north from there gives access to the hills in the east of the area. Most of the other hills can be climbed from the road beyond the west end of Loch Arkaig.

To the north, the A87 road and its branch westwards past Tomdoun and Loch Quoich to Kinloch Hourn gives access to the north side of the area, but Loch Quoich forms a very effective barrier between the road and the hills, so this is not a particularly good approach unless one has a canoe or some other means of crossing the loch.

At the eastern edge of the area, the hills overlooking Loch Lochy can be easily reached either from Clunes at the east end of the Mile Dorcha or from Kilfinnan at the north-east end of Loch Lochy.

From the west, access to the mountains at the head of Loch Nevis is more problematical. There is not, as indicated on the 1:50,000 Ordnance Survey map, a ferry service to the head of the loch. Bruce Watt Cruises do however operate sightseeing cruises from Mallaig up Loch Nevis, and it might be possible to make a special arrangement to be put ashore near the head of the loch. (Bruce Watt Cruises, Mallaig. Telephone 0687 2283). Otherwise it is necessary to take the regular ferry from Mallaig to Inverie, and walk from there to the head of Loch Nevis. (See next chapter).

PUBLIC TRANSPORT

Bus: Glasgow to Kyle of Lochalsh, passes through Laggan and Invergarry. (Scottish Citylink Coaches and Skye-Ways Express Coaches). Daily.

Postbus (4 seater): Invergarry to Kinloch Hourn. Mondays, Wednesdays and Fridays. Invergarry to Kingie. Tuesdays, Thursdays and Saturdays.

ACCOMMODATION

Most of the accommodation near these hills is in the Great Glen, and there are several hotels between Spean Bridge and Invergarry,and near Gairlochy. There is also an abundance of bed and breakfast houses and self-catering chalets, for example at Laggan a few kilometres south of Invergarry. Loch Lochy youth hostel is also situated at Laggan. In Glen Garry there is a camp and caravan site at Faichem two kilometres west of Invergarry, and a hotel at Tomdoun. There are a few informal lochside camp sites beside Loch Garry. Permission to camp along the north shore of Loch Arkaig should be sought from the West Highland Estates office in Fort William. In addition to the bothies mentioned in the last chapter, there is also Kinbreack in Glen Kingie.

THE HILLS

Directly above the Great Glen between Spean Bridge and Laggan the Loch Lochy hills rise very boldly on the west side of that loch, presenting a continuously steep and in some places preciptious hillside with forests clinging to the lower slopes along the lochside. The summits themselves are rather rounded, and not nearly as rugged as those further west, but they have some fine corries. Ben Tee, the pointed hill at the north end of this group, is one of the most prominent landmarks in the Great Glen. To the west and north-west the slopes of these hills are more gradual and drop down to the forests on the south side of Loch Garry. The Cam Bhealach, a pass rising to about 610m between Loch Lochy and the head of Gleann Cia-aig, divides this group of hills into two roughly equal halves.

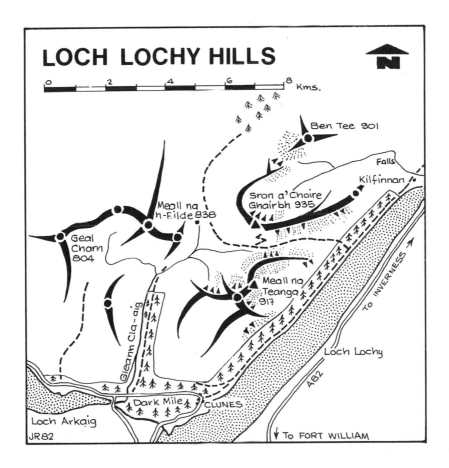

Meall na Teanga *(hill of the tongue)* (917m)
Meall Coire Lochain *(hill of the corrie of the lochan)* (900m)

The highest hill in the southern half of this group is Meall na Teanga, flanked on the south by Meall Coire Lochain and on the north-east by Meall Dubh (837m). The shortest approach is from Clunes. Follow the forest road one kilometre north-east, then back west-south-west to its end at grid reference 200 890. From the end of the road scramble up the steep bank for a few metres to emerge on the open hillside. Climb north to the knoll of Leac Chorrach (586m) and then up a long grassy slope to Meall Coire Lochain, whose summit is at the edge of Coire Lochain. The ridge to Meall na Teanga drops steeply a few metres north of the cairn, and is quite narrow and well-defined for about 300 metres down to the col from which the ascent to Meall na Teanga is quite straightforward. (The descent might be slightly awkward in hard winter conditions). The top of this hill is near the south end of the level summit ridge. One can continue northwards down steep bouldery slopes to reach Meall Dubh or the Cam Bhealach.

An alternative route to Meall na Teanga from the south starts at the Eas Chia-aig waterfall at the west end of the Mile Dorcha. Take the signposted path uphill through the forest on the east side of the waterfall to reach a forest road, and go along it northwards to its end where a path continues up the glen. Once beyond the forest climb eastwards up a steep grassy hillside to reach the ridge of Meall Odhar, which is followed to Meall Coire Lochain.

Ben Tee *(fairy hill)* (901m)

The isolated cone of Ben Tee is a feature of the landscape in the central part of the Great Glen, and it is also clearly seen from distant points far to the west along Glen Garry. It is most easily climbed from Kilfinnan, which is reached by a narrow public road from Laggan Swing Bridge, and cars can be parked beside the road about a hundred metres before reaching the farm. From that point there is a path up the north side of the Kilfinnan Burn, but this leads to the Kilfinnan Fall and is used by those going to look at it. A more direct way to Ben Tee goes north-west directly up the grassy hillside (traces of a path) and then along a more level shoulder to reach a stile over a high fence. Once over this stile continue westwards across level moorland to the steeper and in places rocky cone of the summit. There is an indifferent path on the north side of the Allt a' Choire Ghlais above the Kilfinnan Fall, but it does not offer a quicker route to Ben Tee.

Sron a' Choire Ghairbh *(nose of the rough corrie)* (935m)

This, the highest of the Loch Lochy hills, is formed by a long horseshoe-shaped ridge enclosing Coire Glas. The best ascent is from Kilfinnan, following the upper forest road south-west through the recently clear-felled part of the South Laggan Forest for three kilometres and then climbing the path westwards to the Cam Bhealach. From the top of the pass a stalker's path zig-zags up the hillside to the

Sron a' Choire Ghairbh and Ben Tee from the Great Glen

north for a further few hundred metres and ends just below the smooth mossy ridge a short distance from the summit of Sron a' Choire Ghairbh.

An alternative to this route is to climb due west from Kilfinnan to Meall nan Dearcag and follow the ridge over Sean Mheall, but this is rougher and there is a good deal of up and downhill work along the ridge. Coire Glas is rather a wild and remote corrie, but it has no great climbing interest.

On the other side of Sron a' Choire Ghairbh the north and west slopes are uniformly steep and grassy, and rather featureless. It is possible to make an ascent from the north-west, starting from the bridge across Loch Garry four kilometres east of Tomdoun, but the approach through the forest by Greenfield and up the Allt Ladaidh is fairly long. The forest track up the Allt Ladaidh now reaches the foot of the Allt Bealach Easain (there is new forest planting there) and it is possible to reach that point by bicycle. From there climb south up the broad grassy ridge leading to the north-east end of the level ridge of Meall a' Choire Ghlais which leads in a further three kilometres round the head of Coire Glas to the summit.

The circuit of Ben Tee and Sron a' Choire Ghairbh is a good expedition, Kilfinnan being the best starting and finishing point. However, there is some quite steep and rough ground on both the south-west side of Ben Tee and more especially on the north-east face of Meall a' Choire Ghlais. The latter can be avoided by climbing or descending the north-west edge of this face. This traverse can also be done from Glen Garry, using the approach described in the paragraph above. From the end of the forest track at the foot of the Allt Bealach Easain a path leads towards the col between the two hills.

The traverse from Kilfinnan to either Clunes or the Eas Chia-aig over Sron a' Choire Ghairbh and Meall na Teanga, following routes described above, is the best day's hillwalking in these mountains However, it requires a co-operative car driver if one is to avoid a long walk back to Kilfinnan along the forest roads beside Loch Lochy at the end of the day.

Meall na h-Eilde *(hill of the hinds)* (838m)

The country to the west of the Loch Lochy hills has several rounded hills, of which Meall na h-Eilde is the highest. It forms an undulating ridge with its neighbours Meall Tarsuinn (660m), Meall Coire nan Saobhaidh (820m) and Meall an Tagraidh (761m). The shortest approach to Meall na h-Eilde is up Gleann Cia-aig from the Eas Chia-aig. Follow the route described above for Meall na Teanga to the end of the forest and then continue along a path to the footbridge over the Allt Cam Bhealaich at grid reference 188 929. From there climb due north up a grassy slope to Meall na h-Eilde. (Note that the footbridge shown on the 1:50,000 map at grid reference 186 925 has been washed away).

Geal Charn *(white hill)* (804m)

This rounded hill three kilometres west of Meall na h-Eilde is most easily reached from the south by the path from Achnasaul up the east side of the Allt Dubh, followed by a climb up the south-east side of the hill.

Sgurr Mhurlagain *(peak of the bay-shaped inlet)* (880m)

For fourteen kilometres westwards from Geal Charn the hills on the north side of Loch Arkaig are low and rounded, and of no great interest. The change from these smooth granulite hills to the much more rugged schist mountains further west comes at Sgurr Mhurlagain, which rises above the cottage of the same name (but not the same spelling) near the west end of Loch Arkaig. The shortest ascent is from the road near Murlaggan cottage due north up the grassy hillside direct to the summit. Alternatively, the ascent may be combined with Fraoch Bheinn (see below) by climbing the long south-west ridge from the col between the two hills.

Fraoch Bheinn *(heathery hill)* (858m)

This is a fine little hill, particularly on its north side where two steep ridges enclose Coire a' Chaorainn. The ascent is most conveniently made from Strathan up the south-west ridge. Alternatively, one can climb up the path beside the Dearg Allt and climb the steeper south-east side of the hill, but this route is slightly longer. The most attractive route, however, is the narrow north-north-east ridge, which rises above Kinbreack bothy in Glen Kingie. Near the top of this ridge one can look down the rocky east face at an extensive area of fissured rock fall.

Sgurr Cos na Breachd-laoigh *(peak of the cave of the bonny calf)* (835m) (OS spelling *laoidh* is probably wrong)

This hill and its eastern outlier Druim a' Chuirn (815m) rise directly to the north-west of Glendessarry Lodge. The summit ridge forms a horseshoe round Coire Chicheanais; the central part of this ridge between the two summits is quite narrow and there is a prominent little pinnacle, A'Chioch, on its crest. The traverse can well be done from east to west, starting from Glendessarry Lodge northwards up a stalker's path for half a kilometre before climbing directly up the ridge to Druim a' Chuirn. The traverse westwards is very enjoyable as the ridge is narrow and the north flank above Glen Kingie precipitous. Descend from Sgurr Cos a' Breachd-laoigh down its south-east ridge directly to Glendessarry Lodge.

There are stalker's paths on both the east and west sides of Fraoch Bheinn which lead from Glen Dessarry to Kinbreack in Glen Kingie. They provide very convenient routes to the bothy and to the mountains on the north side of Glen Kingie. However, it is worth bearing in mind when planning any route that involves crossing the River Kingie that there are no bridges over the river and it is likely to be impassable during and after wet weather. At the time of writing Kinbreack bothy is in good condition and is a fine base for climbing the Glen Kingie hills.

Between Glen Kingie and Loch Quoich there is a magnificent range of mountains, seventeen kilometres long from Gairich in the east to Ben Aden far to the west on the border of Knoydart. This is one of the finest ranges in the western Highlands, becoming progressively wilder as one goes from east to west. It may be described briefly as follows:- Gairich at the eastern end is rather an isolated mountain with a low pass (360m) to its west. Then the ridge rises steeply to Sgurr an Fhuarain and continues with only a slight drop to about 720m before rising to Sgurr Mor. There the ridge turns south-west and drops to 750m before the peak of Sgurr Beag (890m), down again to 660m and up to An Eag (873m), which stands close to the pass between the head of Glen Kingie and upper Glen Dessarry. Continuing westwards from An Eag, the ridge forms the watershed between Glen Dessarry and the streams draining northwards into Loch Quoich. The peaks on this ridge are Sgurr nan Coireachan, Garbh Chioch Mhor and finally Sgurr na Ciche. From there the westward continuation of the ridge drops in four kilometres to the head of Loch Nevis, but another ridge goes north-east to Meall a' Choire Dhuibh (740m) overlooking the head of Loch Quoich, and then back west to Ben Aden.

Gairich *(the peak of roaring)* (919m)

This isolated mountain dominates the south side of Loch Quoich, and is prominent in views up Glen Garry from the east. It is most easily climbed from the east end of Loch Quoich, starting from the dam and following a usually rather wet path southwards over moorland to the point where it reaches the Glen Kingie forest. From there a good stalker's path climbs up the Druim na Geid Salaich and ends once level ground is reached on the broad crest of this ridge. The route continues

Looking up Glen Garry to the Glen Kingie hills (centre) and Gairich (right)

westwards along the wide ridge across eroded peat bog until the steepening final slopes of Gairich are reached, with the crags of Coire Thollaidh on one's right. Continue directly up, following a faint path (disregard the path which goes off to the left) and climb a few short rock steps to reach the mossy dome of the summit, crowned by a large cairn.

An alternative route to Gairich from Glen Kingie makes use of the path on the north side of the River Kingie opposite Kinbreack. Follow this path up to the pass, A'Mhaingir, on the west side of the mountain. From there a stalker's path zig-zags steeply up the end of Gairich Beag, from where the ridge to Gairich itself is easy going.

Sgurr an Fhuarain (901m)

This peak is very much the eastern outlier of Sgurr Mor, to which it is connected by a high ridge. There is a stalker's path from the southern shore of Loch Quoich right to the summit, but because of the problem of reaching its starting point, this route of ascent is only accessible to canoeists and others with access to a small boat. (The path continues along the ridge from Sgurr an Fhuarain to Sgurr Mor). The most usual route is from Kinbreack, crossing the River Kingie and taking the path north-east towards Gairich (see above) until the foot of the east ridge of Sgurr an Fhuarain is reached. This ridge leads directly to the summit.

Sgurr Mor from Sgurr an Fhuarain, with Sgurr na Ciche in the distance

Sgurr Mor *(big peak)* (1002m)

As its name implies, Sgurr Mor is a massive mountain, dominating the western end of Loch Quoich and throwing down long and uniformly steep slopes to Glen Kingie. It is rather inaccessible since the enlargement of Loch Quoich, and the traditional approach from the north is now possible only for those with a canoe or dingy in which to cross the loch. The usual route of ascent is therefore from the south. Take the path north from Glendessarry Lodge, and once over the pass make a slightly descending traverse north-west into Glen Kingie. After crossing the river (which at this high point should be possible, even in the wettest of weather) one can either climb directly and tediously up the steep slope due north to the summit, or take a less direct route by the stalker's path onto the ridge south-west of Sgurr Beag. This path continues along the ridge to Sgurr Mor and makes the going easy.

A fine traverse can be made following the high-level stalker's path from Sgurr an Fhuarain over Sgurr Mor and Sgurr Beag to An Eag. This little peak is at a strategic point, with its three sides dropping to Loch Quoich, Glen Kingie and Glen Dessarry. From it the descent to Glen Dessarry goes down the south ridge to the col below Sgurr Cos na Breachd-laoigh. From there the traverse over this peak to Glendessarry Lodge is probably a quicker return to Strathan than the descent of the Allt Coire nan Uth down a steep-sided and trackless corrie which gives rough going.

Sgurr nan Coireachan *(peak of the corries)* (953m)

This is a steep-sided mountain formed by a single ridge running from south to north between Glen Dessarry and the head of Loch Quoich. On the east side of the summit the Coire nan Uth has some impressive glaciated slabs high up. The most direct route of ascent is from Glen Dessarry by the steep grassy south ridge, which rises directly above the footbridge where the path up the glen crosses the Allt Coire nan Uth. High up there are many small rocky outcrops, and the ridge leads directly to the summit. A good traverse can be made by descending the rocky east ridge, climbing An Eag and returning to Glendessarry Lodge as described above.

Garbh Chioch Mhor *(big rough place of the breast)* (1013m)

The col immediately south-west of Sgurr nan Coireachan, the Bealach nan Gall, is easily reached from Glen Dessarry by the stream flowing south from it. West of this col the main mountain ridge becomes much more rugged, with a great deal of outcropping rock, as it climbs to Garbh Chioch Bheag and continues to Garbh Chioch Mhor. There is a dry stone dyke of impressive proportions all the way along this ridge, a memorial and tribute to the toil of estate workers many years ago when landowners jealously staked out their territory. Nowadays hillwalkers may find this dyke of some route-finding help on days when visibility is reduced to a few yards. The north side of the ridge drops steeply into Coire nan Gall in a succession of glaciated slabs, giving this corrie a wild and craggy character. The south side of the ridge overlooking the pass at the head of Glen Dessarry is steep, but less continuously rocky.

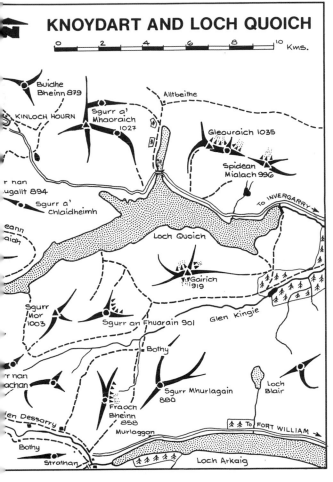

KNOYDART AND LOCH QUOICH

One simple route of ascent to Garbh Chioch Mhor from Glen Dessarry is up to the Bealach nan Gall and along the ridge, following the dyke all the way to the summit. The return can be varied by descending steeply north-west, still following the dyke, to the next col on the ridge, the Feadan na Ciche. The name means *the chanter of the breast,* and is appropriate, for the wind can fairly whistle through this gap. From there descend south-west into a steep-sided, boulder-filled gully which leads quite easily (traces of a path) down to a level grassy terrace below the crags of Garbh Chioch Mhor. Traverse horizontally south-east below these crags until an easy descent leads down to the pass at the head of Glen Dessarry.

Sgurr na Ciche (*peak of the breast*) (1040m)

One kilometre north-west of Garbh Chioch Mhor, across the rocky gap of the Feadan na Ciche, rises Sgurr na Ciche. This is the culminating peak of the great ridge that we have been following along the south side of Loch Quoich, and it is undoubtedly the finest. It rises as a solitary cone above its neighbours, and is the most prominent landmark in this area where the western extremity of Lochaber reaches the Rough Bounds of Knoydart.

The mountain is formed by an eight kilometre long ridge running north-east from the head of Loch Nevis to the head of Loch Quoich, the summit being near the middle. The south-west ridge, called the Druim a' Ghoirtein, rises from the water's edge near Sourlies bothy in a series of steep steps and level sections with a final rocky rise to the summit. The north-east ridge rises directly above the little

Sgurr na Ciche from Garbh Chioch Mhor

dam at the west end of Loch Quoich; it is a good deal more rocky and rugged and passes over the peak of Meall a' Choire Dhuibh where the ridge to Ben Aden branches off. On all sides of the summit of Sgurr na Ciche the slopes are steep and rocky, and on the north-west these slopes drop over a thousand metres to the River Carnach in a single sweep.

The most frequented routes of ascent to Sgurr na Ciche are from Glen Dessarry and from Loch Nevis. From Glen Dessarry follow the path to the pass at the head of the glen (the Bealach an Lagain Duibh) and then climb north-west beside a small stream (traces of a path) to reach a level grassy terrace below the crags of Garbh Chioch Mhor. Traverse north-west along this terrace horizontally and climb a boulder-filled gully following a faint path to reach the Feadan na Ciche. From there climb north-west up the steep hillside among boulders and small crags through which a faint path twists and turns before reaching the short easy-angled ridge to the summit.

From the head of Loch Nevis the obvious route of ascent is the long Druim a' Ghortein ridge. If one starts at Sourlies the ridge is climbed in its entirety, and it will doubtless seem a long climb. If one starts from Carnoch it is more convenient to climb the steep grassy flank of the ridge above the River Carnach to reach its crest just above Lochan na Craoibhe.

Ben Aden with the long ridge of Sgurr a'Choire-bheithe to the left, seen from Loch Nevis

A third route of ascent that was much used before the raising of Loch Quoich is the north-east ridge over Meall a' Choire Dhuibh. Either a ten kilometre walk along the north shore or a suitable boat is needed to reach the small dam at the west end of the loch. From there it is probably best to get onto the crest of the ridge as low down as possible as its flanks are quite steep and rocky. There is a stalker's path leading for a short distance up the Allt Coire nan Gall and onto the east flank of the ridge.

Ben Aden *(the hill of the face)* (887m)

Despite the fact that it does not reach Munro status, Ben Aden is a splendid peak which epitomises as well as any other the character of the Rough Bounds of Knoydart. It is steep and rocky on all sides, remote and withdrawn in its wild fastness between Loch Quoich and Loch Nevis, truly a wilderness mountain. On three sides it plunges down hundreds of metres to deep glens and corries, on the fourth, to the east, a knobbly ridge links Ben Aden to its nearest neighbour, Meall a' Choire Dhuibh.

Practically any route up Ben Aden involves careful route-finding and possibly also some scrambling among its many crags. In misty weather it may be difficult to find an easy route, and this is particularly true of the descent, for the many crags and cliffs are not easily seen from above. Ben Aden is not a mountain of well-defined ridges; more a maze of knolls and crags, humps and hollows.

Probably the easiest route is from the Carnach River, starting at its junction with the Allt Achadh a' Ghlinne. Climb the south-west face of the mountain, making a rising traverse leftwards high up to avoid the steep rocks below the summit, and reach the north-west ridge. At the top of this ridge a couple of knolls or false tops are passed before the summit is reached.

Another route from the same starting point goes up the Allt Achadh a' Ghlinne into a wild corrie enclosed by crags. In one and a half kilometres climb steeply north-east by a little stream which leads to the east ridge of Ben Aden half a kilometre from the summit.

The north face of the mountain overlooking Lochan nam Breac is if anything steeper and rockier than the south face, and it is certainly in a remoter setting. The east-north-east ridge is a good route if one can overcome the problem of reaching its foot.(See above for the north-east ridge of Sgurr na Ciche, with which this route might be combined).

PATHS AND WALKS

Strathan to Loch Nevis. The first part of this route as far as Sourlies bothy has been described in the last chapter. From Sourlies the best route for the next kilometre depends on the state of the tide. If it is out, then walk along the foreshore below a steep crag and then across saltings northwards to the footbridge over the River Carnach. If the tide is in, then one has to climb a short way up the hillside north-west of Sourlies and contour round on a narrow path above the crag, then descend to the saltings. Once over the River Carnach one is in Knoydart, and the route to Inverie is over the Mam Meadail. There is a good path all the way, starting a short distance north of the ruins of Carnoch. The whole path from Strathan to Inverie is a right of way. (27 kilometres).

Loch Quoich to Loch Nevis. This route follows the northern boundary of the area described in this chapter. The starting point is where the road to Kinloch Hourn leaves Loch Quoich. For five kilometres the way along the lochside is trackless, but the going is fairly easy. Beyond the Abhainn Chosaidh, which may well be impossible to cross in spate conditions, the remains of a road built by the Hydro-Electric Board give easier going for four kilometres to the dam at the west end of the loch. The path to Barrisdale built many years ago by James Watt starts at the south end of the dam and goes to the east end of Lochan nam Breac and along its north side. However, one must leave this path near the west end of the lochan and descend very rough terrain into the deep glen of the River Carnoch, where the path is virtually non-existent for much of the way, though it does reappear in places and three kilometres down the river it becomes fairly well-defined on the west bank. In a further four kilometres the ruined houses at Carnoch are reached across level boggy ground that once was cultivated. This is a fine walk through magnificent surroundings, but much of it is rough going. (20 kilometres).

Strathan to Glen Garry by Glen Kingie. From Strathan take the Dearg Allt path to Kinbreack. Cross the River Kingie and after two pathless kilometres follow the path down the glen below Gairich to Lochan where the Forestry Commission plantation is entered. At this point there is a choice of routes: either north to the Loch Quoich dam (18 kilometres), or along the forest road on the north side of the River Kingie, crossing after a few kilometres and continuing to Loch Poulary and Glen Garry two kilometres west of Tomdoun. (22 kilometres).

Loch Arkaig to Kilfinnan by Gleann Cia-aig. From the Eas Chia-aig take the path and forest road up Gleann Cia-aig to the footbridge over the Allt Cam Bhealaich (as described for Meall na h-Eilde). The continuation of the path to Fedden has now almost disappeared, so make a way alongside the Allt Cam Bhealaich (on either side) to join the path just west of the Cam Bhealach. Continue over the pass and down through the South Laggan Forest to Kilfinnan. (15 kilometres).

Loch Arkaig to Glen Garry by Gleann Cia-aig. Follow the route described in the preceding paragraph to the footbridge over the Allt Cam Bhealaich. Continue along the line of the now non-existent path (but still shown on the 1:50,000 map) to the ruined cottage of Fedden. Cross the glen eastwards to join the path which contours round the foot of Sron a' Choire Ghairbh from the Cam Bhealach. Continue north-east along this path down into newly planted forest (where the path is hard to follow) to reach the Allt Bealach Easain. From that point a track continues down the Allt Ladaidh for two kilometres to a shed at a junction of tracks. There either turn west to Greenfield and the bridge over Loch Garry (19 kilometres), or eastwards to White Bridge near Invergarry (21 kilometres).

CLIMBING

Despite their undoubtedly steep and rocky character, the mountains described in this chapter have yielded very little in the way of serious climbing. Certainly no routes have been recorded, and this is surprising. The remoteness of most of the crags is no doubt responsible for their apparent neglect. Nevertheless there is a vast amount of good rough rock on mountains such as Ben Aden, and although the glaciated slabs of Coire nan Gall on the north side of Garbh Chioch Mhor may not rival the Etive Slabs, there is a lot of unexplored rock there too. But not least, there will be a special challenge and pleasure to be found on the crags of these remote mountains.

CHAPTER 5

Knoydart

MAPS: Ordnance Survey 1:50,000 Sheets 33 and 40
Bartholomew 1:100,000 Sheet 50

PRINCIPAL HILLS

Sgurr nan Eugallt	894m	931 045
Sgurr a' Choire-bheithe	913m	895 016
Luinne Bheinn	939m	868 008
Meall Buidhe	946m	849 990
Ladhar Bheinn	1020m	824 041
Beinn na Caillich	785m	796 067
Sgurr Coire Choinnichean	796m	791 011
Beinn Bhuidhe	855m	822 967

If one district in the western Highlands epitomises better than any other the rugged grandeur and remoteness of this part of Scotland, then it must surely be Knoydart. This mountainous peninsula between the sea-lochs Nevis and Hourn is one of the most inaccessible corners of the land, and the wild, rocky and inhospitable nature of much of the terrain well earns for itself the title The Rough Bounds of Knoydart. It is surrounded on three sides by the sea and long narrow sea-lochs, and on the fourth side by the mountains around the west end of Loch Quoich which present a very effective barrier, penetrated only by a single narrow road and three footpaths.

From the mountaineer's point of view, Knoydart is best known for its three great mountains, Ladhar Bheinn, Luinne Bheinn and Meall Buidhe, all Munros. There are, however, several other fine peaks which do not quite reach this status, and several good footpaths which are rights of way penetrate through the area. These footpaths are vital for travel in Knoydart, for there are barely twelve kilometres of roads, and only the locals have cars.

The two sea-lochs which enclose Knoydart, Loch Nevis meaning the *loch of heaven,* and Loch Hourn, *hell's loch,* are scenically two of the finest of Scotland's west coast lochs, being long, narrow and steeply enclosed by mountains. It is these sea-lochs, and a few others like them along the west coast of the Highlands, that

Looking across Loch Hourn to Ladhar Bheinn

gives this part of Scotland its characteristic, one might almost say unique, combination of mountain and glen, sea and loch.

There is more to Knoydart than its landscape, however, no matter how impressive it may be. The character of this peninsula is such that it is one of the most delectable goals in the western Highlands for those who seek wilderness, solitude and adventure, whether it be in climbing the mountains, making long cross-country walks or sailing and canoeing round the coastline.

Although the landscape of Knoydart is unchanged and (one hopes) will remain so, the social fabric of the peninsula has altered in recent years with change of ownership. Parts of the Knoydart estate have been sold, so that the original estate is now broken into smaller parts. Changes in the population and its pattern of life are also evident. Inverie is the only habitation of any size. Its cottages and houses, the estate office and the shop are lined along the edge of Inverie Bay, looking out across the mouth of Loch Nevis towards the Inner Hebrides. The only public road links Inverie with Airor, a tiny village on the Sound of Sleat. Elsewhere there are several isolated houses around the coast, some of them inhabited. The interior of the peninsula is wild and uninhabited.

ACCESS

It is one of Knoydart's distinctive characteristics that there is no road access from outside into the district. The nearest road is at Kinloch Hourn, and it ends at the north-eastern corner of the peninsula. The only other public access that does not involve walking is the boat service between Mallaig and Inverie. As noted in the preceding chapter, the indication on the Second Series edition of the 1:50,000 map of a ferry service to the head of Loch Nevis is incorrect, but it may be possible to make a special arrangement or charter to sail to the head of the loch and land there. Contact Bruce Watt Sea Cruises, Mallaig. Telephone 0687 2320.

The keeper at Barrisdale has his own private boat which he may be willing to make available for sailings between there and Kinloch Hourn and Arnisdale. It may also be possible to arrange with a boatman at Arnisdale or Corran on the north side of Loch Hourn for a crossing of the loch to Knoydart. However, it must be stressed that access to Barrisdale by boat is highly uncertain, and visitors should be prepared to walk.

The principal walking routes to Knoydart are (refer to the map on page 78):

1. The right of way from the west end of Loch Arkaig by Sourlies and the Mam Meadail to Inverie, described in the two preceding chapters.

2. The right of way along the north shore of Loch Quoich to its west end, followed by the path to Lochan nam Breac. From there, either down the River Carnach to Loch Nevis (as described in the preceding chapter) or over the Mam Unndalain to Barrisdale. A variation of this route is to go from Loch Quoich up the Abhainn Chosaidh and down Glen Barrisdale.

3. The right of way along the south shore of Loch Hourn from Kinloch Hourn to Barrisdale.

Owners of canoes or lightweight dingies will find that these forms of transport are ideal for the journey from Kinloch Hourn to Barrisdale and points further west along the shore of Loch Hourn. The upper end of the loch is in a superb setting, seals are often seen and the tiny island of Mhogh-sgeir has a heronry. However, both Barrisdale Bay and Loch Beag at the head of Loch Hourn dry out at low water, and the tide races through Caolas Mor, so it is advisable to check the state of the tide before setting out.

PUBLIC TRANSPORT

Postbus (4 seater): Invergarry Post Office to Kinloch Hourn. Mondays, Wednesdays and Fridays.

Boat: Mallaig to Inverie (Bruce Watt Sea Cruises, Mallaig. Telephone 0687 2320). Mondays, Wednesdays and Fridays.

ACCOMMODATION

Accommodation in and around Knoydart is not plentiful. At Inverie there are a guest house, a hostel and a few cottages to let and offering bed and breakfast. There is a camp site near the village. Enquiries about accommodation at Inverie should be made from the Estate Office (Telephone 0687 2331). There is no shelter or accommodation at Camusrory at the head of Loch Nevis, but Sourlies bothy is about two kilometres away. There is not a Mountain Rescue Post at Camusrory as indicated on some of the earlier editions of the 1:50,000 map. At Barrisdale there is a bothy beside the keeper's cottage, but it is too small to be able to meet the demands made of it. As it may not be possible to pre-book accommodation, it is probably advisable not to rely on finding shelter there. There is, however, a camp site at Barrisdale. It may be possible to get bed and breakfast or bothy accommodation at Kinloch Hourn. Enquiries should be made locally.

THE HILLS

The north-eastern corner of Knoydart is the Barrisdale Estate, and in it there are two very large mountains, judged by their extent if not by their heights, which in both cases are just less than Munro height. They are Sgurr nan Eugallt and Sgurr a' Choire-bheithe, the highest points of two long ridges running from east to west, and separated by Gleann Cosaidh. Both ridges are quite long, seven kilometres or more, and both have many minor bumps and tops along their crests, so that they are really quite substantial mountains, unjustifiably neglected.

Sgurr nan Eugallt *(peak of the precipices)* (894m)

This mountain is quite accessible as it rises directly above the road between Loch Quoich and Kinloch Hourn in a series of rough corries. It was through one of these corries, Coire Beithe at the east end of the ridge, that Prince Charles in July 1746 broke through the cordon of Hanoverian troops that was trying to cut off his escape eastwards from the coast. With his party of five companions he crossed the east end of the Sgurr nan Eugallt ridge in darkness and descended the north-east side of the mountain, slipping past the Hanoverian sentries near Loch Coire Shubh before heading north to Glen Shiel and Affric.

The most straightforward route to Sgurr nan Eugallt is the stalker's path which starts at the ruined roadside cottage of Coireshubh. This path ends just below the north-east ridge of the peak, and this ridge can be followed to the top. A good long traverse can then be enjoyed by going one kilometre north-west to Sgurr Sgiath Airigh (881m) which is the north-west top of the long ridge. Then one can return south-east along the ridge over many little tops to Sgurr a' Chlaidheimh (840m) before descending to the road down one of the steep and rough corries on the north-east side of that peak.

Sgurr a' Choire-bheithe *(peak of the birch tree corrie)* (913m)

This summit is the highest point of the Druim Chosaidh, and is situated nearly at the west end of that remarkably long and rugged ridge, which measures ten kilometres from Loch Quoich to the glen near Barrisdale. Sgurr a' Choire-bheithe is rather inaccessible from the east; a long walk along Loch Quoich followed by an equally long traverse of the ridge over many little knolls and tops. This ridge gives one or two little bits of scrambling if the crest is followed. The descent should be made west for half a kilometre and then south to the path near the summit of the Mam Unndalain, from where it is a long walk back to Loch Quoich.

A much shorter route starts at Barrisdale, taking the path south towards Gleann Unndalain for two kilometres and then climbing the long easy-angled ridge on the north side of the glen. This ridge leads over a small knoll one kilometre west of the summit. This knoll is less than one kilometre north of the Mam Unndalain, and it is accessible from there by a short steep climb.

Elsewhere in the Barrisdale Estate there are a few lower hills worth noting. Just east of Barrisdale, Carn Mairi (502m), An Caisteal (622m) and Meall nan Eun (666m) form a semi-circular ridge round an unnamed corrie. The north side of An Caisteal is a fine slabby face 200m high at an average angle of 45 degrees. To the south-east of this group, Slat Bheinn (700m) lies between Gleann Cosaidh and Glen Barrisdale, and can be climbed from the path up Glen Barrisdale, provided the river can be crossed.

Luinne Bheinn (doubtful meaning, possibly *hill of anger* or *mirth*) (939m)
Meall Buidhe *(yellow hill)* (946m)

The centre of Knoydart is dominated by the two mountains Luinne Bheinn and Meall Buidhe which together extend across the peninsula from the head of Loch Nevis to Barrisdale. They are very rough and craggy mountains, though nowhere are there cliffs of any great size or height. One of their most impressive features is Coire Odhair, on the west side of the ridge between them. This corrie shows extensive areas of glaciated rock with two tiny lochans lying in its depths.

Luinne Bheinn consists of a narrow ridge running west from the Mam Unndalain to the double-topped summit, and then dropping north-west to the Mam Barrisdale. The north and south sides of the summit ridge are very steep and there is a fine corrie, the Coire Glas, on the north side overlooking Barrisdale. The true summit is the west top, marked by a small cairn, with a larger cairn a short distance along the north-west ridge. When descending southwards from Luinne Bheinn it is advisable not to go down directly south from the summit as that side of the ridge drops very steeply in broken cliffs. It is better to go a short distance west and then descend south by a grassy gully for about 100m to reach the top of a broad grassy shelf which drops at an easy angle towards the col at the head of Coire Odhair.

Meall Buidhe has two tops, the north-western one being the higher. The South-east Top (940m) is at the edge of a steep little crag on the north face of the mountain, and stands at the junction of its three ridges. The west ridge drops four kilometres to the junction of the Inverie River and the Allt Gleann Meadail. The south-east ridge drops over Sgurr Sgeithe towards Carnoch, and the north-east ridge goes round the head of Coire Odhair to link Meall Buidhe to Luinne Bheinn; these last two ridges enclose a fine little corrie at the head of the Allt na Sealga where steep slabby rocks plunge down to a tiny lochan.

These two mountains are often climbed together, and will be described accordingly. Being at the centre of Knoydart, they are equally accessible from Inverie, Barrisdale and the head of Loch Nevis. The approach from Loch Quoich in the east is much longer, but it is a very fine route, taking one past lonely Lochan nam Breac, and is quite feasible if one can reach the head of Loch Quoich by boat.

From Inverie take the track up Gleann an Dubh-lochain and the path to the Mam Barrisdale. Climb Luinne Bheinn by its north-west ridge. Descend south as described above and traverse round the head of Coire Odhair; the ridge round the corrie climbs over the top of Druim Leac a' Shith, and this little bit of climbing can be avoided by traversing along fairly obvious grass terraces and ledges on the west side of the ridge to reach the Bealach Ile Coire. From this col Meall Buidhe is climbed by its north-east ridge, which becomes steeper and rockier as it approaches the South-east Top. The summit is across a shallow grassy dip. The descent is down the west ridge which gives pleasantly easy going. It is advisable in wet weather to aim for the bridge over the Allt Coire Meadail.

From Barrisdale take the path up Gleann Unndalain to the Mam Unndalain and climb the east ridge of Luinne Bheinn. This ridge rises at an easy angle, but is quite rocky, especially towards the top where the crest is slabby, but there are no difficulties. Continue to Meall Buidhe as described above. The return journey is best made by descending the easy gully north-east from the col between the two tops of Meall Buidhe into Coire Odhair, aiming for the two lochans amid grand rock scenery. From the lochans traverse north, making use of grassy terraces across the rocky west face of Luinne Bheinn and continue on a slightly descending line below Bachd Mhic an Tosaich to reach the Mam Barrisdale, and so back to Barrisdale.

From Carnoch take the path to the Mam Meadail, then climb steeply north to reach the south-east ridge of Meall Buidhe, which is followed to the top. Traverse round Coire Odhair to Luinne Bheinn, from where the easiest return to Carnoch is back to the Bealach Choire Odhair and then down Coire na Ghaoithe'n Ear to the River Carnach.

From Loch Quoich follow James Watt's old path west past Lochan nam Breac to the Mam Unndalain and climb the east ridge of Luinne Bheinn. Traverse to Meall Buidhe, and return to the Bealach Choire Odhair. From there it is possible, with care, to make a descending traverse north-east to rejoin the path near the Mam Unndalain and follow it back to Loch Quoich.

Ladhar Bheinn (*hoof* or *claw mountain*) (1020m)

Ladhar Bheinn (pronounced Larven) is the finest mountain in Knoydart, and is probably in most climbers' list of the best dozen mountains in Scotland. It is a complex massif of several ridges, peaks and corries, but at its heart and the centre of climbing interest is the horseshoe of ridges and peaks that enclose Coire Dhorrcail. This corrie, facing north-east to Loch Hourn, is one of the finest in the Highlands with great cliffs along its headwall and along the south-east side of the smaller Coire na Cabaig.

The summit of Ladhar Bheinn is near the western corner of Coire Dhorrcail, which is the meeting point of three ridges. The summit cairn is on the west-north-west ridge a short distance from the junction. The north-east ridge drops and rises again over the peak of Stob a' Choire Odhair (960m) and forms one arm enclosing Coire Dhorrcail. The south-east ridge, which forms the headwall of the corrie, drops to the Bealach Coire Dhorrcail and rises to Stob a' Chearcaill (849m) whose ridge runs at right-angles to it, thus forming a letter **T**. The north-east ridge of Stob a' Chearcaill drops very steeply at first and then continues to Creag Bheithe above Barrisdale Bay; the south-west ridge, called Aonach Sgoilte, goes for several kilometres to end at the sharp-pointed peak of Sgurr Coire Choinnichean above Inverie. The complete traverse of this ridge from Barrisdale to Inverie, or vice versa, is a fine expedition, but is probably seldom done.

Altogether Ladhar Bheinn is a complex and magnificent mountain. Its only dull feature is the south-west side above Gleann na Guiserein. The north part of the mountain, Coire Each and Coire Odhar, are very wild and seldom visited, being off the climber's normal routes. There is a magnetic anomaly on the mountain, and the magnetic compass is not reliable.

In recent years part of Ladhar Bheinn, from Coire Dhorrcail north-west to the Mam Li, and from the summit down to Loch Hourn, has been purchased by the John Muir Trust with the aim of conserving and protecting its wilderness qualities. It is fitting that the name of John Muir, a Scotsman and pioneer conservationist, should be linked with this grand mountain. A major contribution towards this purchase was made by the Scottish Mountaineering Trust.

The classic traverse of Ladhar Bheinn is the circuit of Coire Dhorrcail, which is best done from Barrisdale. Take the stalker's path towards Coire Dhorrcail and at the point where it crosses the lower part of the Creag Bheithe ridge turn left and climb this ridge. As one gains height there are superb views towards Ladhar Bheinn, and in due course the ridge abuts against the steep peak of Stob a' Chearcaill. The ascent directly up this peak is quite a scramble, traversing to and fro on grassy ledges and climbing short pitches; however, with good route-finding there are no great difficulties. It would certainly be more difficult to find the best route in mist,

opposite above. Luinne Bheinn from Lochan nam Breac
below. On James Watt's path to Barrisdale looking east beyond Lochan nam Breac to Sgurr Mor

Ladhar Bheinn from Stob a'Chearcaill

or in descent, and it is possible to find an easier route of ascent by traversing round to the south-east for a short distance before climbing up. (An alternative but less fine route to Stob a' Chearcaill is by the Mam Barrisdale and the south-east face of this peak; the last part of the ascent to the summit ridge is also quite steep, but with careful route-finding an easy way can be found).

Once on Stob a' Chearcaill, its fine ridge is followed past the tops of two or three impressively steep gullies, and at Pt 849m turn north-west and descend the broad ridge to the Bealach Coire Dhorrcail. Near the bealach a prominent spur juts out into Coire Dhorrcail, separating it from the smaller Coire na Cabaig, and there is an easy descent northwards from the bealach down steep grass. This is probably the easiest route of ascent or descent in the whole cirque of Coire Dhorrcail. The ascent to Ladhar Bheinn continues along the headwall of the corrie, climbing over the tops of several buttresses and descending slightly between them to look down into the depths of dark gullies. Eventually the last of these clefts is passed, a steep climb leads to the junction of the ridges, and the summit is a short distance along the nearly level ridge to the west.

Returning to the junction, descend the north-east ridge quite steeply and reascend to the narrow peak of Stob a' Choire Odhair, from where there is a particularly fine view down to Barrisdale Bay and beyond to the head of Loch Hourn. Further down the ridge becomes broad and grassy with a few small crags. Below these crags leave the ridge and descend east into the lower part of Coire Dhorrcail to reach the start of the stalker's path back to Barrisdale.

The ascent from Inverie is a lot longer. One route, hardly worthy of the mountain, is to take the track north from the pier over the Mam Uidhe into Gleann na Guiserein and climb the south-west side of Ladhar Bheinn, a steep and rather uninteresting ascent. A better way is to take the road up the Inverie River to the outflow of Loch an Dubh-Lochain, then climb north to the Mam Suidheig (490m) and traverse the ridge east to Aonach Sgoilte and the 849m top of Stob a' Chearcaill, where the Barrisdale route is joined.

Beinn an Caillich *(hill of the old woman)* (785m)

This is a rather remote hill, well to the north-west of Ladhar Bheinn. It is fairly grassy with easy-angled slopes to the south, but steeper and more rocky on the three other sides. The ascent from Inverie is rather long, but follows paths for most of the way, first over the Mam Uidhe to Gleann na Guiserein and the ruin at Folach, then up the Abhainn Beag until a crossing of this burn can be made and the southern slopes of the hill climbed.

A shorter and more interesting route is possible from the east if a landing on the south shore of Loch Hourn near Li can be made. From there climb up the Allt Li, cross flat ground eastwards and finish up the steeper east ridge of Beinn na Caillich, called Carn Dubh.

Sgurr Coire Choinnichean *(peak of the mossy corrie)* (796m)

This is the sharply pointed peak which rises directly above Inverie and looks so impressive as one approaches the village by boat from Mallaig. The ascent from Inverie is short and steep. To avoid the forest behind the village, follow the road past Inverie House for a further half kilometre until clear of the forest, and then strike uphill towards Coire na Cloiche to reach the narrow upper ridge of the peak and follow this to the top.

Beinn Bhuidhe *(yellow hill)* (855m)

This very extensive hill occupies the whole north shore of upper Loch Nevis, Beinn Bhuidhe itself being the highest point of a long undulating ridge. On the north side several rugged corries drop towards Gleann Meadail. If approaching from the head of Loch Nevis, the best ascent is to the Mam Meadail followed by the traverse along almost four kilometres of undulating ridge. If approaching from Inverie, take the route to Gleann Meadail as far as the footbridge at grid reference 813 988, then follow the stream south-east into the corrie to reach the col half a kilometre west of Beinn Bhuidhe.

PATHS AND WALKS

Carnoch to Inverie. This is the last stage of the right of way starting at the west end of Loch Arkaig and leading to Inverie. From the ruined village of Carnoch , take the path which climbs in a well-graded series of curves to the Mam Meadail (550m). On the west side of the pass the path descends gradually into Gleann Meadail and in six kilometres joins the road in the Inverie glen near the prominent monument on Torr a' Bhalbhain. There remain three kilometres down the glen to Inverie. (12 kilometres from Carnoch, 27 kilometres from Strathan).

Kinloch Hourn to Barrisdale. This is an important right of way, as it gives the shortest walk from a public road into Knoydart. The path is well-defined all the way from the road end at Kinloch Hourn

The path along Loch Hourn to Barrisdale

along the south shore of the loch to Barrisdale. There is a good deal of climbing involved, however, as the path goes up and downhill along the lochside. (10 kilometres).

Barrisdale to Inverie. The route is well-defined all the way over the Mam Barrisdale (450m), as there is a good path. Once past Loch an Dubh-Lochain the path becomes a road for the rest of the way to Inverie. (14 kilometres. 24 kilometres from Kinloch Hourn to Inverie)

Loch Quoich to Barrisdale. The first half of this route as far as Lochan nam Breac has been described in the preceding chapter. To go to Barrisdale from the lochan keep on the path which climbs gradually on the north side and in three and a half kilometres reaches the Mam Unndalain. Descend Gleann Unndalain to Barrisdale. (19 kilometres from the road at Loch Quoich).

This path, along with others in Knoydart, was made many years ago by an engineer named James Watt who returned to Scotland from Rhodesia under a cloud and sought employment out of the public eye. He obtained a contract to link the glens in Knoydart, which he did very effectively with the help of only two men.

An alternative to the preceding route leaves Loch Quoich at the foot of Gleann Cosaidh and follows the path up the glen for three kilometres, then over a pass north-westwards to reach the head of Glen Barrisdale, down which the path continues to Barrisdale. (16 kilometres from the road at Loch Quoich). This may be preferable to the previous route in (or after) very wet weather, as it does not involve any big river crossings; just a succession of small ones. The Abhainn Chosaidh may not be crossable at such times.

CLIMBING

The climbing possibilities of the great cliffs of Ladhar Bheinn were recognised long ago, probably as early as the celebrated SMC yachting meet of Easter 1897. In the following year H.Raeburn and his companions made the first ascent of the prominent gully in Coire Dhorrcail which now bears his name. It was realised that the unfavourable strata of the rock and the profuse vegetation made the cliffs quite unsuitable for summer rock climbing, and that the best possibilities would be in winter; however, the remoteness of Ladhar Bheinn and its proximity to the west coast made winter climbing problematical. Many years elapsed until finally in 1963 T. Patey and his companions climbed two fine gullies, and revived interest in the winter climbing potential of the mountain. Since then many fine winter routes have been done.

The main feature of the Coire Dhorrcail cliffs is the great 350m high buttress at their left-hand end. In winter a big steep snowfield forms in the centre of this buttress. To its right is the long *Viking Gully,* one of Patey's routes, and further right is *Raeburn's Gully.* The big buttress, called *Spider Buttress,* has been climbed by five distinct routes between Grade III and V. Several of the corners further right have also been climbed.

On the north-west face of Stob a' Chearcaill both obvious gullies and two other narrower ones have been climbed, all in winter.(Grade III and IV).

In the corrie two kilometres east of Barrisdale the north face of An Caisteal, which is a fine 200m high sweep of slabs, has three routes of Very Severe standard. The west face of Meall nan Eun has some rather small buttresses, the best being the southernmost one on which two short routes of Severe standard have been done.

CHAPTER 6

Loch Quoich to Glen Shiel

MAPS: Ordnance Survey 1:50,000 Sheets 33 and 34
Bartholomew 1:100,000 Sheets 50,51,54 and 55

PRINCIPAL HILLS

Spidean Mialach	996m	066 043
Gleouraich	1035m	040 054
Sgurr a' Mhaoraich	1027m	984 065
Meall Dubh	788m	245 078
Druim nan Cnamh	790m	131 077
Creag a' Mhaim	947m	088 077
Druim Shionnach	987m	074 084
Aonach air Chrith	1021m	051 083
Maol Chinn-dearg	981m	032 088
Sgurr an Doire Leathain	1010m	015 099
Sgurr an Lochain	1004m	005 104
Creag nan Damh	918m	983 112
Sgurr a' Bhac Chaolais	885m	958 110
Sgurr na Sgine	945m	946 113
The Saddle	1010m	935 131
Sgurr Mhic Bharraich	781m	917 174
Beinn Sgritheall	974m	836 126
Beinn na h-Eaglaise	804m	854 120
Beinn nan Caorach	773m	871 122

This is another well-defined region of the western Highlands, the southern boundary being Glen Garry, Loch Quoich and Loch Hourn, and the northern boundary Glen Moriston, Loch Cluanie, Glen Shiel and Loch Duich. As is the case with the neighbouring areas, there is a marked contrast between the eastern and western parts. The eastern part near the Great Glen is mainly high undulating moorland and forests and the landscape has no great character; the western part, however, is entirely mountainous and is one of the most splendid parts of the Highlands. The dividing line between these two areas is the A87 road between Glen Garry and Glen Moriston. To the east of this road there is an extensive tract of rough country rising to its highest point at Meall Dubh, and there are large areas of forest near Fort Augustus and on the hillsides above Loch Ness and Glen Moriston.

West of the A87 road, however, the landscape is very different, and one only has to stop at a roadside parking place near the top of the hill above Glen Garry to appreciate one of the great West Highland panoramas. Many of the mountains described in earlier chapters are arrayed on the south-western horizon beyond Glen Garry, and to their right, looking further north beyond Loch Loyne, are some of the mountains to be described in this chapter.

On the north side of Loch Quoich there are three fine peaks: Spidean Mialach, Gleouraich and Sgurr a' Mhaoraich. To their north, overlooking Strath Cluanie and Glen Shiel, is the South Glen Shiel Ridge, a splendid fourteen kilometre long range of seven Munros. Beyond their western end, and really part of the same chain of mountains, are Sgurr na Sgine and The Saddle. Further to the west there is a broad peninsula between Loch Hourn and Loch Duich where the solitary Beinn Sgritheall towers over the litle village of Arnisdale on Loch Hourn.

All these mountains are very accessible, none of them being more than four kilometres from the nearest road. This no doubt accounts for their popularity, but it must be admitted that, fine as they are, they do not convey the sense of remoteness so characteristic of the peaks of western Lochaber and Knoydart which were described in the last two chapters.

ACCESS

The main route of access from the south to the mountains in this area is the A87 road from Invergarry to Cluanie Inn and westwards down Glen Shiel to Loch Duich. Seven kilometres west of Invergarry a branch road continues up Glen Garry past Loch Quoich to Kinloch Hourn. From Shiel Bridge at the head of Loch Duich another minor road climbs over the Bealach Ratagain to reach Glenelg and Arnisdale.

PUBLIC TRANSPORT

Bus: Glasgow to Kyle of Lochalsh via Invergarry and Glen Shiel (Scottish Citylink Coaches and Skye-Ways Express Coaches). Daily.
Inverness to Kyle of Lochalsh via Glen Moriston and Glen Shiel (Scottish Citylink Coaches and Skye-Ways Express Coaches). Daily.

Postbus (4 Seater): Invergarry to Kinloch Hourn. Mondays, Wednesdays and Fridays.
Invergarry to Kingie. Tuesdays, Thursdays and Saturdays.
Arnisdale – Glenelg – Shiel Bridge – Kyle of Lochalsh. Mondays to Saturdays.

Spidean Mialach and Gleouraich from the north-west

ACCOMMODATION

On the south side of the area there are hotels at Invergarry and Tomdoun, and a camp and caravan site at Faichem two kilometres west of Invergarry. In the north the hotel at Cluanie is right in the heart of the mountains, a traditional mountaineers' inn. Corrielair cottage close to Cluanie Inn is available to let outwith the stalking season. At the foot of Glen Shiel and round the head of Loch Duich there are hotels and many cottages and houses offering bed and breakfast. The youth hostel at Ratagan is one of the SYHA's oldest and most popular, and there is a camp and caravan site at Shiel Bridge. On the far side of the Bealach Ratagain there is a small inn at Glenelg, and in that village and at Arnisdale there are bed and breakfasts and cottages to let. Throughout the area described in this chapter wild camping is possible, provided discretion is used, and for the bothy dweller there is the lonely cottage at Suardalan in Glen More, south of the Bealach Ratagain.

THE HILLS

Spidean Mialach *(peak of deer, or other wild animals)* (996m)
Gleouraich (possibly *uproar* or *noise*) (1027m)

These two mountains form a very fine ridge on the north side of Loch Quoich, and their traverse is a delightful expedition, giving all the pleasures of west Highland ridge-walking with the advantage (in some people's eyes) of a very short and easy approach. The south side of these mountains is mostly grassy with some scree and boulders high up; the north side is very different, for on that side a series of wild corries and rocky spurs overlook the head of the River Loyne.

The traverse of the two mountains is most conveniently done by starting at the foot of the Allt Coire Peitireach, four kilometres west of the Loch Quoich dam. A short distance eastwards along the road a rough track slants up the hillside as far as the electricity transmission line, and above it a good stalker's path continues as far as the headwaters of the Allt a' Mheil. From the end of the path one should climb east for one kilometre up easy grassy slopes, and then north-east to the summit of Spidean Mialach. The ridge westwards drops in a series of scalloped curves to the Fiar Bealach (742m), and there is a zig-zag stalker's path up the ridge to the east top of Gleouraich, called Craig Coire na Fiar Bhealaich (1006m). A further slight drop and rise lead to the main summit. The descent goes north-west at first, down to the junction of two ridges, and then south-west to reach the top of a stalker's path. This turns out to be a splendid path, giving an easy and enjoyable descent. For some distance it goes along the south-west ridge on its west flank which is so steep that there is a feeling of exposure, with Loch Quoich a long way below. Lower, the path zig-zags down the grassy hillside to return to the road through a patch of overgrown rhododendrons, the only remaining signs of the gardens of the long-since flooded Glenquoich Lodge.

Another stalker's path goes from Alltbeithe in Glen Quoich up the north-west ridge of Gleouraich to a height of about 700m, but this route of ascent or descent is rarely used by hillwalkers.

Sgurr a' Mhaoraich *(peak of the shellfish)* (1027m)

This, the third of the trio of Munros on the north side of Loch Quoich, is separated from the other two by the three kilometre long arm of the loch created by the raising of its level. With its two lower tops, Am Bathaich and Sgurr Thionail, it forms a large and isolated mountain. Seen from Loch Hourn it seems to completely block the head of the loch with its great bulk. Like so many of the mountains in this area, its south side is grassy, forming the big open Coire nan Eiricheallach. The west and north sides of the mountain are much steeper and rockier, and the east face holds the steep-sided Coire a' Chaorainn.

The quickest ascent to Sgurr a'Mhaoraich is by its south ridge, starting just east of Loch a' Choire Bheithe on the road to Kinloch Hourn. This route is certainly very direct, but it lacks any features of interest.

A more interesting traverse makes use of two good stalker's paths. Start one kilometre south-west of the bridge over the arm of Loch Quoich, and climb the path up the broad ridge of Bac nan Canaichean to reach Sgurr Coire nan Eirichealach (891m). Continue north-westwards, dropping to 823m along a fine ridge which becomes quite rocky on the rise to Sgurr a' Mhaoraich; at one point it appears that pitons have been driven into the rock, but they are just the visible remains of fence making years ago. The ridge broadens, and a final steeper climb leads to the summit. Descend north-west then north down a steep grass slope to the Bealach Coire a' Chaorainn and climb the ridge north-east to Am Bathaich (899m). Continue east along a narrow ridge and reach the top of a stalker's path which zig-zags steeply down the grassy crest and leads to the private road to Alltbeithe. Return along this road to the starting point.

Glen Quoich divides at Alltbeithe and its two halves, Easter and Wester Glen Quoich, form a deep valley running roughly east to west which with the head of Glen Loyne separate the three mountains just described from the next range to the north, the South Glen Shiel Ridge. This valley was once important as the line of a drove road between Tomdoun and Shiel Bridge. The path from Alltbeithe up Wester Glen Quoich follows the line of this drove road over the pass at its head, the Bealach Duibh Leac (721m), and descends steeply on the north-west side to Glen Shiel. Another path starting at Loch Coire Shubh near Kinloch Hourn crosses the pass north-west of Sgurr a' Mhaoraich and descends a short distance to join the previous one high up in Wester Glen Quoich. These two paths provide walking routes from Loch Quoich or Kinloch Hourn to Glen Shiel. Taken together they give an interesting route round the base of Sgurr a' Mhaoraich. It was by the route north from Loch Coire Shubh to Wester Glen Quoich and Glen Shiel that Prince Charles escaped north-eastwards to Glen Moriston after breaking through the cordon of Hanoverian soldiers between Loch Quoich and Loch Hourn during his epic journey in July 1746.

Meall Dubh *(black hill)* (788m)

This undistinguished hill is the highest point east of the A87 road where it crosses from Glen Garry to Glen Moriston. It can be easily climbed from the road, starting near the dam at the east end of Loch Loyne and climbing due east across rough moorland for four kilometres.

Druim nan Cnamh *(bony ridge)* (789m)

This is the highest point of the large hill, probably better known as Beinn Loinne, which extends along almost the whole southern shore of Loch Cluanie, and has an impressively craggy face above the loch. The ascent can best be made along the old road from Cluanie to Tomdoun; it is possible to take a car for the first two kilometres as far as a locked gate. From there walk to the highest point of the road, and then strike due east across rough moorland to the steeper slopes of the summit.

The South Glen Shiel Ridge is one of the finest mountain ranges in the Highlands, particularly if one includes its westward continuation to The Saddle. The Ridge itself extends for fourteen kilometres from the old Tomdoun-Cluanie road in the east to the Bealach Duibh Leac in the west, and includes seven Munros and two lesser peaks in its length. The drops between the individual peaks are not very great, and only once does the ridge fall below 800m.

The seven Munros, going from east to west are:

Creag a' Mhaim *(rock of the large rounded hill)* (947m)
Druim Shionnach *(ridge of the fox)* (987m)
Aonach air Chrith *(trembling hill)* (1021m)
Maol Chinn-dearg *(bald red head)* (981m)
Sgurr an Doire Leathain *(peak of the broad thicket)* (1010m)
Sgurr an Lochain *(peak of the little loch)* (1004m)
Creag nan Damh *(rock of the stags)* (918m)

The south side of the ridge is steep and grassy along nearly its whole length, forming a continuous and rather monotonous hillside above Glen Quoich. One or two stalker's paths climb steeply up to the ridge on this side, but the ascent is rather tedious and cannot be recommended. The north side of the ridge overlooking Glen Shiel is much more interesting as there are several fine corries with subsidiary spurs between them which give character and shape to the individual peaks.

The ridge itself is well-defined along its whole length, narrow in places, but never difficult. Route finding presents no problems for there are signs of a path the whole way (becoming increasingly eroded), and lines of old iron fence posts in places. Even without these aids to navigation, the ridge is defined by steep grass slopes dropping on the south side and the edge of the northern corries on the other side. Its popularity is due to the quality of this long high level walk, and the fact that one can climb seven Munros in a single day that is not too long nor strenuous, provided suitable transport arrangements make a long walk back through Glen Shiel at the end of the day unnecessary.

The traverse is probably best done from east to west. In this case start by walking up the old road from Cluanie Inn to Tomdoun as far as the bridge over the Allt Giubhais, and then climb fairly directly southwards to the summit of Creag a' Mhaim. (A longer but more relaxing ascent can be made by following the road past its highest point and climbing the stalker's path up the south-east side of Creag a' Mhaim). The ridge westwards is broad as far as the first col, but there is a narrow section leading up to Druim Shionnach, a rather flat-topped peak. The next two kilometres of the ridge go along the top of Coire an t-Slugain, and there are some fine cliffs and gullies in the headwall of this corrie. An interesting feature of Aonach air Chrith is its north ridge, the Druim na Ciche. For a short distance from the summit this ridge is narrow and rocky, and gives some good scrambling as far as the little peak of A'Chioch, but this is a diversion from the westward traverse.

Continuing west, the ridge is quite narrow but perfectly easy over Maol Chinn-dearg to Sgurr an Doire Leathain, whose summit is on a grassy spur about 100 metres north of the main crest. The next mountain, Sgurr an Lochain, is the most shapely of the seven, being a well-defined conical peak with a fine corrie on the east holding the lochan which gives the mountain its name. Sgurr Beag (896m) is next along the ridge, but it is probably bypassed by many, for it is not a Munro and an easy traverse across its south flank saves a bit of climbing and leads to a source of water which may be welcome on a hot day. The ridge continues down to its lowest col (726m) and finally climbs to Creag nan Damh.

Two descent routes to Glen Shiel are possible. The shorter one goes down the north-east ridge of Creag nan Damh which is quite steep and has a narrow rocky crest in places, but leads without difficulty down to about 450m where a stalker's path in Am Fraoch-choire (not shown on the 1:50,000 map) is reached and followed down to Glen Shiel at the road bridge. The other route continues along the ridge west for two kilometres to the Bealach Duibh Leac and goes down the path, steeply at first, to the Allt Mhalagain and Glen Shiel.

For those who do not want to traverse the whole ridge in a single day, there are two or three easy routes on the spurs which drop down from the main ridge towards Glen Shiel. They are equally suitable as routes of ascent or descent, and are listed:

1. The stalker's path starting from the Cluanie Inn to Tomdoun road half a kilometre south-east of the Loch Cluanie bridge leads to the north ridge of Druim Shionnach.
2. The north-east ridge of Aonach air Chrith, reached from the foot of Coire an t-Slugain, leads over A'Chioch with some scrambling (as noted above).
3. The north-east ridge of Maol Chinn-dearg is reached by a stalker's path starting near the summit of the A87, and gives very easy going.
4. The north-east ridge of Sgurr Coire na Feine, the Druim Thollaidh, is also a very easy route with a stalker's path at its foot.
5. The north-east ridge of Sgurr an Doire Leathain is steep and grassy.

Sgurr a' Bhac Chaolais *(peak of the hollow of the narrows)* (885m)

This peak is on the main South Glen Shiel Ridge to the west of the Bealach Duibh Leac. It can be climbed from the Allt Mhalagain bridge in Glen Shiel by the path to this bealach. For its first two kilometres to the crossing of the Allt Coire Toiteil this path is good, but thereafter it becomes rather overgrown and difficult to follow as it zig-zags steeply up to the pass. Continue west along the fairly narrow ridge, following a wall and then the remains of a fence over little rocky humps and hollows to the summit. It is possible to complete a traverse of the hill by descending the west ridge to the broad col at the head of Coire Toiteil and going down this corrie to rejoin the uphill path.

The east face of Sgurr an Lochain

Sgurr na Sgine *(peak of the knife)*
(945m)

The next mountain to the west is
Sgurr na Sgine. It is not well seen
from Glen Shiel as it is hidden
behind the very prominent conical
peak of Faochag (c900m) to which
it is linked by a high crescent-
shaped ridge enclosing the head
of Coire Toiteil. The east face of
Sgurr na Sgine is about 200m
high, the upper half being a crag
of steep grass and loose rock, split
by gullies.

A pleasant traverse of Sgurr na
Sgine and Faochag can be made,
taking the path up the Allt
Mhalagain (see previous paragraph) and continuing up easy
ground towards the head of Coire
Toiteil. From there the short rocky
north-east ridge of Sgurr na Sgine
is a good route direct to the
summit. Alternatively continue
further west up to the head of the
corrie and climb an easy-angled
grassy gully to the ridge a short
distance north-west of the summit,
close to the 944m North-west
Top. Approaching the summit of
Sgurr na Sgine from the north-west, the top is easily recognised even in the thickest
of weather for the east face drops precipitously a few metres beyond the cairn.

Faochag is the sharp-pointed peak which looks so impressive in views down Glen
Shiel, and the return to Glen Shiel from Sgurr na Sgine over its summit is very
enjoyable, the connecting ridge being quite narrow and steep-sided. The descent is
directly down the north-east ridge of Faochag.

Sgurr na Sgine can also be climbed from Kinloch Hourn, though this approach
is rather neglected. The first part of the route uses the right of way from Kinloch
Hourn to Arnisdale, and there are fine views down Loch Hourn as one gains

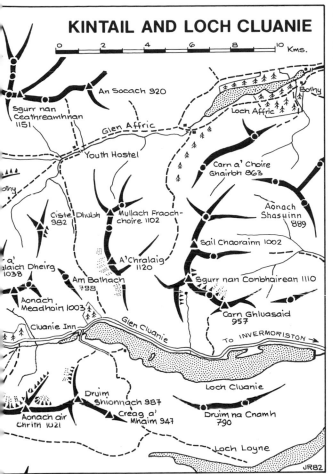

KINTAIL AND LOCH CLUANIE

height. A good circuit can be made by taking the right of way for one and a half kilometres to its highest point above Loch Beag, and then climbing east up a stalker's path onto the south ridge of Buidhe Bheinn (879m). Continue up this ridge and traverse to Sgurr a' Bhac Chaolais along an undulating three kilometre ridge. Traverse west to the col at the head of Coire Toiteil and climb Sgurr na Sgine. The east face of this peak can be outflanked by a rising traverse south-west below the crags to reach easy ground a short distance south of the summit. Descend the broad south-west ridge to reach a stalker's path which leads down across Coire Reidh to regain the right of way two kilometres from Kinloch Hourn.

The Saddle (1010m)

Two kilometres north-west of Sgurr na Sgine one comes to The Saddle, which is the culminating point of the great range of mountains on the south side of Glen Shiel. Although not the highest, it is certainly the finest of these mountains with its narrow rocky ridges and deep corries. The summit is the meeting point of three ridges, and the plan of the mountain is like the letter **E** with the three prongs pointing northwards. Between these three prongs or ridges are two fine corries, Coire Uaine to the west and Coire Chaoil to the east, and the streams from these corries unite to form the Allt Undalain which joins the River Shiel at Shiel Bridge.

The north ridge rises from the Allt Undalain three kilometres south of Shiel Bridge, and at first is steep and grassy with a band of rocks. Then a narrower ridge rises to Sgurr na Creige, and finally a more level section leads to the summit of The

The Saddle from Faochag

Saddle. The west ridge starts a long way to the north-west, rises over Sgurr Leac nan Each (919m) and Spidean Dhomhuill Bhric (940m). These peaks enclose the deep Coire Uaine whose headwall drops steeply from the ridge a short distance west of the summit of The Saddle to the little Loch a' Coire Uaine three hundred metres below. The final section of this ridge over the West Top (c968m) is quite narrow.

The third ridge is the finest; this is the east ridge whose lower part overlooks Glen Shiel.The upper part, called the Forcan Ridge, is narrow and rocky for a few hundred metres as it rises to Sgurr na Forcan (c960m), dips and rises to the East Top (958m) and finally reaches the summit. This is a level crest about 100 metres long with a trig point at its west end and a cairn on a little rocky buttress at the east end. The two points are of equal height.

The best route of ascent of The Saddle is without doubt the Forcan Ridge. Although it is narrow and rocky, and some scrambling is involved if one climbs right on the crest of the ridge, there are no difficulties that cannot be avoided and the ascent has few equals in the northwestern Highlands. In winter, of course, the climb is likely to be much more serious, possibly even difficult. The climb starts in Glen Shiel one kilometre above Achnangart, and a good stalker's path leads up to the ridge between Biod an Fhithich and Meallan Odhar. The latter hill is traversed

The Saddle from Sgurr na Forcan

or contoured on its north-west side to reach the foot of the Forcan Ridge. At first the ridge is easy, though rocky; then after a short drop it narrows almost to a knife-edge and there is fine scrambling along the crest. On the left slabs fall sheer into Coire Mhalagain, but on the right the rocks are more broken and difficulties can be avoided on that side. All too soon this excellent scramble ends at the top of Sgurr na Forcan. The traverse continues with a steep but easy pitch down to a gap in the ridge which continues, still quite narrow but easy, over the East Top and then steeply up to the cairn at the east end of the level summit ridge.

The descent should be made by a different route to complete a fine traverse of the mountain. The best option is to go west along the ridge to Spidean Dhomhuill Bhric and on to Sgurr Leac nan Each and north for two or three kilometres before descending to the Allt Undalain. Alternatively, a quicker descent to Shiel Bridge is down the north ridge over Sgurr na Creige, avoiding the rock band lower down the ridge by a descent eastwards towards the Allt a' Choire Chaoil.

The quickest return to Glen Shiel near Achnangart is to descend east-north-east from the summit of The Saddle into the very top of Coire Chaoil, go down the corrie for one and a half kilometres and then climb to the col between Biod an Fhithich and Meallan Odhar, where the top of the stalker's path is reached.

The Forcan Ridge of The Saddle

The traverse from The Saddle to Sgurr na Sgine is quite straightforward. From the summit trig point descend south at first for a short distance, then south-east to the Bealach Coire Mhalagain. (This is easier and quicker than returning to Sgurr na Forcan and descending its rocky south-east ridge). From the bealach, an ascent south leads to the ridge between Sgurr na Sgine and Faochag. A very good expedition is the ascent of the Forcan Ridge to The Saddle, followed by the traverse to Sgurr na Sgine and descent by Faochag.

Other distant starting points for The Saddle are Kinloch Hourn and Arnisdale. The right of way between these points can be used to reach the ruined cottage in Gleann Dubh Lochain, from where the Mulloch Gorm ridge leads to the West Peak of The Saddle, half a kilometre from the summit.

Sgurr Mhic Bharraich *(peak of Maurice's son)* (781m)

This hill rises above the head of Loch Duich and the dark forests of Ratagan. The most straightforward ascent is along the path from Shiel Bridge which goes up the Allt Undalain to the pass at Loch Coire nan Crogachan, from where a climb due north leads to the summit ridge just south-east of the top.

The peninsula to the west of The Saddle, sometimes referred to as the Glenelg peninsula, lies between Loch Hourn and Loch Duich. It has some very pleasant and varied scenery, particularly round the coast where there are many contrasting features such as the forested hillsides above Loch Duich, the farmland in Glen More and the steep mountains above Loch Hourn. The two brochs in Gleann Beag (south of Glenelg village) are called Dun Telve and Dun Trodden. They are well worth a visit, being the best preserved Pictish Iron Age brochs on the Scottish mainland. At Glenelg there are the stark remains of Bernera Barracks where a Hanoverian garrison was stationed in the 18th century. A third broch, Caisteal Grugaig, is situated in the forest one kilometre west of Totaig at the northern tip of the peninsula overlooking Loch Alsh, but only a small part of the original wall remains.

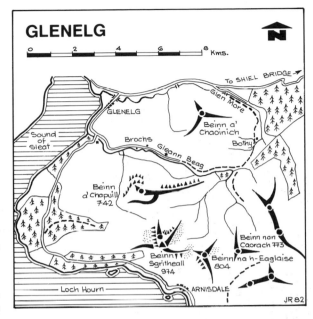

Beinn Sgritheall (probably *scree* or *gravel mountain*) (974m)

The highest and finest mountain in this peninsula is Beinn Sgritheall, which rises directly from the waters of Loch Hourn north-west of Arnisdale in ever steepening slopes. High up below the summit, screes and broken buttresses present a rather forbidding appearance, sufficient to deter anyone from a direct ascent of this face. The remote north side of the mountain has three corries: Coire Min, Coire Dubh and a third corrie, unnamed on the 1:50,000 map, due north of the summit. The North-west Top (928m) rises on the west side of this corrie.

One route of ascent of Beinn Sgritheall starts from the roadside about three kilometres north-west of Arnisdale, near a crag called Creag Ruadh. Climb north-west up the rough hillside to the woods of Coille Mhialairigh and (if possible) find a faint path leading to an old shieling among the trees. Above the shieling the path continues, very steeply in places, and reaches flatter ground just south-west of a little lochan on the west ridge of Beinn Sgritheall. From there the ascent is straightforward up the ridge which is broad and grassy at first, but becomes rockier as it steepens below the summit. On a fine day this climb is rewarded with superb views across the Sound of Sleat to Skye and Rhum.

Beinn Sgritheall and Beinn na h-Eaglaise from Coire Dhorrcail

An alternative ascent from Arnisdale can be made directly up the hillside behind the village to the Bealach Arnasdail. It is probably best to keep on the east side of the stream which comes down from the bealach. From there climb a steep stony slope to reach the east peak of Beinn Sgritheall (903m), and continue along the delightful ridge to the top.

The north side of the mountain is remote, but well worth exploration in spite of the long approaches. Balvraid in Gleann Beag is the nearest starting point accessible by car, and Suardalan bothy in Glen More is a good base for exploring the north side of Beinn Sgritheall. The best route of ascent leaves the glen midway between Balvraid and Suardalan and follows the Allt Srath a' Chomair to the foot of the north-east ridge, which leads directly to the summit.

Beinn na h-Eaglaise (*hill of the church*) (804m)

This steep hill is a small neighbour of Beinn Sgritheall, being separated from it by the Bealach Arnasdail. Its summit is less than half a kilometre from the bealach, but the intervening hillside is very steep and rocky. The easiest ascent is from Arnisdale up the stream to the level ridge of Beinn Bhuidhe just south-east of the summit of Beinn na h-Eaglaise, followed by a short climb up the south-east ridge to the top. This route is quite steep, but there are no major obstacles.

Beinn nan Caorach *(hill of the rowan berries)* (773m)

This hill has a steep, scree-covered south face. It rises three kilometres north-east of the tiny village of Corran, near Arnisdale. The easiest ascent, though not the shortest in distance, is to take the track up Glen Arnisdale for just over one kilometre, then the path north-east up the Allt Utha and Coire Chorsalain to the col at its head. From there climb the easy-angled east ridge of the hill.

A descent north from the summit followed by a traverse anti-clockwise round the head of Coire Dhruim nam Bo leads to the col at the foot of the north-east ridge of Beinn na h-Eaglaise, which can be easily climbed from there.

PATHS AND WALKS

Loch Quoich to Glen Shiel. Start at the road bridge over Loch Quoich's northern inlet, and take the private road to Alltbeithe. Then follow the right of way up Wester Glen Quoich to the Bealach Duibh Leac. On the north-west side of the pass the path descends steeply and is rather indistinct, but it improves lower down, and after crossing the Allt Coire Toiteil the going down to Glen Shiel is good. (14 kilometres).

Kinloch Hourn to Glen Shiel. Take the stalker's path from Kinloch Hourn or Loch Coire Shubh up the Allt Coire Sgoireadail. Cross the pass north-west of Sgurr a' Mhaoraich, and descend a short distance into Wester Glen Quoich where the preceding route is joined. This may be followed north-west to Glen Shiel (10 kilometres), or south-east to Loch Quoich (14 kilometres).

Kinloch Hourn to Arnisdale. This right of way goes steeply uphill behind Kinlochhourn House, climbing almost to 300m behind a little knoll before descending slightly across the foot of Coire Reidh and continuing fairly level to reach the head of Gleann Dubh Lochain. This glen is followed past its two tranquil lochans and down a track in Glen Arnisdale to the road at Loch Hourn just south of Arnisdale. This is a superb walk; it is a pity that the first half is spoiled by the electricity transmission pylons which follow the path on their way from Loch Quoich to Skye. (13 kilometres).

Kinloch Hourn to Gleann Beag (or Glen More). Take the previous route to Gleann Dubh Lochain, but instead of turning south-west down this glen at the ruined cottage, continue north-west over the Bealach Aoidhdailean along the line of electricity pylons and descend the glen on the north side to Srath a' Chomair, where a good track is joined. This track can be followed either west to Balvraid in Gleann Beag (17 kilometres) or north-east past Suardalan bothy to Glen More (19 kilometres).

An alternative to this route is to go north from the ruined cottage in Gleann Dubh Lochain to a pass called the Bealach Casan at grid reference 911 123 and descend the stream at the east end of the Druim na Firean crags to the Glenmore River. This may be approximately the line of an old drove road from Kylerhea to

Tomdoun which was marked on earlier editions of the Ordnance Survey maps, but is not shown on the present 1:50,000 edition, an indication that the path is so seldom used that it has now nearly disappeared.

Totaig to Glenelg. This is a pleasant coastal walk with views across Kyle Rhea to Skye. The first part , which passes the Caisteal Gruagaig broch, is through forest to Ardintoul. Thereafter the way is along the shore to the ferry opposite Kylerhea, and on past Bernera Barracks to Glenelg. (14 kilometres).

CLIMBING

On the South Glen Shiel Ridge, there are several corries with potential for climbing. The easternmost of these is Coire an t-Slugain on the west face of Druim Shionnach, where one rock climb has been done in the south-east corner of the corrie (*The Silver Slab*, 100m, Severe). Winter ascents have been made of some of the gullies in this corrie and in Coire nan Eirecheanach on the west side of Aonach air Chrith. It is likely that one or two of the gullies on the east face of Sgurr an Lochain overlooking the lochan might give pleasant but easy winter routes.

The south-west face of Sgurr a' Bhac Chaolais above Coire Reidh has a deep-cut gully with a well-defined buttress on its right level with the Sgurr na Sgine col. The buttress has been climbed by its right-hand edge (*Mayfly,* 60m, Very Severe).

The east face of Sgurr na Sgine, which in summer is loose and vegetatious, might give some good climbing in cold winter conditions when the loose rocks and turf are well frozen.

On The Saddle the south flank of the Forcan Ridge has given some rock climbs on slabby rock. *Easter Buttress* (100m, Severe) is a fairly well-defined route which finishes a few metres below the horiontal knife-edge near the top of the ridge. Coire Uaine on the west side of the summit has potential for winter routes. The headwall is very steep, but too vegetatious for summer climbing. The spur which drops steeply north-east from Spidean Dhomhuill Bhric has been climbed in winter conditions and is a pleasant route.

The north face of the North-west Top of Beinn Sgritheall has given one recorded climb, *North Buttress,* which consists of three rock steps separated by grassy ledges (130m, Difficult). This route has been climbed in both summer and winter.

CHAPTER 7

Kintail

MAPS: Ordnance Survey 1:50,000 Sheet 33
         Bartholomew 1:100,000 Sheet 54

PRINCIPAL HILLS

Am Bathach	798m	073 144
Ciste Dhubh	982m	062 166
Aonach Meadhoin	1003m	049 138
Sgurr a' Bhealaich Dheirg	1038m	035 143
Saileag	959m	018 148
Sgurr na Ciste Duibhe	1027m	984 149
Sgurr Fhuaran	1068m	978 167
Beinn Fhada	1032m	018 193
A'Ghlas-bheinn	918m	008 231
Sgurr an Airgid	841m	940 227

The splendidly mountainous corner of the Highlands described in this chapter includes the Kintail and Inverinate forests. It is bounded on the south-west by Glen Shiel and Loch Duich, on the north by Loch Long and Glen Elchaig and on the east by the irregular line of glens from An Caorann Mor near the head of Loch Cluanie to the Falls of Glomach above Glen Elchaig. This area is itself divided into two parts of quite different character by Strath Croe and its extension north-east over the Bealach na Sroine to the Falls of Glomach. To the east is Kintail, an area best known for the superb range of peaks on the north-east side of Glen Shiel, the Five Sisters of Kintail. The Inverinate Forest to the north-west of Strath Croe is much less mountainous than Kintail; there are no Munros and only one Corbett in this area, but it is nevertheless rugged country with a few rocky little hills and some fine crags.

The setting of these hills and mountains is enhanced by the two long, narrow sea-lochs that reach into them. Loch Duich is comparable with Loch Hourn and Loch Nevis not far to the south, but it is very different in one respect, namely that it carries along its shore the main road to Skye, and there are habitations along both sides of the loch. These do not detract, however, from its beauty, but impart a rather less austere character. The outer reaches of the loch are unfortunately marred by a large fish farm whose rafts are moored opposite Letterfearn. Loch Long is a narrow offshoot of Loch Duich, and by comparison is very secluded; a quiet backwater of the west coast in every sense, leading to the equally secluded Glen Elchaig.

In many ways Kintail epitomises the West Highland landscape. The Five Sisters seem to be present in every view, but such is their tall, aspiring outline that they do not dominate their surroundings, rather they provide a superbly elegant backdrop to every vista. In the classic views of these mountains Loch Duich provides the essential foreground, white cottages along its rocky shoreline, dark forests above. There is the feeling in Kintail that in this part of the west coast, unlike depopulated areas elsewhere, many people still live and work in harmony with their surroundings.

Much of Kintail, including the Five Sisters and some of the neighbouring mountains, is owned by the National Trust for Scotland, having been purchased by the Trust with funds given by Percy Unna, a past President of the Scottish Mountaineering Club. The normal restrictions which may apply to many of the Highland mountains in the stalking season do not apply to the Kintail mountains which stand in Trust territory. This is fortunate, for many of the surrounding mountains are in deer stalking country, and there are likely to be problems climbing them in late summer and autumn. The boundary of the National Trust for Scotland property is shown on the Ordnance Survey map.

The many and varied features of interest in Kintail and the surrounding country – splendid mountains such as the Five Sisters and The Saddle, the Falls of Glomach, Eilean Donan Castle and the Pictish brochs near Glenelg to name a few – make it one of the most popular parts of the Highlands with climbers, walkers and tourists alike. The combination of mountains, lochs and glens confer a scenic grandeur matched in only a few other parts of the Highlands.

ACCESS

The mountains of Kintail are very accessible, as the main A87 road from the south to Kyle of Lochalsh and Skye passes close to most of them. There is a public road from Ardelve up the west side of Loch Long as far as the little village of Camasluinie (no more than a few cottages). The road on the north side of Glen Elchaig is private and cars are not permitted beyond Killilan. In Strath Croe at the head of Loch Duich the public road on the north side of the strath ends at a Forestry Commission car park near Dorusduain, and on the south side of the strath at Morvich.

PUBLIC TRANSPORT

Bus: Glasgow to Kyle of Lochalsh (Scottish Citylink Coaches and Skye-Ways Express Coaches). Daily.

Inverness to Kyle of Lochalsh via Glen Moriston (Scottish Citylink Coaches and Skye-Ways Express Coaches). Daily.

Postbus (4 Seater): Dornie – Killilan – Kyle of Lochalsh. Mondays to Saturdays.

ACCOMMODATION

There are hotels at Cluanie, at the head of Loch Duich and at Dornie and Ardelve on opposite sides of the mouth of Loch Long. Bed and breakfast houses, and houses and caravans to rent abound, particularly at Ratagan and Inverinate where there are communities of Forstry Commission workers. The Scottish Youth Hostels Association has hostels at Ratagan near the head of Loch Duich and Alltbeithe in the remote upper part of Glen Affric. In Gleann Lichd there is a climbers' hut at Glenlicht House leased by the National Trust for Scotland to the Edinburgh University Mountaineering Club, and at Morvich the Morvich Outdoor Centre is run by the Trust for visiting parties of climbers and others, but the charges make it more suitable for large rather than small parties. Just to the north-east of the watershed at the head of Gleann Lichd the remote cottage at Camban, renovated by the Mountain Bothies Association, provides simple shelter in the heart of the mountains. There are camp and caravan sites at Shiel Bridge, Morvich and Ardelve, and at Balmacara several kilometres west of Ardelve.

THE HILLS

The main mountains of Kintail are those on the north side of Glen Shiel, the Five Sisters and the continuation of that ridge eastwards over four more mountains to end not far north of Cluanie Inn. The entire range from Ciste Dhubh in the east to Sgurr na Moraich, the north-western outlier of the Five Sisters, is fifteen kilometres long and includes six Munros, and it might well be called the North Glen Shiel Ridge. By comparison with the South Glen Shiel Ridge, it is a far finer range; the peaks are higher, steeper and have more individuality, the cols which separate them are lower and on the north side overlooking Gleann Lichd there are some magnificent corries with steep slabby buttresses and gullies.

Although it is quite possible for fit climbers to traverse the whole ridge in a single day, this is a very strenuous expedition, much more so than the South Glen Shiel Ridge. Most climbers prefer to take two days to climb all these peaks, one day for the Five Sisters and a second one for the eastern half of the ridge. The col between the two halves, the Bealach an Lapain (723m), is easily reached from Glen Shiel and makes the fastest route between glen and ridge.

The two other Munros in Kintail are Beinn Fhada and A'Ghlas-bheinn, both north of Gleann Lichd and more retiring than the Five Sisters. Beinn Fhada in particular hides its grandest corries from the roadside viewer, and reveals its secret places only to those prepared to climb high into its northern fastnesses.

Am Bathach *(the byre)* (798m)
Ciste Dhubh *(black chest)* (982m)

These two hills form a narrow ridge to the north of Cluanie Inn, with Bealach a' Choinich (567m) at its mid-point. Ciste Dhubh is the dominant peak of this pair, its sharp-pointed summit can be glimpsed from the road near Cluanie Inn, showing a craggy top split by a steep gully. The south ridge of Ciste Dubh forms a level crest which is remarkably narrow for a few hundred metres and forms the small peak An Cnapach (881m) before it drops to the Bealach a' Choinich. South-east of the bealach, Am Bathach is a long and narrow grassy ridge. On the east side An Caorann Mor is a deep glen through which goes the path from Cluanie Inn to Glen Affric. The west face of Ciste Dhubh is a long steep slope which can be dangerous in conditions of soft snow; there have been records of avalanche accidents on the mountain.

The normal route of ascent of Ciste Dhubh is from Cluanie Inn up the valley of An Caorann Beag. There is no well-defined path up this glen, but the going is fairly easy along the east side of the stream, by grassy slopes, a faint path and some cairns which lead to the Bealach a' Choinich. Little extra effort is required to reach the bealach over the summit of Am Bathach, which is a very pleasant traverse. To do this, start over one kilometre east of Cluanie, just west of the road bridge over the Allt a' Chaorainn Mhoir and follow a stalker's path uphill beside the small Forestry Commission plantation. Continue along the narrow grassy ridge to the summit, and down to the bealach. From there climb a steep slope to An Cnapach at the start of the narrow crest of the south ridge of Ciste Dhubh, and continue along this ridge with a slight drop before the final climb to the summit.

Ciste Dhubh can be climbed from the north, either by the north-west or north-east ridge. Like the west face, the north side of the mountain is steep and avalanche prone in soft snow conditions.

Aonach Meadhoin *(middle hill)* (1003m)

To the south-west of the Bealach a' Choinich are the twin peaks of Aonach Meadhoin and its slightly lower Top, Sgurr an Fhuarail (988m), only the latter being named on the 1:50,000 map.

If coming from the east, Sgurr an Fhuarail will be climbed first, either by its south-east ridge from Cluanie Inn, crossing a small knoll at 855m on the way, or by the broad grassy slope of the north-east ridge from the Bealach a' Choinich. The latter route is the obvious way to traverse from Sgurr an Fhuarail to Ciste Dhubh, or vice versa.

The traverse from Sgurr an Fhuarail to Aonach Meadhoin goes along a short and quite narrow ridge, but there is no difficulty at all. In winter this ridge may form a graceful corniced curve. The summit of Aonach Meadhoin is a small level plateau, and from it the west ridge, which is quite narrow, drops to a col at 831m. The

Saileag and Sgurr a' Bhealaich Dheirg from the west

descent to Glen Shiel from this col is most easily made by traversing south-west for a few hundred metres to reach a knoll (807m) on the grassy crest of the ridge which goes south, then south-east to Meall a' Charra. Descend this ridge to about 600m and then drop down the south side through the gap between two blocks of forest to reach the road.

Sgurr a' Bhealaich Dheirg *(peak of the red pass)* (1038m)

The east ridge of Aonach Meadhoin leads to the next mountain on the north side of Glen Shiel, Sgurr a' Bhealaich Dheirg. The main ridge along the top of the mountain is fairly level for about 400 metres, with its highest point (1031m) at its south-east end, From there the north-east ridge runs out towards the head of the Fionngleann. The summit of the mountain is about 100 metres along this ridge, which is narrow and rocky, and has a dry stone dyke along its crest leading to the splendidly built summit cairn which stands astride the ridge, one of the noblest cairns on any Scottish mountain. A short distance beyond the summit the ridge is cleft by a reddish gully to which the mountain may well owe its name.

The traverse along the main ridge from east to west over Sgurr a' Bhealaich Dheirg is very straightforward. At the north-west end of the level crest the ridge turns sharply south-west and drops over two small knolls to the col at 876m before rising to Saileag.

If one is not traversing the North Glen Shiel Ridge, but simply looking for a quick route to Sgurr a' Bhealaich Dheirg, then the best starting point is the Cluanie - Shiel watershed. There a gap between two blocks of forest gives access to the Meall a' Charra ridge which in turn leads to the main ridge half a kilometre south-east of the summit.

Saileag *(little heel)* (959m)

This is not a very distinguished mountain. It has been described as a mere swelling in the ridge, but it does have a steep west face which looks impressive from the lower reaches of Gleann Lichd. One kilometre west-south-west from the summit down a grassy ridge one reaches the Bealach an Lapain which, as already mentioned, gives a fast and easy route up from or down to Glen Shiel. There is also a perfectly straightforward route on the north side of the bealach which provides the best route onto the North Glen Shiel Ridge from Gleann Lichd.

The Five Sisters of Kintail
Sgurr na Ciste Duibhe *(peak of the black chest)* (1027m)
Sgurr Fhuaran (1068m)

The Five Sisters of Kintail are among the best known mountains in the northwestern Highlands. Their appearance, particularly as seen from Loch Duich or the top of the Bealach Ratagain, is very striking with the peaks showing their full height above sea-level and their remarkable symmetry of outline. In addition to the two highest peaks named above, the three others which make up the Five Sisters are: Sgurr na Carnach *(peak of the stony place)* (1002m), Sgurr nan Saighead *(peak of the arrows)* (929m) and Sgurr na Moraich *(peak of the sea-plain)* (876m).

Surprisingly, for the ridges that join these peaks seem to go up and down a lot, there are only two Munros among the Five Sisters. Another fine peak at the east end of the ridge which is not normally counted as one of the five is Sgurr nan Spainteach *(peak of the Spaniards)* (c990m). The name originates from the little-known Battle of Glenshiel fought in 1719 when a small force of Jacobites supported by 300 Spanish soldiers who had landed on the west coast at Eilean Donan castle was defeated by a Hanoverian army in Glen Shiel. In the heat of the battle the heather on the hillside was set ablaze and the Spaniards had to hastily retreat uphill, some of them doubtless reaching the peak which now bears their name.

On both its sides the ridge of the Five Sisters falls sheer into the glens far below, Glen Shiel on the south-west and Gleann Lichd on the north-east. The south-west face of Sgurr na Ciste Duibhe falls 1000m in a horizontal distance of just over one kilometre, one of the longest and steepest continuous slopes in Scotland. Lower down Glen Shiel the Five Sisters are characterised by the long grassy spurs of Sgurr na Carnach and Sgurr Fhuaran, separated by deep gullies. The Gleann Lichd side is much wilder, and there are some fine corries on this remote side of the ridge.

Looking east from the Bealach an Lapain to Sgurr na Ciste Duibhe

The classic expedition is the traverse of the Five Sisters, and it should be done fron east to west for two reasons. Firstly, the best views are ahead, and secondly the ascent to the Bealach an Lapain from upper Glen Shiel is far easier than the climb to the north-west end of the ridge from Loch Duich or the lower part of the glen. The start of the traverse is at the very obvious gap in the forest plantations on the north side of the glen almost two kilometres east of the site of the Battle of Glenshiel. The ascent is steep and unrelenting up a grassy slope, but there is now quite a distinct path worn by many climbers, and an hour should be sufficient to reach the bealach. The hardest part of the day's work is over, and a grand traverse stretches ahead.

The narrow grassy ridge rises gradually westwards over an intermediate top to Sgurr nan Spainteach, and then drops more abruptly, with one short rocky pitch down to the col below Sgurr na Ciste Duibhe. At this col there is a curious hollow in the crest of the ridge, which one passes either to the left or right before climbing steeply to the big cairn of Sgurr na Ciste Duibhe. (This feature can be very confusing in mist, particularly if one is going from west to east). The main ridge now swings round northwards across the Bealach na Gaoibhe (850m) and is broad and bouldery over Sgurr na Carnach and down to the Bealach na Carnach (868m) below Sgurr Fhuaran, whose ascent is steep for 200m.

The Five Sisters of Kintail from the north-west

The east face of Sgurr nan Saighead

On its north side, in the direction of the continuing traverse, Sgurr Fhuaran is very steep, so descend west-north-west for a short distance down the spur which drops all the way to Glen Shiel. At a short level section of the spur turn right and make a traverse, descending slightly, north-eastwards to regain the main ridge below the steep summit slopes of the peak. The ridge to Sgurr nan Saighead gives a good view of the steep slabby east face of that peak, which appears very much as a pyramid from the south. One gets a good impression of the typical rock structure of the Kintail mountains, flaggy granulites and mica-schists set at a steep angle, presenting smooth slabby faces with a lot of vegetation, and gullies filled with scree and loose rock. It is not surprising that most of the climbing on the crags of the Five Sisters has been done in winter.

Beyond the highest point of Sgurr nan Saighead the ridge turns west, then north-west and is very narrow for a short distance to the lower north-west peak, called Beinn Bhuidhe (871m). This point commands a very fine view, both westwards towards Loch Duich and Skye,and south-east back along the main ridge. The last peak of the Five Sisters is Sgurr na Moraich, a very bulky hill as seen from Loch Duich, which has a long broad summit ridge and continuously steep slopes above the loch. Three possible descent routes from Beinn Bhuidhe are:

1. Down the north-west ridge to the 443m col before Sgurr an t-Searraich, and

then steeply down south-west to a bridge over the River Shiel just above Loch Shiel.

2. Down the Allt a' Chruinn, following a path on the north-east side of the stream down the steep hillside past crags and waterfalls.

3. Over Sgurr na Moraich and down westwards to the Allt a' Chruinn above the steep lower hillside.

Any of the routes described above can be used to ascend to the north-west end of the Five Sisters ridge. The direct ascent to Sgurr Fhuaran from Glen Shiel is noted as one of the longest continuous uphill grinds in the Highlands, 1000m at an average angle of nearly 25 degrees. Routes on the Gleann Lichd side of the Five Sisters are equally long and steep, but have the compensation of superb scenery in a wild and remote setting. The east ridge of Sgurr Fhuaran, starting half a kilometre south-east of Glenlicht House, is a fine way up that mountain.

Beinn Fhada *(long hill)* (1032m)

To the north of the Five Sisters is Beinn Fhada. Its name is very appropriate for it stretches for eight kilometres from the head of Loch Duich to Glen Affric, and in its extent it equals all the Five Sisters together. It has very steep slopes dropping on the south-west side into Gleann Lichd, so steep that there are no reasonable routes of ascent from that glen. On the north-east side there are several fine corries with intervening ridges.

Unlike the Five Sisters, Beinn Fhada does not show its grandeur to every traveller on the road to Skye; its summit is far withdrawn behind outlying tops. From the road causeway at the head of Loch Duich the western peak, Sgurr a' Choire Ghairbh (870m), appears as a fairly level ridge with several rounded knolls, the Faradh Nighean Fhearchair. These knolls are the crests of a series of slabby buttresses dropping on the other side of the ridge into Choire Chaoil, the finest of Beinn Fhada's corries. To the east the spine of the mountain widens and merges into a great plateau, the Plaide Mhor, at whose furthest point is the summit. Beyond there the main crest continues a long way further east towards Glen Affric. A northward ridge from the Plaide Mhor leads to the rocky top of Meall a' Bhealaich which overlooks the Bealach an Sgairne, an important pass through which goes one of the two rights of way from Glen Affric to Loch Duich.

The normal starting point for the ascent of Beinn Fhada is at Morvich in Strath Croe. Two very fine routes are possible, and the following combination of them gives an excellent traverse of the mountain. From the cottage at Innis a' Crotha climb easy slopes eastwards to Beinn Bhuidhe and continue up this broad grassy spur aiming for a knoll at the north end of the Sgurr a' Choire Ghairbh ridge. From this knoll, or the col immediately to its south which can be reached directly by a shallow gully, climb south up a broad rocky ridge to Sgurr a' Choire Ghairbh. (There is a cairn about 100 metres north-north-west of the top, which itself has only a tiny cairn). Continue south along the broad undulating ridge to the Bealach an t-Sealgaire *(the hunters' pass)* where there is a descent of 20m down slabby rocks which calls for care, especially when wet. The ridge rises to Ceum na h-Aon-choise (910m) and beyond there to Meall an Fhuarain Mhoir (956m), and the last two kilometres to the summit are across the wide expanse of the Plaide Mhor, dropping slightly at first and then climbing a gentle slope to the large cairn. The Plaide Mhor may be rather an anticlimax after the earlier fine climb, but if visibility is bad it will give some good navigation practice.

To return to Morvich, descend west for a short distance, then north-west down the broad ridge towards Meall a' Bhealaich until near its lowest point (at grid reference 011 206) the top of a stalker's path is found. This leads steeply down into Coire an Sgairne and then north to join the path in Gleann Coinneachain, which in turn is followed back to Innis a' Chrotha and Morvich.

From the east Beinn Fhada can be climbed easily over Sgurr a' Dubh Doire from either the youth hostel at Alltbeithe or the bothy at Camban. A traverse along the whole mountain combining this route with the ascent route described above is a very fine expedition.

A'Ghlas-bheinn *(the greenish-grey hill)* (918m)

This little mountain, rather knobbly in appearance as seen from Glen Croe, lies to the north of Beinn Fhada in the Inverinate estate. It is most easily climbed from Strath Croe by its west ridge, but this is not a particularly interesting route, and is better used in the descent after climbing the hill by its south-east ridge from the Bealach an Sgairne.

The Bealach an Sgairne is reached from Morvich or from the car park near Dorusduain in Strath Croe by the fine path up Gleann Choinneachain which also leads to the northern corries of Beinn Fhada. The bealach may also be reached from Beinn Fhada by traversing its northern top Meall a' Bhealaich. The north face of this top is steep and rocky, with a prominent gully directly above the pass. The safest descent is well to the east of this gully and its enclosing crags, taking a bearing north-east from the top of Meall a' Bhealaich until below the crags.

From the Bealach an Sgairne climb the very pleasant south-east ridge of A' Ghlas-bheinn, following a faint path which at one point makes a steep rising traverse across a band of rocks, one of several rocky knolls along the ridge. There are fine views down to lonely Loch Gaorsaic and beyond it to the bulk of Sgurr nan Ceathreamhnan. Descend the west ridge, which is broad and grassy. Towards its foot the ridge becomes steeper and narrower, and it is important to adhere to the crest and aim for the point where the path to the Bealach na Sroine leaves the forest (much of which has now been felled). The return to the car park is down the forest road past Dorusduain.

Sgurr a' Choire Ghairbh from the north-east

The ascent of A'Ghlas-bheinn can be combined with a visit to the Falls of Glomach by ascending or descending the long north ridge over a couple of knolls and past two small lochans.

Sgurr an Airgid *(peak of silver)* (841m)

The only other hill of any size in the Inverinate estate is Sgurr an Airgid, which rises directly above Inverinate village and Strath Croe at the head of Loch Duich. The ascent is easily made from a point just west of Ruarach in Strath Croe by the stalker's path which zig-zags up the steep grassy hillside towards the col to the east of Sgurr an Airgid. From the col a fairly narrow rocky ridge with a double crest leads to the summit, which is a splendid viewpoint.

To the north-west of Sgurr an Airgid, beyond Coire Dhuinnid, the landscape of the Inverinate Forest changes. There are several little rocky knolls rising from the undulating moorland, and steep craggy hillsides overlook the head of Loch Long and Glen Elchaig. Two paths cross the hills between Coire Dhuinnid, Camas-luinie and Loch Long, but this is an area which is quite unfrequented by hillwalkers. One of the most attractive features is the little rocky knoll of Boc Beag above the Carr Brae road; it is a splendid viewpoint and gives rock climbers some pleasant short climbs.

PATHS AND WALKS

The Falls of Glomach. There are two routes to the Falls. The shorter one starts at the Forestry Commission car park in Strath Croe four kilometres from the A87 road causeway at the head of Loch Duich. The way follows a forest road for two kilometres, then a good path over the Bealach na Sroine to reach the top of the Falls. To get a good view of them it is necessary to carefully descend a steep path to a superb natural balcony facing the Falls, whose waters plunge over 100m down the chasm in two great leaps. (6 kilometres).

The other route is from Glen Elchaig and is a good deal longer, but it does give a very good walk and a much better approach to the Falls than the preceding one. The nearest starting point is at the tiny village of Camas-luinie at the end of the public road in the glen. Follow a footpath on the south side of the River Elchaig for two kilometres, then cross and walk up the private road to Loch na Leitreach. (This point can be reached more quickly by bicycle from Killilan). Cross the river by the A.E.Robertson Memorial Bridge and follow the path into the narrow gorge of the Allt a' Ghlomaich. The path climbs across the steep west side of the gorge, crosses the Allt na Laoidhre and climbs higher still to traverse far above the stupendous chasm of the Glomach and reach the top of the Falls where the route described above is joined. (9 kilometres).

The traverse from Glen Elchaig to Strath Croe by the Falls of Glomach is a splendid walk, provided suitable transport arrangements have been made for the return journey. (15 kilometres from Camas-luinie to Strath Croe).

Cannich to Loch Duich. The start of this long walk from Cannich village to Killilan or Dornie will be described in Chapter 9 as it passes through Glen Cannich. Once over the pass at the head of that glen, the walk goes down the length of Glen Elchaig which is delightfully quiet and peaceful, provided that fierce Highland bulls which are reputed to roam the glen do not cause trouble. If personal transport is not awaiting one at Killilan, then it may be better to cross the River Elchaig and go to Camas-luinie, from where a footpath goes westwards through the hills and down the River Glennan to Dornie on the A87 road where public transport is available. (47 kilometres from Cannich to Killilan; 54 kilometres from Cannich to Dornie).

Cluanie Inn to Alltbeithe. This is the shortest distance from a public road to Alltbeithe, and follows the eastern boundary of the area described in this chapter. Start from the A87 road one and a half kilometres east of Cluanie Inn and follow a well-defined path north through An Caorann Mor, over the pass at its head and down the Allt a' Chomhlain to the River Affric. There is a bridge at Alltbeithe. (11 kilometres from Cluanie Inn to Alltbeithe).

Alltbeithe to Strath Croe by the Bealach an Sgairne. Go west from Alltbeithe along a path on the north side of the Allt Gleann Gniomhaidh, cross the pass and skirt round the south side of Loch a' Bhealaich. Climb to the Bealach an Sgairne (510m) and descend Gleann Choinneachain under the splendid northern corries of

Beinn Fhada to reach either Morvich or the car park near Dorusduain. (11 kilometres from Alltbeithe to Dorusduain). This pass is one of the oldest and most frequently used in the western Highlands. St Duthac, the Irish saint and missionary of the 11th century, must have used this route between his home in Ireland and his shrine and church at Tain in Easter Ross. Loch Duich is *St Duthac's Loch,* and the Bealach an Sgairne is also known locally as Cadha Dhuich, *St Duthac's Pass.*

Alltbeithe to Strath Croe by Gleann Lichd. Start westwards as for the previous walk, and in half a kilometre follow the left-hand path, cross the Allt Gleann Gniomhaidh and go south-west past Camban bothy to the pass at the head of the Fionngleann. A fine path continues down Gleann Lichd, with the steep slopes of Beinn Fhada on one's right and the corries of the Five Sisters on the left, down through the dramatic gorge of the Allt Grannda waterfalls to the footbridges above Glenlicht House. From there a rough track leads down beside the River Croe to Morvich. (15 kilometres from Alltbeithe to Morvich). A particularly fine circular walk can be made by combining the two preceding walks to circumnavigate Beinn Fhada, starting and finishing either at Morvich or Dorusduain. (26 kilometres).

CLIMBING

In general the rocks in the northern corries of the Five Sisters and Beinn Fhada are more suited for winter than summer climbing. These crags have been described as looking like all rock when seen from below and all grass when seen from above, a sure indication of the amount of vegetation clinging to the ledges. Nearly all the reports of climbing in these corries, particularly the more recent reports, are of winter climbs.

On the Five Sisters there have been winter gully climbs on the north face of both Sgurr nan Spainteach (Grade II) and Sgurr na Ciste Duibhe (Grade III), and on the east face of Sgurr na Carnach (Grade II). The obvious gully on the north face of Sgurr Fhuaran has been climbed by its centre fork (Grade II/III), and on the north face of Sgurr nan Saighead the prominent gully in the centre of the face has been climbed, all in winter.

On Beinn Fhada, the great east-facing crags of Sgurr a' Choire Ghairbh look impressive. *Summit Buttress* is the main feature, cleft by two narrow gullies. It has been climbed in both summer and winter conditions, and the two narrow gullies have been climbed in winter (both Grade II/III). The buttresses to the left (south) have been climbed in summer, Difficult but of no great quality. Much further south, near the hunters' pass, there are some smaller buttresses, one of them giving a good route up its north edge. (*The Needle,* 110m, Severe).

In the Inverinate Forest some pleasant rock climbing has been done on the two tiers of the little rocky knoll Boc Beag above the Carr Brae road. The rock is good and the climbing about Very Difficult to Severe, with splendid views to the Cuillin Hills on a fine day.

CHAPTER 8

Strath Cluanie and Glen Affric

MAPS: Ordnance Survey   1:50,000   Sheets 25,26,33 and 34
            Bartholomew   1:100,000   Sheets 54 and 55

PRINCIPAL HILLS

Carn Ghluasaid	957m	146 125
Sgurr nan Conbhairean	1110m	130 139
Sail Chaorainn	1002m	133 155
A'Chralaig	1120m	094 148
Mullach Fraoch-choire	1102m	095 172
Carn a' Choire Ghairbh	863m	137 189
Aonach Shasuinn	889m	173 180
Toll Creagach	1054m	194 283
Tom a' Choinich	1111m	163 273
Carn Eighe	1183m	123 262
Mam Sodhail	1180m	120 253
Beinn Fhionnlaidh	1005m	115 283
An Socach	920m	088 230
Sgurr nan Ceathreamhnan	1151m	057 229
Mullach na Dheiragain	982m	081 259
Sgurr Gaorsaic	c838m	036 219

To the east and north-east of Kintail the Highland landscape takes on a larger and more spacious scale. The mountains are higher and more massive, the glens and straths longer, wider and in places magnificently wooded. Splendid rivers flow down along these straths through countryside which is as prosperous, in an agricultural sense, as any in the far north of Scotland. The appearance of the country is very different from Knoydart or Torridon, less rugged and precipitous maybe, but having a grandeur that fully compensates and gives these mountains and glens something of the character of the Cairngorms. The mountains have much smoother contours than the steep and jagged peaks of Knoydart and Kintail, and they are characterised by long ridges enclosing many fine corries. However, few of these corries possess much in the way of steep cliffs and crags; rather they are great bowls carved by ancient glaciers out of the mountainsides. The difference between these mountains and their lower neighbours is probably that, because of their central position in the Highlands, an ice-cap could have existed to protect them from the effects of valley glaciation in the Ice Age.

Remote mountainous country at the head of Glen Affric

The area to be described in this chapter is bounded on its south side by Glen Moriston, whose highest part between the west end of Loch Cluanie and the watershed is known as Strath Cluanie. To the north are Glen Urquhart and Glen Cannich, and to the east is Loch Ness. The western boundary is Gleann Gaorsaic, Gleann Gniomhaidh and An Caorann Mor.

Glen Affric is in the heart of this area. It is one of the finest of all Scottish glens, and between its highest reaches and the Beauly Firth where its waters reach the sea there is a richness and variety of scenery that few glens can match. The headwaters of the River Affric rise high in the remotest corries of the Kintail mountains, close under the summits of Beinn Fhada and Sgurr a' Bhealaich Dheirg, and flow down to the great confluence of streams and glens near Alltbeithe, the loneliest of Scottish youth hostels. For the next seven kilometres the river meanders through grassy flats, and several ruined cottages testify that once this part of the glen was inhabited and cattle grazed along the banks of the river. Now only the cottage at Athnamulloch is occupied occasionally. At Loch Affric the forests begin; on the north side are some remnants of the Old Caledonian Forest, and on the south side these fine old pine trees are now mixed with the more densely planted conifers of the Forestry Commission. At the east end of Loch Affric, in a splendid position on a wooded knoll, stands Affric Lodge, and two kilometres further east one comes to Loch Beinn a' Mheadhoin (pronounced Loch Benevain). This is the part of Glen Affric

Looking west along Loch Mullardoch to Beinn Fhionnlaidh

much seen and admired by car-borne tourists, for the public road goes as far as a car park near the head of this loch. From there down to Fasnakyle, where the River Affric enters Strath Glass, there is one of the most beautiful stretches of woodland in the Highlands, a glorious forest of native birch and pine through which the river carves its turbulent way. In fact, the River Affric is distinctly less turbulent nowadays since the North of Scotland Hydro-Electric Board built a dam across the east end of Loch Beinn a' Mheadhoin, and most of the waters of Affric and Cannich now flow down to the power station at Fasnakyle through underground pipes. At the village of Cannich one is in Strath Glass, and this valley continues for almost 30 kilometres to the Beauly Firth, presenting in its length a wonderfully varied landscape of forests and hills, farms, villages and cultivated land.

The other glens in the area of this chapter also have their own distinctive features. Glen Cannich is often spoken of as the twin of Glen Affric, but the similarity between the two is not great. Like Affric, Cannich is forested in its lower reaches, but the predominant impression is of closely planted conifers, with smaller areas of natural woodland. Thirteen kilometres up the glen from Cannich the public road ends at the huge dam which impounds Loch Mullardoch. This greatly enlarged loch, whose waters flow south through a tunnel to keep Loch Beinn a' Mheadhoin topped up, extends for a further 13 kilometres westwards almost to the head of the glen, which is barren and treeless save for some fine old pines on the south side of the loch. Changes in the level of Loch Mullardoch create a rather ugly 'tidemark' along its entire length, and when the water level is low, the head of the loch becomes an extensive muddy area of no great beauty. Nevertheless, despite these features, there is an undeniable grandeur about Glen Cannich: long, wide, remote and surrounded by the five highest mountains of the northwestern Highlands.

Glen Urquhart and Glen Moriston are hardly mountain glens, but they are both beautifully wooded and between them there is a vast tract of rough undulating moorland dotted with innumerable lochs and lochans. This is not hillwalking country, but it is a fisherman's paradise. Some of the high moorland north of Invermoriston is used for military training and access is restricted. The most prominent feature of this whole area is the distinctive rounded dome of Meall Fuar-mhonaidh (696m) which rises steeply above Loch Ness between Drumnadrochit and Invermoriston. It has the distinction of being the highest Old Red Sandstone hill in the country. The upper part of Glen Moriston, namely Strath Cluanie and the enlarged Loch Cluanie, is surrounded by mountains and has some of the same character as Glen Cannich. However, it carries the main road to Skye and thus lacks the wilderness quality of Cannich.

Like many of the districts of the western Highlands, Glen Moriston and Glen Affric have their associations with Bonnie Prince Charlie during his flight after Culloden. His travels in July and August of 1746 took him north from Morar to Glen Shiel where he stayed at Achnangart before moving east through Strath Cluanie and over Sgurr nan Conbhairean to a hiding place in Coire Mheadhoin on the north-east side of that mountain. This spot, known as Prince Charlie's Cave, is marked on the present edition of the Ordnance Survey map and is worth a visit despite its inaccessibility. It resembles the Shelter Stone in the Cairngorms, being formed from several large fallen boulders. After a week in this hiding place the Prince moved north with his bodyguard to Athnamulloch in Glen Affric, then down the glen to Fasnakyle and north over the hills to Glen Cannich. This was the northernmost point of the Prince's travels before he turned south and returned to Loch Arkaig by Glen Moriston and Tomdoun.

ACCESS

The mountains described in this chapter can be reached from roads on three sides. On the east the public road up Glen Affric ends at a Forestry Commission car park just beyond the west end of Loch Beinn a'Mheadhoin. From there a right of way continues west along the north side of Loch Affric and a Forestry Commisssion road, passable on a mountain bike, goes for several kilometres on the south side of the loch, linking with the right of way near Athnamulloch and ending in Gleann na Ciche below Mullach Fraoch-choire. To the south the A87 road passes through upper Glen Moriston and Strath Cluanie close to the southern mountains in this group. In the west the closest access is from Dorusduain in Strath Croe, a few kilometres east of the head of Loch Duich, but only Sgurr nan Ceathreamhnan of the high mountains described in this chapter is readily accessible from there. Glen Elchaig provides a very long route from the west, but refer to Chapters 7 and 10 for information about access up this glen.

PUBLIC TRANSPORT

Bus: Glasgow to Kyle of Lochalsh, passes through Strath Cluanie (Scottish Citylink Coaches and Skye-Ways Express Coaches). Daily.
Inverness to Kyle of Lochalsh, passes through Glen Moriston and Strath Cluanie (Scottish Citylink Coaches and Skye-Ways Express Coaches).Daily.
Inverness to Cannich via Drumnadrochit (Highland Scottish Omnibuses). Mondays to Saturdays.
Inverness to Cannich via Beauly and Strath Glass (W MacDonald, Beauly). Tuesdays and Fridays.

ACCOMMODATION

There are hotels at Struy and Cannich in Strath Glass, and at Cozac Lodge at the east end of Loch Mullardoch. To the south-east of the area, and much further from the mountains, there are hotels at Drumnadrochit and Invermoriston. Cluanie Inn in Strath Cluanie is the best placed hotel for hillwalkers in this part of the Highlands, and there is self-catering accommodation at Corrielair Cottage near this hotel available outwith the stalking season. There are several hotels at Loch Duich. Self-catering and bed and breakfast accommodation and caravans to let abound, particularly in Strath Glass, Cannich, Glen Urquhart and Kintail.

The Scottish Youth Hostels Association has hostels at Cannich, Ratagan at the head of Loch Duich and Alltbeithe high up in Glen Affric. Alltbeithe, at the very heart of the mountains, is the best base for hillwalking in the area described in this chapter. Although officially open only during the summer months, the hostel is unlocked during the rest of the year as a shelter for climbers and walkers. However, it goes without saying that anyone using the hostel at such times is under an obligation to respect this facility and cause no damage. The continued use of the hostel by climbers and walkers depends on their causing no damage to the hostel, nor interfering with stalking and hind culling during the season for these activities.

The deserted cottage at Camban in the Fionngleann, three kilometres south-west of Alltbeithe, is available as an unlocked bothy, and it provides good shelter.

THE HILLS

The mountains described in this chapter can all be climbed from Glen Affric, though the distances to some of them are quite long. However, the use of a mountain bike from the end of the public road westwards to Alltbeithe or Gleann na Ciche brings them all within reach. These mountains, with the exception of the two Corbetts south of Loch Affric, can be divided into two groups.

To the south-west there is a group of five Munros between Loch Cluanie and Glen Affric which are most easily approached from the south. To the north, forming the watershed between Glen Affric and Glen Cannich, there is a long and continuous range of mountains, seventeen kilometres from Toll Creagach to the western slopes of Sgurr nan Ceathreamhnan, and including eight Munros, several Tops and many fine ridges and corries. In its height and scale it is the grandest of the many long east-west chains of mountains in the northwestern Highlands.

Carn Ghluasaid *(hill of movement)* (957m)
Sgurr nan Conbhairean *(peak of the keepers of the hounds)* (1110m)
Sail Chaorainn *(hill of the rowan)* (1002m)

The group of five high mountains between Loch Cluanie and Glen Affric is divided into two halves by Gleann na Ciche and the Bealach Choire a' Chait. The eastern part consists of Carn Ghluasaid, Sgurr nan Conbhairean and Sail Chaorainn. These three mountains form a great crescent-shaped ridge whose northern outpost is Tigh Mor na Seilge (929m), a Top of Sail Chaorainn. The east side of this five kilometre long ridge is a series of fine wild corries in whose recesses rise the headwaters of the River Doe, a tributary of the Moriston. It is high in one of these corries, under the crags of Sail Chaorainn, that Prince Charlie's Cave is to be found. The west side of the ridge is a more uniform grassy slope dropping steeply into Gleann na Ciche.

These three mountains can be easily climbed from the side of Loch Cluanie. Starting at Lundie (where there is nothing more than the foundation of an old cottage near the lochside), follow the old military road, which is now only a footpath, westwards to the junction with a stalker's path which leads up the south side of Carn Ghluasaid. This path gives an easy climb right up to the flat summit plateau, and it ends a few hundred metres south-west of the summit itself. In bad visibility it may be difficult to find the rather small cairn which marks the top,so one should cross the plateau to its abrupt northern edge where there is a cairn, from which the true summit is about 50 metres southwards.

On a clear day the view from Carn Ghluasaid to Sgurr nan Conbhairean is very fine, for there are some grand corries between the two peaks. The ridge north-westwards to Sgurr nan Conbhairean is very easy over the flat top of Creag a'Chaorainn (999m) and across the Glas Bhealach; in places the grass is as smooth and close-cropped as a golf course. The summit of Sgurr nan Conbhairean is crowned by a fine cairn with a little sheltered niche on its east side overlooking Coire Dho.

The traverse north to Sail Chaorainn goes along an easy hummocky ridge, and can be continued to Carn na Coire Mheadhoin (1001m) and Tigh Mor na Seilge, whose summit ridge is very narrow for a short distance, with an impressive drop on the south side overlooking Coire Mheadhoin.

The return to Loch Cluanie should be made by the same route as far as Sgurr nan Conbhairean. From there a different way can be taken by descending south-west to the col above the Gorm Lochan and climbing to the little top of Drochaid an Tuill Easaich (1000m). Descend south by a pleasant grassy ridge to the steep lower slopes, Meall Breac, and then bear south-east to cross the Allt Coire Lair. Follow a path down to the old military road, which leads east to Lundie.

The approach to these mountains from the east, starting at Ceannacroc Bridge in Glen Moriston, is very much longer than the preceding route, but it takes one through remote and unfrequented country along the River Doe and into the wild corries at its head. There is a private Landrover track for about eight kilometres up the River Doe, rough going for a mountain bike, and from its end a stalker's path leads a further four kilometres to the foot of the steep east face of Sgurr nan Conbhairean.

A'Chralaig *(the basket or creel)* (1120m)
Mullach Fraoch-choire *(heather-corrie peak)* (1102m)

These two fine mountains form a high ridge eight kilometres long running from south to north between the west end of Loch Cluanie and Glen Affric. The east side of this ridge drops to the Allt na Ciche, a tributary of the River Affric, in a series of large grassy corries, and the west side falls in long, continuously steep slopes to the deep glen between Cluanie and Alltbeithe formed by the Allt a' Chomhlain and An Caorann Mor. This glen gives the shortest route from a public road to Alltbeithe, and is therefore a useful way of reaching upper Glen Affric. There is a good path all the way.

A'Chralaig is normally climbed from Loch Cluanie, leaving the road near the foot of An Caorann Mor and climbing the relentlessly steep hillside north-eastwards to reach the south ridge at about 700m where it becomes quite narrow and well-defined. Higher up the ridge becomes level for a short distance and a subsidiary spur goes out north-east for one and a half kilometres to A'Chioch (948m). The summit of A'Chralaig is crowned by a huge cairn, visible from afar. The north ridge leads in one and a half kilometres to Stob Coire na Cralaig (1008m) and there turns north-east and drops to its lowest point.

On the south ridge of Mullach Fraoch-choire, looking towards A'Chralaig

The ascent of Mullach Fraoch-choire from this col goes up the south ridge of the mountain, which in its last half kilometre is narrow and pinnacled. The traverse of this series of pinnacles is exhilarating, but not at all difficult, and makes an excellent climax to this fine traverse.

On the north side of Mullach Fraoch-choire two ridges lead out towards Glen Affric and enclose the Fraoch-choire *(the heathery corrie)* between them. The north-west ridge is a good route of ascent from Alltbeithe, and the north-east ridge is an equally good route if one has walked or cycled up the Forestry Commission road in Glen Affric to the foot of Gleann na Ciche.

A very fine circuit of the four highest mountains in the group just described can be made from Glen Affric, starting and finishing at the foot of Gleann na Ciche. Climb the north-east ridge of Mullach Fraoch-choire and traverse to A'Chralaig. Descend its south-east ridge for just over half a kilometre and then drop down eastwards to the Bealach Choire a'Chait (726m). The second half of the traverse goes up the west ridge of Sgurr nan Conbhairean, north to Tigh Mor na Seilge and finally down to Gleann na Ciche. It is advisable to descend more or less due west from the last summit to avoid forestry plantations further north along the flank of the glen.

Carn a' Choire Ghairbh
(hill of the rough corrie)
(863m)
Aonach Shasuinn *(height of the saxon, or sassenach)* (889m)

These summits are the two highest of quite an extensive area of rounded heathery hills between Glen Affric and Coire Dho. They lack the height and character of the other mountains described in this chapter, and are seldom climbed. The most convenient approach, which can be used to give a long traverse of both hills, is from the end of the public road in Glen Affric for two kilometres along the south side of the glen to the foot of the Allt Garbh.

Take the stalker's path on the west side of the burn and climb the steep slopes of Na Cnapain to reach Carn Glas Iochdarach (771m). Continue along the broad ridge to Carn a' Choire Ghairbh where there are two flat tops, the northern one being the higher. Descend south-west to the Cadha Riabhach (664m) and climb south-east up Carn a' Choire Ghuirm to reach a broad ridge just north of Tigh Mor na Seilge at Loch a' Choinich. Continue north-east over a slight rise (863m) and down the An Elric ridge to the Bealach an Amais (652m). Finally climb east up the rounded ridge of Aonach Shasuinn, crossing the 875m west top to reach the summit. Return a short distance west to the col at the head of Coire Gorm, and descend north-north-east into this corrie and down to the Allt Garbh where a path is reached which leads down to Glen Affric.

The ascent of Aonach Shasuinn from the south-east by way of Coire Dho is perfectly feasible, although the approach is quite long. The eight kilometre long track from Ceannacroc Bridge past Ceannacroc Lodge and up the River Doe is rough going, even for mountain bicycles. From the end of this track at the confluence of the Allt Coire Sgreumh and the Allt Coire Mheadhoin, climb north up the broad shoulder of Carn a' Choire Bhuidhe to Aonach Shasuinn. It would be possible to continue south-westwards round the head of Coire Mheadhoin, traversing Sail Chaorainn, Sgurr nan Conbhairean and Carn Ghluasaid in a fine long walk.

Looking down the long east ridge of Mam Sodhail to Sgurr na Lapaich

The long range of mountains between Glen Affric and Glen Cannich starts in the east with one or two low hills of no great interest in the Fasnakyle Forest. The first of the high mountains is Toll Creagach, a large rounded summit between Loch Beinn a'Mheadhoin and Loch Mullardoch. Three kilometres west is Tom a'Choinich and four kilometres further west is Carn Eighe, the highest mountain north of the Great Glen. At this point the main ridge turns south for one kilometre to Mam Sodhail, which is almost the twin of Carn Eighe, while a subsidiary ridge goes north for two kilometres to Beinn Fhionnlaidh, a very inaccessible mountain overlooking the west end of Loch Mullardoch. From Mam Sodhail an important side ridge runs east for four kilometres to end at Sgurr na Lapaich (1036m), a fine peak which is the most prominent of the Affric mountains in views westwards from Loch Beinn a'Mheadhoin. The main ridge goes south-west from Mam Sodhail, and there is a steep drop to the Bealach Coire Ghaidheil (716m), the lowest point of the range. Beyond this col is An Socach, and three kilometres further west is Sgurr nan Ceathreamhnan, a magnificent mountain of many peaks, ridges and corries. One of these peaks is Mullach na Dheiragain, which is situated far out along the north-east ridge of Sgurr nan Ceathreamhnan and is another very remote mountain. The western slopes of Sgurr nan Ceathreamhnan fall steeply into Gleann Gaorsaic, whose streams flow down the spectacular Falls of Glomach on their way to Loch Duich and the western seas.

Tom a' Choinich (centre) and Toll Creagach (right) from Glen Affric

Toll Creagach *(rocky hollow)* (1054m)

This mountain has a very rounded outline with a fairly level two kilometre long ridge extending from the summit to the West Top (952m). It may be that the mountain owes its name to the little rocky corrie immediately north of the summit. The highest point is a cairn a short distance west of the summit trig point.

The ascent is usually made from Glen Affric by the path up Gleann nam Fiadh, starting from the road at the bridge over the Abhainn Gleann nam Fiadh. The path is followed for about three kilometres and then a route taken due north up the lower steep hillside followed by easier grassy slopes.

If one is continuing the traverse westwards, the route goes along the broad level ridge west-south-west over the West Top and down to the Bealach Toll Easa (873m).

Tom a' Choinich *(hill of the moss)* (1111m)

This mountain has a more distinctive outline than its neighbour, with a crescent-shaped summit ridge enclosing an east-facing corrie. In the centre of this corrie a well-defined ridge drops from the summit to the Bealach Toll Easa. The path over this pass was used in former days as a route between Affric Lodge and Benula Lodge, the latter now submerged below the waters of Loch Mullardoch.

From the Bealach Toll Easa, reached either from Toll Creagach or the path in Gleann nam Fiadh, the east ridge gives a very fine and direct ascent leading right to the summit. The south-east ridge, rising above its rocky lower buttress Creag na h-Inghinn, is also a good route of ascent, but care is needed if descending the rocky lower part of the ridge.

Carn Eighe *(file hill)* (1183m)
Mam Sodhail *(hill of the barns)* (1180m)

These two mountains are very similar in height and appearance. From some close viewpoints, for example from Sgurr na Lapaich, their twin-like character is evident and they rise steeply at the head of Gleann nam Fiadh. From distant viewpoints, however, their appearance is undistinguished for, despite their height, they have no very distinctive outline.

Carn Eighe and Mam Sodhail are almost invariably climbed from Glen Affric, either singly or as a traverse which may be extended to include neighbouring mountains such as Sgurr na Lapaich, Beinn Fhionnlaidh and Tom a'Choinich. The best starting point is the end of the public road in Glen Affric, although if the burns are in spate it may be advisable to start at the road bridge over the Abhainn Gleann nam Fiadh and thereby avoid a possibly difficult crossing of that stream.

From the car park at the end of the public road continue west along the north side of Loch Affric for just over one kilometre and then take the stalker's path north over the shoulder of Am Meallan and descend to Gleann nam Fiadh to cross

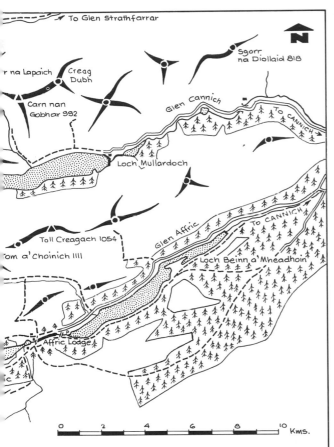

GLEN AFFRIC AND GLEN CANNICH

the stream, normally without difficulty. (If spate conditions exist, it is better to start at the foot of Gleann nam Fiadh and follow the path on the north side of the stream, thereby avoiding this crossing). Continue up the glen for two kilometres and then climb up the stalker's path which leads to the tiny lochan west of Coire Mhic Fhearchair, from where an easy climb leads to the Garbh-bhealach (964m). This point may also be reached by starting the traverse with Tom a'Choinich (qv) and descending its west ridge over Tom a'Choinich Beag (1029m) and An Leth-chreag (1044m).

From the Garbh-bhealach continue south-west along the ridge on a well made stalker's path, which at one point on the steep ascent to Sron Garbh (1132m) is almost a staircase of flat boulders up the rocky ridge. From Sron Garbh the ridge is fairly level for one kilometre and there is a delightful section where the crest becomes very narrow and broken into some sharp little pinnacles. The scramble over these pinnacles is one of the best parts of the traverse, but it can be avoided by a narrow path on the south side below the crest. The next rise leads to Stob a' Choire Dhomhain (1148m), and from there a broad ridge continues to Carn Eighe.

Descend south-west down a broad slope to a col at 1044m, and climb more steeply to reach Mam Sodhail. This summit was an important survey station in the primary triangulation of Scotland in the 1840's, and its huge cairn was once over 7m high. There was also a stone surveyors' shelter on the summit which, on a clear day, commands a widespread view over the northern part of the Highlands. Return to Glen Affric along the long grassy ridge which goes east from Mam Sodhail over the slight rise of Mullach Cadha Rainich (993m) to Sgurr na Lapaich, a fine viewpoint above Loch Affric. Descend south-east round the edge of the east-facing corrie and lower down bear east across rough moorland to rejoin the stalker's path which is followed back to the road beside Loch Affric.

An alternative route to Mam Sodhail from Glen Affric which might be preferred in bad weather is to take the right of way westwards along the north side of Loch Affric to the foot of Coire Leachavie. Then follow the stalker's path up the north-east side of the Allt Coire Leachavie to the col at the head of the corrie where the south-west ridge of Mam Sodhail is reached at 1086m, barely half a kilometre from the summit.

The south-west ridge of Mam Sodhail drops to the flat top of Ciste Dhubh (1109m), and near this point another lateral ridge extends south-cast for three kilometres to end in steep crags above the west end of Loch Affric. An Tudair (1074m) is a fine peak half way along this ridge, which looks very imposing from the south side of Loch Affric. On the south side of this ridge is Coire Coulavie; the Sputan Ban waterfalls at the foot of this corrie are impressive when the Allt Coulavie is in spate.

Returning to Ciste Dhubh, the main ridge continues south-west for half a kilometre to the next minor summit, Carn Coulavie (1069m), and there it turns south-east to Creag Coire nan Each (1056m) before dropping to Loch Affric. There is rather a discontinuity in the main ridge at Carn Coulavie, but the watershed drops steeply westwards to the Bealach Coire Ghaidheil, which is crossed by a path from Glen Affric to Loch Mullardoch. The best route to Mam Sodhail from Alltbeithe is up this path to the bealach and then up another path which makes a rising traverse across the north-west flank of Mam Sodhail's south-west ridge almost to the 1086m col at the head of Coire Leachavie.

Beinn Fhionnlaidh *(Finlay's hill)* (1005m)

Although it is very much on the north side of the main range being described, overlooking the head of Loch Mullardoch, Beinn Fhionnlaidh is most aptly described among the Glen Affric mountains as it is from Glen Affric that it is most usually ascended. It is the terminal point of the north ridge of Carn Eighe, from which it is separated by the Bealach Beag (835m), and it is most conveniently climbed along this ridge over the intervening Top of Stob Coire Lochan (917m). The traverse to Beinn Fhionnlaidh and back to Carn Eighe takes about two hours.

Two other routes to Beinn Fhionnlaidh are possible. The approach on foot from the Loch Mullardoch dam along the south side of the loch is long and tedious across very rough terrain, but if a boat can be hired on the loch and sailed to its west end, then the ascent of Beinn Fhionnlaidh is straightforward, though continuously steep. The approach from Glen Elchaig is very long, but if a bicycle is used to get from Killilan to Iron Lodge, the walking distance from there by the path over the pass eastwards to Loch Mullardoch is about eight kilometres. The Abhainn a' Choillich has to be crossed before the ascent of Beinn Fhionnlaidh is tackled, and if this stream is in spate after heavy rain or in conditions of melting spring snow, the crossing may be very difficult or impossible.

An Socach *(the snout)* 920m

This little peak is the lowest in the range along the north side of Glen Affric, and it is overshadowed by its big neighbours Mam Sodhail and Sgurr nan Ceathreamhnan. An Socach has three principal ridges and is quite steep to the north and east, though the south-west side, Coire na Cloiche, is easy-angled.

The approach from the end of the public road in Glen Affric is quite long, but a bicycle can be used for at least seven kilometres to Athnamulloch, and possibly a further three kilometres to the foot of the Allt Coire Ghaidheil. From there the ascent is straightforward up the south-east ridge along the edge of Coire Ghaidheil to the rather flat, bouldery summit. To vary the return, descend the north-east ridge to the Bealach Coire Ghaidheil and follow a good stalker's path south to reach the track in Glen Affric.

The ascent of An Socach from Alltbeithe is very short. Follow the path northwards from the hostel to the col on the main ridge and then climb the short west ridge of An Socach. Alternatively, this route can be shortened by striking more directly up Coire na Cloiche to the summit.

Sgurr nan Ceathreamhnan *(peak of the quarters)* (1151m)
Mullach na Dheiragain (possibly *summit of the hawk*) (982m)

Sgurr nan Ceathreamhnan, pronounced 'kerranan', is the westernmost high mountain in the great range above Glen Affric, and it is one of the finest mountains in the northwestern Highlands. On the whole it has a more striking appearance than either Carn Eighe or Mam Sodhail, and had it an extra 35m of height it would undoubtedly be regarded as the finest mountain in this part of the Highlands. A glance at the map will show the complex nature of Sgurr nan Ceathreamhnan with its many peaks, ridges and corries. The longest of these ridges goes north-east from the summit for six kilometres to end above Loch Mullardoch, and half way along this ridge is Mullach na Dheiragain. Although classified as a separate mountain in Munro's Tables, it is very much a part of the massif of Sgurr nan Ceathreamhnan. Two other Tops on this very long ridge are Carn na Con Dhu (968m) midway between Sgurr nan Ceathreamhnan and Mullach na Dheiragain, and Mullach Sithidh (973m) at the point where the ridge north of Mullach na Dheiragain divides to form two arms enclosing Coire Aird.

Another ridge leads eastwards from the summit of Sgurr nan Ceathreamhnan for one and a half kilometres to Stob Coire nan Dearcag (940m) and continues to An

Socach, forming the main ridge between Affric and Cannich. Westwards from the summit there is a narrow level ridge for half a kilometre to the West Top (1143m) from which three ridges radiate. The north ridge runs out over Stuc Beag (1074m) to Stuc Mor (1043m) where it splits into two shoulders enclosing the Fraoch Choire. The north-west ridge forms a shoulder enclosing Coire Lochan, and the south ridge leads over Beinn an t-Socaich on the north side of Gleann Gniomhaidh.

By virtue of their remote position, the ascent of Sgurr nan Ceathreamhnan and Mullach na Dheiragain (particularly the latter) is a major expedition unless one happens to be staying at Alltbeithe. Three more distant starting points are Loch Affric, Cluanie Inn and Dorusduain in Strath Croe. Glen Elchaig is also a possibility with the aid of a bicycle.

The routes from Loch Affric and Cluanie Inn both lead first to Alltbeithe, so the traverse from there will be described. Start by climbing the stalker's path north of the hostel to reach the main ridge at the col west of An Socach. From a point on the ridge about a hundred metres west of the col make a slightly descending traverse west towards Loch Coire nan Dearcag. There is a very faint path, but in winter this will be snow-covered and the traverse across a steep snowfield may be difficult. Cross the flat Coire nan Dearcag north-westwards to reach the Bealach nan Daoine by easy slopes. Now traverse the ridge north-eastwards over Carn na Con Dhu to Mullach na Dheiragain. Return to the Bealach nan Daoine and climb the north-east ridge of Sgurr nan Ceathreamhnan which is quite narrow and rocky in places and leads directly to the summit. Descend the east ridge over Stob Coire nan Dearcag and a steep little knoll to its east to reach the col, from where the path leads back to Alltbeithe.

From Dorusduain the route goes up the right of way over the Bealach an Sgairne and down to the south end of Loch a'Bhealaich. Leave the path at the watershed and climb round the southern slope of Sgurr Gaorsaic in a north-easterly direction to reach the West Top of Sgurr nan Ceathreamhnan. A fine short traverse along the summit ridge leads to the top. This is the shortest route from a public road to Sgurr nan Ceathreamhnan, but on the other hand it is a very long route if one wishes to include Mullach na Dheiragain and return to Dorusduain, as this would involve a double traverse of the mountain.

If one can cycle up Glen Elchaig as far as Carnach, a fine long circular traverse can be made. The route goes by Iron Lodge, east to the foot of Gleann Sithidh where there may be a difficult river crossing in wet weather, up to Creag a' Choir' Aird and south along the ridge over Mullach Sithidh to Mullach na Dheiragain. From there to Sgurr nan Ceathreamhnan the route is as described above. Descend north-west from the West Top round the rim of Coire Lochan and continue descending north-west into Gleann Gaorsaic. Leave this glen northwards by a path past Loch Lon Mhurchaidh and continue down the steep path beside the Allt Coir' Easaich to Carnach. This traverse combined with 20 kilometres of cycling gives a rather strenuous, but magnificent day.

Sgurr Gaorsaic *(peak of the thrill)* (c838m)

This hill lies south-west of Sgurr nan Ceathreamhnan, directly above the watershed between Glen Affric and Gleann Gaorsaic, and it is rather dwarfed by its high neighbours; a Corbett between two great Munros. It can be climbed from Dorusduain, either by itself or *en route* to Sgurr nan Ceathreamhnan, by the route described above to the south end of Loch a' Bhealaich with a final climb up the south-western slopes.

PATHS AND WALKS

Glen Affric to Kintail. This cross-country walk is one of the finest in Scotland. It takes one through a wonderful variety of scenery from the forests of Glen Affric to the wild mountains of Kintail. One may chose to start the walk at Cannich, in which case the first eighteen kilometres lead up the public road in Glen Affric; very beautiful, but liable to be busy with cars in the tourist season. An alternative to avoid the traffic is the forest road on the south side of Loch Beinn a'Mheadhoin. However, most people start at the end of the public road and continue along the private road to Affric Lodge and the right of way on the north side of Loch Affric. The path climbs some distance above the loch and its scattered remnants of the Old Caledonian pine forest, and there are good views south-west towards Mullach Fraoch-choire. Beyond Loch Affric the path continues, becoming a rough track near Athnamulloch, and this track continues along the grassy flats of upper Glen Affric past Alltbeithe. There is then a choice of routes, either up Gleann Gniomhaidh and over the Bealach an Sgairne to Dorusduain or up the Fionngleann, past Camban bothy and down Gleann Lichd. Both these routes are described in the preceding chapter, and whichever one choses the way goes through magnificent mountain scenery, leading eventually to Strath Croe and the head of Loch Duich. (28 kilometres from Loch Beinn a'Mheadhoin to Loch Duich).

There are several forest roads, tracks and paths through the extensive Guisachan Forest south of Loch Beinn a'Mheadhoin. One of these goes from Tomich to the small group of houses at Cougie in the heart of the forest. From there one can continue either west to reach Loch Affric, or south-west and south by a long path to reach Coire Dho and Ceannacroc Lodge in Glen Moriston.

From Hilton Lodge, four kilometres south-west of Tomich, a track goes south through forest and across the moors following the electricity transmission pylons to Dundreggan in Glen Moriston.

A good circular walk round Loch Affric can be made from the end of the public road in Glen Affric. Take the Forestry Commission road on the south side of the loch to Athnamulloch where there is a bridge across the River Affric, and return by the path on the north side of the loch. (17 kilometres).

CHAPTER 9

Glen Cannich, Strathfarrar and Strathconon

MAPS: Ordnance Survey   1:50,000   Sheets 25 and 26
Bartholomew   1:100,000   Sheets 54 and 55

PRINCIPAL HILLS

Sgorr na Diollaid	818m	282 363
Carn nan Gobhar	992m	182 344
Sgurr na Lapaich	1150m	161 351
An Riabhachan	1129m	134 345
An Socach	1069m	100 333
Beinn a'Bha'ach Ard	862m	361 435
Sgurr na Ruaidhe	993m	289 426
Carn nan Gobhar	992m	273 439
Sgurr a'Choire Ghlais	1083m	259 430
Sgurr Fhuar-thuill	1049m	235 437
Sgurr a'Mhuilinn	879m	265 557
Meallan nan Uan	840m	264 545
Bac an Eich	849m	222 490
An Sidhean	814m	171 454

The area to be described in this chapter is the northward extension of that described in the last one, and it has many of the same characteristics. The lie of the land is dominated by the long east-west glens and their intervening ranges of mountains, all of which are similar to Glen Affric and its mountains, albeit on a less grand scale. The glens rise far to the west, not far from the Killilan and Glen Carron mountains, and drain to the Beauly and Cromarty firths. There are four of these glens.

Glen Cannich, the southernmost one, has its source at the very remote pass which separates it from Glen Elchaig and its highest stream flows from the tiny Gorm-lochan just under the summit of Sgurr nan Ceathreamhnan. The upper half of the glen is filled by Loch Mullardoch, now greatly enlarged by the damming of its waters for hydro-electric power. This part of the glen is very bare, with few

Loch Monar at the head of Glen Strathfarrar, looking towards Maoile Lunndaidh

habitations and treeless except for some remnants of the Old Caledonian pine forest on the south shore of the loch and a small plantation on the north side. Below the dam, where the public road ends, the glen shows more signs of habitation with a few cottages and quite extensive afforestation in the lowest part before the River Cannich joins the Affric at Cannich village.

Glen Strathfarrar is scenically finer than Cannich, and is a rival to Glen Affric. It has its highest reaches among the remote mountains of Glen Carron, and its upper part is filled by the waters of Loch Monar, another long, narrow reservoir which is very similar to Loch Mullardoch over the hills to the south. Both lochs suffer the same effect that when their water levels are low, very obvious and ugly 'tide-marks' are evident along their lengths. Below the Loch Monar dam, to which one can drive along the private road in the glen, the scenery changes markedly and in its lower part Glen Strathfarrar rivals Glen Affric. There are superb natural woods of pine and birch, in places clinging to the craggy hillside, the River Farrar flows in smooth curves along the glen and two small lochs, Loch a'Mhuillidh and Loch Beannacharan, add variety to the landscape. In winter and spring large herds of red deer graze by the riverside. The only jarring features of the landscape are the power stations of the North of Scotland Hydro-Electric Board. Glen Strathfarrar joins Strathglass at the little village of Struy.

The next glen to the north of Strathfarrar is Glen Orrin. It is quite different, being desolate, uninhabited and almost treeless beyond Fairburn House, whose wooded policies along the banks of the River Orrin are in contrast with the barren glen to the west. Only a private road goes for about five kilometres to the dam at the east end of the Orrin Reservoir and then climbs into the remote country to the south of the reservoir. Glen Orrin itself is pathless until far to the west where tracks and paths reach the glen from the upper part of Strathconon and it is from there that the easiest access into upper Glen Orrin exists. The only habitation in the upper part of the glen is the bothy at Luipmaldrig, but it is far from any hills of interest, and Glen Orrin is without doubt the least frequented of the glens in this part of the Highlands.

Finally, there is·Strathconon, the northernmost of the glens described in this chapter. Like Glen Strathfarrar it has a great variety of scenery. The lowest part is forested and there are hydro-electric power stations on the River Conon. The middle part of the glen above Bridgend is farmed and more populous, and beyond Scardroy Lodge, where the public road ends, the glen continues for many kilometres to the pass beyond which lies Glen Carron. Glenuaig Lodge near this pass is reached by a rough track from Glen Carron (see next chapter).

The main mountains in this area are in two east-west ranges, one on the north side of Loch Mullardoch, and the other on the north side of Glen Strathfarrar. The latter can be reached from Strathconon by crossing Glen Orrin, but this long approach is seldom used. Lower down Glen Orrin the hills on both sides of the glen are low and featureless, and offer no attractions compared with the higher ones further west. At its head, Strathconon penetrates into wild, mountainous country which is described in the next chapter as it is more easily approached from Glen Carron. The middle reaches of Strathconon are dominated by three lower mountains, all Corbetts, Bac an Eich, Sgurr a' Mhuilinn and Meallan nan Uan.

ACCESS

There are four possible routes of access to these mountains. Firstly, up Glen Cannich from Cannich village to the Loch Mullardoch dam. Secondly up the private road in Glen Strathfarrar. Thirdly up Strathconon to Scardroy Lodge, and finally and most remotely up the private road in Glen Elchaig either on foot or by bicycle.

The road up Glen Strathfarrar is private and a gate across the road just above Struy is locked. At the time of writing, access by car up this road is permitted by an agreement between the landowners and the Nature Conservancy Council, who have a small Nature Reserve in the glen. Permission to drive up the glen, and the key of the locked gate, are obtained at the cottage beside this gate, and it is advisable to telephone the gatekeeper beforehand, (046 376 260). The hours when permission is normally granted to drive up the glen are at present:
Weekdays (except Tuesdays) 9.00 a.m. onwards. Sundays 1.30 p.m. onwards. Tuesdays, no access.

Please do not call at the cottage for the key between 1.00 and 1.30 p.m. The above arrangement operates between Easter and the end of October. During the winter months, from the end of October to Easter, the access agreement lapses, but it may be possible to get permission to drive up the glen. It is essential to telephone the above number beforehand. If no reply is received, the Nature Conservancy Council office in Inverness may be contacted (Telephone 0463 239431). At the time of writing there appears to be no restriction to driving across the little curved dam at the east end of Loch Monar and continuing for a further three kilometres to a small power station in Gleann Innis an Loichel. This gives the closest approach by car to the mountains north of the west end of Loch Mullardoch.

PUBLIC TRANSPORT

Bus: Inverness to Cannich via Drumnadrochit (Highland Scottish Omnibuses). Mondays to Saturdays.
Inverness to Cannich via Beauly and Struy (W MacDonald, Beauly). Tuesdays and Fridays.
Inverness to Muir of Ord (Highland Scottish Omnibuses and Rapsons Coaches, Alness). Mondays to Saturdays.

Postbus (11 seater): Beauly – Muir of Ord – Strathconon – Scardroy. Mondays to Saturdays.

ACCOMMODATION

There is a wide selection of hotel, guest house, bed and breakfast and self-catering accommodation at Cannich, Struy, Beauly, Muir of Ord, Conon Bridge and Milltown in Strathconon. There is a hotel at Cozac Lodge just below the Loch Mullardoch dam, and it may also be possible to obtain accommodation at Benula Lodge, beside the Mullardoch dam, and in a self-catering chalet eight kilometres west of the dam on the north side of the loch. (For the last two places, enquiries may be made by telephoning 045 65 347). There is a youth hostel at Cannich and a bothy at Luipmaldrig in Glen Orrin, best reached by a footpath from Inverchoran in Strathconon.

THE HILLS

The range of mountains between Glen Cannich and Glen Strathfarrar starts in the east with a few low rounded hills in the Struy Forest. Going west, Sgorr na Diollaid is the first prominent hill, and far to its west the range rises over Carn nan Gobhar to Sgurr na Lapaich, the highest peak north of Glen Cannich. To its west lie the long level ridges of An Riabhachan and An Socach, beyond which the deep trench of upper Glen Elchaig marks the western end of this range.

Sgorr na Diollaid *(peak of the saddle)* (818m)

Despite its relatively modest height, this hill is nevertheless quite prominent, as it is considerably higher than its neighbours, and its summit is a characteristic pointed rocky tip which is a distinctive landmark. The summit crest is a line of rocky knobs with the highest one at the north end. The ascent of Sgorr na Diollaid is a very short climb compared with others in this area. It can equally well be undertaken from Muchrachd in Glen Cannich, or from Cambussorray in Glen Strathfarrar.

From the bridge over the River Cannich at Muchrachd climb north up the steep hillside. Higher up rocky slabs at an easier angle give pleasant walking and lead to the rocky summit crest which is traversed for about 200 metres over several knolls to the top.

The route from Cambussorry is fairly straightforward, bearing south-west up the hillside through the birch trees of the Coille na Leitire Dhuibhe

Carn nan Gobhar *(hill of the goats)* (992m)

This rounded mountain with its lower north-east top, Creag Dubh (946m), forms a broad ridge midway between Loch Mullardoch and the power station in Gleann Innis an Loichel, and it may be climbed from either the north or south. It is easy to be confused about the summit in bad visibility, for the true top is marked by a small cairn while there is a much larger cairn 200 metres to its south-south-east and only slightly lower along a very broad, featureless ridge.

Starting from the Loch Mullardoch dam, follow the path on the north side of the loch for one and a half kilometres to cross the Allt Mullardoch by a footbridge. Climb north-west to reach the ridge of Mullach na Maoile (761m), and continue over this top, bearing round north-north-west up the broad ridge to Carn nan Gobhar and passing the large cairn shortly before reaching the summit. The return may be varied by traversing the broad ridge to Creag Dubh, descending south-east from there for one kilometre to Pt 814m, then south-west down to Coire an t-Sith to reach the end of a stalker's path which leads down to Loch Mullardoch.

The ascent of Carn nan Gobhar from the power station in Gleann Innis an Loichel is not particularly attractive as the Garbh-choire is an extensive expanse of eroded peat bog which gives rough going. This route may, however, be used as a fairly quick descent, in which case do not follow the Allt Garbh-choire right down to the glen, but leave it to cross a little col one kilometre due south of the power station.

The west-north-west ridge of Carn nan Gobhar leads towards Sgurr na Lapaich, and is traversed if going to or from that mountain. The lower part of the ridge is littered with many huge boulders.

A distant view of Sgurr na Lapaich from Kessock Bridge at Inverness

Sgurr na Lapaich *(peak of the bog)* (1150m)

This splendid mountain is the highest and finest in the area of this chapter. In distant views of the Affric, Cannich and Strathfarrar mountains from the east, for example looking up the Beauly Firth from the Kessock Bridge at Inverness, it is the Sgurr na Lapaich, its eastern corries often snow-filled until late in spring, that appears as the most prominent peak.

Sgurr na Lapaich and its lower tops form a six kilometre ridge running north from Loch Mullardoch to Gleann Innis an Loichel. On the east side of this ridge there are three large corries with high lochans and steep headwalls. One kilometre south of the summit along this ridge, and unnamed on the 1:50,000 Ordnance Survey map, is the Top called Sgurr nan Clachan Geala *(peak of the white stones)* (1095m), whose east face falls very steeply to Loch Tuill Bhearnach.

The shortest approach to Sgurr na Lapaich is from the power station in Gleann Innis an Loichel. Continue up the glen for one kilometre along a rough track to a bridge across the Uisge Misgeach, cross the stream and climb directly up the long north-east flank of the mountain. After crossing a prominent little top called Rudha na Spreidhe *(point of the herd)* (1050m), the narrower north ridge leads to the summit. Although short and direct, this route is rather uninteresting.

A more interesting route goes further up the Uisge Misgeach, and then follows a stalker's path south-west up the steep hillside west of the Allt an Eas Bhain Mhoir to reach level ground north of Loch Beag and Loch Mor in the Toll an Lochain, the fine north-eastern corrie of An Riabhachan. Go south along the level ridge between the two lochans and make a rising traverse south-east among huge fallen boulders to reach the Bealach Toll an Lochain at the head of the corrie. From there a steep climb north-east leads to the summit of Sgurr na Lapaich.

Starting from Loch Mullardoch, the approach is longer than the one just described, but if access up Glen Strathfarrar is not possible, it is the only practicable route. Follow the path west from the dam along the north side of the loch. Beyond the Allt Mullardoch one can either follow a path horizontally to pass just above the little plantation near the site of the former Cozac Lodge, or make a gradually rising traverse across the hillside along the line of a faint vehicle track. Once the Allt Taige is reached, three routes are equally possible; either west to Mullach a' Ghlas-thuill (792m) then north to the summit up the broad ridge of Braigh a' Choire Bhig, or more directly up the south-east ridge of Sgurr nan Clachan Geala and north to the summit, or right up the Allt Taige to the bealach at the head of the Glas Toll from where the east ridge of Sgurr na Lapaich rises directly to the summit, giving a fine route if the rocky crest of the ridge is followed.

It is quite possible to combine the traverse Sgurr na Lapaich and Carn nan Gobhar, in which case the east ridge of the former must be either ascended or descended. The narrow rocky crest of this ridge can be avoided by grassy slopes on the south flank.

An Riabhachan *(the brindled greyish one)* (1129m)

To the west of Sgurr na Lapaich is An Riabhachan, a long level mountain with wide grassy corries to the north and south. The north-western slopes of the mountain are remote and unfrequented, the favourite haunt of red deer, accessible only from the equally remote Pait Lodge on the south shore of Loch Monar. The summit ridge is about two kilometres long, broad, flat and mossy. The highest point is near the middle of this ridge, with the North-east Top (1117m) at one end and the South-west Top (1086m) at the other. At the east end of the mountain a rather narrow ridge drops from the North-east Top to the Bealach Toll an Lochan (820m), and on the north side of this ridge steep cliffs called the Creagan Toll an Lochain drop to Loch Beag and Loch Mor. At the west end of the mountain the main ridge drops north-west to the West Top (1040m) and then south-west to the Bealach a'Bholla (901m), beyond which rises An Socach.

Like Sgurr na Lapaich, An Riabhachan can be climbed either from the Loch Mullardoch dam or from Gleann Innis an Loichel. The chalet on the north shore of Loch Mullardoch mentioned under *Accommodation* is well placed below the southern slopes of the mountain, and the rather long approach from the Mullardoch dam can be shortened by hiring a boat to reach this chalet. It is perfectly feasible to combine An Riabhachan and Sgurr na Lapaich in a single expedition.

The approach to the foot of An Riabhachan along the north side of Loch Mullardoch is eight kilometres along a fairly good path. (The former path was submerged when the level of the loch was raised, and the present path has gradually evolved with the passage of many walkers, sheep and deer). A rather rough stalker's path continues for a further one and a half kilometres up the Allt Socrach, and beyond it the route to An Riabhachan lies directly up grassy slopes to the summit. If continuing the traverse to either An Socach or Sgurr na Lapaich, the main ridge gives easy going in both directions.

The ascent of An Riabhachan from Gleann Innis an Loichel uses the same route to the Bealach Toll an Lochain as that described above for Sgurr na Lapaich. From the bealach the east ridge rises at an easy angle, and higher up it becomes quite narrow, but not at all difficult.

An Socach *(the snout)* (1069m)

This mountain, like its namesake in Glen Affric, is not named on the 1:50,000 Ordnance Survey map. It is even more remote than An Riabhachan, being the westward continuation of that mountain beyond the Bealach a' Bholla. The summit is near the middle of a crescent-shaped ridge which encloses the head of Coire Mhaim, a rather featureless corrie ringed with crags of no great steepness. On all other sides the flanks of An Socach are grassy and uninteresting, and a long shoulder goes out to the south-west to enclose Coire Lungard.

An Socach is usually climbed with An Riabhachan, in which case the ascent from the Bealach a' Bholla between the two mountains is made by the short ridge which rises westwards from the bealach quite steeply to a little knoll and continues across a slight dip to the summit.

The ascent direct to An Socach from Loch Mullardoch is best made from the chalet at the foot of the Allt Socrach westwards for one and a half kilometres along the stalker's path towards Coire Mhaim, and then up the ridge which curves round the southern rim of this corrie. The floor of this corrie is a terrible maze of eroded peat bogs, and any route up or down the middle of the corrie is not advised.

The traverse of An Riabhachan and An Socach from the east end of Loch Mullardoch, with or without Sgurr na Lapaich included, is a long day, and the hire of a boat and outboard motor to shorten the approach walk is quite an advantage.

An alternative approach to An Socach is from Glen Elchaig, but again this is a long way and the use of a bicycle to reach Iron Lodge is a considerable advantage. From Iron Lodge the route goes north-east to Loch Mhoicean from where a long steep climb up grassy slopes leads to the top.

In the desolate country north of An Socach there rises An Cruachan (706m), a hill of more interest to geologists than to climbers. It has some unusual rocks for the area, including a variety containing graphite. It can be reached by way of the long path which goes from Iron Lodge past Loch Mhoicean to Pait Lodge. An Cruachan rises directly above the highest point of this path.

On the north side of Glen Strathfarrar, Beinn a' Bha'ach Ard and its neighbour Sgurr a' Phollain are the eastern outliers of the range. They are prominent in views from the east , rising between Strath Glass and Glen Orrin. Further west there is a compact group of four mountains forming the North Strathfarrar Ridge, and far to the west of these is Maoile Lunndaidh, which is more a part of the Glen Carron mountains and is described in the next chapter.

Beinn a' Bha'ach Ard *(mountain of the high byre)* (862m)

This hill rises to the north-west of Struy and is easily climbed from Inchmore at the foot of Glen Strathfarrar, just before the locked gate across the road is reached. There is a track which can be followed north to Loch na Beiste, and from there one may either continue to Sgurr a' Phollain (the path shown on the 1:50,000 map is virtually non-existent until the ridge is reached) and traverse to Beinn a' Bha'ach Ard, or bear north-west directly towards the summit of the latter. The view from there is one of contrasts: westwards to the mountainous interior of Cannich and Strathfarrar and east to the low-lying lands of Beauly and the Black Isle, with the Moray Firth beyond Kessock Bridge.

The return may be varied by descending south-west down a small stream, the Allt Doire Bhuig, towards the Neaty Burn. The trail of an Argocat is reached at about 500m and followed south to a small dam, and from there a good track leads to the Culligran power station two kilometres up the glen from the starting point.

Sgurr na Ruaidhe *(peak of the redness)* (993m)
Carn nan Gobhar *(hill of the goats)* (992m)
Sgurr a' Choire Ghlais *(peak of the greenish-grey corrie)* (1083m)
Sgurr Fhuar-thuill *(peak of the cold hollow)* (1049m)

These four mountains, known collectively as the North Strathfarrar Ridge, form a compact group which can easily be climbed together in a single expedition, particularly if a car is available to make a six kilometre walk along the road in the glen unnecessary at the end of the day. This traverse will be described from east to west. Sgurr na Ruaidhe and Carn nan Gobhar are both rounded hills with smooth slopes. Sgurr a' Choire Ghlais has more distinction, mainly because of its extra height and steepness. To its west the ridge becomes narrower with steep corries to the north, and the crest continues over Creag Ghorm a' Bhealaich (1030m), and Sgurr Fhuar-thuill to Sgurr na Fearstaig (1015m). At this point the ridge turns south and ends at Sgurr na Muice (891m), a very fine craggy peak with dark cliffs above Loch Toll a' Mhuic.

The east to west traverse is best started near the east end of Loch a' Mhuillidh where a rough track climbs steeply up the hillside to the east of the Allt Coire Mhuillidh. Beyond the end of this track continue along the stalker's path for a further kilometre and after crossing a tributary of the Allt Coire Mhuillidh climb north-east directly up the broad ridge leading to Sgurr na Ruaidhe. Descend north-west down smooth mossy slopes to the Bealach nam Botaichean (775m), and

The summit of Sgurr Fhuar-thuill

climb the broad ridge, very bouldery in its upper part, to Carn nan Gobhar. (Careful map reading is necessary in bad visibility as the ridge over this hill changes direction three times, at one point going from south to north). Go south-west from the summit of Carn nan Gobhar along a level ridge, then down westwards to reach the next col, the Bealach Sneachda (874m), followed by a long steep climb to Sgurr a' Choire Ghlais up the edge of its north face. The summit is crowned by two large cairns and a triangulation pillar.

The second half of the traverse is finer, scenically at least, for the ridge is narrower and views to the western mountains of Glen Carron and Torridon open out. The drops between successive tops are not great and the main crest of the ridge turns south at Sgurr na Fearstaig *(peak of the sea-pinks)*. The descent to the glen can be made from this peak down a stalker's path which starts from the ridge just to its east and makes a descending traverse across its south face towards Loch Toll a' Mhuic. Lower down in the grassy corrie the path tends to disappear, but it reappears again near the loch and continues down to the glen. It is better, however, to continue the traverse south from Sgurr na Fearstaig to Sgurr na Muice *(peak of the pig)* and descend south from there to the col below the little knoll of Carn an Daimh Bhain. To the east of this col a stalker's path leads down to join the main path along the Allt Toll a' Mhuic.

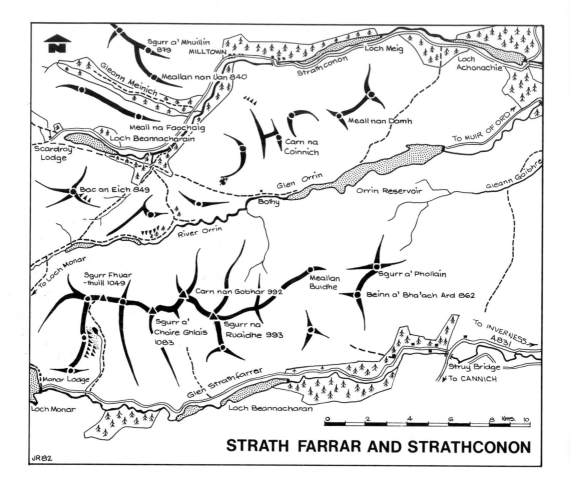

STRATH FARRAR AND STRATHCONON

The North Strathfarrar Ridge may be reached from the north, leaving Strathconon at Inverchoran and following the track south to reach Glen Orrin at the pinewood below Creag a' Ghlastail. From there a bridge across the river gives access to the northern side of these mountains. This approach is seldom used.

Glen Orrin, as already stated, is the least frequented of the glens in this part of the northwestern Highlands. The approach up the lower part of the glen on foot is long and tedious. However, it is possible to reach the upper part of the glen from Inverchoran in Strathconon either by the path to Luipmaldrig bothy, or the track to the bridge over the River Orrin below Creag a' Ghlastail, as noted above. From there a path continues up the glen and at Loch na Caoidhe it forks, one branch going south-west to Loch Monar, the other going north-west to the River Meig above Scardroy Lodge. These paths give cross-country routes through an area which is utterly remote and desolate.

Strathconon has more to interest the hillwalker, with three fine hills, all Corbetts. From Bridgend, where the road crosses the River Meig, there is a good view up the glen to Sgurr a' Mhuilinn and its twin peak, Meallan nan Uan. Further up the strath the view is dominated by the imposing mass of Bac an Eich.

Sgurr a' Mhuilinn *(peak of the mill)* (879m)
Meallan nan Uan *(little hill of the lambs)* (840m)

This is quite an isolated and extensive mountain mass whose pointed peaks are prominent in views from afar, particularly from the south-east along the southern shores of the Moray Firth. In addition to the two peaks noted above which overlook Strathconon, there is a third, Sgurr a' Ghlas Leathaid *(peak of the grey hillside)* (844m) which lies to their north-west above an extensive tract of desolate moorland sloping down to Strath Bran. The northern and western slopes of the mountain above Strath Bran are bare and featureless, and the ascent from that side is not recommended. Strathconon provides a much better approach.

The best starting point is at Strathanmore, on the south side of the Allt an t-Srathain Mhoir. Climb west up a steep grass slope to reach the flatter corrie above. Cross the stream and continue north-west up the easier-angled hillside, which gives rough going across eroded peat bog, to reach the foot of the steep ridge which leads directly to the summit of Sgurr a' Mhuilinn.

From there one can make either a long or a short circuit of the tops. The long alternative goes almost three kilometres north-west along a broad ridge to Sgurr a' Ghlas Leathaid and its twin top (unamed on the 1:50,000 Ordnance Survey map) Sgurr a' Choire Rainich *(peak of the bracken corrie)*. The return should be made as far as the 700m col half a kilometre east of Sgurr a' Ghlas Leathaid, then a long horizontal traverse south-east across the hillside leads to the col at the head of Coire a' Mhuilinn. This point can be reached much more directly by a descent south-west from Sgurr a' Mhuilinn on the shorter traverse. From the col continue south-east over a knoll to the steep cone of Meallan nan Uan and onwards along the fine narrow ridge to Creag Ruadh. From there descend north-east down a broad shoulder to regain the uphill route above Strathanmore.

Creag Ghlas (685m), an outlying top above Gleann Meinich, is of more interest to rock climbers than hillwalkers, for it has a big crag on its south side above the glen. This crag can be reached by a four kilometre walk up the forest road in Gleann Meinich.

Bac an Eich *(bank of the horse)* (849m)

This hill is very prominent in views up Strathconon, seeming to block the glen at the point where it turns west near Loch Beannacharain. It may be climbed from Inverchoran, taking the track south-west up Gleann Chorainn, crossing the stream just beyond the last of the trees on its north bank and making a rising traverse towards Loch Toll Lochain. Climb the ridge to the south of this lochan. It steepens at about 600m, and the easiest line is up the crest; one should avoid going too far right where steep crags overlook the lochan. This leads to the knoll of Sgurr Toll Lochain (727m), beyond which the ridge continues at an easy angle round the rim of the corrie to the summit.

As an alternative route for the descent, go north-west to Corriefeol and return to Inverchoran along the path on the south side of Loch Beannacharain.

An Sidhean *(the fairy hill)* (814m)

To the south-west of Bac an Eich there is a fairly extensive area of rounded hills at the head of Glen Orrin. An Sidhean, the highest of these, is a vast flat-topped hill of no particular interest. It is easily climbed from the road at the Loch Monar dam, passing Monar Lodge and following the good path along the north side of the loch for four kilometres to cross the Allt na Cois. Then climb a stalker's path up the south side of the hill for about one kilometre and continue due north up the broad ridge of Mullach a' Gharbh-leathaid to the top.

The ascent of An Sidhean from the end of the public road in Strathconon near Scardroy Lodge is a lot longer, and the stalker's path up the Allt an Amise onto the hill is not in good repair.

PATHS AND WALKS

The three classic long distance cross-country walks in the area of this chapter are Glen Cannich to Glen Elchaig, Glen Strathfarrar to Glen Carron and Strathconon to Glen Carron. These three routes may rank with the Glen Affric to Kintail walk described in the last two chapters for length and general character, but none of them matches the scenic quality of the Affric route. Only the Glen Cannich route will be described here, the other two being reserved for the next chapter.

Cannich to Killilan. If this walk is started at Cannich village, the first fifteen kilometres are along the road to the Loch Mullardoch dam. The continuation along the north side of the loch follows a path which gives fairly good going as far as the chalet at the foot of the Allt Socrach. Beyond there the way is rougher to the west end of the loch where a path appears at the Allt Coire Lungard. This path keeps above the muddy area at the head of the loch and leads west over the low pass near Loch an Droma and down to Iron Lodge. There remain twelve kilometres to walk along the private road in Glen Elchaig to reach Killilan as described in Chapter 7. (47 kilometres from Cannich to Killilan).

Glen Cannich to Strathfarrar. There is a right of way from Liatrie in Glen Cannich to Ardchuilk in Strathfarrar. Take the path on the west side of the Liatrie Burn through a beautiful stand of Scots pines and keep heading north over the col between Meallan Odhar and An Soutar. Descend the east bank of the Allt Innis na Larach and cross the River Farrar by a footbridge near Ardchuilk. (6 kilometres). A variant of this route goes further up the Liatrie Burn to cross the col west of Meallan Odhar and descend north-west to reach a track leading down to Inchvuilt.

CLIMBING

Most of the climbing in the area of this chapter is on the hills around Glen Strathfarrar. On Sgurr na Lapaich one Grade III winter route has been made in a gully at the head of the Garbh-choire on the flank of the east ridge of the mountain. There would appear to be possibilities for winter climbs on the steep face of Sgurr nan Clachan Geala overlooking Loch Tuill Bhearnach. On An Riabhachan a Grade II gully has been climbed on Creagan Toll an Lochain, the crag on the north flank of the east ridge.

On the opposite side of Glen Strathfarrar there are some climbing possibilities on the east face of Sgurr na Muice and the ridge connecting this peak to Sgurr na Fearstaig. The east face of Sgurr na Muice is a great rocky bastion intersected by two or three grassy ledges or rakes rising from south to north across the face. It is possible to scramble up this face by various routes varying in difficulty from Moderate to Very Difficult, according to one's inclination and route finding ability. Much variation is possible. At the south end of this face two shallow watercourses have given 150m Grade III/IV ice climbs when frozen. Further north, round the nose of the east face of Sgurr na Muice, there is a 250m high slope of mixed grass and rock which has given two Grade III climbs up shallow gullies.

One kilometre further north, on the east face of Pt 880m, there is a steep 120m high cliff where two more winter routes of Grade II and III have been recorded.

Creag Ghlas, the south-western outlier of Sgurr a' Mhuilinn, has two buttresses overlooking Gleann Meinich. The East Buttress is about 250m high and has been climbed by various routes between Difficult and Very Severe standard. The West Buttress is about 150m high, steep, compact and slabby. The rock is very sound and the routes so far recorded on it are all Very Severe.

CHAPTER 10

Glen Carron, Killilan and West Monar

MAPS: Ordnance Survey 1:50,000 Sheets 24,25 and 33
Bartholomew 1:100,000 Sheet 54

PRINCIPAL HILLS

Sguman Coinntich	879m	977 304
Faochaig	868m	022 317
Aonach Buidhe	899m	057 325
Beinn Dronaig	797m	037 382
Bidein a' Choire Sheasgaich	945m	049 412
Lurg Mhor	986m	065 404
Beinn Tharsuinn	863m	055 433
Sgurr na Feartaig	862m	055 454
Sgurr Choinnich	999m	076 446
Sgurr a' Chaorachain	1053m	087 447
Maoile Lunndaidh	1007m	135 458
Sgurr nan Ceannaichean	·915m	087 480
Moruisg	928m	101 499

The mountainous area which is the subject of this chapter is near the watershed at the head of Glen Cannich, Strathfarrar and Strathconon. To the west of this watershed shorter glens run down to Loch Long (an arm of Loch Duich) and Glen Carron, and this long glen forms the north-western boundary of the area. It also forms an important dividing line in the Highlands, for to its south-east are the schistose mountains of Cannich, Affric and Kintail, and to its north-west are the quartzite and sandstone peaks of Applecross and Torridon, very different in appearance and structure.

The eastern boundary of this area is formed by Loch Long, Glen Elchaig and its continuation north-eastwards to Pait Lodge on the south side of Loch Monar; then across the loch to Coire Fionnarach and due north to Achnasheen. This line takes one through some very remote territory, particularly near the head of Glen Elchaig and the west end of Loch Monar, and some of the mountains described in this chapter are among the least accessible in the Highlands, judged by their distance from the nearest public road. The highest of them form a great arc round the head of Loch Monar.

ACCESS

The main routes of approach to this area are along the A87 road from Loch Duich to Kyle of Lochalsh, with a branch up Loch Long to Killilan and Camas-luinie, and along the A890 road down Glen Carron from Achnasheen to Kyle of Lochalsh. From the east there are long walks up Glen Cannich, Strathfarrar and Strathconon, but these routes are more used by cross-country walkers than by climbers.

PUBLIC TRANSPORT

Bus: Glasgow to Kyle of Lochalsh (Scottish Citylink Coaches and Skye-Ways Express Coaches). Daily.
Inverness to Kyle of Lochalsh via Glen Moriston. (Scottish Citylink Coaches and Skye-Ways Express Coaches). Daily.
Inverness to Kyle of Lochalsh via Glen Carron. (Scottish Citylink Coaches and Skye-Ways Express Coaches). Daily.

Postbus (4 Seater): Dornie – Killilan – Kyle of Lochalsh. Mondays to Saturdays.

Train: Inverness to Kyle of Lochalsh. Stations at Achnashellach and Strathcarron.

ACCOMMODATION

There are numerous hotels, guest houses, bed and breakfast houses and cottages to let in the Loch Duich area, including Dornie and Ardelve villages, and at Lochcarron. Camp and caravan sites at Morvich (Loch Duich) Ardelve and Balmacara. Independent hostel at Craig (Glen Carron).

There are two very remote bothies in this area, both renovated by the Mountain Bothies Association. Maol-bhuidhe (053 360) is an extremely isolated cottage beside the headwaters of the River Ling, a 20 kilometre walk from Killilan up Glen Elchaig. Bearnais, unnamed on the 1:50,000 map at (021 430), is four kilometres north of Bendronaig Lodge in the desolate strath of Bearneas. It was restored as a memorial to the climber Eric Beard, and is reached by paths over the hills from either Strathcarron or Achnashellach.

THE HILLS

Between the Inverinate and Killilan forests is Glen Elchaig, at whose head passes lead east and north-east to Loch Mullardoch and Loch Monar respectively. There is a private road up the glen to Iron Lodge, but cars are not permitted along it. (An agreement between the previous landowner and the National Trust for Scotland to allow cars to be driven up the glen to Loch na Leitreach has lapsed). It is, however, a right of way, and was shown on Roy's map of 1755 as part of the road from Strath Glass to Plockton. Bicycles are the ideal form of transport as far as Iron Lodge along this quiet and secluded glen, which in its lower reaches is well wooded along the banks of the River Elchaig. Higher up, towards Loch na Leitreach, the glen has a sterner appearance due to the steep hills and crags on either side.

Sguman Coinntich from Loch Long

Sguman Coinntich *(mossy peak)* (879m)

This hill, with its lower neighbour Ben Killilan, looks very fine as one approaches from the west along the road up Loch Long. The two hills form a big horseshoe ridge enclosing the Coire Mor, and the lower slopes of Sguman Coinntich above Killilan are quite steep and craggy. The most obvious route of ascent is up the stalker's path starting at Killilan and climbing beside the Allt a' Choire Mhoir to the Bealach Mhic Bheathain. From there the ridge leads round to Sguman Coinntich with a short scramble up the crags above the bealach. The return to Killilan may be extended by traversing the horseshoe ridge to Ben Killilan and Sgurr na Cloiche (753m), and then descending south-west from there to return to the foot of Coire Mor.

Faochaig *(the whelk)* (868m)

This hill is five kilometres east-north-east of Sguman Coinntich, and with it forms a high sprawling mass of broad ridges and corries between Glen Elchaig and the River Ling. Faochaig has few outstanding features except its big east-facing corrie which is quite rocky. The most feasible ascent is by bicycle up Glen Elchaig to Carnach, and then north up the stalker's path on the east side of the Allt Domhain. Continue up this stream into a high grassy corrie which is a favourite haunt of red

Looking down Glen Elchaig from the road end near Iron Lodge

deer, and reach the summit plateau of Faochaig, where the cairn is on an outcrop of boulders.

Aonach Buidhe *(yellow hill)* (899m)

The head of Glen Elchaig, between the Allt na Doire Ghairbh and An Crom-allt, is filled by the mass of Aonach Buidhe, a large rounded hill isolated from its neighbours by steep grassy slopes. The most direct ascent is from Iron Lodge, following the path up the Allt na Doire Gairbhe for a short distance before climbing up the broad south ridge. The foot of this ridge is quite steep and there is a small crag not shown on the 1:50,000 map which should be avoided.

The most interesting feature of Aonach Buidhe is its long narrow north-east ridge which extends over An Creachal Beag (870m). This is the best route of ascent for anyone staying at Maol-bhuidhe bothy, but otherwise it is a very inaccessible part of the mountain.

The traverse of Faochaig and Aonach Buidhe is straightforward, particularly if a bicycle is used to reach Carnach or Iron Lodge, although the col between them (465m) is quite low. On the ascent or descent of Faochaig on the west side of this col the stalker's path should be used to avoid steep ground near Leac na Nighinn.

Beinn Dronaig *(hill of the knoll or ragged hill)* (797m)

Going north across the River Ling from the Killilan Forest, one comes to the Attadale Forest and Bendronaig Lodge, a very remote lodge in the heart of some desolate country. The lodge is reached along a rough private road from Attadale House by Loch Carron (12 kilometres). A mountain bicycle could be used with advantage on this road. An alternative route to the lodge is from Achintee near Strathcarron, following the path (a right of way) south-east over the Bealach Alltan Ruairidh.

Beinn Dronaig itself is rather an uninspiring hill rising immediately to the south-east of the lodge, from which it can be climbed in an hour and a half. The summit is towards the east end of an undulating ridge.

Bidein a' Choire Sheasgaich
(peak of the corrie of the barren cattle) (945m)
Lurg Mhor *(big ridge stretching into the plain)* (986m)
Beinn Tharsuinn *(transverse hill)* (863m)

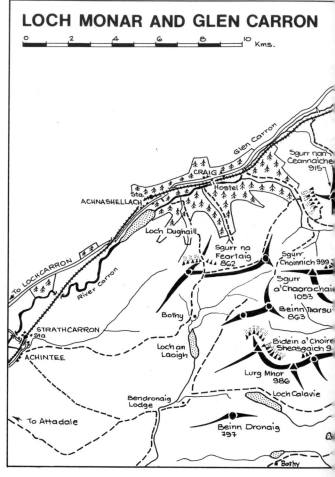

LOCH MONAR AND GLEN CARRON

These three fine mountains rise to the north-east of Bendronaig Lodge on the east side of the wide strath called Bearneas, and form part of the watershed round the head of Loch Monar. Bidein a' Choire Sheasgaich is a steep and rocky peak, particularly to the north and east, and its sharp-pointed summit is a prominent landmark from distant points to the south. Lurg Mhor is a long level ridge which has some steep north-facing cliffs. Beinn Tharsuinn is rather overshadowed by its neighbours, and is usually climbed *en route* to them rather than for itself.

Although they are not far from Bendronaig Lodge, these peaks are seldom climbed from there because of the long way from the A890 road beside Loch Carron to the

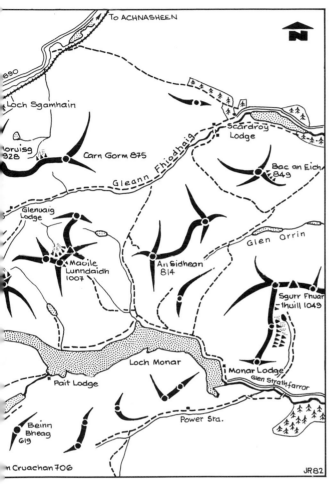

lodge. The ascent is usually made either from Achnashellach or Craig in Glen Carron.

From Achnashellach (or Lair) cross the River Carron a few hundred metres south-east of the Forestry Commission office at Lair either by wading, or (if the river is too deep) by a two-wire bridge a short distance downstream. Enter the forest and follow the path which goes south towards Coire Leiridh. High up in the corrie this path traverses east below some crags and reaches a flat col west of Sgurr na Feartaig. Continue south down to Bearnais bothy. This is a good base for climbing the surrounding mountains, but in very wet weather the Abhainn Bhearnais may be impassable without a long diversion upstream.

The alternative, and more frequented approach to these mountains is from Craig, three kilometres east of Lair. The gate at the level crossing is locked, so one has to walk or cycle up the forest road into the glen of the Allt a' Chonais. There is a good track up this glen, and it is possible to cycle to the pass at its head, and a short distance further to Glenuaig Lodge where the track ends. This effectively shortens the time to reach these mountains.

Going to Bidein a' Choire Sheasgaich, leave the track five and a half kilometres from Craig, cross the Allt a' Chonais and climb the stalker's path which leads south-west up the Allt Leathad an Tobair to the Bealach Bhearnais (596m). Continue a short distance south to the slightly higher Bealach Crudhain (637m); Beinn Tharsuinn rises to the south-west of this bealach. Climb a steep slope of grass and rocks to reach a broad undulating ridge, where a little unnecessary climbing can be avoided by a level traverse on the east side of the ridge to reach the summit. From there drop down to the col between the two tops of Beinn Tharsuinn, and make a descending traverse south-west to reach the Bealach an Sgoltaidh. (This name on the 1:50,000 map is misleadingly shown a long way east of the true pass).

Above the bealach the north ridge of Bidein a' Choire Sheasgaich rises steeply and looks rather forbidding with two bands of crags. Walk up beside a stone dyke and from its top continue uphill through small crags to reach the base of the upper band of rocks, which appears to encircle the end of the ridge. There are at least two ways of surmounting this barrier, both of which involve some mild scrambling on steep grass. More or less directly ahead there is an open grassy gully forming a recess in the cliffs which gives a steep scramble. Alternatively, a traverse to the right below the cliffs for a few hundred metres leads to another grassy gully which in turn provides a fairly easy route up.

Both these routes lead to a tiny lochan lying near the edge of the cliffs at the start of a level section of the ridge. This leads over a minor top, past another lochan and finally up a narrower ridge to the summit of Bidein a' Choire Sheasgaich.

To continue to Lurg Mhor, go a short distance south-west along the summit ridge of Bidein a' Choire Sheasgaich and then descend south-east down a broad ridge to the col from where another broad ridge rises in two steps to the top of Lurg Mhor, one of the remotest and consequently most highly prized of the Munros.

The return from Lurg Mhor to the Bealach Bhearnais may be made by the outward route over Bidein a' Choire Sheasgaich and Beinn Tharsuinn, but this involves a lot more climbing. Alternatively, it is fairly straightforward, and certainly avoids some of this climbing, to descend north from the col west of Lurg Mhor and make a gradually descending traverse across the east face of Bidein followed by a gradually ascending traverse across the east face of Beinn Tharsuinn to reach the Bealach Crudhain. The going is not too difficult across mainly grassy slopes.

The east ridge of Lurg Mhor leads to the 974m east top called Meall Mor. The connecting ridge is narrow, at one point narrow enough to cause slight difficulty which cannot be easily avoided. Further east the ridge runs down gradually to Loch Monar near Pait Lodge. This very remote lodge is reached by boat along Loch Monar.

The ascent of Bidein a' Choire Sheasgaich from Bearnais bothy is relatively short, provided the Abhainn Bhearnais can be crossed. One possible route is to climb up to the Bealach an Sgoltaidh and climb the north ridge as described above. More direct and easier alternatives are to climb Coire Seasgach to the lochan on the north ridge, or to bear south of this corrie to reach the Sail Riabhach ridge which leads easily to the summit.

Sgurr na Feartag *(peak of the sea pink)* (862m)

This long level hill is well seen from Achnashellach in Glen Carron. Its north face has two corries – Coire na h-Eilde and Coire nan Each – with a line of crags high up below the summit ridge. There is a stalker's path right along this ridge, and the traverse is a very pleasant and easy hillwalk. The col at the west end of the summit ridge is reached by the path from Achnashellach (Lair) to Bearnais bothy, and the start of the stalker's path up the north-east end of the hill is reached four kilometres up the track from Craig at a rather frail-looking footbridge across the Allt a' Chonais.

The summit of Sgurr na Feartaig can also be easily reached from the Bealach Bhearnais up a steep slope of grass and boulders, or less directly by a narrow stalker's path from the bealach to a point on the summit ridge a few hundred metres south-west of the summit itself.

Sgurr Choinnich *(moss peak)* (999m)
Sgurr a' Chaorachain *(peak of the little field of the berries)* (1053m)

These two mountains occupy a strategic position between the head of Loch Monar and Glen Carron, and are well seen both from Loch Monar and from the Allt a' Chonais as one climbs above the Achnashellach Forest. Sgurr Choinnich has a steep craggy north face overlooking Coire Choinnich. To their east is the very fine peak Bidean an Eoin Deirg which, although classified as a Top of Sgurr a' Chaorachain, is more impressive, with its pointed summit and very steep rocky north buttress. It is the most striking peak of this group in views westwards along Loch Monar.

The traverse of these three peaks is best made from the Allt a' Chonais. If going from west to east, take the route to the Bealach Bhearnais described above for Bidein a' Choire Sheasgaich. From the bealach climb Sgurr Choinnich by its west ridge, which is grassy with a few small rocky steps. The summit is a narrow level ridge with the top, marked by a very small cairn, near the middle. On the north side steep cliffs drop into Coire Choinnich.

From the south-east end of the summit ridge turn north-east and descend steeply to the Bealach Coire Choinnich. Climb from there to the rounded summit of Sgurr a' Chaorachain. The continuation to Bidean an Eoin Deirg is along a broad stony ridge for two kilometres. The return is probably best made by reversing the traverse as far as the Bealach Coire Choinnich. From there descend north into the corrie, keeping to the east side of the burn high up to avoid the rock bands on the west side. Cross the Allt Leathad an Tobair to regain the stalker's path and descend to the Allt a' Chonais track.

Alternatively, it is possible to descend north from Sgurr a' Chaorachain, but care is required as the steep slopes above the headwaters of the Allt a' Chonais are rather craggy, a fact not evident from the 1:50,000 map. If taking this route, go down the north ridge for half a kilometre, then north-west down steep, but uncomplicated slopes.

Maoile Lunndaidh *(bare hill of the wet place)* (1007m)

This flat-topped mountain is more reminiscent of a Cairngorm-type hill than a west Highland one. It has an extensive flat summit ridge and rounded corries gouged out of its flanks. It is situated in the centre of the remote country between Loch Monar, the head of Strathconon and the Allt a' Chonais, and can be ascended from these three sides.

The ascent from the glen of the Allt a'Chonais is probably the shortest, particularly as one can cycle up the track in that glen to within four kilometres of the summit of Maoile Lunndaidh. Leave the track near the little plantation one kilometre south-west of Glenuaig Lodge and traverse rough peaty ground eastwards to cross An Crom-allt and climb the steep hillside of grass and boulders between the Fuar-tholl Mor on the east and the shallower bowl of the Fuar-tholl Beag to the west. Higher up the climb goes along the edge of the Fuar-tholl Mor to reach the flatter slopes of Carn nam Fiaclan (996m). Continue along the level mossy ridge with the deep hollow of the Fuar-tholl Mor on the left, and Toll a' Choin on the right, to reach the highest point of Maoile Lunndaidh.

The return may be varied by descending north to a col at about 750m and then bearing west down to the outflow from Fuar-tholl Mor and across the rough moor to the track one kilometre south-west of Glenuaig Lodge.

It is possible to combine Maoile Lunndaidh with the three mountains just described in a very good long day's hillwalking. It is probably best to climb Maoile Lunndaidh first, as described above, and then descend west from Carn nam Fiaclan to the col at 600m below Bidean an Eoin Deirg, whose north face gives a steep and rocky climb. From there traverse west to Sgurr Choinnich and return to the Allt a' Chonais by reversing the route described previously.

The approach to Maoile Lunndaidh from the Glen Strathfarrar road at the east end of Loch Monar is longer. There is a good path along the north side of the loch for much of the way, and a stalker's path continues up the Allt Toll a' Choin for two and a half kilometres. From the end of this path the summit plateau may be reached by either of the two bounding ridges of the Toll a' Choin.

Sgurr nan Ceannaichean *(peak of the merchants or pedlars)* (915m)
Moruisg *(big water)* (928m)

These two mountains rise very prominently on the south side of Glen Carron, a few kilometres east of Craig, and their nearness to the glen makes them very accessible. Sgurr nan Ceannaichean has a very steep and rocky west face, cleft by two great gullies, and this mountain looks impressive when seen from Craig or Achnashellach. Moruisg, on the other hand, appears from Glen Carron to be a very flat-topped hill, with a long extension eastwards to Carn Gorm and Carn Liath, two tops which are very seldom climbed. Between Sgurr nan Ceannaichean and Moruisg is Coire Toll nam Bian, a deep corrie with a headwall of steep grass and rock.

The two mountains can be very easily traversed together, and the best starting point for this is on the A890 road in Glen Carron two kilometres up from Glencarron Lodge. There is a footbridge over the River Carron one kilometre downstream from Loch Sgamhain, and a stalker's path leads from there southwards into Coire Toll nam Bian. It is hardly necessary to follow this path, as the direct ascent of the north-western slopes of Moruisg is perfectly straightforward, provided one avoids the deep gullies and minor crags on the right (south-west) of the hillside. The summit is a flat mossy plateau. Continue south-west along the broad ridge to the col (728m) and then up, west at first and then south-south-west, to Sgurr nan Ceannaichean whose summit cairn is right on the edge of the east-facing corrie, looking down to Glenuaig Lodge.

The descent goes north-north-east down the ridge of ascent for half a kilometre, then due north down a broad shoulder, avoiding some crags lower down and bearing north-east to cross the Alltan na Feola. On the east side of this stream the stalker's path leads back to the starting point.

Sgurr nan Ceannaichean can be climbed equally well from Craig by the track up the Allt a' Chonais. One possible route is to leave the track half a kilometre beyond the forest and climb steeply up the north-west shoulder, keeping left of difficult craggy ground and following a very tenuous path up steep grass and scree to reach the more level west ridge which leads easily to the summit. Another longer but in some ways easier route is to continue up the Allt a' Chonais and climb the stalker's path on the south side of the mountain. This path ends high up not far below the west ridge.

PATHS AND WALKS

Loch Monar to Glen Carron. This is the western half of the cross-country route following long established rights of way from Strath Glass to Glen Carron, the eastern half being the road up Glen Strathfarrar from Struy to the Loch Monar dam.

The continuation along the north side of Loch Monar follows a good path for ten kilometres. Five more kilometres of pathless going lead to the west end of the loch, where there is a small rusty corrugated iron shed which might provide shelter *in extremis*. From there follow a path up the east side of the Allt Bealach Crudhain which gives good going half way up to the pass. On the north side of this pass descend a short distance to the Bealach Bhearnais, where there is a choice of routes, depending on one's objective.

If aiming for Craig, descend the stalker's path north-east to the Allt a' Chonais and finish down the track in that glen. (26 kilometres from the Loch Monar dam to Craig).

If aiming for Achnashellach, climb the narrow and rather indistinct stalker's path west from the Bealach Bhearnais to the ridge of Sgurr na Feartaig, traverse this

Looking south-east from Sgurr na Feartaig to Sgurr Choinnich (left) and the distant outline of An Riabhachan above the Bealach Bhearnais

ridge west for just over two kilometres to the flat bealach at the head of Coire na h-Eilde and descend to Achnashellach by the path down Coire Leiridh. (26 kilometres from the Loch Monar dam to Achnashellach).

If aiming for Strathcarron, descend the wide strath of Bearneas to Bearnais bothy and follow the path south-west up the grassy hillside. The path continues across high moorland westwards and eventually descends to Achintee a short distance from Strathcarron station. (32 kilometres from the Loch Monar dam to Strathcarron). This route can be shortened slightly by going from the west end of Loch Monar to Bearnais bothy over the Bealach an Sgoltaidh, but this may involve a difficult crossing of the Abhainn Bhearnais if this stream is in spate.

Strathconon to Glen Carron. This very obvious route, which is a right of way, goes up Strathconon from the end of the public road near Scardroy Lodge. For twelve kilometres the path follows the north bank of the River Meig up featureless Gleann Fhiodhaig to Glenuaig Lodge. From there a track leads over the pass and down the Allt a' Chonais to Craig. (22 kilometres from Scardroy Lodge to Craig).

There are several more rights of way in the Killilan, Attadale and Monar forests:-

1. Bendronaig Lodge to the Allt a' Chonais by the east side of Loch an Laoigh and Bealach Bhearnais.

Bidein a' Choire Sheasgaich from Beinn Tharsuinn

2. Bendronaig Lodge to Pait Lodge by Loch Calavie.
3. Pait Lodge to Iron Lodge (Glen Elchaig) by An Gead Loch and Loch Mhoicean.
4. Bendronaig Lodge to Killilan along the west bank of the River Ling.
5. Loch Monar to Glenuaig Lodge by Loch Mhuillich and the pass between Maoile Lunndaidh and Bidean an Eoin Deirg. This route can be used as a variant on the Loch Monar to Glen Carron walk described above.

CLIMBING

On Lurg Mhor there is a fine crag of rough quartzite on the north flank of the west ridge at (062 405). The crag is recognised by its many parallel slanting grooves and overlapping slabs. Two routes of Very Severe standard have been done on it, one up the left edge and the other a direct central line.

In the Toll a' Choin of Maoile Lunndaidh a route has been done in the left side of the corrie (*Mica Ridge*, 100m, Difficult). There are two prominent gullies on the west face of Sgurr nan Ceannaichean, but it is not certain that either has been ascended completely in summer conditions, although partial ascents have been made. The North Gully has been climbed in winter (420m, Grade III/IV).

CHAPTER 11

Applecross and Coulin

MAPS: Ordnance Survey 1 : 50,000 Sheets 19, 24 and 25
Bartholomew 1 : 100,000 Sheets 54 and 55

PRINCIPAL HILLS

Beinn Bhan	896m	804 450
Sgurr a'Chaorachain	792m	797 417
Meall Gorm	710m	779 409
Beinn Damh	903m	893 502
Maol Chean-dearg	935m	924 498
An Ruadh-stac	892m	922 481
Sgorr Ruadh	962m	959 504
Fuar Tholl	907m	975 489
Beinn Liath Mhor	926m	964 520
Sgorr nan Lochan Uaine	871m	969 531
Sgurr Dubh	782m	979 558

This is a clearly defined group of mountains stretching inland from the Applecross peninsula between Glen Carron and Glen Torridon towards the road from Achnasheen to Kinlochewe which passes through Glen Docherty. It is an area which stands on its own merit for the calibre of its mountain scenery, in no way overshadowed by the giants of Torridon to the north. Here the scale is smaller, but the mountains combine to form a landscape of quality, while still retaining much of their individuality in the overall pattern. The character of the mountains is governed by the predominant rock formation. They lie almost wholly within the line of Torridonian sandstone which stretches along this western coastline from Ardnamurchan to Cape Wrath. Glaciation and subsequent weathering have created a magnificent architecture of terraced cliffs, great scooped-out corries, and monumental tops enhanced in places with a sprinkling of white quartzite.

On the Applecross peninsula, the sandstone forms an elevated plateau which fills the south-eastern corner. This rises up from the western shoreline, and falls steeply to the east towards Kishorn and Glen Shieldaig, creating a virtual barrier between Applecross and the mainland. Until recent years the pass across the highest point of the plateau – Bealach na Ba (*the pass of the cattle*) – carried the only road into the peninsula. This gives a spectacular introduction to the area. It rises up relentlessly from Tornapress at the head of Loch Kishorn and traverses the lower slopes of

Beinn Bhan, crossing the Russel Burn at the mouth of Coire nan Arr to give a glimpse of one of the finest features of the Applecross mountains – A'Chioch Buttrress in the eastern recesses of Sgurr a'Chaorachain.

It continues to rise above the north side of the wild torrent of the Allt a'Chumhaing which drops down between Sgurr a'Chaorachain and Meall Gorm over a series of steep walls and ledges. Terraced faces rise up on either side, and the final section onto the summit of the plateau is accomplished in a spectacular series of four hairpin bends up the headwall of the glen. At this point the way reaches a height of 626m making it the third highest motor road in Britain. The descent to the village of Applecross is less steep but equally spectacular, with sweeping views westwards to the mountains of Skye and the surrounding islands.

The western coastline stretches for almost 25 kilometres along the Inner Sound; the small communities dotted along its length still hold the bulk of the population. A new prosperity touched the area for a time in the wake of the construction yard at Kishorn; with its collapse the economy has reverted to the old pattern of crofting, forestry and estate work, with an increased participation in tourism and fish farming. The Bealach na Ba is no longer the only tenuous link with the outside world, often severed in winter months. Nowadays the north coastal road winds round from Shieldaig by way of Kenmore to join the old road at Applecross village. Mainly scenic in its initial stage, the functional quality improves as it progresses. There are no other ways through Applecross, and the words of the old minister who wrote the statistical account two centuries ago still hold true – 'the foot traveller is guided according to the season of the year, what course to take, over rugged hills, rapid waters and deep marshy burns'. The Gaelic name for Applecross is A'Chomaraich – *The Sanctuary* – and in the past this was a place of refuge for fugitives, recognized as such by the Church until the times of the Reformation. Legend has it that if you take a handful of earth from the grave of St. Maelrubha who lies buried there at Cruarg, you will always return again in safety.

The mountains on the landward side of the area, to the east of Glen Shieldaig, lie entirely within the Beinn Damph and Coulin deer forests, with the usual restrictions on access during stalking seasons. This is compensated for by the exceptionally fine system of cross-country paths which cover the entire area, making for easy access to the main mountains from all directions. Their general direction is north to south, connecting Glen Torridon with Glen Carron, but most of them interconnect along their middle stretches to give good lateral lines. Several of the most important of these are established rights of way. The mountains there are still mainly of Torridonian sandstone, but towards the east side quartzite begins to appear. Long corries and deep glens have been gouged out of the original sandstone layer, significant enough to virtually isolate the individual mountains, and providing natural lines for the web of paths, which are there seen to join across the intervening passes on the ridges. These corries also carry the considerable drainage system of rivers and small burns down to all sides. On the north side, into the River Torridon and Upper Loch Torridon; on the south side, into the River Carron.

Four main glens and corries are seen to establish the pattern of the area. On the west side, Srath a'Bhathaich slants in from Glen Shieldaig for almost ten kilometres to divide Beinn Damh and its satellites from the cluster of hills around the head of Loch Carron. From the mouth of the strath, Loch Damh stretches north for five kilometres between Beinn Damh and Ben Shieldaig, the biggest area of fresh water loch in the area. The River Balgy, a well-known salmon water, flows into Upper Loch Torridon from its north end, carrying most of the drainage from this side. On the south side. Coire Fionnaraich and Coire Lair penetrate inland from Glen Carron for more than six kilometres, effectively separating the main group of mountains in this central section. On the east, the River Coulin and its tributaries stretch across from north to south – a distance of ten kilometres – forming the boundary on that side. There are no important hills in the corner between there and Achnasheen. The north end of the Coulin track provides a most picturesque gateway to Glen Torridon and the mountains of the north; the tree-lined slopes provide a perfect setting for Loch Coulin and Loch Clair , with the ridges of Beinn Eighe and Liathach forming a spectacular background.

ACCESS

Road provides the most convenient access to all of the mountains. The way into Applecross has already been described, the rest of the area is completely circled by good motor roads. Achnasheen is the principal junction on the east side and the trunk road from Dingwall and Inverness (A832) forks there. The main branch of the A832 road carries on west for fifteen kilometres to the village of Kinlochewe, first along the side of Loch a'Chroisg, then down through the narrow defile of Glen Docherty, which opens out to give a splendid view along Loch Maree. The left branch (A890) passes down through Glen Carron past Achnashellach to the village of Lochcarron at the head of the loch, 35 kilometres. The majority of the mountains can be approached easily from this side. Lochcarron is the largest centre of population, with a variety of services and a nearby railstop at Strathcarron. The A896 continues past the village to Tornapress at the head of Loch Kishorn (ten kilometres) then swings north through Glen Shieldaig to Loch Torridon. The road to Applecross turns off at Tornapress across the mouth of the River Kishorn. From Shieldaig the main road continues along the south shore of Upper Loch Torridon through the villages of Shieldaig, Annat and Torridon before turning eastwards along Glen Torridon to Kinlochewe. This northern section of the road gives access to the remainder of the mountains in the area.

PUBLIC TRANSPORT

Rail: There is a daily passenger service from Inverness and Dingwall via Achnasheen – Achnashellach – Strathcarron. Mondays to Saturdays.

The Applecross hills seen beyond the village of Lochcarron

Bus: Strathcarron – Lochcarron – Kishorn – Shieldaig – Annat – Torridon. (D McLennan. Shieldaig). Mondays to Saturdays. All Year.
Inverness – Dingwall – Achnasheen. (MacKenzie and MacLennan. Gairloch). Tuesdays, Thursdays, Fridays. All Year.

Postbus: Shieldaig – Applecross – Toscaig – Shieldaig – Kishorn. Mondays to Saturdays. All Year.
Shieldaig – Tornapress – Kishorn. Mondays to Saturdays. All Year.

ACCOMMODATION

There are hotels at Achnasheen, Strathcarron, Lochcarron, Applecross, Shieldaig, Torridon and Kinlochewe. Bed and breakfast accommodation is readily found throughout. The Scottish Youth Hostels Association has a hostel in Glen Torridon which is open from March to October. There are independent hostels at Achnashellach and at Glen Cottage in Glen Torridon, both open all year. There are camp sites with services at Kinlochewe and at Applecross. The Scottish Mountaineering Club's Ling Hut in Glen Torridon (grid reference 908 563) is available to members of climbing clubs in Britain; bookings should be made with the Honorary Hut Custodian. This is currently D.J.Broadhead, 11 Cradlehall Park, Westhill, Inverness. IV1 2BZ.

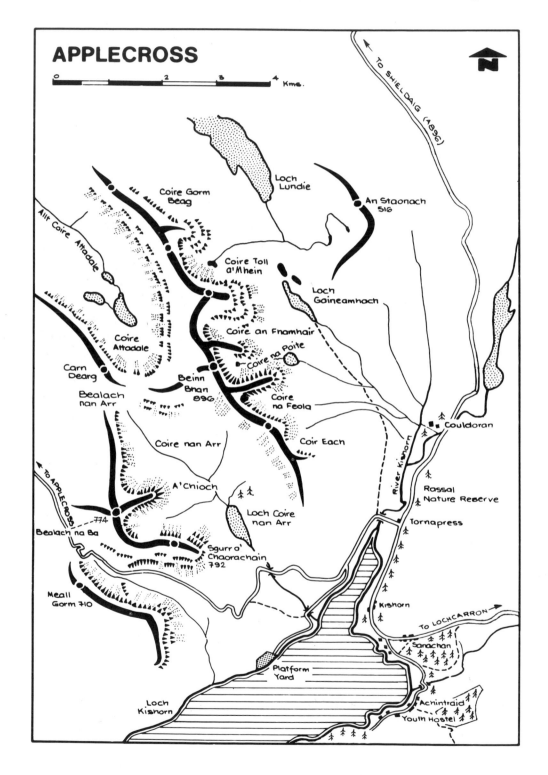

APPLECROSS

0   2   3   4 Kms.

TO SHIELDAIG (A896)

Loch Lundie

An Staonach 516

Coire Gorm Beag

Allt Coire Attadale

Coire Toll a'Mhein

Loch Gaineamhach

Coire an Fhamhair

Coire Attadale

Coire na Poite

Carn Dearg

Beinn Bhan 896

Bealach nan Arr

Coire na Feola

Couldoran

Coire nan Arr

Coir Each

River Kishorn

TO APPLECROSS

A'Chioch

Rassal Nature Reserve

Loch Coire nan Arr

774

Tornapress

Bealach na Ba

Sgurr a' Chaorachain 792

Kishorn

TO LOCHCARRON

Meall Gorm 710

Sanachan

Platform Yard

Achintraid Youth Hostel

Loch Kishorn

THE HILLS

The Applecross mountains lie on either side of the Bealach na Ba, and the summits of all of them can be reached from the head of the pass there with little difficulty. The plateau is relatively flat, but the boulder-strewn surface makes for rough walking in places.

Meall Gorm (*green hill*) (710m)

This is the only mountain on the south side of the Bealach na Ba. The ridge extends for two kilometres in a south-easterly direction towards the head of Loch Kishorn; the summit is on the north-west end, and is quickly reached from the head of the pass with little effort. The south side of the ridge has unbroken slopes; to the north and east a line of imposing cliffs drop steeply towards the bed of the Allt a'

A'Chioch of Sgurr a'Chaorachain

Chumhaing. These are well-terraced, vegetated, and seamed with deep gullies and wide stone-chutes, easily approached along the floor of the corrie from the hairpin bends.

Sgurr a'Chaorachain (*peak of the little field of berries*) (792m)

This fine mountain lies on the north-east side of the Bealach na Ba, its summit ridge forming a crescent with the highest point at its south-east end and a slightly lower top (776m) one and a half kilometres to its north-west. The entire north-east side of this summit ridge falls in a series of great sandstone cliffs down to Coire nan Arr (*the giant's corrie*), and at the centre of this line of cliffs a long spur juts out eastwards into the corrie and terminates in a splendid sandstone tower, A'Chioch. The south side of the mountain, overlooking the Bealach na Ba road, is also a steep and impressive wall of sandstone, and it is only to the north-west, towards the head of Coire nan Cuileag, that the slopes of Sgurr a'Chaorachain are less than precipitous.

The shortest route to the summit, but one hardly worthy of the mountain, is to leave the Bealach na Ba road near its highest point and go east up gradually rising slopes to reach the summit ridge , which is followed south-east then east without difficulty to the summit. The 776m top, on which there is a prominent communications aerial, can be reached very easily from the road by a track leading right to the top.

Another very direct route is up the south-east ridge, starting from the road a short distance west of the bridge over the Russel Burn. Despite the impressive appearance of this ridge, which has steep cliffs on both flanks, the ascent up the true crest involves only a litle easy scrambling up some short sandstone steps, and the angle eases long before the summit is reached.

The finest approach to Sgurr a'Chaorachain is undoubtedly up the Coire nan Arr, following a path from the road bridge along the burn to Loch Coire nan Arr. From the lochside the great tower of A'Chioch shows its full height and grandeur. It is connected to the mountain by the east spur which is itself the crest of several towers, thus forming an undulating ridge with very steep sides and rocky gaps between the towers. It is not a hillwalkers' route, but for rock climbers the ascent of A'Chioch followed by the traverse along the spur is one of the finest climbs in this part of the Highlands. It is possible to reach the summit without much difficulty, however, by bearing south-west below A'Chioch to a tiny lochan high up in the side corrie, and from there one can either climb steeply towards the south-west corner of this little corrie to reach the summit ridge, or go north-west up a grassy gully to reach the 776m top.

Beinn Bhan (*the white mountain*) (896m)

Beinn Bhan is the highest mountain on the Applecross plateau, forming a remarkable rampart along its north-eastern edge. The ridge rises as a long gentle slope from the head of Loch Kishorn and stretches continuously inland for over eight kilometres over the unnamed point (712m) above the west end of Loch Lundie on the edge of the Glenshieldaig Forest. The summit is relatively flat and is easily reached from the Bealach na Ba by way of the north-west shoulder of Sgurr a' Chaorachain to the Bealach nan Arr, a distance of three kilometres and easy walking. From the bealach, climb the broad shoulder which curves up equally easily for a further one and a half kilometres onto the highest point on the ridge.

A straightforward alternative is provided by the long south-east ridge rising from Loch Kishorn for five kilometres; this can be safely attempted in most conditions. The slopes along the west side of the ridge fall into Coire nan Arr and more steeply into Coire Attadale; to the east the mountain presents a series of magnificent cliff-lined corries separated by narrow precipitous sandstone spurs with splendid terminal towers. From north to south these corries are: Coire nan Fhamhair (*giant's corrie*), Coire na Poite (*corrie of the pot*), Coire na Feola (*corrie of the flesh*), Coire Each (*horse corrie*). Terraced cliffs fall sheer into the middle two corries and there is no easy way down into them. Even in winter conditions however, a way can be made

The approach to Beinn Bhan from the head of Loch Kishorn

down the head of Coire nan Fhamhair. The unnamed corrie to the north of Coire nan Fhamhair, below point 843m, is Coire Toll a'Bhein; it presents a steep north-east face towards Loch Lundie. The furthest north corrie is Coire Gorm Beag. Both of these would seem to be of limited interest.

The approach to the east side of Beinn Bhan is by way of a good path which leads in from the west side of the bridge over the River Kishorn for almost five kilometres towards Loch Gaineamhach. This keeps rather low down along the water course, but it can be left at any convenient point to make a way up into the corries. Above Lochan Coire na Poite, a rock barrier guards the mouth of Coire na Poite; this forms the lip of the inner corrie containing two little lochans. Immediately behind, the headwall rises onto the summit ridge for a height of over 350m, its steep walls broken by occasional vertical rifts and narrow terraces. The corrie is enclosed by narrow ridges with precipitous sides, their outer ends forming the castellated buttresses which are such prominent features of the mountain. The right-hand buttress is A'Phoit and the left-hand one is A'Chioch (of Beinn Bhan). The ridges can be gained by scree slopes behind the terminal buttresses, but difficulties are then encountered in gaining the summit. The general angle of the upper wall where A'Chioch joins it is found to be extremely steep. In summer, the upper connecting ridge is an exposed scramble which in winter becomes a Grade II climb; the upper connecting ridge of A'Phoit is a Severe rock climb by any route.

Beinn Damh (*mountain of the stag*) (903m)

Beinn Damh is the most westerly of the mountains which form the skyline along the south shore of Upper Loch Torridon. It rises from the roadside at the head of the loch between Annat and Balgy on the way to Shieldaig. It is separated from Ben Shieldaig (616m) on the west side by Loch Damh, and from Beinn na h-Eaglaise (*mountain of the church*) (736m), on the east side, by Coire Roill. The mountain is encircled by paths and roads, giving easy access from any direction. The track along the east shore of Loch Damh is a right of way for pedestrians; the gate at Balgy Bridge is usually locked against vehicle traffic and the bothy at the south end of the loch (Ceann-loch-damh) is private. The south end of the loch can also be reached by a short stretch of right of way track from the Shieldaig/Kishorn road (grid reference 850 474) which continues around the south end of the Beinn Damh ridge via the Drochaid Coire Roill for over twelve kilometres to join the A896 opposite Torridon Hotel. The normal start to the mountain is by the path which leaves the road through the wicket gate at the bridge over the Allt Coire Roill and rises through some magnificent pine woods along the steep sides of the gorge of the river. Once above the tree-line, the rounded dome of An Ruadh-stac looms up beyond the far end of Coire Roill, framed by the precipitous north-eastern ridge of Beinn Damh and the south slopes of Beinn na h-Eaglaise.

Take the right-hand branch of the main path at the fork beyond the tree-line; this is well marked and climbs steeply onto the saddle between Sgurr na Bana Mhoraire (*peak of the lady*) (687m) and the main summit. To the left of the saddle is a wide scalloped corrie lying between the main ridge and Creag na h'Iolaire, the small north spur of Beinn Damh. The corrie is seen to be broken, but has no significant exposure of continuous rock; Creag na h'Iolaire is impressive and overgrown, but has been climbed. The main ridge now steepens considerably onto the summit of Beinn Damh from where a craggy shoulder drops north-eastwards towards the path across the Drochaid Coire Roill.

Maol Chean-dearg (*bald red head*) (935m)
An Ruadh-stac (*steep red hill*) (892m)
Meall nan Ceapairean (*hill of the bannock*) (655m)

The approach to this compact group of mountains can be made equally well from Annat at the west end of Glen Torridon, or from the bridge at Coulags on the A896 road, eight kilometres to the north-east from Lochcarron. Starting from Coulags, the path follows the east side of the Fionn-abhainn. This is the right of way to Torridon; it eventually links up with the path from Annat on the north side of the Bealach na Lice, between Maol Chean-dearg and Meall Dearg (646m), the midpoint of the twelve kilometre route. The river rises in a series of rocky basins along the west side of the path and is crossed by a bridge after two and a half kilometres, or alternatively by the line of uniformly square stepping-stones conveniently located just below. The path continues up the inner Coire Fionnaraich along the west bank of the river. The cottage which is passed after 800 metres is now a well-maintained open bothy, regularly in use except during the stalking season. Beyond this the path passes a curious forefinger of stone – Clach nan Con-fionn – the stone where the legendary giant Fionn tethered his staghounds while hunting in the glen. After another 800 metres, take the branch of the path which bears west to climb steeply onto the flat saddle between Maol Chean-dearg and Meall nan Ceapairean at a height of almost 600 metres. This is really the junction of the three summit ridges, and makes for easy ascents to all sides. The path from the saddle drops down the west flank of Maol Chean-dearg past Loch Coire an Ruadh-staic then completes the loop north to rejoin the main path to Annat at the end of Loch an Eoin beyond the Bealach na Lice. The approach from this side to the north face of An Ruadh-stac probably requires less effort and certainly provides equally fine views *en route*.

From the saddle, a line south-east soon leads onto the summit of Meall nan Ceapairean in half a kilometre with only 60 metres or so of ascent. The east face of the hill is steep and rocky above the path line and has been investigated, but its main interest is as a fine viewpoint for the mountains lying to the east.

Back on the saddle, the broad ridge northwestwards leads up over a series of steps to the Munro top of Maol Chean-dearg in little over one kilometre. The mixture of sandstone boulders and quartzite blocks makes for rough walking on the final climb to the summit cairn. The view north from the summit to Torridon is panoramic, and the steep quartzite cliffs rising up above Loch an Eoin can give fine climbing on this side.

From the saddle bear south for a short distance then south-west to An Ruadh-stac, which unlike its neighbours is mainly composed of quartzite. From the connecting col the ascent looks forbiddingly steep, but at close quarters it presents a pleasant scramble over large quartzite blocks to the summit cairn – a Corbett top. In winter the highly polished nature of the rock requires care. The north face of the mountain is a more serious proposition, falling in two steep 100 metre tiers towards Loch Coire an Ruadh-staic, and giving excellent climbing rock with seemingly abundant holds. The return to Coulags is best made by retracing the outward path.

Fuar Tholl (*cold hollow*) (907m)
Sgorr Ruadh (*red peak*) (962m)

These two splendid mountains form a five kilometre long ridge which runs north-westwards from Glen Carron between Coire Fionnaraich and Coire Lair. It is possible to gain the ridge by way of the the west side, but the climb up the long steep grassy slopes from the Coulags path is rather tedious and of little interest. The better approach is from Achnashellach Station five kilometres to the north-east of Coulags. From the A890 road, a private road leads up to the railway station.

Cross the railway just west of the platform to the cottage on the north side of the track. Continue west for 60 metres to find the Corrie Lair path which follows the east side of the river. The start of this is rather wet and a drier alternative is by the forestry track which slants in from the east side of the cottage. This is followed for a short distance to a cairned junction ; the unsurfaced vehicle track which continues east-north-east is the right of way route to the Coulin Pass and Glen Torridon. The west branch cuts back through brush and rhododendrons to join the path for the mountains which takes a line along the north-east bank of the River Lair through wild magnificent scenery and fine woodlands. The river follows a turbulent course by way of a deep narrow gorge, broken frequently by waterfalls and bordered by twisted pine trees. It is a formidable barrier to cross and one is well-advised to keep to well-established paths. Two and a half kilometres of steady climbing lead to a junction at the wide mouth of the upper corrie. The east fork goes up over the saddle between Carn Eite and the south-east end of the main ridge of Beinn Liath Mhor; it then continues to the east along the north side of the Easan Dorcha to join the track to Coulin. The main track continues to follow the course of the river to the head of Coire Lair for another four kilometres between the sharply contrasting ridges of Beinn Liath Mhor on the north and Sgorr Ruadh and Fuar Tholl on the south. The path climbs steeply along the head of Coire Lair to cross the Bealach Coire Lair on the narrow col betwen Beinn Liath Mhor and Sgorr Ruadh; it then continues round the lower north-west corner of Sgorr Ruadh onto the Bealach Ban, swinging to the south-west for over a kilometre to link with the Coulags path on the Bealach na Lice. From the junction at the mouth of Coire Lair, the west fork of the path fords the river and climbs steeply up heathery slopes skirting the north end of Fuar Tholl onto the broad saddle with its maze of lochans which lies between Fuar Tholl and Sgorr Ruadh – the Bealach Mor (670m) – a distance of almost three kilometres. From there, either summit can be climbed without difficulty.

Fuar Tholl can be seen to radiate three spurs, to the north-west, to the south and to the east. From the Bealach Mor, the north-west ridge presents an obvious ascent route, either negotiating a way through crags or more normally by following the line of the ridge to the summit keeping to the west side. The south-east face of the mountain immediately below the summit cairn opens into the high, steep-walled corrie which catches the eye from the road at Achnashellach. The north-east facing wall of this is the Upper Cliff of Fuar Tholl, one of the main climbing areas on the mountain. Above the line of the crags there, Fuar Tholl falls southwards towards the road in a long steep slope of exposed sandstone, with steeper exposures of continuous slab towards the east side. These can cause problems in descending from this direction, they require careful route finding, keeping to the west in the event of difficulty. It is probably best to retrace the route down the north-west ridge to the Bealach Mor and the path back to Coire Lair. On the north-east side of the ridge, a superb buttress of terraced sandstone hangs perpendicularly above a tiny lochan just south of the path leading onto the bealach. This is the Mainreachan Buttress; the climbing there is generally considered to be amongst the best on sandstone anywhere.

The approach to Sgorr Ruadh up Coire Lair

The ascent of Sgorr Ruadh from the Bealach Mor is equally straightforward, a steep climb leads directly onto the summit in one kilometre. The approach from the north side requires more careful route finding. From the path on the Bealach Coire Lair, climb south-west towards the small lochan on the north-west ridge of Sgorr Ruadh, continuing steeply south-east up a rough scree slope to the summit cairn, one kilometre. The descent to the Bealach Mor has been described. Loch a' Bhealaich Mhoir, the largest of the numerous lochans on the saddle, makes a useful landmark on the way down. Sgorr Ruadh has an impressive north-east face which throws out several distinctive sandstone buttresses separated by narrow couloirs along this inner corner of Coire Lair. The most northerly of these is Raeburn's Buttress, the high buttress which forms the skyline on the approach up the glen. It occupies the angle between the north and north-east faces of Sgorr Ruadh and is seen in profile with a steep north-east wall bounded on the right by a deep,

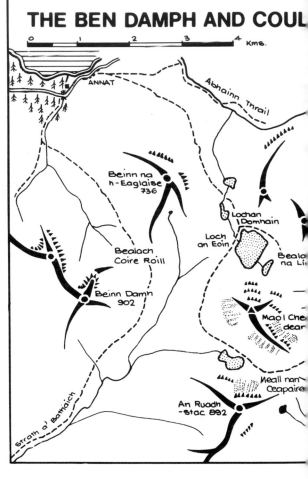

THE BEN DAMPH AND COUL

scree-filled gully. It is separated from the two southerly buttresses by a wide couloir whose steep upper section is usually corniced in winter. The longer of these is Academy Ridge, separated by a steep gully from Robertson's Buttress, which gave the earliest climbing route on the mountain. The winter potential there is obviously considerable.

Beinn Liath Mhor (*big grey mountain*) (926m)

The ascent onto the ridge of Beinn Liath Mhor from the high point of the track from Coire Lair to Coulin is straightforward but strenuous. The slope leading to the high point on this south-eastern end of the ridge (876m) is uniformly steep. The lower slopes have a sparse covering of scrubby heather mixed with small scree; the upper slopes are fairly bald and stony. Generally speaking, the mountain is of

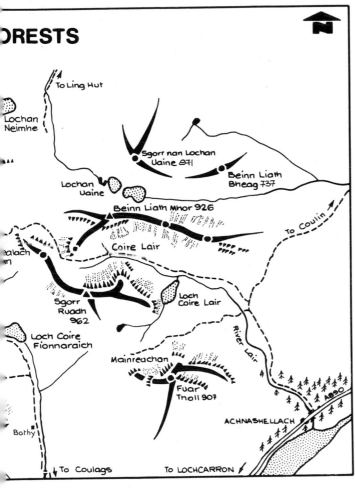

more interest geologically than from any climbing point of view; sandstone and quartzite have been folded together in a complex pattern which can be traced on the bare sides along the ridge. The broad summit ridge with its carpet of quartzite scree stretches to the north-west for two kilometres and is easily followed onto the cairned Munro top. As one would expect, the view all round is breath-taking, with an especially fine prospect of the main Torridon ridges. The descent from the summit takes a line to the south-west onto the Bealach Coire Lair to join the outward path from Achnashellach. This section requires care. The quartzite gives way to sandstone which forms awkward walls and steps, and a small knoll has to be crossed or turned before dropping onto the path. In the event of bad visibility, the lochans at either side of it are useful landmarks. Beinn Liath Mhor is often included in a circuit with Sgorr Ruadh as previously described, making a fine round of over sixteen kilometres.

Sgorr nan Lochan Uaine *(peak of the green loch)* (871m)
Sgurr Dubh *(black peak)* (782m)

These two mountains form an interesting ridge of terraced sandstone which stretches in to the south-west from the road through Glen Torridon to make a right-angled link with Beinn Liath Mhor near the Bealach Coire Lair. Despite their remarkably rugged appearance, their proximity to the loftier Torridon mountains usually causes them to be bypassed or left for some other day. They could be included in a long traverse with Beinn Liath Mhor, but a less exacting ascent is made from the path past the Ling Hut beside Lochan an Iasgair on the south side of Glen Torridon.

This leaves the glen road opposite the well-marked Coire Dubh path (grid reference 960 569) and skirts the lower slopes of the ridge towards the Bealach Coire Lair, continuing much further than is shown on the Ordnance Survey map. A way up from the path to gain the saddle between the two summits is made from any convenient point along the way with a chance of pleasant scrambling among the sandstone outcrops depending on the line chosen. From the saddle the ascent of both mountains is straightforward; the view from either of the summits is equally rewarding, onto the lochans below Sgurr nan Lochan Uaine and along the hidden side of the ridge of Beinn Liath Mhor, then across the remoter corries of the deer forest towards Loch Coulin and Loch Clair among their girdle of conifers.

PATHS AND WALKS

Most of the established rights of way have already been described in conjunction with the mountains. Once aware of these, the combination of routes is largely a matter for individual choice.

Glen Carron to Glen Torridon by the Coulin Pass. The Coulin track is of no great advantage for approaching the mountains which lie to the west of it, but makes in itself a splendid expedition across the area. The start of the route at Achnashellach Station has already been described. This initial section of the route is controlled by the Forestry Commission, who have currently closed the bridge near the west end as being unfit for vehicle traffic, otherwise all gates along the route will normally be found unlocked. At the south end of Loch Coulin the right of way goes across the River Coulin to Torran-cuillinn and then along the north side of Loch Coulin to join the private road at the south end of Loch Clair which leads out to Glen Torridon. The other right of way due north gives six kilometres of rough going to Kinlochewe and makes a less attractive alternative ending for the walk. The exit to Glen Torridon along the two lochs is undoubtedly the highlight of the journey and should not be omitted. The track is in excellent condition throughout and the use of mountain bikes could well be considered. (14 kilometres).

CLIMBING

The mountains on the Applecross Peninsula offer a wide choice of winter and summer routes with tremendous possibilities for further development, especially in winter. Accessibility is good. The terraced buttresses on Meall Gorm are well - explored and give a number of routes of about 150m, grades varying from Very Difficult to Very Severe. The winter routes are all about Grade IV, but some of the gullies to the east give easier Grade II routes of about 200m.

Climbing on Sgurr a'Chaorachain has been concentrated on the south cliffs above the road onto the Bealach na Ba and around A'Chioch in Coire nan Arr. The south face of the mountain has a considerable exposure of steep sandstone, but most of it lacks continuity. Climbing is found mainly on the six steep ribs which rise from the roadside at a point nearly opposite the prominent waterfall on the Allt a'Chumhaing. The leftmost rib starting a mere 30m above the road gives the original route there, *Sword of Gideon* (105m, Very Severe) still considered to be the finest on these crags. The proximity of these cliffs to the road has resulted in so much activity that it is now considered that they have reached saturation point.

The terminal tower of the north spur of Sgurr a'Chaorachain, A'Chioch, is connected with the main mass by a narrow col from which prominent gullies seam both flanks to the corrie floor. From the scree fan of the south gully, a broad heathery ledge, Middle Ledge, cuts horizontally to the right across the face. This Middle Ledge and The Nose are the main landmarks on the south-east face. The Upper Ledge crosses the middle part of the face some 25m higher. The buttress was first climbed at the beginning of the century, but

On the Cioch Nose, Sgurr a' Chaorachain

it was only in the sixties that one of the classic routes in Applecross was pioneered there, *Cioch Nose*. In its original form this gave 180m of sustained Very Difficult climbing, starting from the Middle Ledge and keeping towards the edge of the Nose throughout, with superb situations. It has been described as the finest of its category on Torridonian sandstone. Variations have subsequently been recorded. The south-east face of A'Chioch has also been well explored and has several fine routes varying from Very Difficult to Severe. Routes on the north face are similar in length and standard. Beyond the north face, a recessed corrie has five buttresses, four of which have given routes up to 300m, the standard varies up to Severe. The gullies have given hard winter climbs.

The potential of the eastern corries of Beinn Bhan has long been realised. Earlier activity tended to centre around Coire na Poite and the terminal buttresses on its two spurs. All of these produced a variety of routes, both summer and winter. Summer climbs are generally of Very Dificult/Severe standard, the winter routes vary from Grade III to V. Summer climbs have been mainly on A' Chioch and A' Poite; the back wall of the corrie contains several hard gully climbs, *March Hare's Gully* and *Mad Hatter's Gully*, and other hard routes on the walls. Coire nan Fhamhair is perhaps the most continuously steep cliff of its height on the mainland, with great future potential; most of the routes there are Grade III plus. The centre wall of Coire Each, the most southerly of the corries, has gully routes of about 200m at Grade III/IV. An indication of the possibilites of Beinn Bhan was given some years ago – "the mountain harbours in its great eastern corries an uninterrupted two mile succession of 180m-300m crags whose resources have scarcely been tapped. The winter prospects are exciting, with scope for at least thirty grade IV/V routes of around 300m." Current activity would indicate that many of these new routes will soon emerge.

Beinn Damh has given little in the way of climbing so far, except on Creag na h-Iolaire, although there is a considerable amount of rock in the south-east corrie. Short buttresses on the south-east side of Meall nan Ceapairean have given routes of Difficult standard and its neighbour, Maol Chean-dearg, gives climbing on the quartzite cliff above the lochside on its steep north side. The routes there are of 100m, Severe standard. An Ruadh-stac has a two tier quartzite wall on its north face which gives two routes of delightful climbing, 180m, Severe. Beinn Liath Mhor has given Moderate routes of sorts on some of its features, but harder routes seem unlikely.

Sgorr Ruadh has a variety of climbing routes on its more prominent features. *Raeburn's Buttress* is a long 360m Difficult climb, the winter route Direct is Grade IV. The *Upper Buttress* to its west is 215m, Very Difficult and the winter route is 270m, Grade III. *Academy Ridge* to the south of this is a scramble in its lower section, the narrow upper section is more difficult. *Robertson's Buttress*, next to Academy Ridge, saw the earliest climb on this face; the intervening gully – *Robertson's Gully*, gives a Grade IV winter climb. Around the three buttresess, numerous gullies give Grade I/II climbs. Other lines are possible along this face.

There are three main climbing areas on Fuar Tholl. *The Nose* is the low-lying north-east facing cliff overlooking the path up the lower part of Corrie Lair. Climbs there are sustained and Very Severe, in places vegetated. The Upper Cliff lies immediately below the top of the mountain, and is the north-east facing wall of the high corrie which is prominent from the road. The cliffs have several routes of about 200m up to Hard Very Severe standard and winter routes of Grade V. The small buttress on the right-hand end of the face can be climbed anywhere giving short routes of about 65m varying in standard from Difficult to Severe, and winter lines of about Grade III. *The Mainreachan Buttress* juts out conspicuously northwards from the west ridge half a kilometre west of the summit of Fuar Tholl. The buttress is of terraced sandstone and gives exceptionally high quality climbing. The majority of the routes there are between 140 and 220m with a standard uniformly Severe and above.

CHAPTER 12

Torridon

MAPS: Ordnance Survey 1:50,000 Sheets 19, 24 and 25
              Bartholomew 1:100,000 Sheet 54
              Outdoor Leisure Map 1:25,000 Cuillins/Torridon

PRINCIPAL HILLS

Beinn Eighe	1010m	952 612
Liathach	1054m	929 579
Beinn Alligin	986m	866 613
Beinn Dearg	914m	896 608
Baosbheinn	875m	871 654
Beinn an Eoin	855m	905 647
Beinn a'Chearcaill	726m	931 638
Meall a'Ghiubhais	886m	976 634
Ruadh-stac Beag	896m	973 614

This is an area which has been described as exhibiting more of mountain beauty than any other district of Scotland, including Skye. It lies between Glen Torridon and Loch Maree, and stretches westwards from Kinlochewe to the coastline along Loch Gairloch and Loch Torridon. The four highest mountains are compactly grouped in the southern half, where the majestic sculptured sandstone first encountered in the eastern corries of Applecross is on a much grander scale, and the broken rim of quartzite which has been left along the higher crests forms a distinctive skyline above the edge of the glen.

The importance of Torridon as part of the national heritage is well recognized. In 1951 the Beinn Eighe Reserve, comprising of 10,500 acres, became the first National Nature Reserve in Britain. It contains one of the few remnants of the old Caledonian Forest which once covered large areas of the Highlands, and the study and preservation of this Caledonian Pinewood is one of the main fields of research carried out on the Reserve from the Anancaun Field Station, just north of Kinlochewe. The nearby Coille na Glas-leitire Mountain Trail on the south shore of Loch Maree gives visitors an excellent introduction to the natural habitat and other physical features of the surrounding countryside. Deer management is carried out nowadays in liaison with neighbouring estates. In 1967, the 14,000 acre Torridon Estate was given to the National Trust for Scotland, and a few months later the 2000 acres of Alligin Shuas adjoining its western boundary were added. The Trust property there now includes Liathach and Beinn Alligin, the southern slopes of

Beinn Dearg to its skyline, and the southern slopes of Beinn Eighe from the summit ridge of Sail Mhor to Spidean Coire nan Clach. This last corner is now included in the Beinn Eighe Reserve by agreement, which establishes the Coire Dubh track between Liathach and Beinn Eighe as the present boundary line. There are no restrictions on access within the National Trust for Scotland area, and only limited restriction to paths in the south-west corner of Beinn Eighe during deer-culling periods. Between them, the two bodies work to preserve the natural balance along the whole of the north side of Glen Torridon. The Nature Conservancy Council warden works from the Anancaun Field Station at the east end, and the National Trust for Scotland maintain a very comprehensive Information Centre at Torridon village with a permanent warden resident nearby.

The three mountains which lie in the northern half of the area are of a different character, seen at their best from the roads past Loch Maree. From this direction they seem to stand apart like three watch-dogs guarding the approach to their giant neighbours towering behind. Towards the coast the countryside changes; flatter open moorland stretches out to the north and to the west. The coastline along Loch Gairloch harbours numerous small communities which nowadays live more on tourists than on the older traditional methods. The more isolated communities along the shores of Loch Torridon – Alligin and Diabeg – still carry on the former lifestyle, now augmented somewhat by the work in the developing fish-farming industry. This can be seen as an appropriate occupation here – Diabeg is derived from the Norse, Djup-vik was the Vikings' *deep bay;* across Loch Torridon, Shieldaig was Sild-vik, *herring bay.*

The approach to the area from the north and east is dominated by the sheer beauty of Loch Maree which forms a continuous boundary along this edge for almost twenty kilometres. The view westwards from the top of Glen Docherty remains breath-taking, despite the efforts of the authorities with their low-slung cable lines along the roadside. Mountains fall away on either side, fringed by relics of the former woodlands. It is not too long ago that this was all forest, the landscape then must have been truly remarkable. The track which followed along the north shore of the loch serviced the iron smelting works which finished off the timber there in the early 18th century. Only on the islands in the west end do the old trees still survive. On one of these – Holy Isle Maree – a well can be found which has the reputation for curing insanity. Coins were stuck into a nearby tree as an offering to the spirits. Even Queen Victoria played safe on her visit there in 1877 and left her token. Other rites which existed on the islands right up to the 17th century were less wholesome, relics of earlier pagan worship involving animal sacrifice. The local smith who killed the sacrifical bull is said to have received the head as his traditional payment, an old Druid rite.

ACCESS

The approach to Torridon and the west from Inverness and Dingwall is by way of the A832 trunk road, already described. From Kinlochewe, the A896 branches to the south-west along Glen Torridon for almost sixteen kilometres, skirting the base of the two principal mountain ridges *en route* – Beinn Eighe and Liathach. The road forks when it reaches the Information Centre at the head of Upper Loch Torridon; the main road continues south through Annat to Glen Shieldaig, Tornapress and Lochcarron. The narrow single track road which branches along the north shore of the loch through Torridon village follows a picturesque and airy route for twelve kilometres to the crofting and fishing township of Diabeg, where it ends. Five kilometres west of the Torridon junction (grid reference 869 576) it rises to pass the mouth of Coire Mhic Nobuil which is the west end of the main access path to the remaining two mountains in this corner – Beinn Alligin and Beinn Dearg.

From Kinlochewe, the main A832 road continues for another 30 kilometres to Gairloch, keeping to the south shore of Loch Maree for the greater part of the way. This road passes the starting points for several useful paths which lead towards the northern corries of Beinn Eighe, and also to the mountains in the northern half of Torridon – Beinn a'Chearcaill, Beinn an Eoin and Baosbheinn. Four kilometres south of Gairloch, a very narrow single track road swings sharply to the west at a stone bridge over the River Kerry (B8056) and winds and twists for over twelve kilometres along the south side of Loch Gairloch past Badachro, to the headland at Red Point where it ends. Two kilometres from the turn-off, opposite Shieldaig Lodge Hotel, there is the start of a well-established footpath into the north-west side of the mountains.

PUBLIC TRANSPORT

Rail: There is a daily passenger service from Inverness and Dingwall to Achnasheen and Strathcarron. Sunday services should be checked.

Bus: Inverness – Achnasheen – Kinlochewe – Loch Maree – the west. (MacKenzie and MacLennan, Gairloch). Tuesdays, Thursdays and Saturdays. All Year.
Inverness – Achnasheen – Kinlochewe. (Scottish Omnibuses Limited). Mondays to Fridays. All Year.
Strathcarron Station – Lochcarron – Torridon. (D MacLennan, Shieldaig). Mondays to Saturdays. All Year.

Postbus: Kinlochewe – Coire Dubh – Torridon – Diabeg – Alligin. Mondays to Saturdays. All Year.
Achnasheen – Kinlochewe – Loch Maree – Gairloch. Mondays to Saturdays. All Year.

ACCOMMODATION

There are hotels at Kinlochewe, Torridon, Loch Maree, Shieldaig Lodge, Badachro and Gairloch. Bed and breakfast accommodation is easily found around the perimeter. The Scottish Youth Hostels Association has hostels at Torridon, just north-west of the road junction at the head of the loch; at Craig, four kilometres north of Diabeg (grid reference 774 639) reached by right of way path from

Diabeg, or from Red Point, eight kilometres north; at Carn Dearg, four miles beyond Gairloch along the north shore of Loch Gairloch. All of these are open from April to October. There are camp sites at Gairloch, Taagan, Kinlochewe and Torridon. Camping is permitted in the plantation at the west end of Glen Torridon, but cars are not allowed among the trees there. There is a private bunkhouse three kilometres further along Glen Torridon at Glen Cottage, on the north side of the road at the foot of Liathach; this is open all year. The Scottish Mountaineering Club's Ling Hut on the south side of Lochan an Iasgair (grid reference 958 563) is available to members of British mountaineering clubs on request through club secretaries. The key is held by the Hon. Custodian, D. Broadhead, 11 Cradlehall Park, Milton, Inverness IV1 2BZ. The use of Poca Buidhe bothy at the south end of Loch na h-Oidhche (grid reference 899 644) is restricted. It is now a private bothy, considerably upgraded, and is available on a booking basis from the proprietors. Information regarding use of the facility is obtainable from Mr H. Davies, Creag Beag, Charlestown, Gairloch. One end of the bothy is still open for shelter in case of emergency.

THE HILLS

Beinn Alligin (*mountain of beauty* or *of the jewel*) (986m)

Beinn Alligin is the most westerly of the Torridon mountains; its proportions fall slightly short of those of Beinn Eighe and Liathach, but its splendid ridge contains some fine individual features, and the traverse can be recommended as a good introduction for the longer and more varied expeditions offered by the other two. It curves inland from the Torridon/Diabeg road to form the west side of Coire Mhic Nobuil, a great crescent-shaped ridge of sandstone, stretching for almost five kilometres over four distinct tops, and split dramatically from its highest summit by a deep precipitous cleft – Eag Dhubh – the mountain's most distinctive landmark. This east side of Beinn Alligin falls steeply into three corries; Coir' nan Laogh which lies below the two tops at the south end of the ridge; Toll a'Mhadaidh Mor, the wide central corrie into which plunges Eag Dhubh; and Toll a'Mhadaidh Beag between the main summit and the Horns of Alligin, in the north-eastern bend in the ridge, which falls steeply on its north side into the Bealach a'Chomhla between Beinn Alligin and Beinn Dearg. In contrast to the northern and eastern aspects, Beinn Alligin drops down towards Diabeg in the west in a series of long grassy slopes which continue round on to the southern end of the ridge overlooking Inveralligin.

The ascent of Beinn Alligin from the south starts at the car park on the west side of the bridge which carries the Diabeg road across the Abhainn Coire Mhic Nobuil. A climber's path leaves the north side of the road and rises steadily for one and a half kilometres to the north-west to join the Alltan Glas at the mouth of Coir' nan Laogh (both features named on the 1:25,000 Outdoor Leisure map). Continue up the head wall of the corrie onto the main ridge. From the intervening dip, the two south tops of Beinn Alligin can now be climbed; Meall an Laoigh (*hill of the calf*)

Beinn Alligin across Loch Torridon

(890m) is unnamed on the map, Tom na Gruagaich (*hill of the maiden*) (922m) lies 660 metres to the north-north-east, its summit steeply overlooking Toll a'Mhadaidh Mor giving a magnificent view of Sgurr Mhor and the deep vertical cleavage on its face. From Tom na Gruagaich the ridge narrows towards the north and the path drops steeply to a col (766m) before rising to the north-north-east over the unnamed minor top (858m). Below this point the south-east side of the ridge drops steeply into Toll a'Mhadaidh Mor; the north-west side is bare and more open. A short dip to the north-east leads to a col (833m) from where the path continues on the same line towards the main summit of Beinn Alligin, Sgurr Mhor (*big peak*) (986m). Just west of the cairn the south side of the ridge is split dramatically by the great black-sided gash which is Eag Dhubh. In poor visibility this feature should be kept well in mind.The return to the car park on the Diabeg road is most easily made by retracing the route of ascent.

The complete traverse of the Beinn Alligin ridge from the east end is a much more interesting alternative. The path into Coire Mhic Nobuil leaves the Diabeg road from the east side of the bridge across the Abhainn Coire Mhic Nobuil and enters a small pine forest. The National Trust for Scotland have a signpost at the starting point. The path quickly clears the tree-line and continues along the east side of the river for one kilometre to the first of three bridges. Continue along the main path past the first bridge for another kilometre to reach a second bridge above the junction of the Allt a'Bhealaich. Across this bridge the path forks. The right-hand branch continues in an easterly direction between Beinn Dearg and the northern corries of Liathach, eventualy linking with the path through Coire Dubh from the Glen Torridon road. The left-hand branch follows the east side of the Allt a'Bhealaich towards the Bealach a'Chomhla, crossing the stream by another higher bridge and continuing along the west side into the pass at the north-east end of the mountain. The path continues much further than is shown on the Ordnance Survey map and can be followed right round onto the north side of Beinn Alligin if need be. Leave the path half a kilometre after crossing the Allt a'Bhealaich and climb north-north-west directly up the crest of the ridge, alternative scrambling lines can be found if desired. Once on the ridge, the route is well marked. The way to Sgurr Mhor, the highest top, crosses the Horns of Alligin (Na Rathanan) (866m). These three rocky towers are the highlight of the traverse, the path follows their crest giving an exposed but easy scrambling route, the gullies between can be bypassed if need be at a lower level across steep grassy slopes on the south side. From the col at their west end (757m), a steep ridge rises west-north-west, then swings west onto the summit cairn of Sgurr Mhor. The route of ascent from Tom na Gruagaich (qv) can then be followed to complete the traverse.

The path drops west for a short distance from the summit of Sgurr Mhor then turns south-west past the head of the Eag Dhubh, passing close to the rim of Toll a'Mhadaidh Mor. If in doubt there, it is advisable to move over to easier slopes on the west. The west wall of the Eag Dhubh cleft has areas of clean rock, the east wall is entirely vertical. The corrie at the foot contains a massive boulder field of giant proportions – the reputed lair of one of the last wolves in Scotland. It is strongly advised that parties should not attempt descending from the summit ridges of the mountain into Toll a'Mhadaidh Mor or Toll

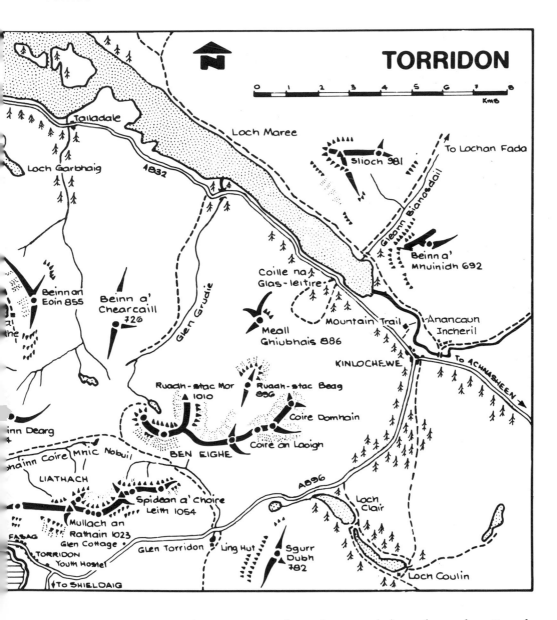

a'Mhadaidh Beag. A safe escape route from the summit is to descend westwards
for one kilometre followed by a gradually descending traverse south-west, then
south round the western flank of the mountain to reach the deer fence. The road is
in sight from there. It is should also be kept in mind that the mountain is prone to
avalanche in winter.

Baosbheinn, Beinn an Eoin and Beinn a'Chearcaill from Beinn Eighe

Beinn Dearg (*red mountain*) (914m)

Beinn Dearg lies across the Bealach a'Chomhla to the east of Beinn Alligin, and like that mountain it tends to be overshadowed somewhat by its proximity to the neighbouring ridges of Liathach and Beinn Eighe to the east. In addition, although the most recent Ordnance Survey map gives its highest point as 914 metres, it remains excluded from the ranks of the Munros. Seen from above, the ridge forms a giant right angle, with the summit as the centre. Two arms swing out to the north and to the east for almost two kilometres in either direction, enclosing an extensive north-east facing corrie – An Coire Mor. The north arm is steep, broken and rocky around either end and along its western flank, which is further split by numerous gullies. The highest point, the top of Stuc Loch na Cabhaig (*peak of the loch of haste*) (889m) lies at the northern end. The east arm falls equally steeply below the summit, the angle becoming easier further along. This spur stretches out onto the secondary top, Carn na Feola (*hill of flesh*)(761m), which looks across rough water-pocked moorland to the mountains in the north of the Flowerdale Forest. The main ridge is found to be remarkably problem-free and gives pleasant walking. Short steeper sections of broken sandstone give some entertaining scrambling in places along the crest; on the east arm of the ridge, two rocky spines appear as formidable obstacles, but the problems are easily bypassed with care. The slopes rising onto the ridge from the floor of An Coire Mor are generally less steep and more open. These give a straightforward climb onto the crest of the ridge at a midway point on the saddle between Stuc Loch na Cabhaig and the main top.

The best approach is along the Coire Mhic Nobuil path already described, following the left-hand branch northwards into the Bealach a'Chomla. The steep western flanks of Beinn Dearg are in full view throughout the walk-in and possible lines of ascent can be assessed. Leave the path four kilometres from the start, taking a line north-east to cross the Allt a'Bhealach to the foot of the north-west shoulder of Stuc Loch na Cabhaig. A steep way up can be found upwards by a succession of short walls and ledges giving some straightforward scrambling in places and the upper ridge is easily followed onto the north top, Stuc Loch na Cabhaig. The way along the main ridge drops to the south for one kilometre onto the saddle at its midpoint then rises to the south-east onto the main top. From the considerable summit cairn, the ridge swings to the east over the rocky towers previously mentioned. These in fact are found to be easier if taken direct, but a bypass can be made at a lower level. As one moves towards the east the ridge becomes broader and easier, rising up onto Carn na Feola on a series of broad heathery steps. The view across to the northern corries of Liathach is superb. The descent to the track leading back can be frustrating if the ridge is left too far to the west, steep heather and sandstone walls become a problem. A line south-south-west from Carn na Feola leads to the top of an open heathery couloir which drops directly south towards a point half a kilometre west of Loch Grobaig to join the path from Coire Dubh. This is followed westwards to the bridge junction in Coire Mhic Nobuil described in the outward route to complete a fine circuit of fourteen kilometres.

Baosbheinn (*mountain of the wizard*) (875m)
Beinn an Eoin (*mountain of the bird*) (855m)

The two mountains which lie on the edge of the Shieldaig and Flowerdale deer forests in the northern half of Torridon, Baosbheinn and Beinn an Eoin, are most easily approached from the Kinlochewe to Gairloch road (A832). Start at Loch Bad an Sgalaig, five kilometres west from Slattadale on Loch Maree side (grid reference 857 720); a conspicuous estate path crosses the neck of water which joins with Am Feur-loch and climbs steadily south-eastwards for almost seven kilometres to Loch na h-Oidhche, which lies between the two mountains. The path continues along the east side of the loch for another two kilometres past Poca Buidhe to the Gorm Lochs. The use of the bothy there at the foot of Beinn an Eoin has already been noted.

Either of the mountains can be climbed without difficulty from the north-west end of Loch na h-Oidhche. Beinn an Eoin rises steeply above the boat house on the north-east bank of the loch, but easier slopes are found round to the north end. The summit ridge is followed easily onto the Corbett top at its south end and a rocky descent can be made from there with care to the Poca Buidhe bothy. The easiest line towards Baosbheinn is from the outflow of the Abhainn Loch na h-Oidhche at the north-west corner of the loch. The stream there can usually be crossed without difficulty. Bear south-west, rising steadily for over one kilometre towards the north-east ridge of Sgorr Dubh (875m), which gives a straightforward climb to the summit of the mountain. Both mountains can easily be climbed together in the course of a day. The south-east ridge of Baosbheinn can be reached by circling around the end of the loch from Poca Buidhe. From the top called Ceann Beag (707m) the ridge climbs steeply up an open slope to a south top then drops onto a broad col before rising onto the summit of the mountain, Sgorr Dubh. The north-east side of Baosbheinn opens out toward Loch na h-Oidhche in a series of small heathery corries, the west flank drops more steeply towards Loch a'Bhealaich and Loch a' Ghobhainn, with a prominent cliff face below the summit. The west side of Baosbheinn can be approached by a well-used stalker's path from Shieldaig Lodge Hotel on the B8056 road (grid reference 808 724). This is followed for ten kilometres to the north end of Loch a'Bhealaich, giving good walking; in contrast the trackless section which skirts the south end of Baosbheinn for eight kilometres to join the Poca Buidhe path is rough going.

Beinn a'Chearcaill (*mountain of the girdle*) (726m)

The easiest approach is by the stalker's path which leaves the A832 road at the west side of Bridge of Grudie (grid reference 963 677). This skirts the east flank of the mountain for almost five kilometres giving a choice of line onto the summit. Beinn a'Chearcaill makes a fine viewpoint for its much loftier neighbours on all sides.

Meall a'Ghiubhais (*hill of the fir tree*) (886m)
Ruadh-stac Beag (*little red peak*) (896m)

Meall a'Ghiubhais, which looks down on the Mountain Trail at the south end of Loch Maree, can be considered as part of Beinn Eighe, but it is too far out on ' a north limb' to be often included in a major traverse. The easiest approach is by the path which leaves the A832 road a short distance to the south of the Anancaun Visitor Centre (grid reference 022 628). This rises for almost four kilometres to the west onto the col to the south-east of Meall a'Ghiubhais, from where it is a straightforward climb onto the summit. On the Ordnance Survey 1:50,000 map only the north-east top is seen to be marked (878m), the true summit which lies to the south-west of this is 886m in height, and is shown on the 1:25,000 map.

Ruadh-stac Beag is another outlier of Beinn Eighe which is more often than not omitted from the traverse of the main ridge. It lies out to the north-east of Spidean Coire nan Clach, a distance of only two kilometres or so, but the intervening dip to Lochan Uaine is somewhat of a deterrent to the approach from the ridge of Beinn Eighe, although it is possible with care to find a way down from there to the connecting saddle. The more feasible approach is up the path from Anancaun described above. Leave this path at its highest point then follow the Allt a'Ghiubhais up the corrie to its head and climb the south ridge of Ruadh-stac Beag. The north face of the mountain is steep and craggy and is not advised. Ruadh-stac Beag and Meall a'Ghiubhais can conveniently be climbed together in a single day.

Liathach *(the grey one)* (1054m)

Liathach is the name given to the whole range of eight tops which stretches for almost eight kilometres from east to west like some great citadel along the north side of Glen Torridon. On its eastern end the boundary with Beinn Eighe is formed by Coire Dubh Mor; on the north-west side it is separated from Beinn Dearg and Beinn Alligin by the length of Coire Mhic Nobuil; the western end of its ridge slopes down towards the head of Upper Loch Torridon.

From east to west, the main points along the ridge of Liathach are:

Stuc a'Choire Dhuibh Bhig	(915m)	942 582
Bidein Toll a'Mhuic	(983m)	933 581
Spidean a'Choire Leith	(1054m)	929 579
Am Fasarinen	(930m)	924 575
Mullach an Rathain	(1023m)	912 577
Northern Pinnacles	(953m)	914 579

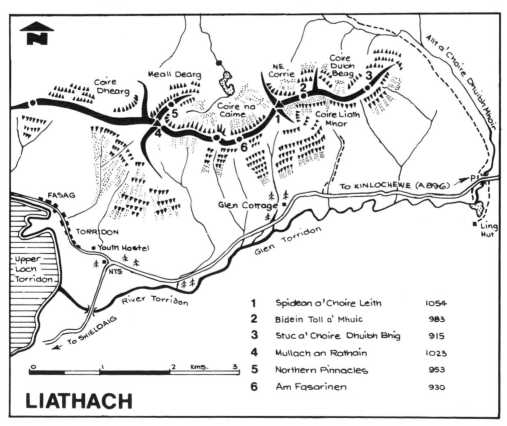

1	Spidean a'Choire Leith	1054
2	Bidein Toll a' Mhuic	983
3	Stuc a' Choire Dhuibh Bhig	915
4	Mullach an Rathain	1023
5	Northern Pinnacles	953
6	Am Fasarinen	930

LIATHACH

The steepness of the southern slopes with their long lines of terraced sandstone is greatly accentuated by their proximity to the road from Kinlochewe. This passes right along the base of the ridge and consequently foreshortens the view of the mountain considerably. Although uniformly steep, at closer quarters it is seen that the summit ridge can be gained by several routes from the floor of the glen with various degrees of difficulty. These are described later.

The hidden side of Liathach has a much more spectacular setting. There the ridge drops into several steep-sided north-facing corries which offer a wealth of climbing. Coireag Dubh Beag lies below Bidein Toll a'Mhuic at the east end and Coireag Dubh Mor opens to the north-east below the main summit, Spidean a'Choire Leith. Coire na Caime (*crooked corrie*) which is one of the finest features of the mountain dominates the central section of the ridge on this side. It is bounded on the east by a north spur of the main summit. The west side is formed by the narrow ridge leading from Mullach an Rathain to Meall Dearg, broken conspicuously by the Northern Pinnacles. The headwall of the corrie is backed by the jagged skyline of Am Fasarinen – The Fasarinen Pinnacles. A small hanging corrie, Coireag Cham, nestles in the upper south-west corner of Coire na Caime immediately below Mullach an Rathain. The buttress at its entrance facing onto the Northern Pinnacles is Bell's Buttress. On the west side of the Northern Pinnacles another small corrie is found high up below the summit, Glas-toll a'Bothain. To the west of Mullach an Rathain the ridge drops gradually onto a broad saddle. A great stone-chute spills down to the village of Torridon on the south side of this and another small corrie, Coireag Dhearg, opens out below the north-west side.

The main mass of the mountain is of highly sculptured sandstone which gives the ridge a russet-coloured tint in certain light. The four highest peaks are capped with white quartzite, which on the main top forms a sharp symmetrical cone of loose angular blocks, awkward to negotiate. The eastern top, Stuc a'Choire Dhuibh Bhig, has a bold terminal buttress but easier slopes on the south side. To the west, the ridge narrows towards the twin tops of Bidein Toll a'Mhuic. The path drops to the head of a prominent gully (833m) and keeps to the crest of the ridge, skirting the rim of Coireag Dubh Beag, which drops sheer to the north as a line of considerable rocky faces. The two tops of Bidein Toll a'Mhuic offer no difficulty apart from awkward walking on the blocks of quartzite which cover the slopes. The final downward slope to the notch in the main ridge between Bidein Toll a'Mhuic and the main summit is looser scree, and the slope up to the summit of Spidean a'Choire Leith has a boulder field of larger blocks which require care. A descent from the west on these can be misleading in bad weather. A mistake in the line down could lead into difficulty there. The prominent flat-topped ridge jutting out below the summit cone, which forms the wall of the upper Coire Leith, is ringed with steep crags around its south end. From the summit of Spidean a'Choire Leith the ridge narrows for almost two kilometres in a more or less westerly direction towards Mullach an Rathain. This section crosses a series of pinnacles (Am Fasarinen) for almost half that distance. These present a fairly sustained scramble

Looking towards the summit of Liathach from Stuc a'Choire Dhuibh Bhig

Mullach an Rathain, the Northern Pinnacles and Meall Dearg from Spidean a'Choire Leith

which can give difficulties in bad weather. There is a fair amount of exposure, especially on the north side, requiring a good head for heights, however holds are plentiful. This section should be avoided by inexperienced parties by traversing along the low level bypass path on the south side of the ridge. This path now suffers badly from erosion, an increasingly common problem throughout Torridon. In winter conditions the pinnacles usually have to be taken direct.Once past the pinnacles the ridge becomes smooth and broad and leads easily to Mullach an Rathain, with a rocky crest near the summit.

Mullach an Rathain sends out a spur to the north-east which leads over another series of pinnacles, extremely shattered and covered with loose blocks, before dropping to a narrow col leading up onto the summit of Meall Dearg. These Northern Pinnacles require a certain amount of rock-climbing technique and should be left alone by parties with no such experience. The spur itself can be misleading in the event of poor visibility. From Mullach an Rathain, the main ridge to the west is uniformly broad, grassy and cairned, giving no further difficulty. There is an easy descent by the north-west slope from Sgorr a'Chadail to the path through Coire Mhic Nobuil leading down to the bridge on the Diabeg road.

The most frequently used route on to the east end of Liathach starts from the roadside 800 metres to the east of Glen Cottage. A well-trodden path starts west of the Allt an Doire Ghairbh, crossing the stream to its east side soon after, then climbing steeply up into Toll a'Meitheach. From the fork in the stream high up in the corrie a steep line to the north-east is taken to the cairn-marked col (833m) on the main ridge slightly west of Stuc a'Choire Dhuibh Bhig. An alternative route from the stream junction is to bear north-west uphill, climbing a short rock band and continuing up steep but easy ground to the prominent col between Bidein Toll a'Mhuic and Spidean a'Choire Leith.

The normal approach onto the west end of the ridge is by following the course of the Allt an Tuill Bhain which falls due south of Mullach an Rathain. Start from the pine wood one kilometre east of the National Trust for Scotland Centre. The route leads up over sloping sandstone pavements into a wide vegetated upper corrie. Open grassy tongues to the left penetrate the steep scree above onto the easier angled ridge leading north-north-east to the summit of Mullach an Rathain.

The north-west slope of Sgorr a'Chadail to the Coire Mhic Nobuil path has already been mentioned. From the north side of the mountain, the scree slope at the head of Coireag Dubh Beag leads onto the ridge between Stuc a'Choire Dhuibh Bhig and Bidein Toll a'Mhuic. This is reached by the path through Coire Dubh Mhor from the parking place at the Allt a'Choire Dhuibh Mhoir, a distance of four kilometres. The ascent of Mullach an Rathain via Meall Dearg and the Northern Pinnacles gives a fine rather indirect approach. The walk from the road into Coire na Caime and the foot of the Meall Dearg ridge takes about two hours.It should be emphasised that this is not a walking route, but a 180m climb of Moderate standard. The route is on the north flank of Meall Dearg; it starts to the right of a small watercourse and follows a steep, narrow shelf diagonally from right to left up the middle of the north face. The Northern Pinnacles are extremely shattered and are covered with large unstable blocks. There are five of them giving a straightforward, pleasant climb. The winter route is Grade II, the first pinnacle being reached by way of a narrow easy gully on the north-west. The last pinnacle is climbed direct, then a little slab is traversed just below the top. A scramble on loose rock follows onto the summit of Mullach an Rathain.

Descent from the ridge requires great care, especially so in bad visibility or in winter conditions. The steep south side has few easy exits. The quickest way from the summit of Spidean a'Choire Leith is to descend the boulder field arête of the main ridge eastwards to the first col (or notch) and retrace the alternative line of ascent described above to the fork in the stream in Toll a'Meitheach, continuing down to Glen Torridon.

Looking south-west from Spidean a'Choire Leith along the main ridge of Liathach, with Beinn Bhan and the Cuillin Hills on the distant horizon

From Mullach an Rathan, the descent to the west via the line of cairns to the head of the large stone chute is inadvisable. The bed of the stone chute is very dangerous but is still attempted by walkers based at Torridon village. The only feasible line is to descend the very steep heather on the west side of the chute itself. The best descent route from this end of the ridge is to go down the ascent route already described up the Allt an Tuill Bhain. Descend one third of a kilometre south-south-west from Mullach an Rathain then descend south-south-east into the Toll Ban to follow the stream back down to the road.

From the east top of Liathach, Stuc a'Coire Dhuibh Bhig, the best route of descent is to retrace the route from the col (833m) south-west into Toll a'Meitheach. An alternative route is to descend the main ridge north-eastwards for half a kilometre from Stuc a'Coire Dhuibh Bhig then make a descending traverse eastwards below the cliffs down to the Coire Dubh Mor track. On Liathach, it should be possible in all cases to use the line of ascent for the return route, keeping in mind the terracing on the steep sides which tends to hide vertical steps from above. The winter traverse of the ridge is a serious mountaineering expedition, and should only be attempted by parties suitably equipped and competent in the necessary techniques.

Beinn Eighe *(file hill)* (1010m)

This is the collective name for an equally magnificent range of tops, nine in all, which stretches away from the east side of Liathach towards Kinlochewe and the south end of Loch Maree, a distance of almost eight kilometres. The boundary along the north-west edge is the line of Glen Grudie and the course of the Allt Coire Mhic Fhearchair. From the road through Glen Torridon, the south side of the ridge is seen fully displayed, uniformly steep and imposing. Graceful curving ridges link its peaks, the overall image enhanced by the covering of white quartzite which almost entirely blankets the summit. This is a major difference between Beinn Eighe and its neighbour. The steady gentle eastward dip of the strata which allows the Torridonian sandstone to form nearly all of Liathach, only brings it to ridge level on Beinn Eighe at the col between Sail Mhor and Coinneach Mhor at its western end, and takes it almost completely out of sight before the eastern end of the ridge is reached, even more so on the south side than on the north. As a result, most of the slopes on Beinn Eighe are of quartzite scree, although on the wider and flatter parts towards the west, a mossy covering makes for easier walking.

The Beinn Eighe range covers nine tops in all, including its two outlying satellites which are seldom climbed in a traverse of the main ridge. From west to east these are:

Sail Mhor	(980m)	938 605
Coinneach Mhor	(976m)	944 600
Ruadh-stac Mor	(1010m)	951 612
Spidean Coire nan Clach	(972m)	965 597
Sgurr Ban	(970m)	974 600
Sgurr nan Fhir Duibhe	(963m)	982 600
Creag Dubh	(907m)	986 608
Ruadh-stac Beag	(896m)	973 614
Meall a'Ghiubhais	(886m)	976 634

The two sides of the ridge display a marked difference in character. The corries on the south send long slopes sweeping down towards the road, steep but open. At the south-east end, the wide crescent of Coire Domhain is prominent between the summits of Creag Dubh and Sgurr nan Fhir Duibhe; to the west, the peak of Spidean Coire nan Clach is seen to form a natural midpoint in the line of the main ridge, sending out a long spur towards the glen road beside Loch Bharranch. From the south-west side of this spur Coire nan Clach opens out above the Coire Dubh Mor track towards Liathach; on the east side Coire an Laoigh tucks close in towards the main ridge below the summit of Spidean Coire nan Clach.

The north side of the mountain is of a more complex pattern, and includes most of the finest features. The corries which fan out towards the north are on a much grander scale, in keeping with the more dramatic scenery on this side. To the north-east, a long significant corrie, almost two kilometres in length, lies between the spurs which terminate on the summits of Creag Dubh and Ruadh-stac Beag,

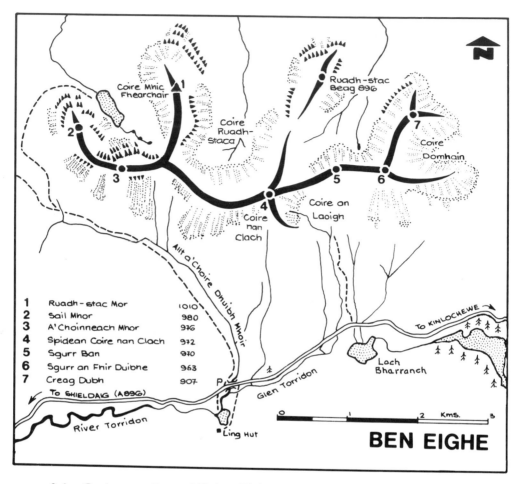

1	Ruadh-stac Mor	1010
2	Sail Mhor	980
3	A'Choinneach Mhor	976
4	Spidean Coire nan Clach	972
5	Sgurr Ban	970
6	Sgurr an Fhir Duibhe	963
7	Creag Dubh	907

BEN EIGHE

one of the Corbett outliers of Beinn Eighe. Though it has no definitive name, its inner corner is Toll Ban, a small scooped-out recess below the pinnacles of Bodaich Dubh and Sgurr Ban. Its outer reaches become the Toll a'Ghiubhais, separating Ruadh-stac Beag from Meall a'Ghiubhais, the second of the two Corbett tops included in the range. The vast expanse of Coire Ruadh-staca fills the central slot; its west wall formed by the north spur of Beinn Eighe which rises to the highest summit of the mountain, Ruadh-stac Mor. This corrie spreads out below Spidean Coire nan Clach, the pivot point on the ridge, for two kilometres northwards and measures over a kilometre across its mouth. To the north lies Maol Cheannan, a barren boulder field.

The most westerly corrie on this side, lying between Ruadh-stac Mor and Sail Mhor, is Coire Mhic Fhearchair, a magnificent amphitheatre where sandstone and quartzite combine to produce one of the finest expressions of mountain grandeur in the Highlands. Beyond the picture-book loch which fills the mouth of the corrie, the spectacular Triple Buttress rises from the back wall of the inner recess, an unsurpassable masterpiece of rock architecture. This ranks among the best known and finest climbing corries in Scotland. The upper buttresses of quartzite stand on a plinth of sandstone rising to almost half the total height of over 300m. The two strata are separated by Broad Terrace, lower and more continuous in its eastern extent, so that the East Buttress is two-thirds composed of quartzite, while almost half of the West Buttress is Torridonian sandstone. The Broad Terrace is an easy scramble which is used as an approach to climbing routes on the upper parts of the East and Central Buttresses. On the main buttresses the quartzite is divided into two layers, the lower half having a more pronounced bedding plane. Their junction is a less-pronounced terrace, the line of the Girdle Traverse. The right aspect of each buttress is well-broken, but the left profiles rise sheer. That of the East Buttress merges with the Eastern Ramparts, a 150m vertical face which stretches back for almost 400 metres to Far East Gully. The cliffs continue slightly less formidable but equally steep – Far East Wall – to merge onto the col on the ridge which leads towards the highest top, Ruadh-stac Mor. The scramble from the floor of the corrie to the col gives an easy way up onto the main ridge of Beinn Eighe, emerging just below the north-east ridge of Coinneach Mhor.

To the right of the West Buttress is Far West Gully, still strewn with wreckage of a crashed bomber from the past. Beyond this lies Far West Buttress, much shorter and less clearly defined. The three main buttresses are separated by East-Central and West-Central Gullies.

The steep broken cliffs of Sail Mhor, which form the west containing wall of Coire Mhic Fhearchair, are not of the same quality for climbing as those of the Triple Buttress itself. They display some of the worst features of Torridonian sandstone, the bands of cliff which encircle the crag are wet and occasionally overhanging, 'all rock from below, all grass from above'. The most practical line of ascent onto the ridge from this corner is by the wide scree fans behind the lochan which can be followed up onto the broken crest to the south below the summit of Sail Mhor.

The most popular line of approach to this north-western end of Beinn Eighe is by the Coire Dubh Mor path which leaves the Glen Torridon road nine kilometres to the west of Kinlochewe. This is probably the most used of all the paths on this side of the glen, the start is from a car park beside the bridge over the Allt a'Choire Dhuibh Mhoir between Beinn Eighe and Liathach. The path crosses the stream by stepping stones after three kilometres of steady ascent, then forks some distance on. The main path continues to swing westwards towards Coire Mhic Nobuil; the right-hand branch contours the buttress of Sail Mhor onto the sandstone rim of Coire Mhic Fhearchair and the side of the lochan. The ascent to the main ridge via the col at the south-east corner of the corrie beyond the Far East Wall is straightforward. From there a broad ridge leads north onto the main summit of Beinn Eighe, Ruadh-stac Mor (*big red peak*) – well-named in respect of the distinctive colouring – a distance of just over one kilometre. Back at the narrow col, a short sharp arête is climbed to the cairn on the flat mossy top of Coinneach Mhor.

The Triple Buttress at the head of Coire Mhic Fhearchair

The continuation of the ridge west then north-west to Sail Mhor involves a steep descent from Coinneach Mhor down to the rocks of Ceum Grannda, *(the ugly step)*. This is an exposed scramble, more awkward in descent, but not really difficult. The steep scree slopes can then be descended to the south end of Loch Coire Mhic Fhearchair, circling the lochan to join the ascent path from Coire Dubh Mor.

From the eastern end of Coinneach Mhor the way along the main ridge of Beinn Eighe drops for one kilometre to the south-east onto the col (821m), then turns north-east. The stony arete leading onto Spidean Coire nan Clach offers no problems, and as has been already said this summit is seen as a natural dividing point for the Beinn Eighe ridge. An easy route up or down can be made from the crest of the small spur which curves out to the south side – Stuc Coire an Laoigh. This route can be followed into Coire an Laoigh then down to meet a path which takes the line of the Allt Coire an Laoigh to the roadside in Glen Torridon opposite Loch Bharranch. Equally well one can descend south into Coire nan Clach by slopes which are almost completely free of quartzite scree and boulders.

A near continuous expanse of white quartzite scree dominates the view to the east along the main ridge from the summit of Spidean Coire nan Clach. This is certainly one of the mountain's most attractive characteristics, but one which can lead to awkward underfoot conditions and tiring climbing; the established paths are

Sgurr nan Fhir Duibhe and the Bodaich Dubh from Sgurr Ban

recommended wherever possible. The way dips down and up onto the top of Sgurr Ban (*white peak*) for over one kilometre, with the inevitable scree slopes on the south side, and steep broken crags and gullies on the north. The ridge continues for another kilometre in the same pattern eastwards towards Sgurr nan Fhir Duibhe (*peak of the black men*). The pinnacled section beyond on the way to the final summit, Creag Dubh, can undoubtedly present problems for hillwalking parties. It becomes necessary to negotiate a series of shattered pinnacles, Bodaich Dubh Beinn Eighe, better known as the Black Carls. They can only be bypassed by a long descent and a tiring traverse, but if in doubt descend south-east to reach the broad easy ridge on the south side of Coire Domhain, from where easy descents go south to Glen Torridon along the east bank of the Allt a'Ghille, or east-north-east to the Allt a'Chuirn where there is a path on the north side. Beyond the summit of Sgurr nan Fhir Duibhe, 10m of exposed scrambling can be avoided by taking the south side of the ridge below the cairn. From the head of the gully at the foot of the steep section, the path crosses over and the next pinnacle is turned on the north before continuing over the final rocky section.

The east end of the Beinn Eighe ridge is normally approached from Cromasaig, one kilometre south of Kinlochewe, leaving the road at Carn Shiel (025 611). The path follows the Allt a'Chuirn for over two kilometres towards the mouth of Coire Domhain and the steep crest of the ridge ahead is climbed onto the summit of Creag Dubh. From the end of the path it is also possible to bypass the pinnacled section of the main ridge if so desired. Bear south-west along the south side of the Allt a'Chuirn and climb the east ridge of Sgurr nan Fhir Duibhe. The continuation westwards to the summit of Spidean Coire nan Clach has already been described, with the option of a descent to Loch Bharranch in Glen Torridon, or continuing the traverse to descend into Coire Mhic Fhearchair and join the path out to Coire Dubh Mor.

PATHS AND WALKS

The main paths in the area have been covered in the course of describing the individual mountains. They offer considerable scope for walkers and backpackers throughout the whole of the area, and can be conveniently linked in numerous combinations offering splendid opportunities to savour the remoter corners of the hinterland.

Coire Dubh Mor to Coire Mhic Nobuil. This walk is a combination of the two most frequented paths into the mountains of Torridon and gives spectacular views throughout its length. Start from the carpark at the bridge over the Allt a'Choire Dhuibh Mhoir on the road through Glen Torridon. The path climbs steeply north-west above the west side of the stream into Coire Dubh Mor, skirting the east end of Liathach. Three kilometres from the start it forks at a prominent cairn. The right-hand branch swings northwards and curves round the shoulder of Sail Mhor of Beinn Eighe into Coire Mhic Fhearchair where it ends. (Seven kilometres from the carpark). The left-hand branch continues north-west to a cluster of small lochans beyond the watershed then swings west along the north side of the Abhainn Coire Mhic Nobuil between Liathach and Beinn Dearg. The views from there into the northern corries of Liathach are particularly impressive. The way continues west along Coire Mhic Nobuil to its junction with the path from the Bealach a'Chomla then crosses a bridge at the confluence of the two streams, continuing south-west along the south bank to exit at the carpark on the Diabeg road. Rough walking in places but easy to follow throughout. (13 kilometres).

Loch Bad an Sgalaig to Coire Mhic Nobuil via Loch na h-Oidhche. This gives a long walking route of quality across the very centre of Torridon from north to south. Start from the A832 road ten kilometres south of Gairloch and follow the well-marked path which climbs inland to the south end of Loch na h-Oidhche. The path continues past the bothy at Poca Buidhe for a short distance and ends at the Gorm Lochs. Follow the east shore of Gorm Loch Fada to the south end of the loch then take a line south-west for one and a half kilometres across the pathless section of the route towards Loch na Cabhaig at the north end of Beinn Dearg. From the west end of this loch continue on the same line for another one and a half kilometres to pass a group of small lochans on the north side of the Bealach a'Chomhla and join the path which leads down between Beinn Dearg and Beinn Alligin. This follows the Allt a'Bhealaich to the junction with the path through Coire Mhic Nobuil, ending at the bridge on the Diabeg road. An overnight camp at Loch na Cabhaig is worth considering to savour the route at leisure.(19 kilometres).

CLIMBING

Most climbing activity in Torridon in the past has been concentrated on Liathach and Beinn Eighe, although the other mountains in the area have certainly been explored. There is a prominent cliff face below the summit of Baosbheinn which would seem to have possibilities, and the quartzite face on the south-west flank of Meall a'Ghiubhais gives several short routes. Two of the earlier gully routes on the Horns of Alligin give pleasant climbing – *Deep South Gully* (250m, Grade I) is on the north-east face between the first and second Horns, *Deep North Gully* (250m, Grade II) is between the second and third Horns. There are several more recent routes there. The north-east face of Tom na Gruagaich has hard winter gully routes. On the left of the upper face, *Giveaway Gully* (350m, Grade IV) is considered to be one of the finest of the Torridonian gullies, even superior to March Hare Gully on Beinn Bhan.

The north face of Liathach offers the best climbing prospects. In Coire na Caime the gullies between the Northern Pinnacles give several winter routes between 90m and 120m up to Grade III standard. *Bell's Buttress*, the original line in the corrie, gives a 90m climb of Severe standard, easier to the left. The gully to the left is a 300m Grade IV climb. There is only one recorded rock climb on the Fasarinen Pinnacles, but the gullies between give Grade II climbs of 120m. To the west is *PC*

Buttress (200m,Difficult). The crag below the summit of Sgorr a' Chadail, at the west end of the ridge, has given short rock routes of Very Difficult standard. The high band of cliffs at the extreme eastern end of Liathach gives a 180m route graded Very Difficult on the edge of a conspicuous gully. The winter gully routes there are graded from I/IV. Despite the limited summer climbing on Liathach, the northern corries hold an abundance of high standard winter lines. Coireag Dubh Beag and Coireag Dubh Mor both have routes of up to 240m, Grade IV/V and the south-east buttress of Spidean a'Choire Leith has also been climbed giving a Grade IV route of 180m. As has been emphasized, a winter traverse of the Liathach ridge is a major mountaineering expedition and not a winter hill walk.

On Beinn Eighe, the quartzite crag lying on the eastern flank of Ruadh-stac Mor is Creag Mhor, Coire Ruadh-staca. This is difficult to see from most directions (grid reference 953 612). The main cliff is described as a jumble of towers, 120m in height, continuing to the right as a steep, continuous 60m cliff. Its prominent features are a gully consisting of a single deep cave, and the two ridges of the main cliffs which come further down the side of the hill than do the rest. A number of routes of around 100m have been climbed there varying from Very Difficult to Very Severe in standard. *Pineapple Chimney* (105m, Very Severe) is the chimney formed by the monolith known as *The Independent Pineapple*. This is a high quality climb with a hard final pitch. The Independent Pineapple gives a fine natural line of Severe standard.

The description in detail of climbing on The Triple Buttress is far beyond the remit of this guide book. On Far East Wall, the routes are generally hard; summer routes are Very Severe standard and above, with more recent winter routes of Grade V/VI. The central section of the 120m quartzite wall is steep. *Far East Gully* gives 60m of straightforward Difficult climbing on good holds. The distinctive and extensive left-hand face of the East Buttress forms what is known as the *Eastern Ramparts*. The routes there vary in standard from Severe to Extremely Severe. The rock is quartzite and the face is split horizontally at just less than half height by the line of the Upper Girdle. A pale diedre near the middle of the upper layer marks the line of *Boggle* (135m, Very Severe) a fine climb on this face. The route starts at the centre of the face and runs to the right as a shelf just above the top of the scree slope. This is now known as Bottom Shelf. The routes on the East Buttress are more difficult on the sandstone tier than on the upper quartzite. The original route there was *Ordinary Route* (210m, Difficult) which starts on Broad Terrace ten metres from the extreme right-hand edge and follows the crest of the buttress. The first ascent avoided the first 30m pitch by going up the gully to the right. *East Central Gully* is basically a winter route but has been climbed in summer, the standard is Severe. The north-east facing left flank of the upper section of Central Buttress has become known as *Central Wall*. It is seen to be triangular in shape with the apex at the bottom, level with Broad Terrace. It is bounded on the left by East Central Gully, and on the right by the crest of Central Buttress. The lower part of the wall is a 45m high tower rising from East Central Gully at the level of Broad

Terrace. The top of the tower is a gently-sloping terrace from which most of the climbs start. A good route there, *East Central Ribs* (105m, Severe) follows the crest of the three prominent quartzite ribs just west of East Central Gully. They are bordered on the left by the gully, and are steep, narrow and exposed. Central Buttress is seen to have more sandstone than the East Buttress, and the quartzite is in three distinct tiers. These are uniform in both size and in the standard of climbing found on them. The lower tier is generally Very Difficult; the middle tier is Difficult or less; the upper tier is Mild Severe. The sandstone tier is conveniently ringed by a broad level grass shelf above the lowest rocks. All climbs start from there, and it is easily reached by scrambling up on the right near West Central Gully.

On Central Buttress, Coire Mhic Fhearchair

The original climb is *Piggott's Route* (Mild Severe) which starts about a third of the way along the shelf from the west end of the buttress beside a large leaning block. The route takes the middle of the face. The 90m on the sandstone is Difficult; the 180m on the quartzite starts from the highest point of the grass on Broad Terrace and goes straight up. West Central Gully has been climbed in winter, and in summer its lower section formed part of the original route on the Triple Buttress pioneered at the turn of the century. West Buttress has more sandstone and less quartzite than the others. It is bounded on the right by Easy Gully which slants rightwards from the foot of the buttress to merge near the rocks which form Ceum Grannda, the ugly step on the main ridge below Coinneach Mhor. At the bottom of the quartzite the Easy Gully forks and a branch comes in from the left which is Far West Gully. Routes there vary from Severe to Hard Very Severe. The quartzite tier of the Ordinary route is Grade III/IV; the winter climb bypassed the sandstone tier.

CHAPTER 13

Loch Maree to Loch Broom

MAPS: Ordnance Survey   1:50,000   Sheet 19
          Bartholomew   1:100,000   Sheets 54 and 58

PRINCIPAL HILLS

Slioch	980m	004 691
Beinn a'Mhuinidh	692m	032 661
Bein Lair	859m	982 733
Meall Mheinnidh	722m	954 748
Beinn Airigh Charr	792m	930 762
Beinn a'Chaisgein Mor	856m	983 786
A'Mhaighdean	967m	007 748
Ruadh Stac Mor	919m	018 756
Beinn Tarsuinn	937m	039 727
Mullach Coire Mhic Fhearchair	1018m	052 735
Sgurr Ban	989m	055 745
Beinn a'Chlaidheimh	914m	061 775
Creag Rainich	807m	097 751
Beinn Dearg Mor	910m	032 799
Beinn Dearg Bheag	820m	020 811
Sail Mhor	767m	033 887
An Teallach	1062m	069 843
Beinn Ghobhlach	635m	055 944

The area between Loch Maree and Little Loch Broom contains a complex group of mountains which lie mainly within the Letterewe, Fisherfield, Strathnasheallag and Dundonnell deer forests. The north-west coastline stretches from the head of Loch Ewe and Gruinard Bay to the Scoraig peninsula at the mouth of Loch Broom. To the south-east lie the mountains of Fannaich. Within these boundaries is an uninhabited maze of mountain and loch which exhibits some of the finest wilderness scenery in the Scottish Highlands.

The coastline swings around a series of wide bays and sea-lochs each of which makes its own contribution to the overall quality of the landscape. At the south end the long sheltered basin of Loch Ewe enjoys the warming effects of the Gulf Stream which was harnessed with such astonishing results last century at Inverewe by the late Osgood Mackenzie, the laird of the time. Around the little headland just north of Poolewe, where the waters of the River Ewe empty from Loch Maree into the sea, he created a garden which is now renowned world-wide for the variety and profusion of plants and trees which it is able to sustain. This is maintained by the National Trust for Scotland and attracts thousands of visitors to the area each year.

To the north of this, beyond Greenstone Point with its fine views of the mountains of Coigach, curves the much broader sweep of Gruinard Bay. Two fine salmon rivers – Gruinard and Little Gruinard – flow into the magnificent sandy beach within a relatively short distance of each other. A third river comes in between them there – the River Inverianvie, known as the Ghostly Burn. No salmon make their way up there; it was cursed to that effect by a local witch, who was helped by the fine 15m waterfall just inland from its mouth. The island in the middle of the bay is a prime example of Man's interference with a wonderful environment. This was the site for an experimental development in germ warfare in the 1940's. Anthrax was introduced to this lovely little islet in the most magnificent of peaceful settings. It has recently been declared clean but not surprisingly there has been no rush to recolonise.

A long narrow peninsula has been formed in the northern corner by two sea-inlets, Loch Broom and Litle Loch Broom, both of them almost 20 kilometres in length. The isolated headland of Scoraig surprisingly supports a thriving litle community whose only links with the 'mainland' are by ferry across the mouth of Little Loch Broom to Badluarach, and by the long path to Badrallach where a narrow road is reached leading to Dundonnell or Ullapool across the Allt na h'Airbhe ferry.

The coastal strip rises up towards the remote inland area of loch and mountain over rough moorlands which give poor quality pasture. In the past the economy there was based on the breeding of cattle and latterly sheep, both of which had to provide their own form of transport to the markets in the east and south. The droving traffic from the whole of this coastline continued well into the 19th century. Lines of communication suitable for man and beast had a host of obstacles to contend with. The droving routes which developed followed the most natural lines along the driest ground of the straths, skirting the sides of loch and avoiding peaks, crossing watersheds by the lower bealachs (passes) at the heads of the glens. The parallel series of great fresh-water lochs which slant across the interior from north-west to south-east were of paramount importance. Their lines follow those of pronounced geological faults; their basins were created as a result of subsequent massive glaciation.

Loch Maree is the largest and most impressive of those areas of waterway which had to be traversed. Its west end is a myriad of islands and in the past its shores were covered by extensive oak forests. There were iron works there in the early 18th century. The daily consumption of oak to service the nearby bloomeries took its toll and the vast forests are no more. The remains of the bloomery at Furnace can still be seen near Letterewe; Cladh nan Sasunnach (*Englishman's grave*) lies to the east end of the loch near the old iron works at the mouth of Gleann Bianasdail. The drove road from Poolewe and the west followed this north shore of the loch and continued east to Achnasheen. The same route was used by the 'walking postman' from Dingwall carrying his weekly satchel of mail to the west.

The two magnificent lochs which lie in the very heart of the mountains were not used as drove routes; the problems there were too great for even the hardy black cattle. The track which follows their line is the best known of the rights of way used in present times, and one of the finest wilderness walks in the Highlands. Fionn Loch and Lochan Fada in the past held a wonderful variety of wild life, much of which has been greatly depleted. There is a fascinating record of the interior in Osgood MacKenzie's account *A Hundred Years in the Highlands*. It is difficult to understand how he created the Inverewe Gardens on one hand, and played the greatest part in decimating so much of the native wildlife on the other, this latter behaviour in the very best Victorian tradition. Both lochs are renowned for their giant trout which have fortunately survived, although the sea-eagle which once fed on them has been less fortunate.

On the north side of the area, the drove road from Gruinard along Loch na Sealga and through Strath na Sealga and the Fannaichs to Achnasheen can still be traced by well-marked paths. This route had several variations, linking in places to a northern branch which followed the edge of Little Loch Broom to Dundonnell, crossing the 'Destitution Road' at Fain to meet the Ullapool drovers at Braemore. The route through Strath na Sealga (*valley of hunting*) must have been particularly impressive with its lines of wild craggy mountains rising up on either side throughout. Droving has long passed from the economic life of the Highlands, but fortunately we can still enjoy its legacy in this part of the country in the form of many rights of way.

ACCESS

A good motor road (A832) passes along three sides of the area, (south, west and east), but as the majority of the mountains lie a considerable distance inland, onward progress depends mainly on the network of stalker's paths which cross from all sides. The A835 road from Dingwall to Ullapool forks at Garve. From there the A832 road branches west through Achnasheen to Kinlochewe at the east end of Loch Maree for access to Slioch and the mountains in the south of the Letterewe forest. The road continues north-west along the side of Loch Maree to the head of Loch Gairloch then winds a twisting way northwards along the head of Loch Ewe and of Gruinard Bay, bypassing most of the little communities on the peninsulas to the west. From Gruinard Bay the A832 road sweeps over the Badluarach headland to the mouth of Little Loch Broom and on to Dundonnell giving direct access to An Teallach and its immediate satellites. From there it rises up from Corrie Hallie to rejoin the A835 road at Braemore Junction. There are no public roads branching off this main A832 road into the interior of the area, although several side roads branch out around the coastal peninsulas.

PUBLIC TRANSPORT

Rail: There is a daily passenger service from Inverness and Dingwall to Achnasheen, The Kyle Line, with onward travel to Kinlochewe and Poolewe by bus and postbus.

Bus: Inverness – Dingwall – Achnasheen – Kinlochewe – Loch Maree – Strath - Poolewe – Aultbea. (MacKenzie and MacLennan, Gairloch) Tuesdays, Thursdays and Fridays. All Year.
Inverness – Dingwall – Achnasheen – Kinlochewe. (Scottish Omnibuses Ltd) Mondays to Fridays. All Year.
Dingwall – Braemore – Dundonnell – Badcaul – Aultbea – Inverewe – Poolewe – Gairloch. (MacKenzie and MacLennan, Gairloch) Mondays, Wednesdays and Saturdays. All Year.

Postbus: Achnasheen – Kinlochewe – Loch Maree Hotel – Gairloch – Poolewe – Aultbea – Laide. Mondays to Saturdays. All Year.

ACCOMMODATION

There are hotels at Kinlochewe, Loch Maree, Gairloch, Poolewe, Aultbea, Laide and Dundonnell. Bed and breakfast accommodation can be found readily around the area. There are caravan/camp sites at Kinlochewe, Gairloch and Laide. The Scottish Youth Hostels Association has a hostel at Carn Dearg, four kilometres west of Gairloch, which is open from March to October. There is a private hostel, Sail Mhor, at Camusnagaul, three kilometres north-west of Dundonnell Hotel. The Junior Mountaineering Club of Scotland (Edinburgh Section) have the Old Smiddy on the east side of Dundonnell opposite the Army Adventure Centre.

There are bothies at Shenavall, at the south-east end of Loch na Sealga (grid reference 065 810)and at Carnmore (in the stable), at the south-east end of Fionn Loch (grid reference 978 769). These are not available in the stalking season. The estate buildings at Achneigie and Larachantivore in Strath na Sealga are not available as bothies, and the lodge at Carnmore is also private. The bothy at the south-west end of Loch a'Bhraoin is seldom locked, but is basically for use by Lochbroom estate stalkers and shepherds. Enquiries regarding its availability should be directed to the owners at Inverbroom Lodge.

THE HILLS

Slioch *(spear)* (981m)

Slioch is undoubtedly the most impressive of the mountains along the north shore of Loch Maree. It towers above the south-east end of the loch like a fortified keep, steep buttressed slopes falling to the south and to the west; its unseen northern flank a similar mixture of steep crag and scree. The view from the east is no less fine, but certainly more encouraging for the climber. From the main summit of the mountain two spurs swing out to the east above Gleann Bianasdail, containing a wide heathery corrie, Coire na Sleaghaich, unnamed on the 1:50,000 map. These are the breaches in the defences through which to reach the summit ridge. The approach is by the path from Incheril. This follows a pleasant route along the Kinlochewe River for four kilometres then crosses the Abhainn an Fhasaigh by a footbridge at the entrance to Gleann Bianasdail. Beyond this the path forks; the main path continues towards Letterewe, the right-hand branch climbs upwards along the side of the stream to the head of the glen and eventually reaches the south-east end of Lochan Fada. Follow the path up the glen for one kilometre, then make a rising traverse due north to the little col between Meall Each and Sgurr Dubh. An easy traverse then leads into Coire na Sleaghaich.

A direct ascent can be be made from there by following the Allt Coire na Sleaghaich to the head of the corrie and the band of crags below the main summit.These are climbed, or turned on the right onto the spur of the mountain which leads to Sgurr an Tuill Bhain *(peak of the white hollow)* (934m). The main summit of Slioch lies just over a kilometre along the ridge to the west. A better alternative is to ascend from Coire na Sleaghaich up a short steep grass slope to the two lochans on the south-east ridge of the mountain and continue from there to the main summit. There are two tops, both of them are 981m. The south top has the triangulation point, the north top is the better viewpoint, looking down the length of Loch Maree and across to the northern corries of Torridon.The descent from the ridge is best made from Sgurr an Tuill Bhain taking a fairly direct line south down into Coire na Sleaghaich to retrace the outward line of approach. It should be noted that the small corrie below that top on its north side is Coire an Tuill Ban, a name mistakenly given to the large central corrie, which is Coire na Sleaghaich.

To reach the foot of Slioch's steeper west face, continue along the Letterewe path for over one and a half kilometres to where it crosses a stream slanting down below the cliff line from the north-west. This stream is followed to its source which is marked by a cairned boulder below the first buttress. The Main Buttress of Slioch forms the skyline to the left. Stepped Ridge lies beyond this, entirely hidden. The pinnacle which is so prominent on the skyline in the view from across Loch Maree is on a broken buttress lying well to the north of the latter. A direct ascent can be made from the cairned boulder by scrambling up steep slopes of grass, rock and short crags to the south of Main Buttress.

Looking across Loch Maree to Slioch

Beinn a'Mhuinidh (*mountain of the heath*) (692m)

This is the mountain which forms the east side of Gleann Bianasdail, a sprawl of featureless slopes rising up from the end of Lochan Fada onto its un-noteworthy summit above the mouth of the glen. The normal rock sequence of gneiss, sandstone and quartzite has acquired a final capping of gneiss, marking the line of a thrust zone, and the crags which line the corner of the tilted plane of the mountain above the end of Loch Maree are of considerable climbing interest. There the bands of quartzite which run for most of the length of these south-west and north-west sides have their largest and finest exposure of rock on the Bonnaidh Donn Buttress. The buttress on the south-west slope, marked by the conspicuous 90m waterfall above the mouth of the Kinlochewe River, is the Waterfall Buttress. This was one of the original routes on the cliffs, first climbed at the end of last century by Glover and Inglis Clark and still considered to be remarkable for its standard and conception. The summit of the mountain can be best climbed from Incheril starting from the track which follows the north side of the Abhainn Bruachaig north-eastwards towards the Heights of Kinlochewe. Leave the track after two kilometres and climb north-west for three kilometres on an open rising plateau scattered with clusters of lochans to the summit of the mountain overlooking Gleann Bianasdail. A descent north-north-east can be made to the south-east end of Lochan Fada to join the stalker's path through the glen for the return to Incheril.

Beinn Airigh Charr (*mountain of the rocky shieling*) (792m)
Meall Mheinnidh (*grassy* or *solitary hill*) (722m)
Beinn Lair (*mountain of the mare*) (859m)

These three mountains form a continuous ridge which rises more or less gradually towards the north-east from the tree-fringed shores of Loch Maree. The shoreline there follows a marked geological faultline; unlike the mountains to the south and to the east the ridge has been scoured out of gneiss, forming characteristically undulating slopes of bare rounded rock and heathery hollows. In contrast, the north-east side falls steeply from all three summits and has finely sculptured features at both ends on Beinn Airigh Charr and on Beinn Lair. On that side, the rock faces are of horneblende schist, a result of metamorphosis of the basic gneiss. This rock is sounder and less vegetated than one would expect, with a profusion of incut holds; protection is scarce however, and the rock requires special care in wet conditions. Beinn Airigh Charr has extensive cliffs culminating in the north top known as Martha's Peak. This rises as a huge rock tower above Loch an Doire Crionaich, four kilometres along the path south-east from Kernsary. Martha was a legendary local lass who tended her herds on the 'rocky shieling' of Beinn Airigh Charr and fell to her death while retrieving her cromag on the first recorded traverse of the tower. The lower part of the peak is split in two by a wide grassy scoop with climbing in the left branch. *Staircase Gully*, which is basically a scree gully with occasional rock pitches, separates Martha's Peak from the rest of the crags, which diminish in height towards the east. The face of Beinn Lair contains more than twenty buttresses, ridges and ribs, separated by deep-cut gullies, varying

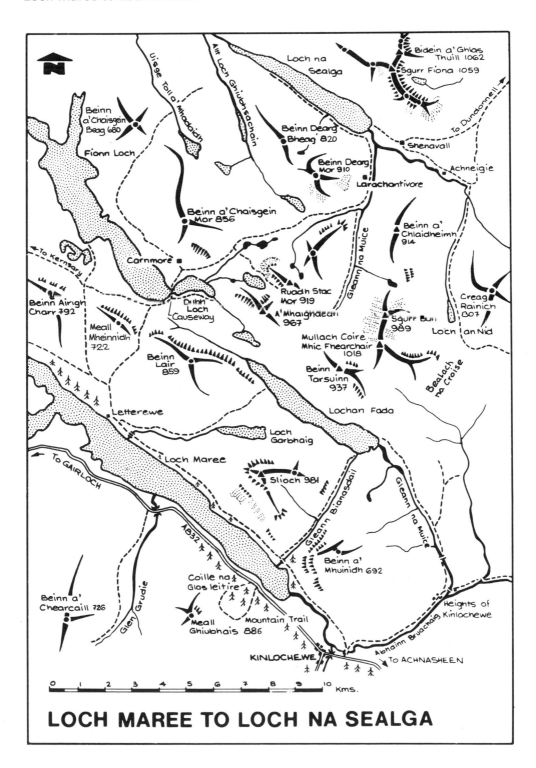

LOCH MAREE TO LOCH NA SEALGA

in height from 120m to 420m. The cliffs fall into two sections: the Fionn Loch cliffs at the north-west end of the escarpment, and the Lochan Fada cliffs at the south-east end. There is a profusion of rock-climbing routes of all standards; winter exploration has been somewhat retarded over the years by reason of general inaccessibility.

The mountains are best approached from Kernsary by the path to Carnmore which is connected to Loch Maree by several other shorter paths across the passes which conveniently divide the range throughout its length. At the west end, Srathan Buidhe crosses between Beinn Airigh Charr and Mheall Mheinnidh, the central summit, which in turn joins to Beinn Lair across the Bealach Mheinnidh. To the east, a good stalker's path from Letterewe Lodge to Lochan Fada skirts the west end of Loch Garbhaig and separates Beinn Lair from Slioch. The right of way from Kinlochewe to the west goes along the north shore of Loch Maree to Letterewe Lodge, and then links with the path over Srathan Buidhe. There is no link with the south shore of the loch other than an estate boat. The path along the Loch Maree side of the ridge from Srathan Buidhe is probably more easily followed from its west end at Kernsary. A signposted path goes to the south from the ford below the stalker's house at Kernsary and leads towards Ardlair Lodge on Loch Maree-side, a distance of just over four kilometres. Three kilometres from Kernsary there is a junction in the path marked by a small shelter - The Postman's Shelter (grid reference 894 769); from there the north-east branch of the path leads into the western corrie of Beinn Airigh Charr, stopping 800 metres short of the west top, Spidean nan Clach (703m). The loch path passes Ardlair Lodge and follows the shoreline to the Rubha Chailleach *(witch's point)* at grid reference 919 742. From there it climbs from the shoreline up the side of the Allt Rubha Chailleach to the top of the crags at about 300m, then takes a line to the east for two kilometres to the corner of the Srathan Buidhe path (grid reference 941 735).

The best and shortest route onto Beinn Airigh Charr is from Kernsary by way of the path to the Postman's Shelter and then up the stalker's path into the western corrie. From the end of the path the way onto the west top (703m) is easily followed; the main top lies 500 metres south-east of this across a slight dip in the summit ridge. An alternative way up to or down from Beinn Airigh Charr can be made from the path across Srathan Bhuidhe. 500 metres north of the junction with the path from Witch's Point, a faint stalker's route makes a rising traverse through rocky hummocks to the north-west for just over two kilometres onto the summit. This is of more interest as a descent route for the return to Kernsary.

The ascent of Meall Mheinnidh is straightforward. From the north end of the Srathan Buidhe path, the north-west ridge leads to the summit in less than two kilometres. From the Bealach Mheinnidh the way up the south-east ridge is just over half that distance.

From the summit of the Bealach Mheinnidh, broad slopes on the west side of Beinn Lair lead to the edge of the cliffs and these can be followed to the summit

Beinn Lair (left), with Meall Mheinnidh and Beinn Airigh Charr beyond, seen from A'Mhaighdean across Gorm Loch Mor

cairn giving unsurpassed views down across remote rocky sanctuaries, with hidden lochs and bare gnarled surrounding crags. The cliffs of Beinn Lair line the south side of Gleann Tulacha, a wonderful corner. This very private glen stretches back from the west end of Lochan Fada, hemmed in on its north side by the steep broken slopes of gneiss which form Beinn Tharsuinn Chaol. From the head of the glen at Bealach a'Chuirn a stalker's path swings up to join the main path onto the Bealach Mheinnidh. To the north of this a series of smaller crags drops towards the Carnmore Causeway. These are all of climbing interest. From the top of Beinn Lair, continue eastwards over a small dip to the subsidiary top, Sgurr Dubh (c800m). A line down to the south to skirt two small lochans leads to the boathouse at the west end of Loch Garbhaig and the stalker's path back towards Letterewe Lodge. If the Abhainn na Fuirneis is fordable, a more direct line can be made towards the Kinlochewe path along Loch Maree-side. A traverse of the mountains on this side is obviously open to many variations dictated by transport arrangements and accommodation used; regardless of choice, be prepared for a testing day's walk.

Beinn a'Chaisgein Mor (*big forbidding mountain*) (856m)

This is the most central mountain in the area of the Fisherfield Forest, and must be a strong contender for the title of most remote of the Corbetts. The summit rises immediately above Carnmore Lodge at the south-east end of Fionn Loch. The easiest route to this mountain is from a point on the path between Carnmore and Shenavall at grid reference 002 775. From there the grassy slopes give an easy climb north-west onto the rounded summit of the mountain in just over two kilometres.

Seen from the west, Beinn a'Chaisgein Mor presents a very different picture. This side of the mountain is a long hump of broken slopes which fall to the north-west down a succession of short rounded outcrops and awkward heather faces which makes it difficult to keep a direct line. The north ridge drops for almost three kilometres onto the connecting saddle with its equally rugged satellite Beinn a'Chaisgein Beag (680m), then continues northwards towards the shore of Loch a'Mhadaidh Mor. An approach from this direction from Gruinard Bay by way of the rather interesting track along the Inverianvie River, with its spectacular Witch's Waterfall, makes a testing challenge of almost eighteen kilometres for aspiring wilderness walkers. The shepherd's route onto the summit is by boat from the west shore of Fionn Loch and then by way of the path from the east side of the loch onto the saddle.

The main importance of Beinn a'Chaisgein Mor is seen to be the existence of two extremely fine exposures of gneiss cliffs which have given some of the finest climbing in Britain in recent years. Carnmore Crag (grid reference 980 773) rises above the stable at Carnmore. It has an upper and a lower wall with a central bay. The central nose of the crag is its most prominent feature – Fionn Buttress. Torr na h'Iolaire (grid reference 984 773) is the great rocky tower which falls south and west from the summit of Sgurr na Laocainn directly above Carnmore Lodge. The rock is excellent for climbing, well broken by terraces and it faces the sun.

A'Mhaighdean (*the maiden*) (967m)
Ruadh Stac Mor (*big red peak*) (919m)

Even in this area of quality, these two mountains enjoy a particularly splendid setting along the south-east side of the Carnmore to Shenavall path across the head of the pass from Beinn a'Chaisgein Mor. By virtue of their shared central position, these are undoubtedly the most remote of the Munros. The branch path to the south-east from the junction with the Carnmore path winds in pleasantly to Fuar Loch Mor and is found to go much further than is indicated on the map. It continues up steeply onto the broken col between A'Mhaighdean and Ruadh Stac Mor giving good walking throughout its three kilometres. The atmosphere in this little corrie is one of utter seclusion. The deep changing colours of Fuar Loch Mor are seen to be in stark contrast to the red crags of Ruadh Stac Mor on one side of the path and the grey coloured gneiss of A'Mhaighdean on the other. If the temptation to remain cannot be resisted, the huge cairn-marked boulder at the col makes an excellent bivouac.

Once on the col either summit is easily reached. A more or less direct line to the trig point on Ruadh Stac Mor can be followed involving some minor detouring through the sandstone crags around the top. The way onto the crest of A'Mhaighdean is a pleasant clamber up an easy-angled rocky ridge, followed by steeper grassy slopes to the dome-shaped summit. This has a marvellous situation overlooking sheer drops along its western flank to the Dubh Loch and Carnmore.

Seen from the west, A'Mhaighdean rises as a rather graceful crested ridge in a series of rocky steps onto the summit at the south-eastern end. The north-west approach gives a scrambling route to the summit, starting from Fuar Loch Beag. This is a much more interesting ascent and any difficulties encountered in negotiating the numerous little crags are always avoidable.

The summit of A'Mhaighdean is of gneiss, the highest point in the whole country where this ancient rock type is found. So too is the Pillar Buttress which falls for 150m southwards from just below the summit. In contrast, the four buttresses along the south face of the north-west ridge are of clean rough sandstone, giving good climbing.

From the col previously mentioned between these two mountains, a circular route back towards Shenavall can be made via the head of Gleann na Muice, following the west bank of the stream to pick up a stalker's path which leads to the foot of Gleann na Muice Beag and the main path from Carnmore.

Beinn Tarsuinn (*transverse mountain*) (937m)
Mullach Coire Mhic Fhearchair (*top of the corrie of the son of Farquhar*) (1018m)
Sgurr Ban (*white peak*) (989m)
Beinn a' Chlaidheimh (*mountain of the sword*) (914m)

These four mountains form a continuous ridge which stretches for almost nine kilometres along the east side of Gleann na Muice from Lochan Fada to Strath na Sealga. They can be climbed in the course of a complete traverse of the ridge starting from either end. When linked with an ascent of A'Mhaighdean and Ruadh Stac Mor, this makes a particularly fine but long expedition, best attempted in good weather conditions. If the shorter expedition is undertaken, then the best approach to these four mountains from Shenavall is by way of the path leading south into Gleann na Muice. Follow the Abhainn Gleann na Muice onto the col at the head of the glen, then join the route described from A'Mhaighdean.

A direct line to the south-east from A'Mhaighdean for three kilometres crosses the broad saddle at the head of Gleann na Muice leading onto the foot of the ridge of Beinn Tarsuinn. The way across is made awkward by the succession of considerable pavements and walls of sloping sandstone which have to be descended. The ridge ahead looks unremarkable at first glance, but once on the crest it is found to narrow considerably where it curves around the rim of a small hanging corrie on its north side. The ridge is somewhat exposed, requiring care in strong winds; it falls in a series of sandstone crags broken by long sweeping slopes of scree down past Lochan Coireachan Odhara towards Gleann na Muice.

Mullach Coire Mhic Fhearchair and Beinn Tarsuinn from Beinn Dearg Mor

An easy shoulder leads down from the mossy summit platform to Bealach Odhar, the col below Meall Garbh (852m). This rocky bump blocks the angle of the ridge leading onto Mullach Coire Mhic Fhearchair. A traverse below the north-west face of Meall Garbh along a narrow path leads to a second col from where the main ridge climbs steeply on the unpleasant quartzite blocks which cover the summit cone. The distance to there from the summit of Beinn Tarsuinn is two kilometres. The west face of the mountain below the summit is of craggy sandstone; the south-east ridge which juts out for almost two kilometres towards Loch a'Bhraoin has exposures of gneiss which terminate in distinctive pinnacles, easier to climb than to bypass. This ridge contains the other two tops of Mullach Coire Mhic Fhearchair. Tom Choinneach (981m) lies 600 metres to the east of the main top, the ridge then narrows to the south-east across the pinnacled section to Sgurr Dubh (918m). Tom an Fhiodha, the eastern shoulder below this top, gives a line of approach from the track leading past Lochivraon bothy to Loch an Nid. This side can also be approached from the south-east end of Lochan Fada by the path through Gleann Bianasdail from Incheril, or alternatively by way of the Heights of Kinlochewe.

Back on the main ridge, the summit of Sgurr Ban lies one kilometre to the north of Mullach Coire Mhic Fhearchair, involving a steep drop and re-ascent from the intervening col – Cab Coire nan Clach. Like its neighbour, Sgurr Ban is mainly of sandstone, with an inevitable topping of quartzite blocks which makes extremely

Beinn Dearg Mor and Beinn Dearg Bheag from Shenavall

rough walking on all sides, particularly unpleasant when wet. The highest point on the mountain is on the north-east corner of the flat summit plateau.

The summit of Beinn a'Chlaidheimh lies three kilometres to the north at the end of the main ridge overlooking Shenavall. Two small lochans on the intervening saddle mark the line of descent. Together with Loch a'Bhrisidh which nestles in the hollow of the corrie on the west side of the ridge, these make good landmarks in the event of bad visibility. The way to the saddle passes continuous sheets of unbroken quartzite dipping down towards Loch an Nid from the slopes of Sgurr Ban; they should be given a wide berth if at all wet. The summit ridge of Beinn a'Chlaidheimh is found to be narrower than is indicated by the map, dropping steeply to the west. The easiest line of descent is to drop north-east from the summit, steeply at first, then by a long descending traverse to reach the glen one kilometre south-east of Achneigie at the point where the track from Corrie Hallie swings down to the Abhainn Loch an Nid. The crossing of the river is a problem to be kept in mind if planning a start or a finish to the traverse of the ridge at this point. There are no bridges and the river is virtually impassable in any kind of spate condition, and should not be attempted.

Creag Rainich (*bracken crag*) (807m)
Corbett status has now drawn belated attention to this previously bypassed mountain which lies isolated in the corner of the Dundonnell Forest between Loch a'Bhraoin

and Loch an Nid. The easiest ascent is from the A832 road near Loch a'Bhraoin. Take the path along the lochside to Lochivraon bothy and from there climb north-west directly up the hillside, over a knoll at 749m, to the summit. Uncomplicated heathery slopes stretch north-east to give a good line of return with a final descent to the old boathouse at the east end of Loch a'Bhraoin.

Beinn Dearg Mor (*big red mountain*) (910m)
Beinn Dearg Bheag (*little red mountain*) (820m)

These two splendid mountains rise along the south-west shore of Loch na Sealga and on the north-west side of Gleann na Muice Beag, the border of the Fisherfield and Strathnasheallag Forests. They are in no way overshadowed by the cluster of Munros which surround them; on the contrary, it is they who tend to steal the limelight. The profile view of their north-eastern spurs seen along the river from Gruinard is tantalising; the view of their great northern corries from the track to Shenavall dominates the surrounding landscape; from all directions for miles around they always seem to get into the picture to some extent. The mountains are of sandstone as the names would imply, exhibiting all the characteristics of that formation. The unbroken line of the south-west side of the ridge slopes steeply down into Srath Beinn Dearg – aptly named the Lost Valley – to the west of which rise the long heathery slopes leading onto Beinn a'Chaisgein Mor; on the north-east side are two fine open corries which contain a selection of steep buttressed walls and gullies. The two wings of Beinn Dearg Mor meet on the central summit point enclosing Coire nan Clach; to the north-west the broad shallow corrie which contains Loch Toll an Lochain opens out below the connecting pass between the two summits.

The east side of Beinn Dearg Mor gives the most feasible ascent routes for hillwalkers. The north-east ridge can be climbed from the bothy at Larachantivore. The south-east ridge is approached from the path through Gleann na Muice Beag, which is left before it begins its final steep zig-zag up the headwall of the glen. Both of these are steep and quite rocky, and the south-east ridge has several towers on its crest which require care. The wide corrie between the north-east ridge and the south-east ridge gives the easiest route. This is reached by a rising traverse south-west from Larachantivore. The headwall of the corrie is not particularly steep and offers a way up onto the summit ridge. The view from the summit cairn perched on its spectacular rocky spur is particularly fine. The crests of both mountains create a jagged skyline, the ridges are narrow, but are less intimidating than they at first appear. A steep rocky slope at the west end of Beinn Dearg Mor gives 300m of descent to the bealach and the long south-east ridge of Beinn Dearg Bheag. The rocky outcrops *en route* are easily surmounted and a descent can be made with care from the west end or from the subsidiary east ridge which drops towards the shores of Loch na Sealga. The winter ascent of these two remote mountains becomes a much more serious undertaking.

Sail Mhor (*big heel*) (767m)

Descending eastwards along the road from the mouth of Litle Loch Broom, the rotund steep-sided summit dome of Sail Mhor stands like a rather portly sentry at the north-west end of the massive elevated sandstone plateau which culminates in the turreted ridges of An Teallach. The best approach to this Corbett is to climb the path along the Ardessie Falls which starts from the roadside four kilometres west of Dundonnell Hotel. Park in the layby just past the entrance to the fish farm and take the path up the east bank of the roadside fall, the first of the series. The path keeps to the east side of the Allt Airdeasaidh for almost two kilometres and this stream is crossed at the first possible ford after its junction with a burn coming down from the col between the south side of Sail Mhor and Ruigh Mheallain. From the col, a stiff climb northwards leads to the rather broken summit and a truly panoramic view. The slopes on the north side are steep and bouldery, the easiest descent is made by retracing the four kilometre route to the road.

An Teallach (*the forge*) (1062m)

An Teallach towers above the head of Little Loch Broom to the south of Dundonnell, rising in successively steeper bands and walls of red sandstone onto the crest of the sharply pinnacled, twisting ridge with its occasional dusting of light coloured quartzite. This in its turn sends long slopes sweeping down to the more open western side along Loch na Sealga, greener and less steep, but equally magnificent. It is the dominating feature in the landscape from all directions, a magnificent example of Torridonian architecture which is justly considered to be one the half dozen most splendid mountain ridges in Scotland.

The main ridge of the mountain extends from upwards of five kilometres in a line running roughly north to south forming a crescent-shaped backbone with projecting spurs to the west and to the east. On the east side of the ridge these spurs contain two corries of Olympian proportions – Glas Tholl and Toll an Lochain – lying immediately below the two Munro summits, Bidein a'Ghlas Thuill and Sgurr Fiona. The view of An Teallach's cliffs towering above Toll an Lochain should not be missed; this is undoubtedly the mountain's most spectacular corner.

From north to south, the principal points along the ridge of An Teallach are as follows:

Glas Mheall Mor	979m	076 854
Unnamed Top	919m	069 850
Bidein a'Ghlas Thuill	1062m	069 844
Glas Mheall Liath	962m	078 841
Sgurr Creag an Eich	1017m	055 838
Sgurr Fiona	1059m	064 837
Lord Berkeley's Seat	1048m	064 834
Corrag Bhuidhe	1020m	065 833
Corrag Bhuidhe Buttress	937m	066 831
Top above Cadha Gobhlach	960m	068 825
Sail Liath	954m	071 825

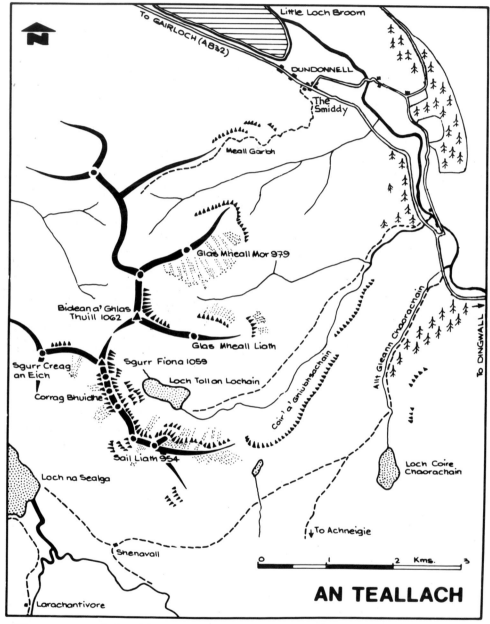

AN TEALLACH

The traverse of the ridge makes a long expedition in the best of conditions; in winter it becomes a serious mountaineering exercise for experienced parties. The choice of approach is open and can be governed by weather, ability or inclination on the day. The normal path leaves the A832 road near the JMCS hut at The Smiddy, east of Dundonnell Hotel. This winds steeply up over the shoulder of Meall Garbh then swings in a south-westerly direction up the broad sandy slopes

An Teallach from Toll an Lochain

ahead to gain the ridge beside the unnamed top (919m) five kilometres from the road. From there a spur juts out to the north-east giving a level stroll onto the quartzite-topped summit of Glas Mheall Mor, which forms the north wall of Glas Tholl. The slopes to the east of the summit are steep but negotiable and can be used as the finish of a traverse of the ridge from the other end. An easy ascent from the unnamed top leads onto Bidein a' Ghlas Thuill, which stands at the base of the middle spur on the east side of the ridge. The way along this spur to Glas Mheall Liath is straightforward. There are some fine buttresses in the south-west corner of Glas Tholl, the most northerly of which culminates in two or three pinnacles on the spur, but these do not impede progress. On the north side, a series of long narrow gullies drop to the floor of Glas Tholl; these are climbing routes in winter. A way down the headwall into the corrie can be made by way of the steep slopes descending from the col on the north side of Bidein a'Ghlas Thuill below the unnamed top (919m). From there, the course of the burn from the corrie can be followed eastwards to the waterfall on the Allt Coir' a'Ghiubhsachain to pick up the path leading to the roadside near Dundonnell House.

The summit of Bidein a'Ghlas Thuill is the highest point on An Teallach. Sgurr Fiona, the second highest, lies one kilometre to the south-west involving a steep descent and reascent on the narrow rocky connecting ridge. From there, the west spur of An Teallach leads over the summit of Sgurr Creag an Eich and continues

The peaks of Corrag Bhuidhe and Sgurr Fiona

more to the north-west for almost two kilometres to Sgurr Ruadh (758m). The wide corrie along its north-east side is an important section of the Dundonnell Forest, best avoided during the deer-culling season.

From Sgurr Fiona, the main ridge narrows significantly, undulating sharply over the series of spectacular sandstone pinnacles which form the mountain's distinctive skyline. These pinnacles include Lord Berkeley's Seat, a pointed turret which overhangs Coire Toll an Lochain, and the four tops of Corrag Bhuidhe, descending in order of height towards the south-east. In summer conditions these give interesting exposed scrambling; difficulties can always be bypassed by dropping westwards onto easier terrain where a fairly continuous narrow path traverses along the south-west flank of the ridge. The continuation south-east from the last of the four tops of Corrag Bhuidhe involves a steep descent to the short level rocky ridge of Corrag Bhuidhe Buttress, which juts out above Toll an Lochain. From the outer end of this short ridge return a short distance before continuing the descent steeply to the next col and then over the top above Cadha Gobhlach (*forked pass*) to reach the pass. In winter conditions this section of the ridge is not for inexperienced climbers, the time factor introduced by short days is an added problem.

The small flat-topped tower at the top of the pass is Stob a'Cadha Gobhlach, which is crossed to the shattered slope leading up to the flat summit of Sail Liath,

On the narrow crest of Corrag Bhuidhe

the south end of the ridge. Descend the south-east slope from the summit of Sail Liath to reach Lochan na Bradhan which nestles on the upper end of the long quartzite escarpment seen stretching down between Coir' a'Ghiubhsachain and Gleann Chaorachain towards the road at Corrie Hallie. A descent to either side is feasible; to the east, a straightforward line leads towards Loch Coire Chaorachain and the path from Shenavall; a way down through the the walls along the north-west side of the scarp is readily found and the side of the Allt Coir' a' Ghiubhsachain followed to the road. By either route the distance from the summit of Sail Liath is almost the same, over six kilometres; either way makes for an enjoyable descent, more interesting by far than the uphill path from Dundonnell.

Beinn Ghobhlach *(forked mountain)* (635m)

This shapely little mountain is the prominent terminal point on the Scoraig Peninsula between Loch Broom and Little Loch Broom. The hill is remarkably well-formed, dropping steeply seawards, and a landmark for a considerable distance to both north and south. To climb Beinn Ghobhlach, start from the road end at Badrallach and walk along the path to Scoraig for almost two kilometres. Then climb easy but quite steep grassy slopes north to pass round the west side of the knoll (336m) on the south side of Loch na h-Uidhe. Bear north-east between this loch and Loch na Coireig and climb easily to reach the west ridge of Beinn Ghobhlach less than half a kilometre from the summit. The final climb up a rocky ridge leads to the top with several small cairns.

PATHS AND WALKS

Many of the principal paths in the area have been mentioned in describing the routes to individual mountain groups. Their condition is generally good and their maintenance is dependent wholly on the various sporting estates. Except where they are rights of way, their use during the main stalking season is obviously restricted. In several cases they can be conveniently linked to give fine long walking routes of particular importance.

Kinlochewe to Corrie Hallie via Bealach na Croise. This route starts from the A832 road 600 metres east of Kinlochewe. A side road crosses the Abhainn Bruachaig to Incheril and swings north-east to join the right of way which follows the north-west bank of the river to the Heights of Kinlochewe. There the landrover track forks, both branches continuing as rights of way. The right-hand branch goes eastwards to Leckie at the mouth of Srath Chrombuill, then swings north-east as a path at first, then eastwards to reach Loch Fannich. The left-hand branch turns north up Gleann na Muice and crosses onto the north-east side of the Abhainn Gleann na Muice, continuing past Loch Gleann na Muice to the south-east end of Lochan Fada. Climb the pathless slopes to the north-east to Loch Meallan an Fhudair and continue on a more level line to the Bealach na Croise (420m) which crosses between Sgurr Dubh, the south-east peak of Mullach Coire Mhic Fhearchair, and Beinn Bheag. Descend the west side of the stream from the bealach to join the stalker's path from Loch a'Bhraoin which leads north to the end of Loch an Nid Continue north past the loch and on along the east side of the Abhainn Loch an Nid to join the vehicle track at the head of Strath na Sealga (grid reference 091 788). This climbs steeply up along the east side of the glen onto a plateau, passing on the west side of Loch Coire Chaorachain before descending the stream which flows north down Gleann Chaorachain to exit at Corrie Hallie on the A832 road south-east of Dundonnell. (30 kilometres).

Kinlochewe to Braemore via Bealach na Croise. This route follows the previous walk to the junction with the path leading to Loch an Nid. Follow the path eastwards past the ruined bothy at the foot of the south slopes of Creag Rainich.This is Feinasheen, unnamed on the Ordnance Survey map. Cross the stream which descends the grassy corrie on the south side of Creag Rainich and continue along its north bank to Lochivraon bothy at the south-west end of Loch a'Bhroain. The path skirts the north-west shoreline to the ruined boathouse at the east end of the loch. A private vehicle track leads out from there for one kilometre to meet the A832 road five kilometres south-west of Braemore Junction. (25 kilometres).

Gleann na Muice to Loch a'Bhraoin via Bealach Gorm. This is another right of way which offers an interesting variation to the middle part of the previous route. A stalker's path branches north-east from the path through Gleann na Muice leading to Lochan Fada at the point where the landrover track ends (grid reference 071 666). This crosses the ridge of Meall an Odhar to Gleann Tanagaidh and stops at the west side of the stream there. The right of way continues pathless to the north-east across the Bealach Gorm between Beinn Bheag and Graban then descends, still in a north-easterly direction, to join the path from Loch an Nid which leads to Lochivraon bothy and the A832 road south-west of Braemore Junction (22 kilometres).

Kinlochewe to Poolewe by Loch Maree. Take the road to Incheril from the A832 road and branch north-west just before reaching the school. Follow this road to its end at the last of the farm buildings and join the path along the north side of the River Kinlochewe to the bridge across the Abhainn an Fhasaigh at the south-west end of Gleann Bianasdail. The right of way follows the north shore of Loch Maree 14 kilometres to Letterewe Lodge. The path is no longer used as much by the estate as it was in the past and is now somewhat neglected. It keeps on the upper edge of the tree-line then drops towards the lochside beyond the old ironworks at Furnace to cross the bridge at the mouth of the Abhainn Fuirneis before continuing along the shore past the lodge. The path rises steeply up the east side of the Allt Folais which is crossed by a bridge, then traverses north-west to the Srathan Buidhe pass between Meall Mheinnidh and Beinn Airigh Charr. This section of the route is much used by stalking parties and is well-maintained. At the south-east end of Srathan Buidhe the path forks. The postman's route continues north-west along the top of Creag Tharbh before descending the side of the Allt Rubha Chailleach towards the loch above the Witch's Point (grid reference 919 742) as previously described under Beinn Airigh Charr. The route then continues via Ardlair Lodge to Kernsary and the private road past Inveran to Poolewe. (30 kilometres).

The main right of way continues north-west through Srathan Buidhe to join the boggy section of path which leads westwards to Kernsary along the north-east side of Beinn Airigh Charr. By this route the overall distance from Kinlochewe to Poolewe is approximately the same. (30 kilometres).

Poolewe to Corrie Hallie via Carnmore. This is the best known transverse route in the area and one which is frequently walked. Leave the A832 road at the north side of the bridge over the River Ewe at Poolewe and take the private road which follows the east bank of the river. Cars should be left near the school there unless prior permission has been obtained from Scatwell Estate to take them a further two kilometres to the gate at Inveran Lodge. The rough road continues for three kilometres to the stalker's house at Kernsary. The last gate reached is at the Ardlair Estate boundary fence; it is usually locked, but there is a stile for hillwalkers. The track leads east past Kernsary to enter a forestry plantation. There a forestry track turns north towards Fionn Loch; the path to Carnmore follows the side of the Allt na Creige to the south-east skirting the foot of Beinn Airigh Charr. This section beyond the trees is boggy and difficult to follow but gives easier walking than

Looking east across the head of Fionn Loch and Dubh Loch to Ruadh Stac Mor and A'Mhaighdean

diversions to the side. The path loops southwards into Srathan Buidhe to cross the stream by a bridge then returns northwards. The stream can usually be forded to give a more direct line and the detour is unnecessary. The way now bears down towards the south-east end of Fionn Loch to join another stalker's path descending from the Bealach Mheinnidh. Cross north over the causeway between the south-east end of Fionn Loch and Dubh Loch to Carnmore. The use of the bothy in the stable there has already been noted. The path skirts the north side of Dubh Loch and swings steeply north-east above the east side of the Allt Bruthach an Easain then bears east-north-east past Lochan Feith Mhic'illean towards the head of Gleann na Muice Beag. Steep zig-zags lead down the headwall of this glen and the path is then followed to its junction with Gleann na Muice. From there the path continues along the east side of the Abhainn Gleann na Muice past the locked estate buildings at Larachantivore at the foot of Beinn Dearg Mor. Cross the Abhainn Gleann na Muice near Larachantivore and bear north-east across flat boggy ground towards Shenavall. The Abhainn Srath na Sealga is now forded with care; the danger there in spate conditions should be kept well in mind. From the bothy at Shenavall on the north side of the river, the path climbs steeply east and then north-east to join with the vehicle track previously described at Loch Coire Chaorachain. This leads down through Gleann Chaorachain to Corrie Hallie on the A832 road south-east of Dundonnell. (45 kilometres).

CLIMBING

The west face of Slioch which falls from the summit towards Letterewe has a prominent buttress at the junction of the Loch Maree and the north-west faces. *Main Buttress* is seen to overhang its base for a horizontal distance of over 100 metres and is insurmountable except at the extreme right which gives a Severe route of 240m. *Stepped Ridge*, which lies hidden to the left, is a 240m route graded Very Difficult if taken direct.

The north-west slope of Beinn a'Mhuinidh has a horizontal band of steep quartzite running high up for most of its length to the summit plateau. The best exposure is at the corner of Glen Bianasdail on the *Bonnaidh Donn Buttress*. A lower band on the south-west slope is marked by *Waterfall Buttress*. *West Route* (90m, Severe) was the original climb here, done in 1899. Above and to the right of this is the most interesting part of the Upper Band. The buttresses at either end of this are North and South Buttress; *Little Buttress* is the first compact mass of rock to the west of the waterfall on the Lower Band. There are routes on all these, the quartzite giving good climbing on clean-cut holds. The standard is generally Very Difficult to Severe with some harder routes also possible.

On the way from Gairloch to Poolewe, a detour to the right along the road marked 'Tollie Bay' leads to the old pier at the west end of Loch Maree. This gives good access to Creag Mhor Thollaidh (grid reference 864 776) known as the *Tollie Crags*. The rock is of unusually smooth gneiss giving a standard of climbing universally Very Severe. There are four main crags: *Loch Maree Crag* (grid reference 880 768) which lies one and a half kilometres east from Tollie Bay and reached by a path from the bay through and beyond the huge lochside boulders. *Upper and Lower Tollie Crags* rise above Tollie Bay. High up on the right is *Gully Crag* (grid reference 864 778).

The original route on the Main Tower of Martha's Peak on Beinn Airigh Charr was climbed in 1910 by Glover and Ling's party and gave 330m of Difficult climbing. The route follows a line almost straight up from the broadest part of Lochan Doire Chrionach to the top of the tower. The left branch of the lower bifurcating grassy scoop gives a Severe climb of 150m which can be linked to the original route. *Staircase Gully* to the east gives a 360m route which varies in Grade from Very Dificult to a Severe overhanging chimney in the upper section. There is a very fine route on the steep arete to the east of this – *The Beanstalk* (105m, Very Severe). *Square Buttress* is contained in the last small face of the mountain, to the south-west of a small unnamed lochan (grid reference 938 765) This gives a Difficult climb of 120m, the difficulties there are in the lower half.

The Fionn Loch Cliffs of Beinn Lair have over twenty buttresses and gullies giving a profusion of routes. The main features are easily identified from north-west to south-east.

Excalibur Buttress is the obvious clean-looking mass of rock to the north-west of the crags. There is a deep-cut gully on the left and a buttress beset with overhangs on its right. *Excalibur* (120m, Very Difficult) starts at the side of the gully, Moderate at first then becoming steeper. Between Excalibur Buttress and next buttress to the left, which is *The Tooth*, lies *West Chimney* (Difficult). *Cavity Chimney* and *Wisdom Wall* starts at the base of the chimney to the left of the Tooth. *Wisdom Buttress* (210m, Very Difficult) is a magnificent exposed climb of continuous interest. It starts at the bottom right corner of the buttress which is conspicuous on account of its slender cigar-shaped aspect. The buttress to the east of this is *Angel Buttress* which has three routes of Difficult standard and one Severe. *Molar Buttress* is the broad buttress to the left of Angel Buttress and right of the Amphitheatre. It has five routes (about Very Difficult) and another which starts up the right-hand gully and then continues up the minor buttress, *Y Buttress*, which lies between the upper parts of Molar and Angel Buttress. The gully on the left is *The Amphitheatre*, a suitable means of descent.

The large mass of rock to the left of The Amphitheatre and right of the great bulk of the *North Summit Buttress* is *Butterfly Buttress*. This is in fact four buttresses; the two outer ones running the full height of the cliff, and the two smaller ones inserted between them at top and bottom. The first gully left of the Amphitheatre running the full height of the cliff is seen to fork about 150 metres below the plateau. Both give fine winter routes Grade II to Grade III. *Butterfly Gully* takes the more interesting left fork. The prominent cone-shaped buttress which falls from the north summit of Beinn Lair to upper Gleann Tulacha is North Summit Buttress. A 420m route of Moderate standard starts at the bottom left-hand corner of the rocks where a stream emerges from the left-hand gully. It is recommended as a pleasant way onto the summit of the mountain rather than as a rock climb. It gives an excellent winter route of Grade III standard.

Between the Fionn and Fada cliffs, rather nearer the western end, is *Marathon Ridge*. This is the first on the left of two prominent buttresses to the south-east of the spur forming the higher part of the cliffs, and in a straight line between the summit of Beinn Lair and that of Beinn Tharsuinn Chaol. To the left is a thin buttress, *Olympus*. The highest buttress visible from the head of the loch, distinguished by a large steep ridge in its upper section is *Stag Buttress*. Two clean buttresses come low down near the head of Loch Fada, the right-hand one is *Falstaff*, the left-hand one is *Sesame*. Climbs there are Severe and Very Severe. The distinctive rock tower high up on the slopes above the upper part of Lochan Fada is *The Keep*.

Enjoyable climbing on excellent rock is found on Craig na Gaorach (grid reference 972 747) below the Fionn Loch cliff. There are two buttresses, *West Buttress* and *Nannygoat Buttress,* with a smaller buttress between, and below the col there is a second small buttress. Little Crag (grid reference 970 753) lies above the path junction at the south-west corner of Fionn Loch. *Ghost Slabs* (grid reference 977

Looking south-east from the foot of Carnmore Crag to Dubh Loch and A'Mhaighdean, whose summit is just hidden by cloud

756) lies to the east of the causeway between Dubh Loch and Fionn Loch. There are three recorded routes of Very Severe standard.

The two crags on Beinn a'Chaisgein Mor at the end of Fionn Loch, Carnmore Crag and Torr na h'Iolaire, give close on a hundred routes of varying standard and character. Detailed descriptions of these cannot be attempted here.

Carnmore Crag has some exceptionally fine routes. *Fionn Buttress* (225m, Very Severe) is considered to be one of the finest climbs in Scotland. The route is on the great central nose of the crag which is one of its prominent features. It is steep and exposed, the rock is perfect and the interest is sustained. *Dragon*, one of the classic routes on the Upper Wall of the crag, is found to be very steep and in places overhanging with great exposure. This 100m route is graded Hard Very Severe. On the Lower Wall, *Black Mischief* is a fine route (130m, Very Severe). *Carnmore Corner* (65m, Very Severe) is a prominent feature on the steep upper section, considered one of the hardest routes on the crag.

The great rocky tower of Torr na h'Iolaire falls south and west from the summit of Sgurr na Laocainn. The rock is well-broken by terraces and many of the original routes find their way up several or all of the rock tiers thus formed. This adds to the difficulty of detailed descriptions. An excellent introduction is *Ipswich Rib* (375m,

Very Difficult) the longest climb on the crag, well defined on the Lower Wall followed by easier ground to the foot of the Upper Summit Buttress which it climbs. The nature of the crag makes possible other similar combinations. A recommended route on the Upper Buttress is *Hieroglyphics* (130m, Very Severe) which gives a fine variety of climbing.

The four sandstone buttresses on the south-west flank of the north-west ridge of A'Mhaighdean are best approached by contouring round below the ridge. There is no climb on the first butress. The second one is *Breccia Buttress* on which *Conglomerate Arete* (90m, Very Difficult) starts from the right-hand corner.The third buttress is *Red Slab* which is identified by a single sheet of slab ending in a steep wall on the right. A huge pinnacle lying against the lower left-hand corner forms a small subsidiary buttress. There are two routes there of 90m, Difficult and Very Difficult. *Gritstone Buttress* has three routes of Severe standard. There are two longer routes to the right of this on the left of West Gully – *Whitbread's Aiguille* and *Vole Buttress*. The prominent gully to the left of West Gully is a winter route – *Ermine Gully* (300m, Grade III). *Octave Ribs* are on the upper of two bands of coarsely crystalline rock which slants across the Dubh Loch face under the sandstone cap. There are routes of Mild Severe standard on ribs four and five.

The best approach to the south-facing *Pillar Buttress* of A'Mhaighdean is from Carnmore. Traverse along the steep side of Dubh Loch and follow the stream up to Gorm Loch Mor, then climb up to the crags from the shore of the loch. The true nose of the buttress gives a 150m route of Difficult climbing, finishing at the summit cairn. *The Slot* (180m, Mild Severe) follows a straight natural line which starts a few metres to the right of Pillar Buttress route at a deep-cut chimney, then continues to the left of the true crest as a line of chimneys and cracks. An earlier route there was *Triple Cracks Route* (120m, Very Difficult). There are two routes of Severe standard on the west face of the Pillar Buttress.

The original route on the Coire nan Clach cliffs of Beinn Dearg Mor was on the South Peak, a climb on the left-hand mass of the corrie wall of a Moderate scrambling nature. Most of the subsequent climbing has been done in winter conditions. The narrow gully first on the left in Coire nan Clach is *Twisting Gully*. This finishes at a fierce-looking notch in the skyline well below the South Peak. The gully to the right of this was also climbed (Difficult). The whole of this east face of the corrie is somewhat broken and although impressive from below, the general angle is easy.

South of the east face there are broken craggy slopes leading to a very slender buttress, *Flake Buttress* (but also known as *Book-end Buttress*). It is cut on both sides by deep gullies. The left-hand one gives a loose and vegetated route of Difficult standard. The east and west walls of the buttress are vertical and Flake Buttress itself gives one of the best routes on Beinn Dearg Mor, (105m, Severe). The *Central Buttress* which lies to the right of this also gives a Severe climb. The left wall of this buttress comprises numerous snow fields in winter separated by short vertical walls. A climb there is *Left Flank* (240m, Grade II).

Central Buttress is bounded on the right by *Trident Gully*, almost 300m long, the lower half being steep snow in winter and scree in summer. The gully forks 90m up, the right branch being the main gully while the left branch is a chimney between the top of Trident Gully wall and a slender buttress, *Tower Buttress*. About 150m up the Trident Gully above the first fork is the triple fork which gives it its name. All three branches are of equal size, the summit of Beinn Dearg Mor lying between the central and right-hand branches. *Left Branch* has a pitch at the bottom but above that it is easy; the *Central Branch* is similar; the *Right Branch* appears harder. The narrow buttress to the right of Central Buttress has been climbed. To the west of this is the more broken *Wedge Buttress*.

Toll an Lochain, the southern of the twin corries on the east side of An Teallach, has little continuity on its sandstone tiers. Its climbing potential is chiefly in winter in the long gullies which drop from the ridge. The prominent gully which reaches the col between Sgurr Fiona and Lord Berkeley's Seat is known as *Lord's Gully*. The rock here is clean and sound and the gully is sheltered even in bad conditions. The summer route follows the line of the watercourse over many pitches, one of which near the top is Severe. Winter routes there are Grade II. Ling and Glover's early route which goes from the edge of Loch Toll an Lochain direct to the summit of Corrag Bhuidhe Buttress is of an indeterminate nature whose difficulties can all be avoided. The long shallow couloir on the right of the buttress occupying the angle between the prominent shoulder and the main crags of Corrag Bhuidhe is *Constabulary Couloir*. It is a snow ribbon throughout most winters and is one of the few consistent winter lines on the mountain. The only real pitch is an easy avoidable lower ice-fall, but the gully should certainly not be treated as a route of descent. A 450m Grade III/IV route on the main face of Corrag Bhuidhe is identified by a snow patch, *The Triangle*, set above a rock barrier. Above this a rightward sloping ramp reaches the crest of the buttress immediately left of Lord Berkeley's Seat. A grade II gully climb, *Lady Gully*, starts at the apex of The Triangle and bears left.

The south-east corner of Glas Tholl contains a number of buttresses separated by steep gullies. *Hayfork Gully* divides the largest of the buttresses - South Crag on its left and Central Buttress on its right. This was the first climb in the corrie. It also gives a winter route. The gullies form a set of vertical prongs towards the left of the cliff. The fourth prong from the left is the steepest of these. *Checkmate Gully* (210m, Grade IV) gives a fine winter climb following the long chimney on the back wall of the corrie. It is the first obvious major line to the left of the easy slopes at the back of the corrie and is frequently in good condition.

There are two fine crags near the roadside to the west of Dundonnell at Gruinard Bay. *Gruinard Jetty Buttress* (grid reference 961 927) and *Goat Crag* (grid reference 962 920) have between them over fifty short climbs varying from Difficult to Very Severe standard on clean gneiss.

CHAPTER 14

The Fannich Forest

MAPS: Ordnance Survey   1:50,000   Sheets 19, 20 and 25
          Bartholomew   1:100,000   Sheets 54, 55 and 58

PRINCIPAL HILLS

A'Chailleach	997m	136 714
Sgurr Breac	999m	158 711
Meall a'Chrasgaidh	934m	184 733
Sgurr nan Clach Geala	1093m	184 715
Sgur nan Each	922m	184 697
Sgurr Mor	1110m	203 718
Meall Gorm	949m	222 696
An Coileachan	923m	241 680
Beinn Liath Mhor Fannaich	953m	219 724
Beinn Liath Mhor a'		
Ghiubhais Li	766m	281 713
Fionn Bheinn	933m	147 621

The Fannaichs form an exceptionally fine cluster of high mountains contained within a well-defined triangle which fans out southwards from Braemore Junction on the Ullapool/Dundonnell road towards Strath Bran and the Kyle of Lochalsh railway line. This particular area of Wester Ross is exclusively deer forest and within its boundaries is completely uninhabited. The only two communities of any size are found at either corner of the base line formed by the railway through the Strath Bran. At the east end lies Garve with its road junction to the north; to the west Achnasheen has importance as a rail stop and road junction. The Kyle Line is a considerable tourist attraction and an important service link to the scattered houses along its route. It still manages to exist despite frequent attempts at closure, probably surviving under the protection of the Brahan Seer who predicted its building almost four centuries before. He forecast that "every stream shall have its bridge, balls of fire will pass rapidly up and down Strath Peffer and carriages without horses shall leave Dingwall to cross the country from sea to sea". A fair description of what came to pass.

Loch Fannich, a twelve kilometre stretch of water which is partially man-made, runs parallel to the base of the area three kilometres north of Strath Bran, and is

Looking across Loch Fannich to Sgurr nan Clach Geala (centre) and Sgurr Mor (right)

seen to be the most significant natural feature of the area. Its central position affects the pattern of land use and mountain access. Fannich Lodge on its north shore is the only regularly occupied building to be found in the interior. Aultdearg at the east end of the loch (grid reference 289 653) is intermittently occupied by an estate stalker; the cottage at the west end of Loch Fannich on the through path to Loch a'Bhraoin, The Nest (grid reference 164 678) was used by Lochrosque estate during the stalking season and at other times by hillwalkers, but it was recently gutted by fire and almost totally destroyed.

Loch Fannich is undoubtedly one of the least frequented of the great freshwater lochs of the north. In the past it was the natural drainage basin for the surrounding hills and was much acclaimed for the quality of its trout fishing. With the building of the dam at the east end, the water level rose considerably, but the overall area of the loch did not increase in proportion. Cabuie Lodge, which previously stood at the west end beneath the ridge of An Sguman at the mouth of the Nest of Fannich, was dismantled in anticipation of submersion. In fact this never happened, and although the loch can certainly experience extremely wild conditions of high wave and wind, the level never lapped the site of the old shoooting lodge. The water from Loch Fannich now supplies the power station at Grudie Bridge via pipe line and tunnel leading over six kilometres through the hills, and accounts for a high percentage of the power produced by the Conon Valley Scheme.

Loch Fannich gives a perspective to the landscape. Along the south shore, the smaller more rounded hills rise westwards onto Fionn Bheinn, the solitary Munro, which presents its most interesting profile to this side. The more impressive outline of Slioch fills the skyline beyond the west end of the loch along the border with Torridon. The main ridge of the Fannaichs opens out above the north shore in a succession of great corries, each one progressively deeper, until eventually at the western end the mountains divide, the narrow line of a pass disappearing towards the north. The view across into these very secluded corries from the Strath Bran hills on the south side is remarkably fine. In winter the sharp lines of the inner buttreses and the clearly etched curving ridge line is an unforgettable picture. This is undoubtedly the finest side of the Fannaich mountains.

Seen from the north-east side, the main ridge becomes rather undulating, the line of rounded tops giving little impression of their true height. The one break in the symmetry is at the north end, where Sgurr Mor stands out like some gigantic pixie's hat above Braemore. Open moorland stretches in from the road along the whole of this side of the mountains, making for rather uninteresting long approaches and rough walking. Like the rest of the Fannaichs, the landscape is virtually treeless. The streams drain into Loch Droma and Loch Glascarnoch as part of the Conon Valley power scheme; Loch Glascarnoch is an artificial loch and Loch Droma at one time drained naturally towards Loch Broom. The top of the Loch Droma dam which diverts the direction of flow provides a good start towards the mountains.

In the past, the Fannaichs were considered to be a fine high-level walking area, with little else to offer. This has long been disproved, and it is now accepted as a fine all-round mountaineering area, offering testing ridge walks, summer and winter climbing and the opportunity for high quality ski-mountaineering expeditions.

ACCESS

The A835 road from Dingwall to Ullapool via Garve and Gorstan Junction passes along the north-east side of the mountains over the Dirrie More between Loch Glascarnoch and Loch Droma. The A832 road branches west towards Dundonnell and Gairloch at Braemore Junction. The five kilometre stretch of road between there and Loch a'Bhraoin gives a direct approach to the mountains on their north-west side.

The A832 road from the east coast branches west at Gorstan and follows the railway line towards Achnasheen and the west along the base of the Fannaichs. A private road leaves the main road just east of the power station at Grudie Bridge (grid reference 312 626). This winds in through deer forest for six kilometres to the infill dam at the east end of Loch Fannich, then on for another six kilometres to Fannich Lodge. The gate at the road end is locked and access can be obtained by contacting the various estate stalkers, not the Power Station. These are: The head stalker at Fannich Lodge; the head stalker of Lochluichart estate at Grudie Bridge

Cottage; the head stalker at Strath Bran Lodge. There is an additional gate beyond the dam on the road towards Fannich Lodge which may be locked, contact Fannich Lodge for access there.

Twelve kilometres to the west of Grudie Bridge, another private vehicle track, the Cabuie track, crosses over towards Loch Fannich (grid reference 198599). It runs slightly west of the line of the old right of way which it eventually joins 800 metres south of the loch and it has limited use for approaching the east side of Fionn Bheinn and the west end of Loch Fannich. The gate at the start of the track on the A832 is normally locked and information regarding its use can be obtained from the head stalker of Lochrosque estate at Achnasheen

PUBLIC TRANSPORT

Rail: There is a daily passenger rail service from Inverness to Kyle of Lochalsh with stops at Garve, Achanalt and Achnasheen.

Bus: Ullapool – Braemore – Dirrie More – Aultguish – Garbat – Garve – Inverness. Mondays, Fridays and Saturdays. All Year.
Gairloch – Braemore – Dirrie More – Aultguish – Garbat – Garve – Inverness. Mondays, Fridays and Saturdays. All Year.
Poolewe – Achnasheen – Grudie – Lochluichart – Inverness. Tuesdays, Thursdays and Fridays. All Year.
These three services are operated by MacKenzie and MacLennan, Gairloch.

ACCOMMODATION

There are hotels at Garve, Aultguish, Inchbae, Leckmelm, Ullapool and Achnasheen. Bed and breakfast accommodation can be found at most of the houses around the perimeter. The Scottish Youth Hostels Association has a hostel at Ullapool which is open from March to October. Bothy accommodation could previously be found at the west end of Loch Fannich at The Nest cottage, eight kilometres beyond Fannich Lodge on the north shore and the end of the hill path to Loch a'Bhraoin (grid reference 164 678). It should be noted that this is no longer available because of fire damage. The bothy at the west end of Loch a'Bhraoin (grid reference 117 734) is Lochivroan. It is used by Lochbroom estate stalkers and shepherds and is not usually locked. Enquiries regarding its use should be directed to the estate proprietors at Lochbroom Lodge.

THE HILLS

The main ridge of the Fannaich mountains rises along the north shore of Loch Fannich on the east side of the track which leads across from The Nest to Loch a'Bhraoin. It consists of ten tops over 914m, seven of which form the spine of a

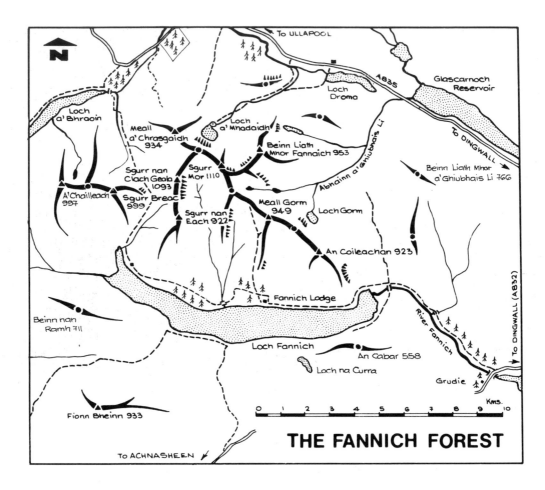

THE FANNICH FOREST

continuous chain (with short side ridges) stretching north-west from the east end of Loch Fannich for thirteen kilometres to the A832 road south-west of Braemore Junction. From north to south these are:

Meall a'Chrasgaidh	*(hill of the crossing)*	(934m)
Carn na Criche	*(boundary hill)*	(961m)
Sgurr Mor	*(big peak)*	(1110m)
Meall nam Peithirean	*(hill of the thunderbolt)*	(971m)
Meall Gorm West Top	*(blue hill)*	(949m)
Meall Gorm East Top		(922m)
An Coileachan	*(the cockerel)*	(923m)

From Carn na Criche, a side ridge reaches four kilometres south-west towards the north-west end of Loch Fannich and crosses two of the other summits:

Sgurr nan Clach Geala	*(peak of the white stones)*	(1093m)
Sgurr nan Each	*(peak of the horses)*	(922m)

The Fannaichs from Dirrie More; Sgurr Mor in the centre, and Beinn Liath Mhor Fannaich on the left

From Sgurr Mor, a short ridge to the north-east passes over the remaining Munro in this group:

Beinn Liath Mhor Fannaich *(big grey hill of Fannich)* (953m)

The mountains are seldom climbed individually, the nature of the area makes it more practicable to combine the ascent of two or three summits to give a full day's hillwalking. Routes described are open to variation in respect of groupings of mountains and of starting points.

Meall Gorm *(blue hill)* (949m)
An Coileachan *(the cockerel)* (923m)

These two mountains form the south-east end of the main Fannaich ridge. When seen from the south-east the view is dominated by Garbh Choire Mor. The massive rocky corrie opens to the east below the narrow south-east spur which An Coileachan sends out towards Loch Fannich dam. This is an impressive corner, with steep overlapping slabs and deeply-cut gullies and the heathery slopes on either side slanting deceptively onto rocky ground below. Surprisingly the two mountains hold no other difficulty, and they can be climbed easily either from the south or from the north-east.

The approach from the north-east starts at the bridge over the Abhainn an Torrain Duibh on the A835 road just west of Loch Glascarnoch. The river is followed upstream by a rough path on its west side. Cross the Allt an Loch Sgeirich and then continue south-west along the north side of the Abhainn a'Ghiubhais Li to a recently built footbridge over the stream at grid reference 254 713. Continue up the south side of the glen along an ill-defined path until after crossing the outflow of Loch Gorm the path improves and climbs more steeply in zig-zags past Loch an Eilein to reach the flat top of Meall Gorm at a large stone-built stalker's shelter. The summit of Meall Gorm is about 200 metres to the west of this along the broad mossy ridge. Alternatively one can follow the Abhainn a' Ghiubhais Li past Loch Li towards Loch an Fhuar Thuill Mhoir. From the lip of the little upper corrie which holds this lochan climb south-south-west onto the col to the west of Creachan Rairigidh. (The route to Meall nam Peithirean and Sgurr Mor lies north-west from there). The way to Meall Gorm follows the stalker's path south-east to the junction on the col (836m) then continues more steeply for another 400 metres onto the summit. Continue east past the shelter to the south-east top of Meall Gorm and descend south-east around the head of Coire Riabhach to a broad grassy col. An easy rise lies ahead which swings to the south for the final 150 metres to the summit cairn of An Coileachan. From there descend north past Gorm Loch to the bridge over the Abhainn a' Ghiubhais Li. An alternative is to continue 300 metres south-east from the summit of An Coileachan down on to the flat crest of the narrow shoulder which leads towards the north side of Garbh Coire Mor. Bear east, descending steep slopes of heathery steps and keeping well north of the edge of the corrie.The lower ground gives rough walking across moorland to gain a stalker's path from Loch Fannich. This follows the west side of the Allt a' Choin Idhir northwards onto the flat top above its source (600m). Descend the slopes on the north side for 300 metres to reach the Abhainn a'Ghiubhais Li and the outward route.

If permission is obtained to drive to Fannich Lodge, the ascent of these mountains from Loch Fannich is much easier. An excellent stalker's path starts in the trees just east of the Lodge and can be easily followed up the south ridge of Meall Gorm. The path divides on the steep upper section of the ridge, the left branch going almost horizontally across the south-west face of Meall Gorm to the col (836m) south-east of Creachan Rairigidh. The right branch continues by well-cairned zig-zags to reach the shelter on the crest of the ridge east of the summit of Meall Gorm. The return to Fannich Lodge from An Coileachan is down the easy south-west shoulder.

Meall a'Chrasgaidh (*hill of the crossing*) (934m)
Sgurr Mor (*big peak*) (1110m)
Beinn Liath Mhor Fannaich (*big grey hill of Fannich*) (953m)

The starting point for the traverse of these three mountains is Lochdrum on the A835 road at the west end of Loch Droma. Cross the dam and follow the private road westwards along the pipeline for two kilometres to the bridge across the Allt

The summit ridge of Sgurr Mor

a'Mhadaidh. The road follows the north side of the stream for another two kilometres then ends. Cross the stream and follow a narrow path to the outflow of Loch a'Mhadaidh. The path is faint in places and the ground around there gives rough walking. Climb west onto the north-east ridge of Meall a'Chrasgaidh and join a stalker's path from Creag Raineach Mor which starts at Braemore Junction. This makes a rising traverse across the east face of Meall a'Chrasgaidh to reach the col (cairn) half a kilometre south-east of its summit. From there an easy climb is made on smooth broad slopes.

Return to the col and follow the broad ridge easily to the south-east to Carn na Criche (961m). The route dips slightly to the south-east then winds steeply up the boulder strewn slopes on the north-west ridge of Sgurr Mor to the large summit cairn perched close to the edge of the precipitous north-east face. In bad visibility great care is required there. Descend the main ridge south-east for a short distance then turn east on the ridge leading to Beinn Liath Mhor Fannaich. The north side of the ridge is very steep and care is required in selection of line in bad visibility. A path is joined on the col lower down and this is followed easily on the stony slopes leading to the flat summit of Beinn Liath Mhor Fannaich. Descend the grassy corrie on the north-east side towards Loch Sgeireach. This is pleasant at first but becomes rougher towards the north-west end of the loch. From there continue northwards down rough heathery slopes to rejoin the private road at the small barrage on the Allt a'Mhadaidh.

Sgurr nan Clach Geala (*peak of the white stones*) (1093m)
Sgurr nan Each (*peak of the horses*) (922m)

These two mountains form the side ridge which swings south-west from the main Fannaich ridge just west of Carn na Criche. Along with Meall a'Chrasgaidh, they can be climbed easily from Loch a'Bhraoin. Leave the A832 road from Braemore to Dundonnell at the start of the private road to Loch a'Bhraoin (grid reference 162 761). Cross the footbridge at the outflow of the loch and follow the stalker's path south along the Allt Breabaig (unnamed on the Ordnance Survey 1:50,000 map), crossing the stream one kilometre from the start and continuing along the east side to the bealach (550m) at the head of the glen. Climb the easy grassy slopes on the east to the col (Cadha na Guite) north of Sgurr nan Each and follow the ridge southwards onto the summit. Two small corries lie to either side of this ridge, with steep crags dropping to the east into Coire Mhoir. Return to the col and climb the uniform grassy slope northwards onto the short level summit ridge of Sgurr nan Clach Geala. This is undoubtedly the finest of the mountains of Fannaich. The high hanging corrie and the steep buttresses below and north-east of the summit present a magnificent backdrop along the west side of the head of Coire Mhoir. The buttresses give the finest rock climbing in the Fannaichs. Descend the graceful narrow curve of the north-east ridge to the wide grassy col below. This is Am Biachdaich (*the place of the fattening*); its rich grazing attracts large herds of red deer from the lower ground throughout the summer. Continue north past the lochan on the broad grassy saddle to climb Carn na Criche and then Meall a'Chrasgaidh, descending easy grassy slopes north-west to rejoin the outward path to Loch a'Bhraoin.

A'Chailleach (*the old woman*) (997m)
Toman Coinich (*little mossy hill*) (993m)
Sgurr Breac (*speckled peak*) (999m)

These mountains lie on the west side of the path from Loch Fannich to Loch a'Bhraoin. They form a continuous ridge which extends westwards from Sgurr Breac over Toman Coinich (unnamed on the Ordnance Survey 1:50,000 map) onto A'Chailleach, a distance of two kilometres. To the south, this ridge sends steep slopes down into the Nest of Fannich, the long U-shaped corrie which opens out onto the west end of Loch Fannich. To the north side, two spurs enclose the rugged corrie of Loch Toll an Lochain; these are Sron na Goibhre and Druim Reidh. The ridge is connected to the main Fannaich ridge at its eastern end. A bealach (550m) which is crossed by the path between Loch Fannich and Loch a'Bhraoin links the narrow south-east ridge of Sgurr Breac to the south-west flank of Sgurr nan Clach Geala. This bealach is seldom used to combine the ascent of the mountains on the west with any of those on the main ridge to the east. The amount of descent and reascent involved is unappealing to most hillwalkers.

The mountains are most easily approached from Loch a'Bhraoin by the private road already described. Cross the footbridge at the outflow of the loch and follow the stalker's path south-east for a short distance before climbing south-west on steep grassy slopes to reach the broad lower shelf of Druim Reidh. Continue south along the grassy ridge which leads easily onto Toman Coinich, the central top. From there descend south-east and climb the west ridge of Sgurr Breac then return to Toman Coinich and descend west-south-west to a col (810m). There are steep grassy slopes on the south side of the broad ridge, the north side in contrast has steep crags. The summit of A'Chailleach lies to the west and is reached just beyond the junction of its east and north ridges.

The descent from A'Chailleach can be made down the Sron na Goibhre ridge bearing steeply down towards the stream which flows from Toll an Lochain, avoiding the outcrops at the north end of Sron na Goibre. The stream is crossed after a few hundred metres and the east bank followed to the mouth of the corrie. A diagonal descent to the north-east across the grassy north end of Druim Reidh leads to the footbridge at Loch a'Bhroain.

Bheinn Liath Mhor a'Ghiubhais Li *(big grey hill of the coloured pines)* (766m)

This rounded top lies close to the roadside at the north-west end of Loch Glascarnoch and is easily climbed from any convenient starting point between the plantation at the end of the loch and the bridge over the Abhainn an Torrain Duibh. Its status as a Corbett now attracts an interest which was previously absent. The view from the flat, stony summit is surprisingly fine, giving some unusual angles along the main Fannaich ridge and across to the north onto the mountains of the Beinn Dearg group. The name of this mountain is rather intriguing; there is not a tree in sight.

Fionn Bheinn *(light-coloured hill)* (933m)

Fionn Bheinn is the only mountain of the Fannaich group to lie south of Loch Fannich. It rises directly from the north side of the A832 road just opposite the railway station at Achnasheen. A gate beyond the stalker's house (grid reference 162 586) leads across parkland towards an obvious water course which gives a steep grassy climb onto a flat plateau. The summit can be climbed any way from there on. It is probably more interesting to follow the broad ridge which runs up onto Creagan nan Laogh, a grassy spur which pushes out to the south of the summit ridge itself. From there a broad col leads easily onto the summit of Fionn Bheinn in just over one kilometre. This south side of the mountain is uniformly rounded, with short heather and moss stretching right onto the top. The two wide corries which are the redeeming features of the north-east side of the mountain – Toll Mor and Toll Beag – fall steeply from the summit towards Loch Fannich, but are virtually unbroken.

Fionn Bheinn improves considerably given snow, the nature of the slopes making for good ski-mountaineering. It is interesting to note that the mountain receives a mention in the prophecies of the Brahan Seer, the famous soothsayer of the 17th century; he predicted that " the day will come when a raven, attired in plaid and bonnet, will drink his fill of human blood on Fionn Bheinn, three times a day, for three successive days". There are no reports of sightings to date.

PATHS AND WALKS

There are two main rights of way through the centre of the Fannaich mountains which offer good long walking routes.

Grudie to Loch a'Bhroain. The start of the route from Grudie Bridge on the A832 road to the west end of Loch Fannich has already been described. The locked gate there has a pedestrian stile. The private road follows the north-east side of the River Grudie to the east end of Loch Fannich and forks at the bridge one kilometre to the east of the dam. The right of way keeps to the north shore of the loch to pass Fannich Lodge, skirting the foot of the main Fannaich ridge throughout. The vehicle track ends at the site of the Nest cottage at the north-west end of Loch Fannich, the right of way continues as a path to a footbridge over the Allt Leac a'Bhealaich, which is followed to the head of the pass between Sgurr Breac and Sgurr nan Clach Geala (550m). From there the path continues down the east side of the Allt Breabaig (unnamed on the Ordnance Survey 1:50,000 map) to the bridge at the east end of Loch a'Bhraoin and the track which leads out to the Dundonnell road (A832). (32 kilometres).

Strath Bran to Kinlochewe via Loch Fannich. Follow the Cabuie track which has been previously described to the south side of Loch Fannich. The landrover track swings west from the small boathouse at the lochside and continues for two kilometres to a bridge (grid reference 180 651). There is a choice of routes from there, running parallel and both rights of way. The main landrover track continues to follow the pipeline through Srath Chrombuill, skirting Fionn Bheinn at its north-west end to reach a dam on the Allt a' Chlaiginn. A pathless section for three kilometres leads to Leckie to pick up a good track along the north side of the Abhainn Bruachaig to Kinlochewe via the Heights of Kinlochewe.(25 kilometres).

Strath Bran to Loch a'Bhraoin via Loch Fannich. The previous route is followed to the bridge on the south side of Loch Fannich. An alternative right of way follows the south side of the loch to the north-west as a faint path and crosses the Abhainn a' Chadh Bhuidhe by a rough girder bridge. Follow the pathless shore of Loch Fannich northwards to the Abhainn Nid, crossing the stream inland to the north-west. This can be difficult if the water is high. Turn east for a short distance to join the right of way from Loch Fannich to Loch a'Bhraoin. The middle section of the route has several burn crossings and is best walked in dry weather conditions. (21 kilometres)

Sgurr nan Clach Geala, with the Geala Buttresses directly in front of the summit ridge

CLIMBING

The Geala Buttresses of Sgurr nan Clach Geala are not marked on the Ordnance Survey map; they lie to the north-east of the summit of the mountain, rising 240m above the more broken lower crags. The six narrow buttresses are of mica schist; the summer routes are Severe standard, winter routes are Grade IV and V. The five deep gullies which separate them give superb winter climbing, Grade II up to Grade V. The long rock step which guards the foot of the main cliffs is found to be awkward in winter, and is best breached on the right by a slanting rake which is the recommended approach to all the climbs.

The west face of Beinn Liath Mhor Fannaich has three climbable gullies whose standard varies from Grade II to IV.

Garbh Choire Mor of An Coileachan has produced a deluge of routes of up to 360m, grade IV and V with several shorter routes of 150m, grade II/ III.

The north-east face of Sgurr Mor gives Grade II/III climbs of up to 300m, and some harder routes of Grade IV/V.

CHAPTER 15

Beinn Dearg and Easter Ross

MAPS: Ordnance Survey   1:50,000   Sheets 16, 20 and 21
          Bartholomew   1:100,000   Sheets 54, 55, 58 and 59

PRINCIPAL HILLS

Beinn Dearg	1084m	259 812
Cona'Mheall	978m	275 816
Meall nan Ceapraichean	977m	257 826
Eididh nan Clach Geala	927m	257 843
Beinn Enaiglair	890m	225 805
Iorguill	874m	239 816
Am Faochagach	953m	304 794
Carn Gorm-loch	909m	319 801
Beinn a'Chaisteil	787m	370 801
Meall a'Ghrianain	772m	366 776
Carn Chuinneag	838m	484 833
Seana Bhraigh	926m	282 879
Carn Ban	842m	338 876
Ben Wyvis	1046m	463 684
Little Wyvis	764m	430 645

The mountains described in this chapter all lie to the north and east of the main road from Dingwall to Ullapool – the Dirrie More. The area is seen to cover the whole of the north-eastern part of Ross-shire from coast to coast but the principal mountains are more or less concentrated in the central section. The coastal belt which stretches eastwards from Dingwall along the north shore of the Cromarty Firth is of little importance to the text. This is the most highly populated part of Ross-shire, basically an area of farms and smallholdings, with concentrations of industrial and oil-related communities along the coastline. Dingwall and the immediate hinterland around Strathpeffer have a certain relevance for access, and for onward travel along the south-western border.

In the north-west, the hills of Cromalt, Strath Kanaird and the Rhidorroch Forest rise gradually from the Ullapool/Ledmore road (A835) to form a buffer between the monolithic skyline of Assynt and Coigach and the more compact mass of mountains inland. This is a delightful corner, seldom explored, with lots to offer for those who like trackless walking among remote hills and empty glens. There is a scattering of crofting communities along the roadsides at Strath Kanaird, Knockan and Elphin; inland there are only sheep and deer and hills for as far as the eye can see. There is nothing to attract the rock climber, but there is a wealth of natural interest, and modest ski-touring can be enjoyed most winters. It covers an extensive area between Loch Broom and the head of Strath Oykel and stretches in to the foot of the larger mountain ranges along Glen Einig, Strath Mulzie and Glen Achall, the line of the right of way across the shortest neck of land in Scotland.

The broad valley of Strath Oykel, which carries the River Oykel to the Kyle of Sutherland at the head of the Dornoch Firth, makes a natural boundary along the border of Sutherland on the north-east side. In the past this was the route followed by one of the main drove roads from the north-west and is still the main line of communication from the east coast communities through Bonar Bridge and Ardgay. The salmon rivers which flow into it – Oykel, Cassley, Shin and Carron – are amongst the most famous in the north and play an important part in the local economy. On a more sombre note, this is the route followed by the ill-fated Marquis of Montrose when he fled from his final battlefield at Carbisdale Castle, only to be imprisoned in Ardvreck Castle on the shore of Loch Assynt before being turned over to his eventual execution in Edinburgh. Legend has it that his jewelled orders of chivalry still lie buried there on the ridge above the River Oykel.

From Ardgay, two other straths form a line parallel to Strath Oykel and lead closer to the principal mountains lying to the south-west. These are Strath Carron and Strath Cuileannach; they do not however provide a cross-country motor link to Ullapool and the west. Ardgay can be seen as an important road and rail junction for onward travel in the north, and it is also a busy service village for both locals and visitors. Strath Carron is remarkably well-populated and is the main artery of communication for a whole network of more remote glens which follow the usual pattern of uninhabited deer forest and sporting estate. Strath Carron is important in local sheep breeding circles, as it has been for the last 150 years. This was an area which featured prominently in the Clearances, and witnessed one of the most tragic incidents of those unfortunate times. Croick, at the end of the strath, is the meeting place of the surrounding glens. There in 1845 whole families who were to be evicted to make way for the introduction of sheep spent their last night in the little churchyard before leaving the area for ever. Some scratched their names and pathetic messages on the windows of the church, and these have been preserved to this day.

Before those times Strath Carron and Strath Cuileannach formed an important part of the droving route from Ullapool and Wester Ross and they still open up many possibilities for cross-country walking routes. The smaller mountains are seen to roll westwards from these glens in waves of fairly rounded slopes. The rock formation throughout the area is schist, exposed in places along the maze of side glens to form isolated crags. This is still very much explorer's country, for walker and climber alike.

Beinn Dearg and Cona' Mheall from the Glascarnoch Reservoir

The western boundary, which follows a line from the village of Garve to Ullapool, skirts the foot of the principal mountains. On this side of the area forestry contributes to the local economy and in places considerable plantations of conifers cover the lower slopes of the mountains to break the otherwise empty landscape. This also was an old droving route, the Dirrie More (*the big climb*). Livestock is still transported from the north and the west, but fish lorries now add to the traffic; fish farming and a growing tourist industry both play a big part in the new style economy of the north. Ullapool at the mouth of Loch Broom has been re-generated in recent years. It is the ferry terminal for Stornoway, the base for the huge seasonal fishing fleet from Eastern Europe, the Klondykers, and a very busy tourist centre; a big step up from being the experimental fishing station established 200 years ago on the site of the Viking settlement of Olave's Bol.

ACCESS

The trunk road from Dingwall to Ullapool via Garve and Braemore Junction (A835) gives easy access from the south and west to the majority of the mountains described. The section of the road which continues north to Lochinver is of limited use.

There are restrictions on the use of most of the side roads on the south side of Ullapool. The road from Morefield Bridge towards Loch Achall is certainly a pedestrian right of way, but becomes a private vehicle road. Permission for use past the quarry should be obtained from Rhidorroch Estate. At the head of Loch Broom the Forestry Commossion road at Inverlael has a locked gate and is only of use for hillwalkers. Further south beyond Aultguish Inn, the road along Strath Vaich from the Black Bridge is strictly private. Although there is no gate at the road end, cars should be left there and not taken to the locked gate across the landrover track to Loch Vaich further along the glen. Further information can be obtained from Strathvaich Estate.

On the east side the main trunk road (A9) follows the coastline; a shortcut is provided by the A836 road from Evanton on the Cromarty Firth across the Struie Hill to Ardgay, often closed in winter months. Two side roads should be noted: From Evanton, a road signposted 'Assynt' leads north-westwards from a bridge in the centre of the village for eight kilometres to Eileanach Lodge gate near the end of Loch Glass for the start of a long walk-in over the Ben Wyvis range. On the Struie Hill, the road which goes west through Strath Rusdale does not carry on through for vehicles to Glen Calvie, there is a barrier at Garbhan Mor (grid reference 537 823).

The main road from Ardgay to the west along Strath Oykel (A837) provides a useful start for Strath Mulzie and the mountains around Seana Bhraigh. A motorable track from Oykel Bridge Hotel can be taken as far as Corriemulzie Lodge (ten kilometres). If the gate at the start is locked (possibly during winter) the head stalker can be contacted nearby. The side roads into the heart of the area from Strath Carron have limitations for motor transport, certainly none of these are through routes to the west. The telephone box at The Craigs (grid reference 474 910) fifteen kilometres from Ardgay is the end of most of the good road. The way through Strath Cuileannach goes on for another eight kilometres then becomes a walking route towards Strath Mulzie. The vehicle track to Glen Calvie and Alladale has restrictions. From Glen Calvie Lodge, two kilometres south of The Craigs, there is no further vehicle traffic allowed along the track into Glen Calvie towards Carn Chuinneag. The gate reached one kilometre past the Glen Calvie turn-off towards Alladale Lodge could well be locked during winter months for deer control. The gate at the bridge over the River Carron just before reaching the Lodge is always locked; no cars are allowed on the track through Gleann Mor to Deanich Lodge and Gleann Beag.

PUBLIC TRANSPORT

Rail: There are daily passenger services north from Inverness to Dingwall and Ardgay. There is a passenger service to the west from Dingwall to Garve, The Kyle Line, Mondays to Saturdays.

Bus: Inverness – Dingwall – Strathpeffer – Garve – Ullapool (Scottish Citylink Coaches). Daily.
Inverness – Dingwall – Strathpeffer – Contin – Garve – Braemore – Ullapool. (Rapsons) Mondays to Saturdays.
Inverness – Muir of Ord – Contin – Garve – Braemore – Ullapool – Lochinver. (MacKenzie and MacLennan, Gairloch). Mondays, Fridays and Saturdays.
Ardgay – Bonar Bridge – Invershin – Lairg – Rosehall – Oykel Bridge – Ledmore – Elphin – Lochinver. (Rapsons, Brora). Mondays to Saturdays.

Postbus: Ardgay – Braelangwell – Croick – Glencalvie – Dounie. Mondays to Saturdays. All Year.

ACCOMMODATION

There are hotels at Ullapool, Leckmelm, Aultguish, Inchbae, Garve, Struie, Ardgay, Bonar Bridge, Invershin, Rosehall and Oykel Bridge. There is a wide choice of bed and breakfast accommodation all round the area. The Scottish Youth Hostels Association has hostels at Ullapool and at Carbisdale Castle, both open from March to October. The hostel at Strathpeffer is open all year.

There are four useful bothies in the area which are regularly used. Knockdamph (grid reference 286 954) at the north-east end of Loch an Daimh, between Glen Achall and Strath Mulzie. Permission is not normally required. Corriemor (grid reference 305 888) at the head of Strath Mulzie on the east shore of Loch a'Choire Mhoir is very small and is not suitable for parties of any size. Permission is not usually required, but enquiries should be made to the head stalker, Mr D. Snody, at Oykel Bridge. Alladale (grid reference 426 895) one kilometre west of Alladale Lodge. Permission can be obtained from the head stalker, Mr R. Munro, at Alladale Lodge. Glenbeg (grid reference 313 834) reached by foot from the bridge at Alladale Lodge via Gleann Mor, Deanich Lodge and Gleann Beag. Permission is not normally required. None of these bothies is available during the stalking season – September/October. All four are maintained by the Mountain Bothies Association.

THE HILLS

The majority of the mountains described here are best approached from the west side, taking a direct line in from appropriate points along the A835 road. The exceptions are the mountains at the head of Strath Mulzie, Seana Bhraigh and Carn Ban, and Carn Chuinneag, the Corbett summit at the head of Glen Calvie.

Beinn Dearg (*red hill*) (1084m)
Cona'Mheall (*hill of the dog*) (978m)
Meall nan Ceapraichean (*hill of the stumps or hummocks*) (977m)
Eididh nan Clach Geala (*web of white stones*) (927m)

This compact group of Munros forms a crescent around the upper end of Gleann na Sguaib, which opens onto the head of Loch Broom, ten kilometres south of Ullapool, at Inverlael. Cars should be left by the roadside there, and an obvious vehicle track is taken through the forestry plantation which covers both sides of the mouth of the glen. The prominent gneiss outcrop which guards the south end is Strone Nea (*the nose of the nest*) a haunt of ravens and offering several climbs. The trees continue for two kilometres and tracks inside the plantation can be confusing. The third crossing place over the river leads to the forest edge and both of the main paths which lead into the mountains. The right-hand path follows the north side of the River Lael for six kilometres onto the bealach between Beinn Dearg and Meall nan Ceapraichean – Bealach a'Choire Ghranda. The path leaving the forest to the north of this leads on towards the back of Seana Bhraigh, giving good walking throughout its marked length and a straightforward final section onto the summit ridge of that mountain – a distance of 12 kilometres from the road.

The Gleann na Sguaib path forks at the waterfall, Eas Fionn, two kilometres south-east of the forestry fence. The left-hand path, which is unmarked on the Ordnance Survey map, rises up towards Lochan a'Chnapaich and the bealach between the two Munros on this side of the glen. A route can be made onto the long rather uniform west ridge which leads with little difficulty onto the summit of Eididh nan Clach Geala making up towards a little lochan on the spine of the ridge, then on through the quartzite boulder field which gives the mountain its name. The north-west cairn is the summit. Across the glen, the prospects of Beinn Dearg become progressively much finer. There are broken rocks below the summit above the path along Loch a'Chnapaich, but there is no significant crag; the descent onto the bealach follows an easy grassy slope towards the first of two small lochans (grid reference 265 838). From there the climb onto Meall nan Ceapraichean is steep, but straightforward. Meall nan Ceapraichean has a subsidiary north-east top – Ceann Garbh (967m) – which is unnamed on the Ordnance Survey map. This overlooks Lochan a'Chnapaich and is seen to have several bands of crag along its north face. The ascent from the bealach bypasses these, and then follows a line south-west onto the summit of Ceann Garbh. A broad stony ridge continues south-westwards for another half kilometre onto the summit of Meall nan Ceapraichean.

Beinn Dearg from Coire Ghranda

Ceann Garbh sends a long shoulder out towards the east to another lesser top, Cnap Coire Loch Tuath (885m), a distance of two kilometres. The ridge then continues in an east-northeasterly direction for three kilometres to give an easy line of descent towards Glenbeg bothy, with a final section of walking through unpleasant peat hags. On the south side of the ridge steep craggy slopes drop down towards Loch Tuath and Loch Prille at the head of Coire Lair.

The descent from the summit of Meall nan Ceapraichean is straightforward; a broad slope leads south-eastwards onto the Bealach a'Choire Ghranda with its cluster of tiny lochans. Here one meets the end of the path from Gleann na Sguaib.

To climb Cona'Mheall and return to the bealach is an easy diversion to the east, four kilometres there and back. Regular slopes with short bands of small scree lead up onto the flat topped ridge, with its summit cairn at the north-east end. The ridge narrows considerably towards the south-east to give the mountain a much more distincive character, dropping steeply over broken rock into Coire Lair. The slopes to either side of the ridge are uniformly very steep and craggy; those on the west form one wall of Coire Ghranda (*gloomy corrie*) the other wall being formed by the imposing line of cliffs which are the east face of Beinn Dearg. These rise directly from the west side of Loch a'Choire Ghranda in two tiers: the lower crag is steep and slabby, its upper section broken by grooves and chimneys; the upper crag extends further up the corrie towards the bealach, its steep walls frequently overhung and vegetated. This is certainly the wildest and most striking corner of the whole range.

To savour its full quality, Cona'Mheall is best approached from the south, leaving the A835 road near the south-east end of Loch Droma. A path which is unmarked on the Ordnance Survey map starts some 400 metres from the end of the loch. This leaves the north side of the road by a rather inconspicuous stone causeway across the roadside ditch and climbs to the north-east for a short distance, improving in quality as it climbs uphill. It then swings to the north, descending to a ruined shieling at the north-west corner of Loch a'Gharbhrain. The next section of the way is tedious, but unavoidable and eventually found to be worth the effort. First cross the Allt a'Gharbhrain. This can be difficult to accomplish with dry feet even in normal conditions, in wet weather the river can flood very quickly and in spate conditions it may well be found impassable.

The way north to Loch Coire Lair is virtually trackless across peat and heather. The side of the loch should be left about half way along and a rising traverse is made towards the lip of Coire Ghranda by way of steep grassy ledges and fine exposures of slab. The stream which flows out of the corrie over a succession of slabs is crossed to reach the foot of the rocky south ridge of Cona'Mheall. This gives an enjoyable route onto its crest, but one which requires some experience. The way up the slabby slopes can be well seen during the ascent, but the rock requires care if wet or in descending. Alternative lines can be found with care up the broken slopes within the mouth of the corrie above the north-west side of the loch, through steep heather and rocky outcrops. Once on the crest, pleasant scrambling on steep grass and easy rocks leads to the broader upper ridge and the bouldery summit of Cona'Mheall.

Any descent along the south-west side of the south end of the ridge of Cona'Mheall requires great care, making for the outflow of the stream from the south-east corner of Loch a'Choire Ghranda at the mouth of the corrie. Short exposures of steep rock along the lower section can all be bypassed, but are not readily seen from above. If this is used as an exit route from the mountains, the nature of the six kilometres back along Coire Lair to the roadside at Loch Droma should be remembered – rough and trackless until past the Allt a' Gharbhrain.

Cona'Mheall may be climbed from Loch Droma in conjunction with Beinn Dearg to make an enjoyable circuit of 17 kilometres. On the Bealach a'Choire Ghranda the route up Beinn Dearg is found to be well-marked. A substantial dry-stane dyke climbs directly up the north-east ridge, and its west side is followed onto the dome-like summit plateau. The dyke does not reach the actual summit cairn which lies almost 300 metres south of the angle made where it turns sharply in a north-westerly direction along the edge of the cliffs which form the south side of Gleann na Sguaib. From the summit of Beinn Dearg go east-south-east for half a

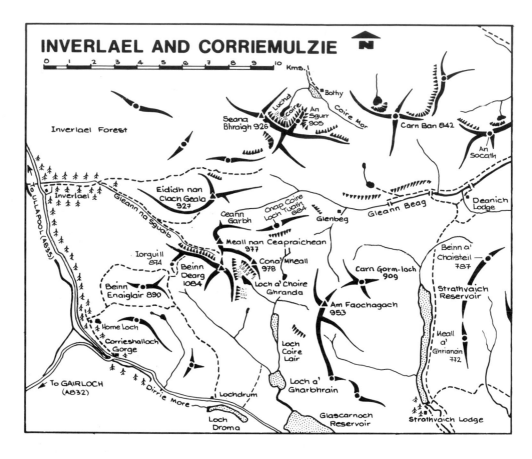

kilometre then turn south-south-east to descend the long ridge which skirts the cliffs along the west side of Coire Ghranda. This requires care in bad visibility. The crags at the south-east end of the ridge above Loch nan Eilean are bypassed on the west side and a steep descent is made south-east towards the crossing place on the Allt a'Gharbhrain and the outward path from Loch Droma.

Other ways off from the summit of Beinn Dearg are possible. The ascent route from the Bealach a'Choire Ghranda may be retraced to join the path down Gleann na Sguaib to Inverlael. As an alternative, the dyke from the summit plateau can be followed north-west for two kilometres to the point where it terminates abruptly against a huge boulder - a useful landmark if climbing up onto the ridge from Gleann na Sguaib by the forestry fence at the east end of the plantation at Inverlael. By either route the distance to the road is just over nine kilometres. In its upper reaches, the dyke passes the top of a prominent wide scree gully which splits the main line of the Gleann na Sguaib crags from the impressive West Buttress of Beinn Dearg. This is the Cadha Amadan, *the fool's pass* (grid reference 249 819); it can be a useful way off the mountain to the north, but one which should be treated cautiously in winter conditions.

Beinn Enaiglair (*hill of the timid birds*) (890m)
Iorguill (*hill of the turmoil or the battle*) (874m)

The ascent of these two mountains makes a splendid expedition starting from Braemore Junction, eight kilometres south of Inverlael. It is worth making a preliminary detour there to see the Falls of Measach in the Corrieshalloch Gorge, a National Trust for Scotland property, which can be reached in minutes from the roadside. The narrow gorge which carries the Abhainn Droma down to join the River Broom is crossed by a suspension bridge giving a spectacular view into the river bed and the 80m cascade of the main fall. Now take the private road through the lodge gates at the road junction and climb up through the forest for one and a half kilometres towards the site of the former Braemore Lodge. A path leaves the track at the side of the only estate building still standing (grid reference 201 790) and passes quickly through trees and dense rhododendrons to open ground beside the Home Loch. A good stalker's path leads north-eastwards for one kilometre then splits to circle Beinn Enaiglair, providing a convenient start for the straightforward ascent of that mountain from any side. There are rocky outcrops along the crest of the north-east spur of the mountain, but these need not offer any problem. It is worth climbing for the view of the Fannaichs alone, which in winter becomes especially fine.

The left-hand branch of the path contours the north side of Beinn Enaiglair for over four kilometres onto the heathery col which joins it with Iorguill, the rounded outlier of the north-west ridge of Beinn Dearg. The path onto Iorguill from the col is unmarked on the 1:50,000 Ordnance Survey map but is easily traced, cairned in places, climbing steadily up the heathery west shoulder onto the flat summit. A continuation north-east from Iorguill for one kilometre around the rim of a wide heathery corrie leads onto the north-west ridge of Beinn Dearg. This is probably the least strenuous approach to Beinn Dearg, certainly as good as the route along Gleann na Sguaib described earlier.

Starting from either Inverlael or Braemore Junction, it becomes perfectly feasible to enjoy an exceptionally fine long hill walk including all of the mountains described. In the event, organisation of transport at either end of the route would be necessary.

Am Faochagach (*whelk shaped hill*) (953m)
Carn Gorm-loch (*hill of the green loch*) (909m)

These two summits lie at the north end of the great range of rounded hills between Coire Lair and Loch Vaich which rises up along the north shore of Loch Glascarnoch and stretches northwards to Gleann Beag. They can be included in a mammoth circuit with the rest of the Beinn Dearg Munros, crossing the head of Coire Lair from Cnap Coire Loch Tuath.

However, the straightforward approach is from the A835 road starting beside the bridge across the Abhainn an Torrain Duibh at the north-west end of Loch Glascarnoch. Whichever line is taken, the ground to the foot of the mountains is flat, but rough and boggy. There is no escaping the necessity for a river crossing; in wet weather this can be a major obstacle. The shortest line is to the end of Loch a'Gharbhrain, crossing the Abhainn a'Gharbhrain where possible then following the line of the Allt na h'Uidhe onto the smooth heathery upper slopes of the main ridge. Once up, the main ridge of Am Faochagach stretches for three kilometres or so without obstacle onto the summit.

Carn Gorm-loch lies one and a half kilometres to the north-east and can be reached by descending to the saddle from which the Allt Glas Toll Beag flows down to Loch Vaich. The use of paths from this side is restricted, and the road along Strath Vaich is closed to cars. To the north side Carn Gorm-loch sends a long shoulder down to the bothy in Gleann Beag – a distance of three kilometres. The views across the inland area here are remarkably revealing and the sensation of remoteness is striking. In winter conditions the outlook becomes spectacular and the mountains assume a much finer and more serious character giving opportunities for ski-mountaineering expeditions.

Seana Bhraigh (*old slope*) (926m)
Carn Ban (*light-coloured hill*) (842m)

Seana Bhraigh can quite feasibly be approached from Inverlael, using the branch of the path from Glensguaib which bears north-east through the end of the plantation and initially climbs east-south-east on the narrow ridge of Druim na Saobhaidhe before rising along the north side of the Gleann a'Mhadaidh and up into Coire an Lochain Sgeirich. The trackless final section requires careful navigation but is not difficult. From the end of the path the way become rough, dropping steeply down through peat hag and hummocks to Loch a'Chadha Dheirg (grid reference 284 858). There are crags above the south bank of the stream flowing into the loch and steep drops from the col on the north side into Cadha Dearg. From the small lochan half a kilometre up to the east-north-east, easier slopes rise north onto the central dome of the mountain (906m) above the south-east corner of Luchd Choire. The summit lies one kilometre to the north-west along the edge of the crags which form the headwall of the corrie. Two spurs push out to the north-east to form the sides of this impressive corrie. The north-west spur rises steeply, but unbroken above Loch Luchd Choire and falls away to the north in broad heathery slopes towards the head of Strath Mulzie; the south-east spur is formed by the narrow rocky ridge of Creag an Duine which rises immediately above Loch a'Choire Mhoir onto the sharply pointed peak of An Sgurr. The east side of An Sgurr is less steep, and easier slopes drop into Feich Coire (unnamed on the Ordnance Survey map) on that side, which in its turn opens out along the south side of Coire Mor. The north side of this long open corrie rises steeply from the bothy at the track end at Loch a'Choire Mhoir onto the north-westerly ridge leading down from the summit of Carn Ban. An ascent of this hill from the bothy has little in the way of difficulty.

Illustrations: (Above) The summit plateau of Seana Bhraigh, looking towards the Coigach peaks.
(Below) The top of An Sgurr at the edge of the Seana Bhraigh plateau

Seana Bhraigh is undoubtedly one of the most remote Munros. The western approach described from Inverlael involves a round trip of over 26 kilometres; an approach from the east is only slightly shorter, but certainly gives a more interesting view of the mountains throughout. Leave the A837 road from Ardgay to Lochinver at Oykel Bridge Hotel. An unsurfaced road follows the south bank of the River Einig for almost seven kilometres to Duag Bridge. The gate at the start has already been noted. The old building at Duag Bridge was once a school, but is now sometimes a hay shed with possibly useful outbuildings. The driveable track continues south-west for three kilometres into Strath Mulzie, following the north bank of the river to Corriemulzie Lodge. This is usually uninhabited during winter months. The track continues for a further three kilometres along the strath and forks. The north branch continues for almost five kilometres to reach the west end of Loch an Daimh; the south branch follows the river for another five kilometres to the outflow of Loch a'Choire Mhoir at the foot of An Sgurr. The track is good throughout its length and has restricted use by estate vehicles. The crossing of the river halfway between the fork and the bothy (grid reference 293 905) only becomes difficult in spate conditions.

This side of the mountain offers many interesting possibilities: an approach on ski can be continued up the north-west spur leading to the summit. The terminal arête of An Sgurr gives a fine scrambling ascent; at close quarters it becomes less formidable, and a line can be taken from the mouth of Luchd Choire on the north-west edge. The only unavoidable difficulties occur on the last 45 metres from the summit tower to the plateau. The winter climbing potential in Luchd Choire is well-known.

Carn Chuinneag (*hill of the churn*) (838m)

This Corbett, which lies on the south side of Glen Diebidale at the head of Glen Calvie, is yet another fairly remote mountain on the east side of the area. It is best approached from Ardgay following the road along Strath Carron for sixteen kilometres to Glen Calvie Lodge. A private estate road carries on south for four kilometres to Diebidale Lodge and the foot of the mountain. A good stalker's path leaves the vehicle track and follows the steep north shoulder onto the summit ridge then eastwards over both tops. Descend easy slopes to the north-east and join the stalker's track at the west end of Loch Chuinneag. Despite its fairly modest height, the twin-topped ridge is a landmark from a remarkable distance, especially in winter. The mountain has good snow-holding potential and gives interesting ski-touring of a moderate nature. The two unbroken corries on the north-west face overlooking Glen Diebidale are reminiscent of the Cairngorms in miniature and give pleasant short ski runs – well worth a visit for the rewarding views into normally hidden corners.

Beinn a'Chaisteal (*castle hill*) (787m)
Meall a'Ghrianain (*sunny hill*) (772m)

These are the highest points on the ridge along the east side of Loch Vaich.They are most easily approached from the road into Strath Vaich already mentioned. The gate across the right of way leading along the east side of the loch is locked for vehicle access. The two hills lie right in the heart of the two deer forests and access is strictly controlled during the stalking seasons. Enquiries should be made during this period at Strathvaich Lodge. The two mountains are gracefully outlined, forming a single ridge which stretches for three kilometres and links the two tops. Both summits are easily climbed from Lubachlaggan on the track along Loch Vaich eight kilometres in from the road end. Stalker's paths on their western flanks greatly facilitate the ascent.

Ben Wyvis (*awesome hill*) (1046m)

Ben Wyvis dominates the landscape as one approaches Ross-shire from the south. It stands apart from the remainder of the mountains in this group, forming a sprawling rounded ridge which stretches for almost seven kilometres from Garbat towards Loch Glass and the lower hills of the Easter Ross peninsula. Seen from most directions it displays no distinguishing feature. The long north-western flank falls in steep unbroken grassy slopes to meet the forests which now skirt the roadside to the north of Garve; the south-eastern face is largely hidden by its own foothills, which stretch round and down towards the shore of the Cromarty Firth. This side of the mountain is split by a series of wide corries, all of which open out to the south-east. The two largest, Coire Mor and Coire na Feola, lie to the north and south of the central eastern spur – An t-Socach (*the beak*) (1007m). These have impressive crags of folded Moine schists along their south sides. A wide grassy corrie opens down from Glas Leathad Beag (928m), the top on the north end of the ridge above Loch Glass. At the south end, An Cabar (*the antler*) (946m) looks down into Coire na Faeraich (unnamed on the Ordnance Survey map), which is currently seen to have considerable possibility for future commercial ski development.

The easiest approach is from Garbat on the A835 road from Garve to Ullapool. The forest has to be negotiated in the first part of the ascent, either by following the path along the north bank of the Allt a'Bhealaich Mhoir from the road just south of Garbat, or by way of one of the Forestry fire breaks which lead in from the fence on the right of the croft buildings on the east side of the road opposite the parking place. Once clear of the tree line, cross open moorland to the foot of An Cabar at the north side of the Bealach Mor, three kilometres from the road. The steep shoulder gives a straightforward ascent onto the summit ridge itself, one kilometre of bare heathery slope offering a variety of path lines to the cairn. The summit ridge stretches out to the north-east for two kilometres onto the main top, Glas Leathad Mor (*big green grassy slope*) (1046m); a broad mossy thoroughfare which gives pleasant easy walking. It is worth making an easy detour for an extra kilometre along the flat spur terminating in An t-Socach; this gives splendid views across to Easter Ross and beyond that across the breadth of the Moray Firth.

Looking north-west from Ben Wyvis to the Glascarnoch Reservoir and An Teallach

Continue for one and a half kilometres to climb onto Tom a'Choinnich (*mossy hillock*) (954m). An undulating ridge swings to the east for three kilometres onto the final Munro – Glas Leathad Beag (unnamed on the Ordnance Survey map). A descent from there towards the end of Loch Glass and the road to Eileanach Lodge and Evanton is only practicable if transport has been organized beforehand. Otherwise return to the summit of Tom a'Choinnich and continue down the steep heathery slopes of the north-west ridge towards Carn Gorm for just over one kilometre onto the saddle. From there descend south-west and follow the Allt na Bana-mhorair for three kilometres across rough open ground to its entry into the forest (grid reference 427 692). A faint path follows the north-west side of the stream for one kilometre to join with a forestry track. This winds down for another kilometre to a gate in the deer fence at the west end of the forest 200 metres north of Garbat. In event of difficulty inside the forest section one should keep to the river course, haphazard detours can lead to confusion among the trees – more frustrating than hazardous.

Care should be taken in winter. Ben Wyvis with its broad summit ridge and open slopes makes a fine introduction to winter walking, but the upper slopes can be prone to avalanche and have already claimed victims.

The approach to Ben Wyvis from Evanton on the A9 road has already been mentioned. Between the main road and Eileanach Bridge the way passes along the

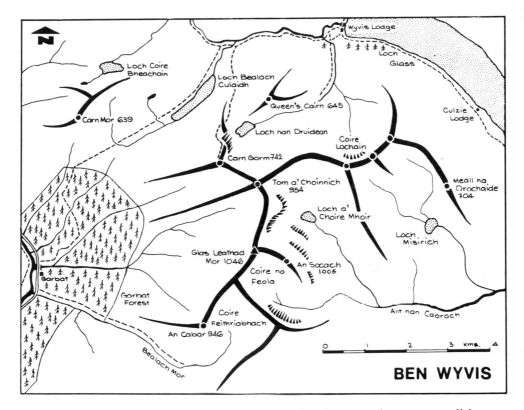

north side of the River Glass through extensive forestry close to a well-known feature of the Easter Ross landscape which is well worth visiting. Leave the road at Assynt House and make for the river bed. At first this seems to have gone underground, but closer inspection will show it running along the foot of a deep, narrow gorge – The Black Rock of Novar – a long chasm which cuts through the Old Red Sandstone for almost two kilometres. The walls drop vertically for almost 40 metres in places, often undercut. A local man from Evanton once jumped across the gorge above a 30m drop; it was subsequently traversed at water level by a group from Ferranti Mountaineering Club. From Eileanach Lodge a long circuitous route leads in towards Ben Wyvis, mainly by way of the course of the Allt nan Caorach. An interesting expedition for a long summer day.

Little Wyvis (764m)

The only redeeming feature of this mountain is its inclusion in Corbett's Tables. Even then it must be the only Corbett which has a vehicle track leading onto its summit. Any ascent from the deer farm entrance at the bridge over the Blackwater River is discouraged by the owner. The most obvious route is by the path leading to the Bealach Mor between Ben Wyvis and Little Wyvis followed by a trudge southwards up open slopes of rough grass and heather onto the flat featureless ridge. A reasonable way to fill a half day.

PATHS AND WALKS

Ullapool to Oykel Bridge via Glen Achall and Glen Einig. From the north side of Ullapool the private estate road is followed along the north shore of Loch Achall for five kilometres to Rhidorroch House. An unsurfaced vehicle track then continues for eight kilometres along the north side of the Rhidorroch River through Glen Achall and swings to the north-east across the mouth of Glen Douchary towards Loch an Daimh. Before it reaches the south-west end of the loch the track forks and a stalker's path loops off to the north. After two hundred metres the track forks again, the right of way descending north-east towards the shore of Loch an Daimh before rising to Knockdamph bothy at the north-east end of the loch. Still as a landrover track, it continues along the north side of the Abhainn Poiblidh for another three kilometres. The path crosses the river one kilometre further on, then follows the south bank of the Rappach Water to the junction with the Corriemulzie track at Duag Bridge. (An alternative avoiding the wet path at the Abhainn Poiblidh crossing starts at the south-west end of Loch an Daimh. Take the track south and keep left at the fork after 250 metres. The way follows the north-east bank of the Allt nan Caorach for one and a half kilometres before swinging east. From the cairned junction (grid reference 277 921) a landrover track is followed through Strath Mulzie to Duag Bridge). From Duag Bridge, the way then follows the south bank of the River Einig to the A837 road at Oykel Bridge Hotel. (30 kilometres).

Duag Bridge to Croick. This was the alternative route taken by drovers to reach Strath Carron and their crossing place at the head of the Kyle of Sutherland. Leave the right of way 1½ kilometres to the east-north-east of Duag Bridge. A link path branches right in an easterly direction then swings south-east to join the track leading to Lubachoinnich at the head of Strath Cuileannach. From there it continues south-east along the north-east side of the river to reach the church at Croick. Transport is necessary at this end. The church is a fine example of an old-style Highland house of worship, designed by Thomas Telford at the beginning of the 19th century, well worth visiting for its unique atmosphere and its poignant memories of the Clearances. (12 kilometres from Duag Bridge to Croick Church).

Strath Vaich to Gleann Beag. The right of way starts at the Black Bridge on the A835 road (grid reference 374 707). A private road goes north-west along the strath for three kilometres. The road continues to Strathvaich Lodge and there is a locked gate on the east side of the the bridge across the Abhainn Srath a'Bhathaich at this turn-off. The right of way continues north for ten kilometres, skirting the east shore of Loch Vaich to its north end, then swinging to the north-east before climbing up round the east side of Meall a'Chaorainn. There it joins the right of way through Gleann Mor to Deanich Lodge from Alladale (ten kilometres). From the junction (grid reference 365 834) the track swings west-north-west to a bridge over the Abhainn a'Ghlinne Bhig (1¼ kilometres), then continues west along the north bank of the river for two kilometres to another crossing where it stops. Glenbeg bothy lies two kilometres to the west. (20 kilometres).

CLIMBING

Strone Nea, at the mouth of Gleann na Sguaib, has several short routes up to Severe standard. The obvious line on the crest of the steep pillar on the left of the main face is *The Shaft* (75m, Very Difficult).

The south side of Gleann na Sguaib is fringed for most of its length by precipitous cliffs. These hold six well-defined gullies, all of which give popular winter routes of up to 240m. The first two gullies are Grade I; the remainder vary from Grade III to IV.

The cliff line terminates in 'an imposing corner tower' on the west of a wide scree gully, the Cadha Amadan. This is the principal feature of the cliffs, giving a fine route 'airy and varied' on good rock, *Tower of Babel* (135m, Very Difficult). The north-west face immediately to the east of Cadha Amadan has two long gully climbs – Grade I/II. Further east the north face contains *West Buttress* (390m, Difficult) on clean rock giving a 'sporting line to the summit of Beinn Dearg'. Various gullies to the east give routes of up to 360m, Grade II to IV.

There are winter routes on the crags of Coire Ghranda on the east side of Beinn Dearg. The lower crag there has Grade III gully climbs (220m). The twisting gully from the summit of Beinn Dearg is *Spaghetti Gully* (Grade I) Summer routes are curtailed by the nature of the crags – steep, dripping walls, frequently overhung and vegetated. The crags on the Cona'Mheall side are drier and more feasible for climbing, but offer little continuity. Most of the routes explored on the series of ribs and faces are about Difficult. There would seem to be winter posibilities in the larger gullics.

The rocks on Seana Bhraigh would seem to hold litle potential; they are mainly of schist, and highly vegetated in summer. There are however extensive winter possibilities there. Despite its low altitude, snow conditions are better than one might expect, and the gullies of Luchd Choire have produced some fine long routes. The main gully climbs lie around the Central Massif of the corrie, routes of 300m up to Grade III. The inner corrie lying to the east of this has several easier lines. The other main feature of the Luchd Choire is *Diamond Buttress*, to the right of the Central Massif. Climbs here are of similar length, but the standard is Grade III to IV. There are easier lines of Grade I to II to the right.

The Alladale Wall (grid reference 375 870), a 250m cliff on the north-east face of An Socach at the head of Glen Alladale, is of steep, smooth-polished glaciated quartzite, giving delicate balance climbing of fine quality, with little in the way of protection. Routes are long, and generally hard.

Gleann Beag Crags, (grid reference 319 848) lie south of Carn Loch Sruban Mora, on the north side of the glen. Also on this side, but one and a half kilometres to the east, is *Niagara Slab*. *Cottage Slab* is on the south side of the glen beyond the Glenbeg bothy. The climbing there is not on the same scale as that at Alladale.

CHAPTER 16

Coigach

MAPS: Ordnance Survey   1:50,000   Sheet 15
           Bartholomew   1:100,000   Sheet 58

PRINCIPAL HILLS

Ben Mor Coigach	743m	094 043
Sgurr an Fhidhleir	705m	094 054
Beinn an Eoin	619m	105 064
Cul Mor	849m	162 119
Cul Beag	769m	140 088
Stac Pollaidh	612m	107 106

Coigach forms a very compact mountain area in the extreme north-west tip of Ross-shire along its boundary with Assynt in Sutherland. The two areas have several marked similarities. The mountains are relatively modest in height; they stand isolated; they are highly individual in character. Along with the neighbouring mountains of Assynt they combine to form a rather unique landscape.

The area is basically a peninsula, jutting out to the north-west onto the blunt sandstone point, lined with cliffs, which stretches from Reiff to Rubha Coigeach. Two thirds of the peninsula is flat moorland; the mountains lie inland along its south-eastern base. From Rubha Coigeach the coastline falls back into Ardmair Bay and the mouth of Strath Kanaird. The attractive little island there is Isle Martin, the property of the Royal Society for the Protection of Birds. St Columba ministered there at one time, and it is thought that the island derives its name from the cleric who built his chapel on the island, having been banished from Iona until such time as he could give proof to the holy saint that he had changed to a more tasteful way of life. Whatever the outcome, he died on the island, and the ruins of the chapel and the graves of his followers are found close to the three cottages still occupied there. Offshore, a sprawl of fish pens detracts somewhat from the tranquility of the setting. Further to the north, the Summer Isles fill the outer bay. These are now inhabited from time to time, but frequently undergo interesting changes in use.

The north coastline of the peninsula curves around Enard Bay towards Inverkirkaig. This was once a thriving crofting community; now both the River Kirkaig and the nearby River Polly have considerable salmon and sea trout hatcheries. The cluster of islands in the bay itself provides nesting grounds for colonies of seabirds, with certain restrictions on visitors during the breeding season.

Cul Mor, Stac Pollaidh and Cul Beag, the three peaks of the Inverpolly National Nature Reserve

The northern half of Coigach forms the Inverpolly National Nature Reserve, the second largest in the country after the Cairngorms. This lies to the north of a line of lochs which interconnect to bisect the area - Loch Lurgainn, Loch Bad a'Ghaill and Loch Osgaig; its own central point is Loch Sionascaig, one of the largest fresh-water lochs in the north. Coigach is formed of some of the oldest rocks in Britain, extremely hard and producing a meagre, infertile soil. Glaciation left a legacy of gouged out hollows, fresh-water lochans and large expanses of bare rock. After the ice-age had played its part, great forests developed, creating a cover which stretched well up the sides of the mountains. Dramatic changes in climate made the next major impact on the vegetation pattern. Wet peat bogs spread upwards to cover many of the lower woods; the upper levels survived. Over the past 1000 years man made his contribution, first by clearing and burning, latterly by excessive grazing. Now only relics of the former forests remain. Regeneration of woodland and re-creation of habitat are two of the most important projects undertaken within the Reserve.

Geology is also of paramount interest. The varied rock exposures along Knockan Cliff on the eastern edge of the Reserve are an important feature, providing a window for the study of the great thrust movements which played a major role in the formation of this rather special landscape. The limestone belt which is found east from there forms an intriguing line of pavement, rich in plant life, caves and impressive sink-holes. The Nature Conservancy Council own this small Knockan section of the Reserve, the remainder is established in agreement with three private estates – Drumrunie, Inverpolly and Eisg-brachaidh. There are resident wardens at Inverpolly and at Knockan Cliff, and a small interpretive visitor centre at Knockan Cliff beside the Nature Trail.

As one would expect, the central part of the area which makes up the bulk of the Reserve is uninhabited. The south-west coastline has the now thriving tourist village of Achiltibuie as the focal point of a scattering of smaller communities. The crofting township of Knockan straddles the Ross/Sutherland border on the north-east corner of the Reserve, and provides a variety of visitor facilities. To the north-west Lochinver is the nearest village of size; to the south a few small crofts lie along Strath Kanaird and Ardmair Bay.

ACCESS

The easiest approach to Coigach is by the road from Ullapool to Ledmore Junction (A835) which continues north to Lochinver and Kylesku. It passes along the south-east edge of the area and the base of the three principal mountains. At Drumrunie, seven kilometres to the north of Ardmair Bay, a secondary road, single track with passing places, branches north-westwards to Achiltibuie, and this provides access to the remaining Coigach hills. It follows a twisting scenic line along the loch-sides between the highly eroded sandstone crags which rise along its route.

At the shepherd's house at Badnagyle, thirteen kilometres from Drumrunie, the road forks. The north branch rises steeply from the end of Loch Bad a' Ghaill, and continues northwards past Inverpolly to Inverkirkaig and Lochinver. This route is equally scenic and twisting, but does not get very close to any of the mountains; however it is useful for walking and fishing expeditions around Loch Sionascaig and the isolated north-west corner of the Reserve. The main branch of the road continues for another five kilometres onto the Achiltibuie peninsula at Achnahaird Bay. Here it loops south-eastward for almost ten kilometres, continuing past the village to the road end at Culnacraig.

PUBLIC TRANSPORT

Bus: Inverness to Ullapool (Scottish Citylink Coaches and Rapsons Coaches). Mondays to Saturdays.
Lochinver to Ullapool via Ledmore and Drumrunie. (Spa Coaches). This is a school bus carrying fare-paying passengers. School days only.
Lochinver – Ullapool – Inverness (MacKenzie and MacLennan, Gairloch). Mondays, Fridays, Saturdays. All Year.

Minibus: Ullapool – Strath Kanaird – Drumrunie – Badnagyle – Achiltibuie.
(J. MacKenzie, Loan, Achiltibuie). Mondays to Saturdays. All Year.

ACCOMMODATION

There are hotels at Achiltibuie, Lochinver, Inchnadamph and Ullapool. There are guesthouses at Knockan, Lochinver and Ullapool. Bed and breakfast accommodation is plentiful all round the perimeter. Bunkhouse accommodation is available at Altandhu, near Reiff, and the Scottish Youth Hostels Association has a hostel at Acheninver, three kilometres south-east of Achiltibuie. This is open from March to September. The hostel at Ullapool is open from Easter to October. There are official camping and caravan sites at Achnahaird, on the road to Altandhu and Reiff, and at Ardmair Point, seven kilometres north of Ullapool.

THE HILLS

The mountains of Coigach are predominantly of well-weathered Torridonian sandstone in various stages of erosion. This reaches its ultimate stage on Stac Pollaidh, that remarkable 'mountain in miniature' which stands out prominently on the skyline to the west. In general, the sandstone is exposed as terraced cliffs facing north and west; the exception is Ben Mor Coigach, which presents its finest features to the north-east and south-west.

Ben Mor Coigach (*big hill of Coigach*) (743m)

This deceptively extensive mountain dominates the north side of Ardmair Bay, nine kilometres beyond Ullapool. From this direction it appears as a continuous line of steep, gully-seamed sandstone, stretching inland for almost three kilometres from Garbh Choireachan at its blunt seaward end to Speicin Coinnich, the shapely rocky point which marks the east end of the ridge. From there, long heathery slopes drop gradually for a further five kilometres towards the road junction at Drumrunie.

The approach to Ben Mor Coigach from the east side is long and rather tedious, but has no difficulty. Leave the A835 road at its highest point, two kilometres to the north of Strath Kanaird, and bear west to cross the River Runie by the newly reconstructed bridge (grid reference 149 036) then follow the line of the Allt a'Phollain Riabhach towards Beinn Tarsuinn, the broken heathery ridge which juts out to the east for more than two kilometres below Speicin Coinnich. A path is eventually found climbing up from the connecting saddle onto the narrow col between Speicin Coinnich and the main ridge of Ben Mor. The first two kilometres from the roadside are wet and boggy, the final section of the path onto the ridge can be difficult in winter; there are steep slopes to the north leading down to Lochan Tuath. A more direct line from the bridge towards the summit of Speicin Coinnich gives interesting scrambling on the rocky upper steps and requires a good head for heights. The distance from the road is six kilometres.

The peaks of Ben Mor Coigach seen from Loch Bad a'Ghaill

The summit ridge of Ben Mor Coigach has an excellent walking surface. The east end is a broad sandstone table, falling steeply along its south side and sending open heathery slopes down to the north. The main top of Ben Mor Coigach stands on a small open plateau which bends out to the north from the main ridge one kilometre west of Speicin Coinnich. From the cairn the line of the remainder of ridge comes into full view, seen narrowing westwards for over a kilometre onto the summit of Garbh Choireachan. The crest becomes a series of delightful small rocky towers all of which can be bypassed on the north, but they are not difficult and are certainly more entertaining if tackled direct. The outlook from the ridge is superb; the mainland hills curve all around in a giant arc; the Western Isles fill the far horizon. If continuing the descent westwards, the outcrops on the west end of Garbh Choireachan are easily negotiated, then make for the top of the deep gorge of the Allt nan Coisiche, above the houses at Culnacraig. Continue due west for another kilometre, descending steep heather to the parking area at the point where the road from Achiltibuie crosses the Allt a'Choire Reidh.

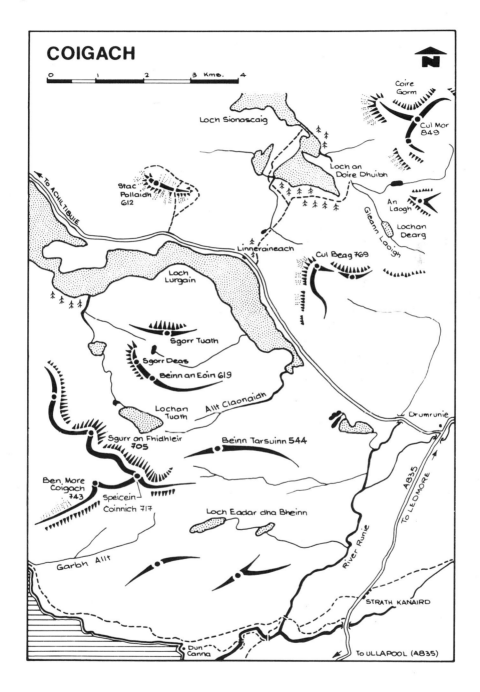

COIGACH

0   1   2   3 Kms.   4

N

Coire Gorm

Cul Mor 849

Loch Sionascaig

Loch an Doire Dhuibh

An Laogh

Stac Pollaidh 612

To ACHILTIBUIE

Gleann Laoigh

Lochan Dearg

Linneraineach

Cul Beag 769

Loch Lurgain

Sgorr Tuath

Sgorr Deas

Beinn an Eoin 619

Lochan Tuath

Allt Claonaidh

Drumrunie

Sgurr an Fhidhleir 705

Beinn Tarsuinn 544

Ben. More Coigach 743

Speicein Coinnich 717

Loch Eadar dha Bheinn

To LEDMORE

A835

River Runie

Garbh Allt

STRATH KANAIRD

Dun Canna

To ULLAPOOL (A835)

Sgurr an Fhidhleir (*peak of the fiddler*) (705m)

The north-east side of the Ben Mor Coigach range is seen as a line of steep broken sandstone split by prominent easy-angled gullies. The dominating feature is Sgurr an Fhidhleir, a forbiddingly steep tooth-shaped peak which dominates the whole mountain on this side and much of the surrounding landscape. From Achiltibuie its presence is not particularly obvious; it rises in a fairly gentle heathery slope to end as just another bump on the undulating line of the ridge above. The car park at Culnacraig makes a good starting point for an easy ascent directly up the heathery slopes contained by the Allt a'Choire Reidh and the Allt nan Coisiche, a distance of three kilometres. The unexpected prospect from the summit cairn is a quite sensational contrast.

The approach from the north-east is of much greater interest. The way is longer and is rougher walking, but in normal conditions has no difficulty. Leave the road from Drumrunie to Achiltibuie two kilometres past the junction (grid reference 145 062). Bear west on an easy line to meet the Allt Claonaidh before it drops more steeply between Cioch Beinn an Eoin and Beinn Tarsuinn, then follow the side of the burn to Lochan Tuath between Ben Mor Coigach and Beinn an Eoin. Sgurr an Fhidhleir becomes progressively more impressive during the four kilometre approach. Go round the south end of the loch and make for the prominent earthy gully which skirts the south face of Sgurr an Fhidhleir; this provides a relatively straightforward but dirty way up onto the level plateau above, from which easy slopes lead onto Ben Mor Coigach and Sgurr an Fhidhleir. From the top of the gully the slopes on either side give firm walking on flat sandstone steps and short heather onto both tops.

A complete circuit of the Coigach ridge is best tackled from Culnacraig. This can reasonably include the two lesser tops which join on to the north-west shoulder of Sgurr an Fhidhleir, Beinn nan Caorach and Cairn Conmheall. A fine expedition for a long day.

Beinn an Eoin (*hill of the bird*) (619m)

This twin-topped hill is the northern outlier of Ben Mor Coigach and displays all of the typical features of Torridonian sandstone on a minor scale. It flings out a long heathery spur towards the south end of Loch Lurgainn ending in a steep craggy bluff, Cioch Beinn an Eoin. This offers the easiest line onto the ridge from the Drumrunie road along the Allt Claonaidh. A gentle traverse up its south side leads directly onto the summit of Sgorr Deas (619m) the south top. This has a craggy west side, but the rock is dirty and vegetated; the view across Lochan Tuath to Sgurr an Fhidhleir is exceptionally revealing. Sgorr Tuath (589m), the north top, has steep ribs towards Loch Lurgainn, but the rock there is also deceptively vegetated and broken. There is an intriguing little gendarme on the broken summit ridge, and the connecting, steeply-sided saddle drops into a miniature lochan-filled hanging corrie. A complete round of the mountain is a delightful six kilometre walk.

Sgurr an Fhidhleir across Lochan Tuath

Cul Mor seen across Loch Veyatie

Cul Mor (*big hill back*) (849m)

Cul Mor fills the north-east corner of Coigach on its boundary with Assynt along Loch Veyatie. Seen from the east, its two quartzite-capped peaks with their smoothly curving connecting saddle, form a most distinctive landmark. To the west, Cul Mor drops in a line of steep muralled sandstone cliffs into Gleann Laoigh (*the glen of the calf*). This lovely secluded glen leads into the heart of the Nature Reserve between Cul Mor and its smaller neighbour to the south-west, Cul Beag. It offers an interesting approach to the foot of both mountains. Sron Gharbh (*the rough nose*) (849m), the highest top, lies on the north side of the mountain above Coire Gorm, a wide deep corrie, circled by crags and hidden from the road. A deep gully formed by a weathered-out dyke drops steeply west from the north-west shoulder of Cul Mor, beyond Coire Gorm; a distinctive rock pinnacle is formed near the point where it meets the ridge. Seen in profile it takes a human shape, Bod a'Mhiotailt (*the old man*). Creag nan Calman (*crag of the dove*) (786m), the south top, rises gently from the connecting saddle and drops steep rocky steps to Lochan Dearg a'Chuil Mhoir in the strange 'lost valley' which is formed with An Laogh (*the calf*) the rocky satellite of the main mountain which curves round the north side of Gleann Laoigh.

Cul Mor is usually climbed from Knockan. Leave the A835 road through the metal gate at the start of a well-used stalker's path close to the Visitor Centre at

Cul Beag and Stac Pollaidh from Knockanrock

Knockan Cliff (grid reference 189 094). This path is followed north for almost two kilometres – rough in places, but good walking – to the foot of Meallan Diomhain, the broad heathery south-east shoulder of Cul Mor; a line of cairns continues for another two kilometres onto an open plateau at the foot of Sron Gharbh. From there the summit cone can be tackled easily from either side. The way across onto the north-east ridge is clearly seen, involving little loss of height, and the slope leads steadily onto the summit along the edge of Coire Gorm. The central approach onto the saddle between Creag nan Calman and Sron Gharbh climbs steeply initially up a rocky watercourse, then keeps to the middle of the wide heathery upper section onto the summit ridge. The ascent of both main tops is then straightforward, the rough sandstone staircases changing suddenly to quartzite just short of the tops. The north-west ridge of Cul Mor is a surprisingly extensive plateau which makes an exceptionally fine viewpoint for the surrounding area. The surface is mainly of rough flat sandstone giving pleasant walking.

Cul Beag (*little hill back*) (769m)

Cul Beag is undoubtedly the most easily accessible of the Coigach mountains. It rises to the north-west from the road junction at Drumrunie as a long heather-covered dip slope for a distance of some four kilometres onto the summit.

It can be climbed from practically any point of the road between Drumrunie and Loch Lurgainn keeping in mind the crags of Creag Dhubh above the south-east end of the loch. An easy line leaves the road shortly after crossing the bridge over the Allt Liathdoire. A rising traverse of the open heathery slopes above the north-east side of the road curves easily round into the broad central corrie on the south-east side of Cul Beag. From the head of the corrie a climb on steep heather from the bed of the Allt Leathad Doire Ruaidhe leads to the little lochan on the saddle between the summit cone of Cul Beag and Meall Dearg, the shapely craggy outlier to the east. From there a steep slog on rather bare heathery slopes leads easily onto the top. From the summit cairn, built on the edge of the steep north-facing slope, the foreground is dominated at first glance by the end-on view of Stac Pollaidh; the remainder of the splendid panorama is taken in later. A way back to the road can be made by way of the steep heather gully leading down just west of the crags of Creag Dhubh.

The north-west side of Cul Beag offers a steeper climb than that from Drumrunie. The slope rises in two sections from the pathside which leaves the road some distance east of the cottage at Linneraineach (grid reference 127 089). A cairn marks the start of the path at the edge of a straggly clump of conifers. The path climbs steeply up north-east and can be left at any point once past the small lochan on the crest. Steep grass and broken crag are negotiated onto the flat top of the first hump, then equally steep, rather bare slopes lead directly to the summit cairn.

Stac Pollaidh (*peak of the peat moss*) (613m)

Despite its modest height, Stac Pollaidh probably attracts more people each year than most other mountains in the north. It is undoubtedly a mountain of special character. The enthusiasm which it arouses amongst climbers, hillwalkers and sightseers alike is both remarkable and yet understandable. The first impression is one of unreality. The summit ridge rises from an encirling apron of steep talus slopes lying at an angle of 45 degress and is an outstanding example of sandstone in the final stages of erosion. The clean rough rock has been highly weathered, sprouting up along the crest of the ridge for 800 metres to form an amazing succession of weird towers and pinnacles interconnected by a maze of narrow gullies, steep slabs and broad ledges, aptly likened to 'a porcupine in a state of extreme irrascibility'.

Its proximity to the roadside along the north shore of Loch Lurgainn greatly facilitates access. Most people start at the carpark on the south side of the road, eight kilometres from Drumrunie. The way up is obvious, towards the saddle near the East Buttress. It is steep and direct, but has little to recommend it. The 'path' is loose and dirty even in dry weather, and becomes a quagmire when wet. It has done nothing to help the already severe erosion problem. Halfway up the slope the way forks. The right-hand line makes for the corner of the East Buttress and improves slightly. A line of cairns is then followed round to the north side of Stac Pollaidh and various paths zig-zag up onto the saddle on the summit ridge. A low

Cul Beag from Stac Pollaidh

level branch skirts the foot of screes to a large cairn beneath the West Buttress, from where a circuit can be completed, picking a way round the west end of the mountain to meet a faint path leading back to the car park.

A slightly longer but definitely more relaxing approach can be made from the house at Linneraineach, one and a half kilometres east of the car park. Cross the stile on the hill fence at the roadside, and take a long slanting line upwards directly to the foot of the East Buttress. Underfoot conditions are good, the gradient easy, the view of the mountain progressively finer, and the time taken is the same. From the foot of the East Buttress a scrambling route onto the top can be made with care, the succession of slabs and ledges is fairly complex and route-finding needs continuous attention to prevent arriving in a 'blind alley'. Horizontal ledges usually offer convenient escape lines towards the north side.

Once on the ridge, the paths to either end are well-defined and countless combinations of walking, scrambling and climbing are possible. Most of the rock problems encountered on the way to the west end of the ridge can be by-passed at lower levels. The final obstacle before reaching the summit is the exception. The small tower which blocks the way to the top of the West Buttress requires definite scrambling and should be treated with care. The drop below the small connecting col to the south side is not immediately obvious, to the north side it can be seen.

In normal weather conditions, routes down from the ridge can be found via most of the gullies on either side. On the south side, the large gully east of the buttress before West Buttress, leads into Pinnacle Basin past some of the mountain's most spectacular features. The resemblances of many these sandstone sculptures are remarkable – *The Sphinx, Tam O'Shanter, Madonna and Child, Lobster Claw, Andy Capp* – the names vary according to the beholder.

A traverse of Stac Pollaidh from west to east is definitely a climbing expedition. The south-west corner of the West Buttress can be climbed above the prominent pinnacle – *The Forefinger* or *Baird's Pinnacle*; the broken nature of the buttress gives a choice of line, the standard is Difficult. The crest of the ridge can be taken by as direct a route as inclination and ability dictate. Needless to say, the views from the ridge in all directions are extensive and superb.

PATHS AND WALKS

Loch Lurgainn to Knockanrock. There is no continuous path across the Inverpolly Nature Reserve, but an obvious line can be followed through Gleann Laoigh to give an exceptionally fine walking route. Start from the roadside at Loch Lurgainn and ascend the path which leads in towards Cul Beag. This is followed for four kilometres, skirting the foot of the mountain then winding through the birch woods covering the south shore of Loch an Doire Dhuibh into the very heart of the Reserve. The situation is unbelievably fine, with a sense of complete isolation. Stac Pollaidh presents a new silhouette, the western cliffs of Cul Mor fill the foreground, the prospect to the north-west is one of endless lochs. There is no bridge where the path ends and fording is necessary, alternative bridges shown on the map do not exist. Once over the stream, keep up on the north side all the way through Gleann Laoigh; the climb is gradual and the walking gets progressively better. Once past Loch nan Ealachan – easily identified by its islands – cross the stream and climb out of the head of the glen onto the lip of quartzite which brings the road at Knockanrock into view. The way across the last 800 metres to the end of Loch an Ais is rather wet, but unavoidable. (10 kilometres).

Culnacraig to Strath Kanaird. A well-established footpath leads from Culnacraig southeastwards, following close to the coastline below Garbh Choireachan to Ardmair Bay, then on to cross the River Runie at Blughasary. From the car-park there, a motor road continues for another kilometre to the main road at the foot of Strath Kanaird. This is a right of way which used to be walked by the local postman. The line is scenic throughout, but is wet and muddy at its east end and exposed in places and somewhat indistinct at its west end. (8 kilometres).

CLIMBING

The first direct ascent of the North Buttress of Sgurr an Fhidhleir – *The Fiddler, Direct Nose Route*, (300m Very Severe) – was the climax to a series of attempts there over the last century, and is seen as a landmark in the development of climbing in the Northwest Highlands. The line follows the central spur above the key feature of the direct route – *The Pale Slabs*. These lie about mid-height on the buttress, and only come into view as one continues along the small subsidiary lochan beyond Lochan Tuath. Routes on the north-east face of Sgurr an Fhidhleir, the formidable sweep of high-angled slabs which confront Lochan Tuath, are uniformly hard. Several Grade III winter routes are recorded on the west and north-west face and the gully to the left of Sgurr an Fhidhleir is Grade II.

Cairn Conmheall, to the west of Sgurr an Fhidhleir, is distinguished by the prominent pinnacle – *The Acheninver Pinnacle* – which flanks the hill on its left. There are several routes there up to 150m, standards vary from Very Difficult to Hard Very Severe. Other shorter routes of the 30m variety have been made on the right-most south-facing buttress.

Climbing on Cul Mor centres on the south-west face of Creag nan Calman, with obvious possibilities all along the mountain's western flank.

The western crags of Cul Beag provide scrambling routes split by the usual heather ledges. The upper reaches of the far west face are split by a prominent Y-shaped gully which sends a long scree tail down to the lower slopes; it encloses a wedge-shaped buttress, its apex at the bottom. This face was the scene that attracted most of the early pioneers in Coigach and gives a variety of climbing routes. Routes on the lower tier of rock below *Wedge Buttress* vary in standard from Very Difficult to Very Severe and up to 200m in length. Other routes there are possible.

The south-east corner of the *West Buttress* of Stac Pollaidh has several routes of over 100m of high standard. The two early routes followed two long converging diedres – *November Groove* and *Enigma Groove*. The rib between the south-east and south-west faces gives a Very Severe climb of 110m – *Jack the Ripper*. Recent activity there has increased considerably. Most of the pinnacles have been explored, and it is unlikely that many new prospects remain undiscovered. Scrambling variations are limitless.

The Rubha Mor peninsula has been the scene of great activity over recent years, and the sea-cliffs of Reiff and Rubha Coigeach have produced a veritable flood of climbs ranging from very short to four pitch. Single pitch climbs between 10m and 25m would appear to be the norm. The cliffs around Ardmair Bay to the west of Dun Canna have produced short hard climbs, and the crags on the south side of the road above the fish farm have also been explored.

CHAPTER 17

Assynt

MAPS: Ordnance Survey 1:50,000 Sheet 15
                Bartholomew 1:100,000 Sheet 58

PRINCIPAL HILLS

Suilven	731m	153 184
Canisp	847m	203 188
Quinag	808m	209 292
Glas Bheinn	776m	254 265
Beinn Uidhe	741m	282 252
Beinn an Fhurain (Na Tuadhan)	860m	303 216
Conival	988m	303 199
Ben More Assynt	998m	318 202
Creag Liath Breabag	815m	287 158

Assynt forms the south-west corner of the district of Sutherland, separated from the adjacent area of Coigach in Ross-shire by the boundary line along Loch Veyatie, Fionn Loch and the River Kirkaig to Enard Bay.

The western coastline stretches around the Point of Stoer to the head of Loch a' Chairn Bhain. In the past, drovers from the north swam their cattle across the narrows there; the 400 metre gap between Kylesku and Kylestrome is now spanned by a fine road bridge. To the east of the narrows the loch divides, sending two fingers probing inland for almost seven kilometres. The north inlet is Loch Glendhu; the south inlet is Loch Glencoul. The dividing peninsula is Aird da Loch which gives a classic exposure of the Sole and Glencoul Thrust Planes, one of the most important viewpoints in the structural geology of the Highlands.

Assynt's eastern boundary follows the watershed along the summit ridges of Beinn Uidhe, Conival and Breabag, paradoxically excluding Ben More Assynt, the highest mountain in Sutherland. In this account the official line will be ignored. At Altnacealgach, on the south-eastern corner, the border of Ross-shire is seen to make an unlikely invasion of Assynt as far as the slopes of Ben More and Conival. A dispute in the past over boundaries was settled there by two witnesses who swore they were walking on Ross-shire soil; they were indeed, for their boots were filled with earth. Altnacealgach means *'burn of the cheat'*.

In Norse, 'Ass' means *rocky*; in Ancient Gaelic, 'As-sint' means *in and out*. Either derivation is apt. Assynt presents the most remarkable mountain skyline in the Highlands, making it easy to accept the legend that the old Norse gods came here when the world was still malleable to practice mountain modelling. The area is a compact geological showpiece, internationally acclaimed, where Lewisian gneiss, Torridonian sandstone, quartzite, limestone and Moine schists all contribute to the making of this strange, prehistoric setting.

Gneiss, one of the oldest surface rocks in Europe, forms a base of low hummocks and water-filled hollows. On top of this the sandstones have weathered to form magnificently terraced isolated shapes with quartzites along their crests and on their eastern flanks. Where limestones outcrop, the surface vegetation is a rich green with a wealth of varied plant life. Below the surface a maze of caves, pot holes and watercourses has developed. At Knockanrock on the Ross-Sutherland border the Moine schists push over the upper limestone crags, and the natural sequence of the various layers of rocks is seen to have been upset. Early observations there played a major part in unravelling many basic geological complexities.

The Inchnadamph Nature Reserve in the north-east corner is limestone orientated. It covers the foothills of Breabag and Conival, encompassed to north and south by the glens of the River Traligill and the Allt nan Uamh. The River Traligill follows a contorted course both over and under the prevailing limestone to its outlet in Loch Assynt; its glen is rich in cave features and in plant life. The Norsemen called this 'Troll's Gill', *the giant's ravine*. The glen of the Allt nan Uamh, three kilometres to the south, has one of the most important archaeological sites in the country, the Allt nan Uamh Bone Caves, which have provided evidence of the presence of early man and of the long-extinct wildlife which once roamed the surrounding countryside.

As one would expect, the area is sparse in people and in houses. Lochinver is a busy fishing port and tourist centre, the one main centre of population on the west coast. In the north, the Drumbeg/Stoer peninsula has a peripheral scattering of small crofting communities; inland is a maze of fine fishing lochs. Between Inchnadamph at the end of Loch Assynt and the two crofting communities of Knockan and Elphin, there are almost 300 square kilometres of wilderness, the domain of sporting estates and the Nature Conservancy Council. Tourism now has begun to take the traditional place of shepherding in the local economy, as is the case in so many other parts of the north.

ACCESS

Two good roads lead into Assynt from the south. The road from Ullapool (A835) with its branch from Drumrunie to Lochinver and Achiltibuie has been described in the previous chapter. The road from the east coast (A837) starts from Ardgay at the head of the Kyle of Sutherland, and follows the valley of the River Oykel north-westwards to Lochinver, an undulating route of almost 80 kilometres. At Ledmore junction, three kilometres past Altnacealgach, it is joined by the A835 road from Ullapool. From this point it very conveniently passes between all the principal mountains and gives comparatively easy access to them on both sides.

At Skiag Bridge, three kilometres north of Inchnadamph, the road forks. The A837 road continues along the side of Loch Assynt to Lochinver; the A894 road climbs over between Quinag and Glas Bheinn towards Kylesku bridge and the far north-west. Three kilometres before the bridge is reached a single track road (B869) branches westwards. This makes a most spectacular circuit of the Drumbeg/Stoer peninsula, winding and switchbacking its way through all the small communities, beneath the towering northern buttresses of Quinag, then past a succession of secluded rocky inlets and unspoiled sandy beaches towards Lochinver. Highly recommended, but not for caravans.

PUBLIC TRANSPORT

Rail: There are daily passenger services from Inverness and the south to Ardgay and Lairg.

Bus: Inverness – Ullapool (Scottish Citylink Coaches and Rapsons Coaches). Mondays to Saturdays.
Lochinver – Ullapool – Inverness (MacKenzie and MacLennan, Gairloch). Mondays, Fridays and Saturdays. All Year.
Lochinver – Lairg – Ardgay. (Rapson of Brora). Mondays to Saturdays. All Year.

Postbus (4 seater): Lochinver – Stoer – Drumbeg. Mondays to Saturdays. All Year.
Kylesku – Inchnadamph – Elphin. Mondays to Saturdays. All Year.

ACCOMMODATION

There are hotels at Inchnadamph, Kylesku, Drumbeg and Lochinver with guesthouse accommodation at Knockan, Lochinver, Kylesku and Stoer. Bed and breakfast accommodation is available practically everywhere throughout the area. There are caravan sites at Clachtoll, Stoer, and Achmelvich. Campsites can usually be negotiated locally. The Scottish Youth Hostels Association has a hostel at Achmelvich which is open from March to September. The Mountain Bothies Association maintain a bothy at Suileag near the base of Suilven and Canisp (grid reference 150 211) This is usually reached by a well-surfaced path from Glencanisp Lodge. The possible alternative approach from the north is by a stalker's path which leaves the A837 road at the west end of Loch Assynt (grid reference 158 250). Use of the bothy is restricted by Assynt Estate during the stalking season.

Ardvreck Castle on the shore of Loch Assynt

THE HILLS

The mountains which rise on either side of the road between Ledmore Junction and Kylesku fall into two distinct groups. To the west, gneiss forms the platform for predominantly sandstone monoliths capped in varying degrees with Cambrian quartzite; to the east, the gneiss is found rising to a much greater height as a result of mighty thrust movements and on Ben More Assynt rises close to the summit, the highest occurrence in Britain. Elsewhere on this side crystalline schists of the Moine series begin to appear; this is the rock formation which is found to form extensive areas of the northern hills.

Suilven (*the pillar*) (731m)

Suilven is the most westerly of the Assynt mountains. It completely dominates the surrounding landscape and is one of the most remarkable and best-known peaks in the British Isles, chameleon-like in its ability to display a changing shape when viewed from differing directions. From the west it appears as a great rounded dome of sculptured sandstone which to the native Gael was Caisteal Liath, *the grey castle*: to the Viking invaders from the sea it was Sul-Fhal, *the pillar*. The ridge is greatly foreshortened when seen from the east, and shrinks to become a single sharp cone-like peak. From the north or south the entire length of the triple-topped ridge is unfolded.

The main top, Caisteal Liath (731m), lies at the west end of the mountain. It is separated from Meall Mheadhonach (723m), the pointed central top, by a prominent col, the Bealach Mor, with steep stone chutes down both its flanks. The easy route onto the summit ridge lies up either; their descent requires care on account of loose rock. At the east end of the ridge Meall Bheag (610m) stands detached from Meall Mheadhonach across a sharply cut, steep-sided notch.

Suilven is usually approached from Lochinver. A single-track road goes to Glencanisp Lodge, a distance of three kilometres. Cars should be left at the parking area 800 metres before reaching the lodge gate. The Suilven path passes behind the lodge, continuing for just over three kilometres to a cairned junction with the path coming from Little Assynt on the Inchnadamph to Lochinver road. Suileag bothy stands 400 metres to the north side of this. Continue along the north side of the Amhainn na Clach Airigh for three kilometres to the bridge at the north-west end of Loch na Gainimh. The main path can be seen to carry on south-eastwards along the loch side. This eventually reaches Elphin, on the eastern edge of Assynt, by way of Loch Fada and Cam Loch, a distance of ten kilometres. The path is suitable for mountain bikes, certainly as far as the ridge beyond the east end of Loch Fada. The Little Assynt track, previously mentioned, starts at a footbridge across the river flowing from the west end of Loch Assynt. After 800 metres, the ford over the Allt an Tiagaich can cause problems during wet weather.

The way onto Suilven from the end of Loch na Gainimh is well marked, climbing steeply through rough ground in a direct line to the foot of the gully on the north side of Bealach Mor, which as previously noted gives a steep, but not difficult

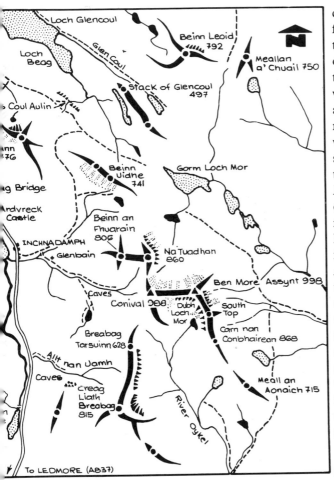

climb to the ridge. An easy climb from the top of the bealach leads to the cairn on the broad summit of Caisteal Liath, passing en route through a gap in the drystone dyke which has intriguingly been built across the ridge there. Retrace the route down to the bealach, from where a splendid ridge walk with some easy scrambling leads on to the central peak, Meall Mheadhonach, with spectacular outlooks to either side. The ridge now drops steeply towards Meall Bheag, and the ascent of the latter from the col requires great care. An awkward corner is turned on the north side, along a rocky ledge, and a way up can then be made onto the top of Meall Bheag by a series of terraces. The situation is somewhat exposed, but affords no great technical difficulty. A little way down the east ridge, a narrow transverse gap is easily crossed and the remainder of the descent is straightforward.

Once down off the ridge there is a choice of route for the return journey. The path to Suileag can be rejoined at either end of Loch na Gainimh. Alternatively a west to east trip can be completed by continuing down the east ridge of Suilven towards Cam Loch. The north shore of the loch is then followed to regain the path to Elphin which has already been described. Alternatively, a line overland from the south shore of the loch may be taken towards the waterfall between Cam Loch and Loch Veyatie (grid reference 211 122). This has now been bridged, and a private vehicle track leads out to the road at Elphin. By either route this eastern approach to Suilven is long and arduous, not advisable in winter.

An interesting alternative is to approach by boat or canoe, either from Elphin Bridge along Cam Loch, or along Loch Veyatie for four kilometres, then take a line overland to the east end of Loch nan Rac and the ridge onto Meall Bheag. This makes for a delightful day's expedition. One other approach to the south side of

Looking east along the ridge of Suilven

Suilven can be made from Inverkirkaig, five kilometres south of Lochinver. A well-signposted path leaves the road from the carpark beside the bridge at the district boundary. It follows the north bank of the River Kirkaig for five kilometres, passing the Falls of Kirkaig with their 20m perpendicular drop, before continuing towards the Fionn Loch. The path then swings round to the north shore of the loch, whence a way can be made to the foot of the stone chute on the south side of Bealach Mor.

A traverse of Suilven from west to east including the ascent of Caisteal Liath with its near vertical cliffs is undoubtedly a classic of its kind, but one which is not within the scope of hillwalkers. The gullies which initially breach the terraced sandstone walls around the north-western end of the mountain tend to run out, leaving the climber faced with three problems; steep vegetation, exposure and little protection. Any attempt to descend from Caisteal Liath by any route except along the ridge to the Bealach Mor requires definite climbing techniques and ability.

Canisp (*white hill*) (847m)

Canisp is an integral part of the Assynt landscape, but holds little of interest apart from its height which earns it a place in Corbett's Tables. Its position across the glen five kilometres to the east of Suilven makes it an ideal viewpoint for the latter. The normal approach is from the north end of Loch Awe, three kilometres north of Ledmore on the road to Inchnadamph. The River Loanan can be crossed by a footbridge there, and after a short boggy start the long south-eastern slope gives good walking directly onto the summit, a distance of almost six kilometres from the road. This side of Canisp is entirely composed of quartzite which on the summit forms a short band of steep shattered crag dropping to the north-west, often a haunt of the golden eagle. These rocks are easily circumnavigated onto the north-west ridge of Canisp, which gives a straightforward descent to pick up a path leading down to the north-west end of Loch Gainimh, and the junction with the track from Lochinver to Elphin. Follow this for six kilometres past the east end of Loch Fada, with a choice of either continuing on to Elphin, or wending a route back to Loch Awe, following the line of small lochans to the east. A direct descent from the summit of Canisp back to the road can be made in its lower stretch along the Allt Mhic Mhurchaidh Gheir which drops in a series of small falls and pools into Loch Awe.

Canisp becomes a much more attractive mountain in winter garb. It holds snow well and frequently offers possibilities for good ski-mountaineering. The south-east slope is relatively open, giving a long ski descent to Loch Awe.

Quinag (*the water stoup*) (808m)

Quinag is the guardian of the northern border of Assynt, the last distinctive 'mountain' in the chain of Torridonian sandstone which stretches the length of the western seaboard from Applecross up to Cape Wrath.

In shape it is like a gigantic Y. The main leg is formed by a long slope which rises north-westwards from Loch Assynt for two kilometres onto the summit of Spidean Coinich (764m), seen standing out boldly at its southern end like the spout of a gigantic bucket. This is the feature which gives the whole mountain its name – 'Cuinneag' is Gaelic for a narrow-mouthed water stoup. The slope has an overlying cover of white quartzite, widely exposed to give pleasant walking when dry. When wet it becomes extremely slippery and dangerous. The quartzite also appears as an impressive cliff on the north-east side of Spidean Coinich. From there the ridge continues north-westwards for one kilometre, narrowing over a small subsidiary point (713m) then dropping steeply to cross the broader saddle, Bealach a'Chornaidh, which bisects the ridge, providing easy access from east to west. A steep, mainly heathery climb leads onto the flattish, unnamed junction top (746m). There the ridge divides and sends out two broad spurs to the north and north-east These form a great fork – the Byre – a broad, steep-sided corrie out of which flows the Allt a'Bhathaich. The north spur continues on the line of the main ridge for almost two kilometres, over the second highest top, Sail Gorm (776m) and ends in an impressive rocky buttress which has easier slopes leading off at either flank. On the north face the underlying gneiss rises to a height of 600 m.

The western flank of Quinag extends for three kilometres as a line of well-seamed crags, rising in places to a height of over 200m, and passing over several well-defined features. From the junction top, the main ridge crosses a small col onto a 'truncated' top which can be taken direct, or contoured along its east side if need be. Beyond a second col the ridge leads over a hummocky top to a small col before rising onto the final long slope and the summit cairn of Sail Gorm. Just beyond this final col, the path passes close to the top of a prominent steep gully; care is required over this section in bad visibility.

From the junction top the ridge drops steeply to the east for 40m onto an open flat connecting saddle. From there the north-east spur rises gradually and easily over one kilometre onto the broad summit of Sail Garbh (808m), the highest point on Quinag; it then continues for another kilometre to form a magnificent terminal buttress – the Barrel Buttress – the mountain's most impressive feature. The main top of Sail Garbh is of quartzite; the deeply gullied face of the buttress is of sandstone which drops in bold steps broken by heathery ledges.

Quinag is usually climbed from the east, with a choice of two routes. Both start from the high point on the road leading to Kylesku (A894) three kilometres north of Skiag Bridge (grid reference 232 274). A narrow stalker's path leaves the west side of the road opposite a convenient large parking area. A short distance from the start a cairn marks the point where the routes split. A line of cairns may be followed to the left towards the foot of the gently rising south-east dip slope. This continues up along the edge of the quartzite crags to the top of Spidean Coinich at the south end of the ridge – a distance of three kilometres.

Alternatively, the stalker's path may be followed further than is indicated on the Ordnance Survey map. It is mainly good, but deteriorates in places along the way.

Pass round the north shore of the lochan to climb the steep slopes beyond onto the Bealach a' Chornaidh, just below the junction point on the main ridge – a distance of almost four kilometres from the road. This approach to Quinag is favoured by hillwalkers who do not plan to make a complete traverse of the main summits. The descent from the bealach is a useful exit route in the event of bad weather.

This point on the ridge of Quinag can be reached equally well from Tumore, six kilometres west of Skiag Bridge on the road to Lochinver. From the solitary cottage at the north side of the road a clearly marked right of way climbs steeply for over one kilometre onto the Bealach Leireag at the base of Creag na h'Iolaire. It then continues north-westwards through Gleann Leireag along the foot of the three kilometre line of cliffs which form the west flank of Quinag. Leave the path at its highest point and make a rising traverse to the north-east for 800 metres up progressively steeper heathery slopes onto the Bealach a'Chornaidh.

Glas Bheinn (*green grassy hill*) (776m)
Beinn Uidhe (*hill of the ford*) (741m)
Beinn an Fhurain (*hill of the spring*) (806m)
Na Tuadhan (*the hatchets*) (860m)
Conival (*hill of the dog*) (988m)
Ben More Assynt (great mountain of Assynt) (998m)

These mountains form a continuous line for more than seventeen kilometres along the eastern boundary of Assynt. Throughout its length the range never drops below 600 metres, rising from either end to over 914 metres on the summits of Conival and Ben More Assynt, the highest points in Sutherland. Despite its height, Ben More does not stand out conspicuously in this Assynt landscape. Even from Inchnadamph its summit ridge is hidden by Conival, and only unfolds when viewed from a distance.

The two Munros are normally climbed from Inchnadamph. Leave the A837 at the bridge 200 metres north of the hotel. A vehicle track follows the River Traligill for almost two kilometres to the cottage at Glenbain, continuing as a path along Gleann Dubh for a further kilometre to a Nature Conservancy signpost, where it forks. The right-hand branch crosses a wooden bridge and continues on past several conspicuous cave entrances (grid reference 276 206) then winds south to reach Loch Mhaolach-coire, better known locally as Loch Gillieroo, the home of a rare breed of red-speckled trout. The left-hand branch, of variable quality, follows the north side of the River Traligill along the floor of the glen for almost two kilometres before swinging steeply upwards to the north-east between Beinn an Fhurain and Conival through a short line of quartzite cliffs onto their connecting saddle. This way is steep and direct and low down it is often soft and wet. A better plan is to leave the path shortly after the fork and make a long rising traverse up and across the hillside on good ground.

From the top of the saddle an obvious way leads up the broad north ridge of Conival for over one kilometre onto the summit. There is no well-defined single path up the lower section where countless feet have made many diversions up the screes; these come together on the narrower crest, and the final approach to the summit is well-marked through the shattered quartzite outcrops. To the south-west a line of steep broken ribs drops down to the narrow dividing pass beyond which the broad ridge of Breabag sweeps on southwards in an unexpectedly magnificent line of crag and corrie along the headwaters of the River Oykel. The stepped rocky ridge, broken by heathery bands, which continues down from the summit of Conival to form the south wall of Garbh Choire, offers interesting scrambling, but not for walkers. To the north, across the steeply curving slopes of Coire a' Mhadaidh, the foreground is dominated by Na Tuadhan (860m) – a steep buttress of highly folded quartzite which juts out above the line of the main ridge to the east of Beinn an Fhurain.

A narrow ridge of shattered quartzite blocks now runs eastwards onto the main top of Ben More Assynt, a distance of one and a half kilometres. Its south side drops steeply into Garbh Choire at the head of Glen Oykel; on the north side the loose stony slopes are more easily angled. The broken crest between the two Munros makes for rough walking, but there are no difficulties in dry conditions; some easy boulder scrambling is necessary in the initial stretches. The summit of Ben More itself is rather indeterminate but the view is panoramic.

The main ridge continues for nearly one kilometre to the South Top of Ben More (960m) (grid reference 324 193). In places it becomes narrow, crossing two or three steps of exposed slab where the ridge drops steeply to Dubh Loch Mor, the source of the River Oykel. This section of the ridge has been compared (probably flatteringly) to the Aonach Eagach in Glencoe: it should not be treated lightly however. The western flanks are deeply-gullied, but a way can be found down with care, any descent becoming progressively easier as one moves south towards Carn nan Conbhairean. To continue the traverse southwards, follow the stream from Dubh Loch Mor to join a stalker's path which descends south-east towards the River Oykel and follows the river to reach Benmore Lodge and the road from Loch Ailsh leading out to the A837 road. (thirteen kilometres). The direct way back to rejoin the Traligill path is to make a rising traverse from the Dubh Loch Mor to the bealach between Conival and Breabag Tarsuinn. The way can be boggy, but the narrow defile is easily followed to regain the outward route from Inchnadamph.

The traverse of the entire range from north-west to south-east makes a fine long ridge walk. Start beyond the highest point on the road from Skiag Bridge to Kylesku (grid reference 238 284) beside Loch na Gainmhich. A stalker's path is soon left for a direct line up the easy north-east slopes of Glas Bheinn onto the open summit plateau. This gives unexpectedly pleasant walking along its length. A narrow rocky ridge leads east down to the cairned saddle and a long boulder-strewn slope climbs gradually onto the summit of Beinn Uidhe. From there the way on past Mullach an Leathaid Riabhaich and Beinn an Fhurain becomes tedious in comparison until one reaches the saddle leading onto Conival. If need be a

Looking towards the summit of Ben More Assynt from the south-east ridge

retreat can be made from this point down towards the Traligill track and Inchnadamph; a commitment to continue and complete the remainder of the ridge should be carefully considered.

Creag Liath Breabag *(grey crag of Breabag)* (815m)

This is the highest point on the rather neglected ridge which forms the south-east corner of the Assynt border. It is best appreciated as seen from the summit of Conival, when all its varied features spread out in plan along the west side of the upper River Oykel. From the roadside by Ledmore Junction it appears as a round grey whale-backed hump, giving no indication of the fine line of hidden corries which are scoured out along its eastern flank, nor of the wide pavements of shattered quartzite which cover the north end of the ridge, in sharp contrast to the more open heathery slopes along its southern end. The ridge can be gained from either end with little difficulty, but the line which follows the Allt nan Uamh glen offers the greatest variety of interest. Leave the road at the fish hatchery six kilometres north of Ledmore, then follow the path along the stream for almost two kilometres to the prominent limestone crag on the south side. The entrances of the Bone Caves are obvious at the top of the steep glacis slope. The bed of the burn is followed eastwards to reach a small loch just below the central saddle. From there the way south onto the Corbett is over easy slopes of alternating grass and flat boulder field.

PATHS AND WALKS

Many of the paths which skirt the mountains have already been mentioned in part. Those which serve as approaches to Suilven offer several interesting combinations at low level, giving the possibility of longer expeditions requiring a degree of fitness. The Inverkirkaig path ends along the north side of the river which flows out of Loch Veyatie into Fionn Loch, Uidh Fhearna. Any expedition involving a link up with the paths along the north side of Suilven necessitates trackless going over rough ground.

Tumore to Nedd via Gleann Leirig. The walk along the right of way from Tumore which passes along the western flank of Quinag requires transport organised at both ends. It gives very easy walking, rather wet at the north end in places, and superb views of the cliffs of Quinag. The path reaches the B869 road some two kilometres east of Nedd, a tiny crofting community standing at the head of an enchanting inlet from the sea. The exit point of the right of way is marked by a prominent cairn. (7 kilometres).

The Stoer Peninsula. The extreme north-west corner of Assynt provides a pleasant circular walk of no difficulty. Starting from the lighthouse, the cliff-line is followed for three kilometres to the Point of Stoer, giving impressive views of the sandstone stack, the Old Man of Stoer, which rises just offshore, 800 metres south of the headland. A circuit can be continued along the north shore towards the scattered crofting community of Culkein, then back overland by peat track and heather past Loch Cul Fraioch. The view south is of the entire sweep of the Assynt landscape with a backdrop of the hills along Loch Broom. (11 kilometres).

The wilderness which lies along the north-eastern edge of the Ben More Assynt range offers scope for testing north to south walks of great interest and quality. To make adequate safe allowance for the time and distance involved in any expedition on this very remote side of the mountains, an overnight camp is advisable and transport requires to be arranged at either end. Paths exist as shown on the Ordnance Survey map, which makes variations possible at both start and finish. Any start from the north end is usually combined with a short detour to the Eas a'Chual Aluinn, the highest waterfall in Britain. This cascades over the cliffs of Leitir Dhubh, making a drop of almost 200 metres to feed into Loch Beag at the head of Loch Glencoul. Directly across the narrow glen, the unnamed ribbon of water which falls from Loch nan Caorach on the plateau above the Stack of Glencoul is only slightly less impressive.

Eas a'Chual Aluinn from the north. To visit the falls, the most usual start from the north is by the path which leaves the A894 road five kilometres north of Skiag Bridge. This skirts the south end of Loch na Gainmhich, then climbs steeply over the Bealach a'Bhuirich (*pass of the roaring*) past small secluded lochans and the unusually fine rock architecture along this north-eastern side of Glas Bheinn. From the head of the pass, the path continues down steeply for almost one kilometre until it crosses a small stream which comes from two lochans on the south side of the path. This point is cairned, but can be easily missed. The way down either side of this stream leads to the top of the Eas a'Chual Aluinn, which can be crossed with care just above the actual lip of the cliff. An obvious path leads further along to the east, and a way can be made down by grassy terraces to get a clearer view of the fall. It is possible with great care to continue down to the floor of the glen by steep vegetation and rocky steps, but only in dry conditions. (5 kilometres).

The foot of the fall can also be reached by boat from Kylesku, or by a rough overland route, leaving the road at the bridge across the Unapool Burn (grid reference 235 303) and crossing in a direct line towards the narrow neck at the head of Loch Glencoul. (five kilometres from the A894 road to the foot of Eas a'Chual Aluinn). The route along the loch-side is mainly trackless and requires care; at one point there is a steep traverse some 50m above the water. As already mentioned, it is possible to gain the top of the fall by steep broken slopes to the south-east beyond the foot of the fall. The alternative is to continue up the Abhainn an Loch Bhig to the head of the glen and join the track from Loch na Gainmhich which continues past the junction to Eas a'Chual Aluinn for almost four kilometres.

One kilometre to the south-east of the junction (grid reference (279 271) a cairn beside two lochans marks the start of a fairly obvious path seen climbing up to the south-west for two kilometres over the bealach between Glas Bheinn and Beinn Uidhe. This drops in a long slanting rake across the lower slopes of Beinn Uidhe to Loch Fleodach Coire. A well-marked line can then be followed for another five kilometres southwards over a flat ridge, giving good walking, to descend towards the track from Gleann Dubh to Inchnadamph.

The path from the junction at grid reference 279 271 continues south-east to a point just short of Gorm Loch Mor, leaving a gap of almost two kilometres – rough, but not difficult – before picking up the south section of the path at the Loch Bealach a'Mhadaidh. It continues along the foot of the ridge for its entire length, generally easy to follow except in snow conditions. The final stretch climbs over the lower slopes of Meall an Aonaich, the south end of the Ben More range, and continues in a south-westerly direction to follow the upper waters of the River Oykel to Benmore Lodge on the shores of Loch Ailsh. (25 kilometres from the A894 road). An estate vehicle road reaches the A837 in another four kilometres; permission to make use of this road can usually be obtained from Assynt Estate. (29 kilometres from the A894 to the A837)

An alternative finish to this walk can be made by taking the path which branches to the east from the junction north-east of Carn nan Conbhairean (grid reference 346 196). This leads to Duchally, at the head of Glen Cassley, a distance of five kilometres. From there, a single track road leads south-east for 18 kilometres along the side of the River Cassley to the village of Rosehall on the A837 road.

Quinag from Loch a'Chairn Bhain. Sail Gharbh, with the Barrel Buttress prominent, is the left hand peak

CLIMBING

Climbing on Suilven is found mainly on the terraced sandstone of the north-west buttress of Caisteal Liath. The earliest route, pioneered in 1892, was by way of the steep open gully on the southern side. The best routes were subsequently found on the middle of the buttress itself; the standard is generally Severe.

Quinag's most impressive rock feature is undoubtedly the *Barrel Buttress* at the north end of Sail Garbh. Most of the climbing is found on the upper of the two tiers, which is split by two long chimney faults to form a central 'stave'. There are two fine steep climbs there of over 100m, on excellent rough sandstone; the standard is Very Severe. The buttress also has several Grade I/II winter routes of up to 300m. The buttress to the east of the Barrel Buttress has also been climbed, frequent ledges allowing for much variation on original lines. The three kilometre line of cliffs along the western flank of Quinag holds a number of features which have produced routes. The buttresses on the whole are too heathery to be of interest, but several of the prominent ribs and gullies give climbs. Routes vary in standard from Very Difficult to Very Severe, with some Grade II winter gullies.

Few climbs have been recorded on the mountains in the eastern side of Assynt. Exploration of the corries on the east side of Breabag and of Garbh Choire could prove fruitful, probably more so in winter. Breabag usually holds snow, and the winter traverse of the Ben More range is a serious undertaking.

Assynt's one sea-stack, The Old Man of Stoer, gives 67m of fine climbing on excellent sandstone. To gain the supporting plinth, a deep channel has to be crossed. This is eight metres wide at its narrowest point, and has proved to be extremely hazardous. A number of routes have now been climbed on the stack.

The Old Man of Stoer

CHAPTER 18

Northwest Sutherland

MAPS: Ordnance Survey   1 : 50,000   Sheets 9, 15 and 16
Bartholomew   1 : 100,000   Sheets 58 and 60

PRINCIPAL HILLS

Foinaven	911m	317 507
Arkle	787m	303 462
Meall Horn	777m	353 449
Sabhal Beag	732m	373 429
Meallan Liath Coire Mhic		
Dhughaill	801m	357 392
Carn Dearg	797m	377 389
Meall Garbh	754m	368 403
Ben Hee	873m	426 339
Ben Stack	721m	270 423
Ben Leoid	792m	320 295
Meallan a'Chuail	750m	344 293
Cranstackie	801m	351 556
Beinn Spionnaidh	773m	362 573

This is the most remote corner of mainland Scotland. The coastline stretches from Eddrachillis Bay, around Cape Wrath to Loch Eriboll – measured straight a distance of some sixty kilometres, but double that if all the indentations are taken into consideration. The southern boundary with Assynt can be taken as a line drawn eastwards from the head of Loch Glencoul to the north end of Loch Shin. The eastern boundary is formed by a winding line of four straths – Strath Tirry, Strath Vagastie, Glen Mudale and Strath More – which stretches for almost 80 kilometres from Lairg in central Sutherland to Loch Eriboll on the north coast.

These were the traditional hunting forests of the Lords of Reay, chiefs of Clan Mackay. In the early 19th century a large part of the area passed into the hands of Lord Stafford, First Duke of Sutherland. Nowadays the Westminster family are the biggest landowners there and the greatest part of the area is still preserved for its sporting potential. Inland, the estates play a major part in the local economy; the few centres of population, which are found mainly along the coastal strips, reflect the marked growth in the current importance of fishing and tourism. Kinlochbervie, at the mouth of Loch Inchard on the southern corner of the Cape Wrath peninsula, has developed into being the largest white fish port in the country. Scourie, in the south-west, and Durness, on the north coast, now augment their traditional role as crofting communities with a healthy tourist trade.

Four great sea-lochs indent the coastline, their names pure Norse in origin, a legacy of the Viking raiders who swept through the Pentland Firth from their Jarldom in Orkney. Eriboll was Eyrr-bol or *beach town*; Durness was *deer's point*; Laxford was aptly named Lax Fjiord – *salmon loch*; Inchard was Engi-fjiord – *meadow loch*. The magnificent stretch of sea-cliffs around Cape Wrath, the ultimate point on the mainland, they named Hvarf – *turning point*, in Gaelic it became Parph. The Cape Wrath lighthouse, built there in 1828, marks the end of Scotland. The tiny island of North Rona, often visible some 70 kilometres to the north-west, is the only landfall before the North Pole.

Inland from Cape Wrath spreads the Parph Moor, an empty wilderness where fact and legend draw close. This is the haunt of the Cu-Saeng, that terrible creature whom no one has lived to describe. It is reputed that its shadow was seen there once on a hillside, it had two heads. Nowadays the area stretching from Kearvaig to the Kyle of Durness is a bombing range which creates a different deterrent to travellers on foot or cycle.

The coastline shows a considerable variety in its rock formation. Lewisian gneiss predominates along the southern half of this western seaboard – from Eddrachillis Bay to Loch Laxford. The result is a complex seascape of bays, inlets and small islands. Inland, the gneiss has produced a harsh rocky landscape typified by a maze of hillocks and lochan-filled hollows. In Gaelic this is Ceathramh Garbh – *rough quarter*.

Around Cape Wrath the gneiss rises to form great multi-coloured cliffs veined with pegmatite, reaching a height in places of over 120m. To the west and to the south of there, long lines of cliff have been sculptured from Torridonian sandstone by the joint action of wind and wave. At Clo Mor along the northern coastline, these cliffs stretch for almost three kilometres to attain their greatest height at the eastern end, Cleit Dhubh. There they reach a height of 280m, the highest sea-cliffs on the mainland of Britain, described by climbers as both formidable and unfriendly.

South of Cape Wrath the sandstone cliffs stretch for over 16 kilometres to the mouth of Loch Inchard. Along this part of the coastline the Torridonian rock forms several noteworthy sea-stacks. A'Chailleach and Am Bodach (*the old woman* and *the old man*) jut up from the shoreline just one kilometre from the lighthouse. Twelve kilometres further, Am Buachaille (*the herdsman*) guards the entrance to the south side of Sandwood Bay. A tapering 60m high obelisk with overhanging base, it is separated from the shore by an eight metre channel. The stack has been climbed, giving a route of Very Severe standard. The channel can be crossed at low tide by a choice of three methods – swim, ladder or fixed rope – with a time limit of four hours in which to complete the exercise.

The Torridonian sandstone is seen at its most spectacular on the bird sanctuary of Handa, which lies to the north of Scourie. There the stratified sandstone has been tilted upwards from the south-east to rise gradually over heathery moorland to Sithean Mor (*great hill of the fairies*) on the north-west corner of the island. On the east side of the point, an inlet with sheer 100m walls, the nesting place for countless sea-birds, encloses the mighty Stack of Handa. It was first surmounted in 1876 by a party of Lewis men collecting sea-birds for salting. A rope was secured over the flat top of the Stack, and the 25 metre gap on the west side was crossed hand over hand, without protection, by one Donald Macdonald. The feat was re-enacted in 1967 by the late Dr Tom Patey using modern aids; the original effort was considered to be incredible. Both the Great Stack and the nearby mini stack - Stacan Geodh Bhrisidh, an elegant detached flake - have been subsequently climbed by more traditional methods.

To the east of Durness the coastline is a mixture of limestone, Moinian rocks and quartzite. The most spectacular of the natural limestone features is undoubtedly the Smoo Cave. The name is predictably Norse in origin – smjuga being a *narrow cleft to creep through*. It is conveniently reached from the roadside at the head of a small bay two kilometres from Durness. At Whiten Head, the end of the Moine Thrust Plane, the great line of sea-cliffs reaches a height of 257m, only slightly lower than the sandstone of Clo Mor. The twin sea-stacks there, known collectively as *The Maiden*, are of a startlingly light-coloured quartzite. Inland, the main mountain ridges follow the general line of the Moine Thrust, and are bisected by a continuous line of inland waterway stretching diagonally across Sutherland from Laxford Bridge on the Atlantic coast to the head of the Dornoch Firth and the North Sea.

ACCESS

Two roads follow this line of waterway and give ready access to the mountains. The main trunk road from Inverness and the south (A9) passes through Ardgay at the head of the Kyle of Sutherland. From there the A836 road branches northwards to Lairg then continues by way of Crask and Altnaharra to Tongue on the north coast. Three kilometres north of Lairg, a single-track branch road (A838) cuts off in a north-westerly direction towards Laxford Bridge. There it is joined by the A894, the road from Assynt and the west, by way of Kylesku and Scourie. From Laxford Bridge, the A838 road swings north-eastwards to Rhiconich at the head of Loch Inchard, and then takes a direct line across the base of the Parph peninsula to Durness, where it becomes the north coastal road to Caithness. With two exceptions, the mountains lie along the eastern side of the A838 road.

The Cape Wrath peninsula is virtually roadless. The greatly improved B801 road follows the north shore of Loch Inchard to the busy fishing port of Kinlochbervie. From there a single-track road continues for a further eight kilometres to serve the crofting communities of Oldshore, stopping short of the coast at Sheigra. One other road across the north of the peninsula leads to Cape Wrath lighthouse. This has no direct motor link with the mainland. A ferry for pedestrians operates across the Kyle of Durness from Keoldale, near the Cape Wrath Hotel (grid reference 377 661). This links with the Cape Wrath minibus service which runs daily, Sundays included, weather permitting, from May to September. Outwith this period the local contact is Mrs I Mackay, Durness (097181) 287.

Four kilometres to the north-east of Scourie, a signposted single track road branches to the tiny harbour at Tarbet. This gives access to the sanctuary on Handa Island which is the property of the Royal Society for the Protection of Birds. A small ferry-boat operates daily (except Sunday) throughout the tourist season, weather permitting. Outwith this period the local contact is Mr W Macrae, Scourie (0971) 2156.

PUBLIC TRANSPORT

Rail: A passenger rail service runs daily from Inverness to Ardgay and Lairg with connections from the south.

Bus: Daily express coaches (Rapsons and Scottish Citylink) from Inverness to Ardgay and the East Sutherland coast are of limited use for onward connections to the north-west.
Lairg – Overscaig – Laxford – Scourie – Rhiconich – Kinlochbervie – Durness. (Rapsons). Mondays to Saturdays.

Postbus: Scourie – Tarbet – Kylestrome. Mondays to Saturdays. Kinlochbervie to Sheigra. School Days only.

ACCOMMODATION

There are hotels at Lairg, Overscaig, Rhiconich, Kinlochbervie, Durness and Scourie. Elsewhere in this area, houses are thinly scattered near the mountains, but where they do occur, particularly around Achfary, between Loch More and Loch Stack, and all along the shore of Loch Eriboll, bed and breakfast accommodation can usually be negotiated. There are organised camping/caravan sites at Scourie; Oldshore more, beyond Kinlochbervie; Achnairn on Loch Shin-side, north of Lairg; and Durness. These are generally open from March to September. The Scottish Youth Hostels Association has a hostel to the east of Durness, near the Smoo Cave, open March to September.

The Mountain Bothies Association maintains bothies at Kearvaig, near Cape Wrath (grid reference 292 727); Strathan, near Sandwood Bay (grid reference 247612); and Strabeg, near the head of Loch Eriboll (grid reference 391 518). There is an open bothy at Lone, on the east side of Loch Stack (grid reference 309 422). This is approached by a private estate vehicle track which leaves the A838 one kilometre north of Achfary, over a bridge across the mouth of the loch – (grid reference 299 403). The use of all of these bothies during the deer culling season could be restricted.

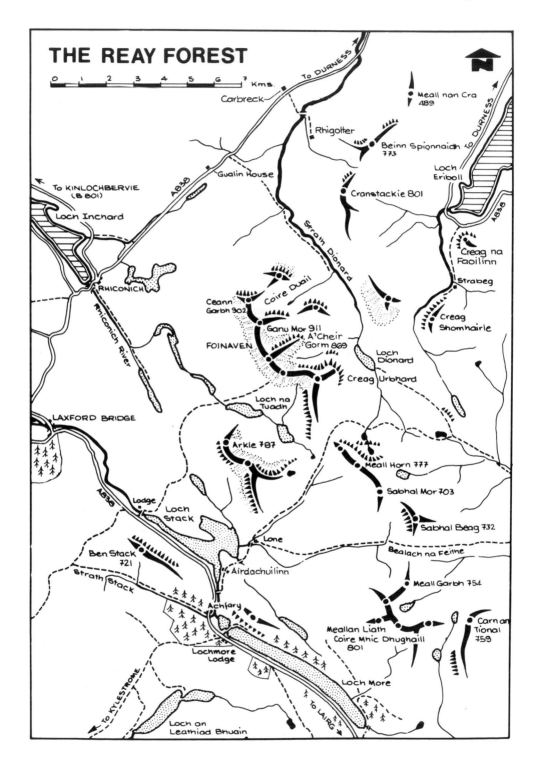

THE REAY FOREST

THE HILLS

Foinaven (*white hill*) (911m)

This is the collective name for the sprawling, E-shaped mass of mountains which forms the western boundary of Srath Dionard, on the south side of the road from Rhiconich to Durness (A838). The ridge stretches for more than five kilometres. To the west it presents continuously steep slopes unbroken by any outstanding feature. On the east side great corries have been bitten deeply into its flanks, the result of considerable glacial erosion. The rock is predominantly quartzite which has shattered in places to form distinctive scree slopes and broken crags whose light colouration gives the mountain its name.

The traverse of the Foinaven ridge can be made from either end; it gives a long and testing day and ample time should be allowed for contingencies. Approached from the west, it is better if transport can be organised at either end; from the north side it is possible to make a circular route.

The approach from the south-west starts at Achfary, at the head of Loch More, on the Lairg to Laxford road (A838). Leave the road one kilometre to the north of the village and take the track previously described leading to Lone. This is a pedestrian right of way only and, although the gate past the bridge is seldom locked, permission for any vehicular use should be sought at the stalker's house at Airdachuilinn, one kilometre on. From there another kilometre of vehicle track leads to the bothy at Lone where the track forks. The right of way carries on for thirteen kilometres due east over the Bealach na Feithe, to Gobernuisgach Lodge, at the end of Glen Golly. The north branch rises steadily up along the north-west side of the Allt Horn for six kilometres onto the saddle between Creagan Meall Horn and the south end of the ridge of Foinaven. From there to the summit of Creag Dionard (778m) is a steady pull of just over two kilometres.

The main points on the ridge can now be followed without great difficulty to Ceann Garbh (902m) at the north end. The ridge rises over an unnamed top (809m) before dropping to the Cadha na Beucaich (*pass of the bellowing*) at the head of Coire na Lice (unnamed on the Ordnance Survey map). Immediately north of the col the ridge is dominated by a small rocky peak known as Lord Reay's Seat. Like many of the features on Foinaven it is unnamed on the Ordnance Survey map. The east face is a cliff of clean quartzite, continuously steep in its lower half, which falls over 200m into Coire na Lice. The pinnacle guarding the ridge is easily bypassed on its west side, and immediately north is an unnamed top (869m). From there the main ridge drops steeply to a bealach, then narrows at the base of the short ridge leading to the north-east which rises onto the highest point of Foinaven, Ganu Mor (*great wedge*) (911m). The narrow crest continues northwards for almost one kilometre to Ceann Garbh (*rough head*) (902m), the final point on the ridge. The line of descent down the north-west slopes of Ceann Garbh is a matter of choice according to any pre-arranged pick-up point along the Rhiconich

Foinaven from the north across Srath Dionard

to Durness road in the vicinity of Gualin House. Care is required on the lower part in poor visibility. The way is down steep grass and loose rocks with a lower band of short cliffs which are difficult to see from above. The final three kilometres from the foot of the slope to the road are rough, boggy and not really pleasant.

The main ridge of Foinaven has several interesting features along its eastern flank. Cnoc a'Mhadaidh, on the north side of the entrance of Coire Duail, is an extension at a lower level of the north-east shoulder of Ceann Garbh. Along with Creag Dubh, a 200m high cliff of gneiss on the east face of Ceann Garbh at the head of Coire Duail, exploration of their climbing potential has proved fruitful. To the south of Ganu Mor, a long quartzite ridge, A'Cheir Ghorm, stretches out from the unnamed point (869m). Its sides are mainly of steep scree, but the east buttress has three fine ridges converging onto the apparent summit. A detour from the main ridge for one and a half kilometres along to this point is well worth the effort, with interesting scrambling if taken direct, splendid impressions of the full scale of the mountain and a magnificent panorama of the surrounding area.

The north face of Creag Dionard is a cliff well over one kilometre in length, but only continuous at its two ends. The complex mass of quartzite which forms the east face of Creag Dionard is Creag Urbhard – the hidden jewel in Foinaven's crown. The Dionard Buttresses, five in number, lie between Creag Urbhard and

Foinaven (left) and Arkle from above Lochstack Lodge

Creag Alistair, which forms the east face of Plat Reidh. This lies some one and a half kilometres south of Loch Dionard.

A descent north-eastwards into Srath Dionard can be made from several points along the ridge. From the base of the spur leading to A'Cheir Ghorm, a more or less direct route leads down into Coire Duail by way of the watercourse which breaches the crags between Cnoc Duail and Ganu Mor. Continue down the Allt Coire Duail to pick up the end of the fishing track which follows the bank of the River Dionard back to the roadside just north of Gualin.

A third route on the north-east side of the Foinaven range starts at Loch Eriboll. A rough track (unfit for cars) leaves the coastal road (A838) at the foot of Creag na Faoilinn, the mouth of Srath Beag (grid reference 394 539). This continues as a wet footpath for two kilometres to the bothy at Strabeg and carries on for a short distance beneath the quartzite crags of Creag Shomhairle. An ill-defined path then crosses over the lower slopes of Conamheall by way of the Bealach na h'Imrich, to the north end of Loch Dionard and the base of Creag Urbhard. For rock climbers, this gives access to all the Foinaven cliffs; for hillwalkers, it offers the possibility of linking up with the paths through Srath Dionard or Glen Golly. Alternatively, from the south end of Loch Dionard the west side of the Allt an Easain Ghil can be followed upwards for some two kilometres to join the right of way to Lone and so gain the south end of the main ridge of Foinaven.

Ben Stack from the north-west

Arkle (*hill of the level top*) (787m)

Arkle stretches along the shore of Loch Stack three kilometres to the north-east of the road from Achfary to Laxford Bridge. Seen from this side it is a particularly distinctive mountain, rising as a uniform slope for more than two kilometres onto the first top. The whole length of the south-west flank is split by prominent gullies, and finely banded by starkly contrasting layers of quartzite screes. The mountain links onto the south-east end of the ridge of Foinaven to form a magnificent amphitheatre of stepped corries and lochans opening out to the north-west. Seen from above, the ridge is sickle-shaped, bending to the north-east, and narrowing considerably, with steep drops to the east, and easier slopes to the west. In winter it makes a particularly fine expedition with extensive views westwards.

The north branch of the track from Lone gives the easiest approach. Leave it one kilometre past the bothy and climb steadily north-west, skirting the edge of the crags, to reach the cairn marking the southern top of Arkle (757m) a distance of just over two kilometres. The summit of this top is flat and open. The ridge is followed down to the west-north-west over bouldery slopes to the head of a wide heathery gully, a useful means of descent towards Loch Stack. It then rises more steeply, narrowing considerably before reaching the main top (787m) almost one and a half kilometres further on. Three small rocky outcrops could cause slight difficulty in windy or wintry conditions, but they are easily bypassed. The quartzite near the summit has been shattered as if by some gigantic hammer to form an unusual series of deep cracks, some broad enough and deep enough to fall into.

From the summit, the prospect all around to the north and west is one of a myriad of lochans. A well-marked stalker's path can be seen winding westwards for almost eight kilometres from the foot of Foinaven, skirting the base of the terminal slopes of the summit ridge of Arkle, then back through a final patchwork of water to Lochstack Lodge and the roadside, five kilometres to the north of Achfary. To gain the path the ridge can be descended either by way of the north-east end and on past Loch na Tuath, or more easily by way of the north-west slopes of Sail Mhor. It is also possible to retrace the route along the ridge to the first top, then descend to Meall Aonghais at the head of An Garbh-choire; from there continue eastwards to rejoin the track from Lone seen climbing towards Foinaven.

Meall Horn (Fhir-Eoin) (*hill of the eagle*) (777m)
Sabhal Beag (*little barn*) (732m)
The circuit of these mountains is easily made from Lone, using the north fork of the track already described. From the highest point at the south end of the Foinaven ridge, a way is made up onto the summit of Creagan Meall Horn (729m). From there, Meall Horn, the Corbett, lies one kilometre to the south-east, steep craggy slopes falling down on the north-east side into An Dubh Loch and Lochan Ulba. The ridge now winds easily on for another three kilometres over Sabhal Mor (703m) and Sabhal Beag, then drops in a final kilometre to the Bealach na Feithe (450m). This is the halfway point on the thirteen kilometre track between Lone and Gobernuisgach Lodge – one of the two rights of way across the Reay Forest. From there it would be perfectly feasible to tackle the remaining mountains in the southern part described below, but in that event judicous route planning is required.

Meallan Liath Coire Mhic Dhughaill (*grey hill of the coire of the son of Dugald*) (801m)
Carn Dearg (*red hill*) (797m)
Meall Garbh (*rough hill*) (754m)
An ascent of Meall Garbh is most easily accomplished from the Bealach na Feithe. The two other main summits on this side of the track, Meallan Liath Coire Mhic Dhughaill and Carn Dearg, could well be included in a round trip, but these are most usually climbed from the south end of Loch More. An estate vehicle track leaves the road near the cottage at Kinloch, seven kilometres south-east of Achfary, skirting the lochside for two kilometres to the cluster of buildings at Aultanrynie from where two well-defined stalker's paths can be seen to climb steeply. The left-hand path slants up towards the west ridge of Meallan Liath for more than two kilometres. The route to the summit from the end of the path is rough but fairly straightforward. The summit ridge stretches for almost two kilometres to the summit of Carn Dearg, narrowing in places, and giving splendid views along its broken northern flank into several high secluded corries. A descent can be made by way of the south ridge of Meallan Liath Beag towards the Allt an Reinidh to pick up the return path to Aultanrynie.

Ben Hee from Mudale

Ben Hee (*fairies' hill*) (873m)

This is the only mountain of note in the south-eastern corner of the Reay Forest. It rises on the south side of the track across the Bealach nam Meirleach (*robber's pass*) which stretches for more than eleven kilometres from the north end of Loch Merkland to Gobernuisgach Lodge and the head of Strath More. This was an old drove road, still a pedestrian right of way, but only suitable for landrover traffic. The gate at the West Merkland end is usually locked.

Ben Hee is a relatively undistinguished mountain, with no special features. Starting from Loch Merkland, the main summit is easily reached by way of an obvious hill path which leaves the right of way close to the first bridge, one and a half kilometres from the start. The path follows the south side of the Allt Coir a'Chruiteir for another two kilometres then ends near a small stone shelter. Cross the stream and climb the steep broad slopes above over short heather and flat stones to the main top. Immediately below the summit, the east face of Ben Hee is split by the broken, but easy-angled slopes of the Ghorm-choire,with a fine prospect down onto the remote basin of Loch Fiag and along the length of Loch Shin, one of the largest inland waterways in Scotland. To the north there is a splendid outlook onto Ben Hope. A broad saddle leads over to the north-east top (843m), a pleasant detour of only one and a half kilometres of easy walking. From there it is best to retrace the outward route, taking a direct line across the upper slopes of Sail Garbh to regain the path along the Allt Coir a'Chruiteir.

Beinn Leoid (*sloping hill*) (792m)
Meallan a'Chuail (*hill of the cudgel*) (750m)

Beinn Leoid suffers from being in a No Man's Land between the Reay Forest and Assynt. It is probably most easily approached from the eastern side. Leave the road midway between Loch More and Loch Merkland (grid reference 357 334). A well-marked path zigzags very steeply upwards between two plantations for just over one kilometre. It then follows a more level course for one kilometre further, finishing rather abruptly beside a prominent cairn. From this point onwards the way is pathless and the broken terrain makes for tiring walking. A stalker's path which comes from Lochmore Side in the north-west can be seen dropping round the shoulder of Meall na Leitreach and making its way along past Loch Dubh, to finish steeply on the saddle between Meallan a'Chuail and Beinn Leoid. From the cairn, a direct line is taken countouring the west slopes of Meallan a'Chuail to reach the saddle, a distance of three kilometres. Once on the saddle, both summits are easily reached. The long east slope of Beinn Leoid follows the edge of broken crags to the top, giving fine views into the wilderness at the head of Loch Glendhu. This is the mountain's most impressive side, in contrast to the rather dull mass seen from the Assynt approach. Meallan a'Chuail is a very shapely peak, steeper and more broken at either end than its neighbour, but with no difficulty. From the summit of Meallan a'Chuail the return to the starting point on the A838 road can be made by following the broad north ridge of the mountain to the prominent cairn on the path of ascent. Together these two mountains make a delightful circuit, especially in winter conditions.

If approached from Assynt, the walk in to Beinn Leoid is certainly scenic and of fine character, but by any line taken from this western side the way is found to be long and indirect.

Ben Stack (*steep hill*) (721m)

This is undoubtedly the most prominent feature on the west side of the road just to the north of Achfary. Its isolation gives this rocky conical peak a disproportionate impression of grandeur. It can be climbed from either end without difficulty, although scrambling can be found if desired. The approach from the south-east has a rather boggy start, then easily follows the dyke of outcropping gneiss up to the first terrace, then on to the crest. The approach from the north-west starts from the path seen leaving the north end of Loch Stack (grid reference 264 437). Follow this path for one kilometre to Loch na Seilge, then climb directly and steeply through the outcrops to the summit. By either route the climb can be made in not much over an hour.

Beinn Spionnaidh and Cranstackie from the west

Cranstackie (*rugged hill*) (801m)
Beinn Spionnaidh (*hill of strength*) (773m)

These hills lie on the north-east side of Srath Dionard, the highest points on the long grassy ridge which drops gradually for almost fourteen kilometres towards the coastline between Loch Eriboll and the Kyle of Durness. They offer pleasant hillwalking combined with fine views across the Cape Wrath peninsula to the north-west. A rough band of gneiss and quartzite is exposed along the long south-western flank of Cranstackie which overlooks Strath Dionard, but there are no prominent crags. The western slopes are uniformly steep grass and boulders; the eastern slopes fall away more gradually towards Loch Eriboll.

The easiest approach is to leave the A838 road opposite the cottage at Carbreck, ten kilometres past Rhiconich. A rough vehicle track leads to the shepherd's house at Rhigolter, a distance of two kilometres. From the back of the house, a direct line leads steeply up the side of the stream coming from the broad, boulder-strewn corrie which lies between Cranstackie and Beinn Spionnaidh. Follow the steep north-west shoulder of Cranstackie which gives pleasant scrambling on the final 100m to the summit. An easy boulder slope leads down to the saddle with similar terrain to follow on the slope up to the flat boulder-covered summit of Beinn Spionnaidh, a distance of almost two kilometres.

The ridge can be followed north-eastwards from there, descending to the Durness road when so inclined. The way across to Meall nan Cra passes over Carn an Righe. Legend has it that Robb Donn, the famous Celtic Bard, filled his beloved rifle with tallow, and buried it deep in the rocks there when his poaching days were over. It has never been found.

PATHS AND WALKS

An extensive network of well-kept stalker's paths makes this an area of particular interest to walkers. Many permutations of route are possible, giving considerable scope for variety in both length and degree of difficulty.

Gobernuisgach Lodge to Loch Merkland via Bealach nam Meirleach. The three main paths across the mountains from west to east have already been mentioned. These converge on Gobernuisgach Lodge at the south-east end of Glen Golly, which is reached by a private road joining the Altnaharra to Hope road near the ruined bothy at Altnabad 14 kilometres north-west of Altnaharra. The lodge is mainly in use during the stalking season, and although it is occupied by a gamekeeper for most of the remainder of the year, the gate across the approach road may be found locked.

From the west side of the lodge, the right of way is followed in a southerly direction for the first kilometre before swinging to the south-east under the crags of Sail an Ias for two kilometres to join the Allt a'Chraois. The track then follows the north side of the stream to the south-west for almost three kilometres to its outflow from Loch an Aslaird, the first in a chain of three interconnected lochans. Beyond lies Loch an t-Seilg into which feeds Loch an Tuim Bhuidhe from just below the highest point of the pass (266m). Along this section of the way the track is bounded by the mountains of the southern edge of the Reay Forest, Beinn Direach, Meall a'Chleirich and the rounded mass of Ben Hee. From the head of the bealach the way continues on its south-westerly line for another three kilometres to reach the A838 road at the east side of the bridge across the Allt nan Albannach at West Merkland. The gate across the track there is locked, but there is a pedestrian's stile. From start to finish the way gives good walking. (13 kilometres).

Gobernuisgach Lodge to Achfary via Bealach na Feithe. This right of way gives an easy and direct route across the mountains of the Reay Forest from east to west. Half a kilometre from the start at Gobernuisgach Lodge the track previously described under Ben Hee leading onto the Bealach nam Meirleach is found to fork. The west branch is followed for just over one kilometre to the bridge across the Abhainn Srath Coir an Easaidh from where the path continues to climb steadily for over five kilometres due west to the head of the Bealach na Feithe (450m) on the saddle between Sabhal Beag and Meall Garbh. The way descends the broad grassy valley of Srath Luib na Seilich for six kilometres to the bothy at Lone on the south-east corner of Loch Stack at the base of Arkle. From there, the vehicle road is followed past the stalker's house at Airdachuilinn to reach the A838 road at the bridge across the outflow of Loch Stack, half a kilometre north of Achfary. The path is well-maintained and gives pleasant walking. (16 kilometres).

Gobernuisgach Lodge to Achfary via Glen Golly. This is the most northerly of the three transverse paths; it gives a longer and less direct walk across the mountains. In its initial stage the path follows the east side of the River Golly which drops in a series of waterfalls on its way through Glen Golly, a deep rocky glen fringed with birchwood. The river is crossed some four kilometres north-west of Gobernuisgach and the path continues steeply up the south-east shoulder of Meall an Lochain Sgeireich for two kilometres to the east end of Lochan Sgeireich. At this point the path forks. The north branch carries on over Creag Staonsaid for almost five kilometres to the south end of Loch Dionard where it ends. The main west branch continues to rise steadily for almost six kilometres onto the saddle (510m) between the south end of the ridge of Foinaven and Creagan Meall Horn. The steep final rise from the crossing of the Allt an Easain Ghil where it flows out of An Dubh Loch in the north-east corries of Meall Horn is particularly impressive. The path now drops down to the south-west for almost one kilometre into the hanging corrie between Foinaven and Arkle then continues its descent for another five kilometres to Lone following the north-west side of the Allt Horn throughout. From Lone the vehicle road previously described is followed out to meet the A838 road north of Achfary. (20 kilometres).

Gobernuisgach Lodge to Gualin House. Take the path along Glen Golly to the fork at Lochan Sgeireach, then follow the north branch to the south end of Loch Dionard. There is no continuous link with the track from Gualin House, which comes in along the River Dionard for six kilometres from the north-west. Srath Dionard is notoriously muddy hereabouts, and vehicle tracks have already created an ugly wide gutter running parallel to the river bank. The middle section of the route necessitates careful choice of line. The way skirts the shore of Loch Dionard and the base of Creag Urbhard giving a fine view of the magnificent cliffs. (26 kilometres).

There are two fine paths on the west side of the Achfary road (A838) which are well worth exploring. Both of these are rights of way.

Achfary to Kylestrome. From Lochmore Lodge, at the north end of Loch More, one kilometre south-east of Achfary village, a well-defined path climbs westwards to the Bealach nam Fiann, then continues in a south-westerly direction to reach the road to Scourie (A894) just to the north of Kylestrome Lodge. (10 kilometres). A lower branch of the path drops steeply down to Loch an Leathid Bhuain and follows the line of the Maldie Burn for two kilometres to the north shore of Loch Glendhu, then forks once more. The right-hand branch continues westwards to Kylestrome along the shoreline; the left-hand branch crosses at the fine waterfall at the mouth of the Maldie Burn and probes eastwards along the north shore of Loch Glendhu for four kilometres, continuing for another five kilometres to the very end of Gleann Dhu in the remote foothills leading onto Ben Leoid. (16 kilometres).

Loch Stack to Duartmore. An obvious stalker's path leaves the A838 road at the north-west end of Ben Stack (grid reference 265 437) and follows a direct line south-west past a succession of lovely secluded lochans to reach the A894 road at Duartmore Bridge, four kilometres north-west of the bridge between Kylesku and Kylestrome. (10 kilometres).

Cape Wrath to Sandwood Bay. To walk along the north-west coastline from Cape Wrath to Sandwood Bay is an unforgettable experience. The way is pathless for over twelve kilometres, the conditions underfoot are uniformly good, the outlook seawards is one of a continuous stretch of magnificent cliff scenery and inland one savours the complete emptiness of the Parph Peninsula. There are two possible water problems in wet weather. The River Keisgaig, halfway along the coast, can usually be crossed at the head of the bay at a point below the stone shelter. The river flowing through Strath Chailleach, three kilometres to the south, can cause greater problems. The series of rocky falls found as the river drops to the sea can usually be negotiated with care. If this is found to be impassable, the only alternative is to make a long detour inland along Strath Chailleach. The final approach to Sandwood Bay is best over the inland end of the band of finely coloured pegmatite crag which drops down to the river flowing out of Sandwood Loch. From the south end of the bay, a track leads on for two kilometres to Loch a'Mhuilinn where it becomes practicable, with care, for cars. A further three kilometres and it reaches Blairmore and the road to Kinlochbervie. The starting time for this walk is dictated by the ferry times at Keoldale; allow seven hours for detours and contingencies. Transport waiting at the south end is usually appreciated. (17 kilometres from Cape Wrath to Blairmore).

From Sandwood Bay, an alternative walk-out by way of Strath Shinary to the bothy at Strathan allows one to pick up a path leading to the Kinlochbervie road by Oldshore Beg. A more adventurous exit route is feasible by continuing south-east towards Creag Riabhach, then out to the Durness road (A838) at the start of the Dionard path. (22 kilometres from Cape Wrath to the A838 road).

CLIMBING

With the obvious exception of Foinaven, the majority of the mountains described here have offered little in the way of climbing to date; the area is so widespread and relatively remote however, that possibilities, especially in winter, cannot be dismissed.

The north-eastern side of Ben Stack is flanked by two bands of rock within easy reach of the road, with several short routes up to Very Difficult standard.

The rib which forms the right edge of the largest gully on the west flank of Arkle gives a Moderate route of 180m onto the ridge, with more difficult alternatives.

Creag na Faoilinn and Creag Shomhairle, both along the Strabeg track, have a number of routes ranging from 60m up to 240m, with standards varying from Difficult to Very Severe.

It is on Foinaven however, that the greatest potential has been discovered over the past twenty-five years. Seen from the west, there is no hint of the extent or

Sandwood Bay and Am Buachaille

quality of the crags which stretch along its eastern flanks overlooking Srath Dionard.
Cnoc a'Mhadaidh, the most northerly of the crags, has at least six routes of about
200m at Very Severe Standard. Routes on Creag Dubh, the gneiss cliff at the head
of Coire Duail on the east face of Ceann Garbh (unnamed on the Ordnance
Survey map) are also of about 200m in length with standard ranging from Very
Difficult to Very Severe. The three ridges which converge on the summit of the
east buttress of A'Cheir Ghorm have all been climbed; these were amongst the
earliest routes on Foinaven giving up to 180m of climbing from Moderate standard
on *Cave Ridge* to Difficult and Very Difficult on the *North* and *South Ridges*. The
steep quartzite cliff on the east face of Lord Reay's Seat attracted the first of the
later explorers, with several fine routes up to 225m being developed. The north
face of Creag Dionard has two easier routes of 150m, both Difficult. The face is
seen to have winter potential.

Creag Urbhard, the complex mass of quartzite cliff which forms the east face of
Creag Dionard, is the dominating feature of this inner sanctum of Srath Dionard.
It is described as having the greatest potential of any cliff north of Carnmore, and
the majority of the routes climbed on Foinaven are found there. Despite continuing
increase in activity, both in winter and in summer, it is unlikely that any two parties
would take exactly the same line. The crags range from 200m to 300m in height
and stretch for over one and a half kilometres. The strata rises steadily from south

to north and climbing lies along left-slanting lines of weakness rather than being truly vertical. Route-finding interest, scale, variable rock quality and remoteness all combine to make any climbing there a serious undertaking.

The five Dionard Buttresses, which lie between Creag Urbhard and Creag Alistair, give varied climbs both in winter and summer. Creag Alistair, the last cliff of any significance along the length of Srath Dionard, has slanting rakes of rock of Moderate standard reaching to almost mid-height; above this for 120m there is very steep rock, often overhanging, and giving several hard routes.

The Cape Wrath peninsula offers much scope for future exploration. Am Buachaille, the guardian stack of Sandwood Bay, has been described. The northeast face of Creag Riabhach, 4 kilometres to the north-east of Strathan (grid reference 279 638) gives universally hard lines, not for the novice. The superb seacliffs along Clo Mor present an obvious challenge. The Smoo Cave, near Durness, boasts a route of 36m, aptly named *The Hole*, and fraught with hazards. In the event of failure, swim seawards.

CHAPTER 19

Northeast Sutherland and Caithness

MAPS: Ordnance Survey   1:50,000   Sheets 9, 10, 11, 12, 16 and 17
Bartholomew   1:100,000   Sheets 59 and 60

PRINCIPAL HILLS

Ben Hope	927m	477 502
Ben Loyal	764m	578 489
Ben Klibreck	961m	585 299
Ben Armine	713m	698 240
Morven	706m	005 286
Scaraben	626m	066 268
Maiden Pap	484m	048 293
Beinn Dhorain	628m	926 156
Ben Griam Mor	592m	806 389
Ben Griam Beg	580m	832 412

In relation to its size, the north-eastern corner of the mainland of Scotland, comprising half of the district of Sutherland and the whole of Caithness, contains fewer high mountains than almost any other area described in this guidebook, the exception being the sea-girt peninsula of Morvern at the mouth of Loch Linnhe in the diagonally opposite south-western corner. It is however an area of marked contrasts, exhibiting a rich variety of landscape form closely related to the underlying geology, in which two main rock types can be clearly identified.

The hilly inland region consists mainly of stratified schists and quartzites; the lowland country stretching to the coastline is composed mainly of sandstone conglomerate. This lowland area, which covers most of Caithness, is similar in many ways to the Orkney Islands, Easter Ross and the countryside around the Moray coast. The principal mountain groupings are found along the western landward boundary – a diagonal line drawn across the central Sutherland plain from Lairg, by way of Altnaharra and Strath More, to meet the north coastline at the mouth of Loch Eriboll near Whiten Head. Lairg has long had a national reputation for is annual sheep sales. It has now developed into a thriving tourist centre, and its strategic position at the south end of Loch Shin makes it the true gateway to the north and west of Sutherland. The small community of Altnaharra,

32 kilometres to the north of Lairg, is the hub of several sporting estates, and is well known as a fishing centre.

Loch Eriboll is probably one of the finest natural harbours in the whole country – its potential undeveloped. It is also the only mainland breeding ground for the Atlantic Grey Seal. To the native Gael, Whiten Head was 'Kennagal' – *'the headland of the stranger'*, the *'stranger'* being the Norsemen who harried the coastline hereabouts over the course of four centuries. From the sea they saw two light-coloured quartzite stacks backed by a line of cliffs, in places 150 metres in height. They named the landmark 'Hvitr', or *white headland*, as it remains today.

Whiten Head marks the north-western corner of the Moine Thrust Zone, one of the classic features of Highland geology. It derives its name from the surrounding peninsula – A'Mhoine – a large, virtually uninhabited peat moss which stretches from Loch Eriboll to the Kyle of Tongue. This also gives its name to the Moine series of rocks – mainly schists – which form much of Sutherland. These Moinian rocks are generally uniform in character over large areas, and weathering has been even. It has resulted in the formation of great stretches of fairly low-lying moorlands, which are seen as a feature typical of the landscape of north-east and central Sutherland. The pattern is broken however along the eastern side of Strath More and Strath Vagastie, near Altnaharra. There the Moine attains much greater heights, with two of the three main summits being Munros. Along Strath More, the schists are exposed as a line of steep crags, rising to the summit ridge of Ben Hope in two steps; elsewhere there are few clean exposures of any great significance.

Away from the inland boundary, rounded heather-clad hills split by wide corries, peat moss, lochs and bogs, roll down towards the more cultivated coastal region, opening at intervals to form long broad straths carrying rivers of exceptional quality; each one a by-name in salmon fishing circles country-wide. Northwards, feeding into the Pentland Firth are Strath More, Strath Naver and Strath Halladale; eastwards into the North Sea are Strath Kildonan, Strath Ullie, Strath Brora and Strath Fleet.

This was the classic area of the Highland Clearances which took place during the first half of the 19th century. The straths were emptied of their native inhabitants to make way for the introduction of great flocks of sheep from the south. The people were evicted from their homes without pity, then forced to move in conditions of appalling hardship, first to the inhospitable coastal areas, where they tried with limited success to establish new communities. Melness, on the east side of the A'Mhoine Moss was settled by the evicted tenants from Strath More; Bettyhill, further along the coast, was graciously donated by the Marchioness of Sutherland to accommodate the evicted tenants from Strathnaver.

Eventually, in sheer desperation, they left in their thousands to make a new life overseas, often taking with them the names of those places they had been forced to leave; New Kildonan in Canada is now the city of Winnipeg. Some of the previous homes can still be found in the pre-clearance villages of Grummore, Grubeg and

Rosal in Strath Naver. The present-day population remains sparse. Flocks of cheviot sheep still graze the straths and the surrounding hillsides, which they now share with the native red deer. The greater part of the area has now been taken over by large sporting estates, and estate work, crofting and the tourist trade provide most of the local employment. In recent years, an increase in private speculative forestation has brought little in the way of obvious employment, but a great deal of concern over the long term effects on the habitat of such areas as the Flow Country in Caithness. A strong lobby has already developed to safeguard the excellent fishing lochs and the breeding areas of several species of rare birds, now seen to be under threat.

As one moves towards the coastal areas, the rock type and the environment are seen to change. In the north, syenite is found. It is an igneous rock, not unlike the granite of the Cairngorms, which forms Ben Loyal, a solitary mountain of exceptional quality. Towards the east, between Strath Naver and Strath Halladale, twin cones of Old Red Sandstone sprout up from the moorland. This is the rock type which now predominates, and just to the north of Strath Kildonan, between Knockfin Heights and the River Berriedale, it forms the only hills of note in the whole of Caithness.

The sandstone breaks down to form rich farming land, and agriculture still plays an important part in the economy of Caithness. Like the Orkneys, there are few trees to break the flat, rather uninspiring outlook. The straths are rich in archaeological remains. Chambered cairns, burial mounds, hut circles, hill forts and brochs are plentiful, many in remarkably good condition, a record of Man's presence over the ages. There in the fertile stretches the place names display a marked Norse flavour; on the inland heights the names are mainly the Gaelic of the native Celts, who were pushed there by the invaders.

The coastline stretches for more than 160 kilometres, from Whiten Head to Dornoch, round Duncansby Head and John o'Groats. Throughout its length, it is indented with deep geos or bays, lined with heather-topped cliffs ending in massive headlands of near-vertical cliffs of weathered sandstone, the nesting place of numerous varieties of seabirds. Weirdly shaped stacks have become isolated from the mainland by the action of the sea, and where the process is still incomplete great natural arches have formed to add to the variety of the scene. Isolated coves and stretches of unspoiled beach complete a truly magnificent seascape

ACCESS

Although the most northerly area on the Scottish mainland, access is relatively easy. A passenger rail service runs daily from Inverness to Lairg; the track then meanders through the centre of Sutherland before turning north-eastwards towards Wick and Thurso. Lairg is the best stop for onward travel to the high mountains along the west side of the area; the use of request stops further north, particularly Kinbrace and Forsinard, gives access to some of the remoter corners of interest inland.

Ben Loyal

A side benefit of oil development in the North Sea has been improved air services. The airport at Wick has regular flights from the south, and Dornoch, at the mouth of the Kyle of Sutherland, has an authorised landing-strip for small planes.

Road travel remains the most convenient method of exploring the area described. The main trunk road from Inverness and the south enters Sutherland at Ardgay, continuing through the centres of population along the east coast to Wick and Thurso. This is supplemented by a network of cross-country roads, mainly connecting with the north coastal route – A836/A838 – which leads to the north-west corner of Sutherland and Cape Wrath. The most useful road for access to the mountains of the north and west (A836) passes north from Ardgay through Lairg, then on to Altnaharra, the road centre for the surrounding area and its mountains.

From the junction some 800 metres north of the small village, three single track roads continue to meet the north coastal route already mentioned. The A836 road continues directly northwards and follows the shore of Loch Loyal to reach the village of Tongue on the east side of the Kyle of Tongue; the left-hand branch passes through Glen Mudale and Strath More, along the side of Loch Hope to reach the coast at Loch Eriboll; the right-hand branch (B873) skirts the shore of Loch Naver, then continues northwards along the river through Strath Naver to reach the village of Bettyhill, one of the main communities on the north coast.

Two other roads can be of use to the motorist or cyclist in the central part of the area – the A897 road through Strath Kildonan and Strath Halladale from Helmsdale on the east coast, to Melvich on the north coast. From Kinbrace junction at the head of Strath Kildonan, the B871 road cuts cross-country to Syre on the Strath Naver road; this is the only direct motorable east-west link in the area.

PUBLIC TRANSPORT

Rail: There are daily passenger services from Inverness and the south via Lairg to Wick and Thurso, with request stops *en route*. Those at Kinbrace and Forsinard are especially of interest.

Bus: There are daily bus services from Inverness to Thurso and Wick. (Rapsons and Scottish Citylink Coaches). All Year.
Thurso to Bettyhill. (Morrison's Coaches). Mondays to Saturdays. All Year.
Thurso to Tongue. (Dunnet's Coaches). School-days only.
Helmsdale to Kinbrace via Strath Kildonan. (Macleod's, Helmsdale). Friday only.

Postbus: Lairg – Crask – Vagastie – Altnaharra – Loch Loyal – Tongue. Mondays to Saturdays. All Year.
Altnaharra – Mudale – Strath More – Hope. Mondays to Saturdays. All Year.
Bettyhill – Strath Naver – Syre – Kinbrace. Mondays to Saturdays. All Year.
Melvich – Forsinard – Kinbrace. Mondays to Saturdays. All Year.

ACCOMMODATION

There are hotels at Lairg, Crask, Altnaharra and Tongue. Garvault Hotel, on theSyre/Kinbrace road, and Forsinard Hotel on the Kinbrace/Bettyhill road are useful for the central area. For the Caithness hills, there is a wide choice of hotels along the A9 road from Helmsdale to Dunbeath. Bed and Breakfast accommodation is generally plentiful, but at the height of summer it is wiser to book in advance in the more remote corners.

The youth hostel at Tongue is seasonal – Mid March to end of September.

There is an open bothy at Strabeg (grid reference 391 598) as previously mentioned, and also at Achnanclach, at the foot of Beinn Stumanadh (grid reference 631 511). A track leaves the roadside some nine kilometres south of Tongue, on the A836, crossing the causeway between Loch Loyal and Loch Craggie.

Camping can usually be found locally on request.

THE HILLS

Ben Hope (*hill of the bay*) (927m)

Ben Hope is the most northerly of the Munros. As with so many of the mountains in the north, it stands well apart from any neighbour, and its appearance is enhanced accordingly. It towers above the east side of the road through Strath More, at the south end of Loch Hope, from which it derives its name, rising in two great tiers from a height only just above sea level. The lower tier has a fine natural birch wood covering reaching a height of some 300 metres; the upper tier starts at 600 metres and rises to the summit in a series of rocky ribs and crags. Ben Hope presents its steepest face to the west and north-west; to the east and south-east the mountain slopes away more gradually, offering a generally easier approach to the summit. The north ridge is both steep and narrow, requiring greater care. The two eastern ridges present little difficulty, but are too remote to be of much use as a means of ascent to hillwalkers, although they provide the normal line of approach for stalking parties, and should certainly be kept in mind.

Ben Hope is best approached from the south, by way of the single track road which branches west from the crossroads at Altnaharra, already described. Halfway along Strath More this passes close to Dun Dornaigil (grid reference 457 450) an outstanding example of the type of fort architecture known as brochs. Pre-Pictish in origin, of the sixty sites recorded in Sutherland, this is one of the best examples. The walls still stand more than six metres in height, and the huge triangular lintel placed over the entrance passage is an unusual feature. From the stalker's house at Alltnacaillich, 800 metres further along the strath, a well marked path can be seen climbing steeply up the side of the burn on the right-hand side of the road. This is the Allt na Caillich, *the burn of the old woman*, which drops from the long south ridge of Ben Hope, Leiter Mhuiseil, over a fine waterfall. The broad ridge rises in a straight line to the summit of the mountain, well clear of the line of the western crags – a straightforward, rather uninspiring route, just over five kilometres from the roadside.

The normal route starts about two kilometres north of Alltnacaillich and is easily located. Stop before reaching a large steading and park in the lay-by on the south side of the burn crossing the road beside a sign post – 'Ben Hope – way up'. The path winds its way up the lower tier past a succession of delightful pools and waterfalls onto the end of the central terrace. It then takes the obvious line through the upper crags onto the steep dome-like summit slopes. The path is wet and unpleasant in its lower sections with little room for deviation. The upper slopes give firm dry walking – a line of cairns marking the edge of the crags. The largest of these cairns is sometimes mistaken for the actual summit of Ben Hope – an Ordnance Survey pillar standing more than 100 metres to the north-east. In bad visibility it should also be remembered that to the north of the relatively wide flat summit the ridge narrows, becomes more broken and drops steeply. To the trig point, three kilometres climbing from the roadside is easily accomplished in under two hours.

Ben Hope from the north end of Loch Hope

The north ridge of Ben Hope gives by far the most interesting line. The previous route is followed to the terrace, then north to follow the stream which skirts the foot of the upper tier crags to Dubh-loch na Beinne. Once past the loch, the ridge can be gained from various points according to inclination and ability. If in doubt, it is prudent to continue further round the base of the slopes almost to Loch na Seilig before starting to climb from the foot of the ridge.

This route can also be reached from a starting point at the south end of Loch Hope. A broad grassy track can be seen leaving the road towards the foot of the mountain in a north-easterly direction. This is the Moine Path, an established right of way from Loch Hope to Kinloch Lodge at the head of the Kyle of Tongue. Leave the track after one kilometre and climb the first tier on steep heather to the Dubh-loch terrace, then continue onto the north ridge as previously described.

Once gained, the ridge presents no difficulties as far as the cairn above the dip to the steep, rocky 'bad' corner – ten metres of exposed scrambling requiring a good head for heights. The escape line is to the left and is well-marked. Move thirty metres across the head of the corrie into a shallow gully, which is then followed upwards to bypass the difficult section. From there, the ridge gradually broadens towards the summit.

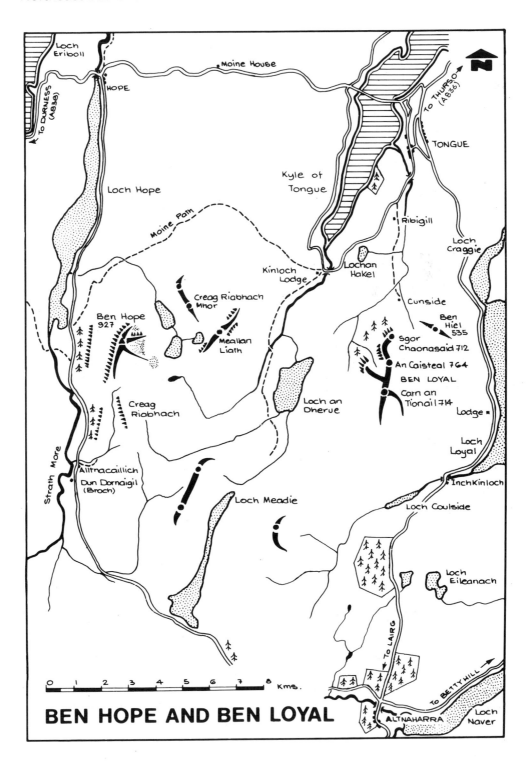

BEN HOPE AND BEN LOYAL

Ben Loyal (*hill of the elm tree*) (764m)

Despite its comparatively modest height, the isolated position and impressive profile of Ben Loyal, rising from the moorland just inland from the Kyle of Tongue, has earned it the title 'Queen of the Scottish Peaks'. The splendid outline presented by the ridge, rising and falling over its four distinctively sculptured granite tops, is only fully appreciated when viewed from the north or from the west. From the east, it loses its clearly defined outline. It rises from the roadside beside Loch Loyal up long featureless slopes. The approach across the three kilometres of wet, intervening moorland is not recommended. Beinn Stumanadh (*modest hill*), its nearest neighbour to the east across Loch Loyal, is aptly named and has little to attract the hillwalker.

Ben Loyal is normally approached from Tongue, a busy little holiday village providing a variety of useful tourist services. Nowadays the main north coastal road crosses the Kyle to Melness by bridge and causeway; the old road still winds round the head of the Kyle from the centre of the village.

Leave this road two kilometres south of Tongue and follow the farm road to Ribigill. A good footpath is taken for another two kilometres to the shepherd's cottage at Cunside. Pass the cottage on the right and climb steep grass and heather up the line of the burn coming down the face of Sgor Chaonasaid (712m) the north end of the ridge. From there, a circuit of the six main tops can be accomplished without difficulty. An Caisteal (*the castle*) (764m), the highest top, lies one kilometre south of Sgor Chaonasaid. On its south side is an intriguing line of smooth steep 15 metre faces of dark syenite. The way along to it passes the twin tors of Sgor a'Bhatain (*the boats*) – these lie slightly to the west of the main line of the ridge, with two steep buttresses near the summit. From An Caisteal, the Corbett top, Ben Loyal continues along the same line for another kilometre. First over Heddle's Top (744m), and finally onto Carn an Tionail (716m), the featureless southerly point on the ridge. From Heddle's Top, a branch ridge dips in a north-westerly direction onto the sharply cut peak Sgor a'Chleirich (663m); its south-west face overlooking Loch Fhionnaich is undoubtedly the best crag on the mountain.

To the west, Sgor a'Chleirich drops steeply for 200 metres onto the connecting ridge with the shapely terminal cone of this branch ridge. From Sgor a'Chleirich, the south-east ridge can be descended with care, then continue steeply down through the apron of birchwood to level ground. From Cunside, the round trip is just over ten kilometres.

For a more direct approach from the west side of Ben Loyal, leave the road from the bridge across the Kinloch River (grid reference 557 523) and take a line south-east across level moorland for two kilometres, then climb straight up through the birchwood into the corrie between Sgor a'Bhatain and Sgor a'Chleirich to come out on the summit below the north side of An Caisteal.

Ben Klibreck from Altnaharra

Ben Klibreck (*hill of the speckled stone*) (961m)

Ben Klibreck is the most conspicuous landmark in the central Sutherland landscape. It is a sprawling mass of mountain, bounded on the north-west by the road from Lairg to Altnaharra (A836) and Loch Naver. To the south-east it is separated from its nearest neighbour, Ben Armine, by Loch Choire. From the roadside just past Crask Inn, the main ridge stretches in a line north-eastwards for over 12 kilometres with Meall nan Con (961m), the summit of the mountain, as its midpoint. Three broad shoulders are flung out to the south-east, forming a gigantic E-shape. They enclose wide grassy corries with little in the way of exposed rock. The western slopes of Ben Klibreck are steep, but mainly heathery, with one significant exposure of crags rising onto the main ridge at a point just below the summit.

The mountain is usually climbed from its west side with a choice of three starting points – Altnaharra, Vagastie or Crask.

As one approaches Altnaharra turn east down the rough motor road sign posted 'Klibreck Farm'. This can be followed for one and a half kilometres along the south shore of Loch Naver to the farm buildings, whence a path is followed across a ford just past the shepherd's house. This is indistinct to start with, but the line soon becomes well-marked, and a good track leads directly up steep heathery slopes onto the flat summit of Meall Ailein (721m), on the north-east end of the ridge. A monument is found at the end of the spur which goes out in a south-easterly direction towards Loch Choire; a memorial to crashed airmen. The traverse of the ridge now develops into a pleasant walk along broad, richly vegetated slopes, with a stiffer final pull onto the summit. Just below the trig point a substantially-built stone shelter is found rather unexpectedly on the south-east side of the ridge. From this point the broad central spur of Ben Klibreck pushes out south-eastwards towards Loch a'Bhealaich, terminating in Meall an Eoin (774m). From the Munro top, the main ridge continues for another two kilometres onto Creag an Lochain (808m). From there, it is best to return to the saddle leading back to Meall nan Con and pick a way down the heathery western slopes to Loch nan Uan. A faint path can be followed back to Klibreck Farm to complete a fine 15 kilometre circuit. The overall distance can be curtailed as inclined.

Starting from Vagastie, the approach towards the mountain is open to variation. A new footbridge has been built across the River Vagastie at grid reference 537 289, and from there a more or less direct line is taken over the rough moorland to Loch nan Uan, then continue onto the lowest point of the ridge above.

The approach from Crask has normally little to recommend it, involving several kilometres of flat, uninteresting walking to start and finish. The logical line onto the ridge is by way of Cnoc Sgriodain (544m) at the south-west end. A circular expedition can be contrived by descending the clear grassy slopes on the south-east to gain the path which follows the side of Loch Choire and Loch a'Bhealaich. This is followed back over the Bealach Easach - a remote and picturesque corner - with a final five kilometre stretch along Srath a'Chraisg. A covering of snow makes it a far more interesting proposition.

Ben Armine (*hill of the warrior*) (713m)

Ben Armine is the collective name given to the broad ridge of hills which stretches from the north-eastern end of Loch Choire towards the great straths which open onto the east coast of Sutherland. There is no outstanding feature to catch the eye, but the overall sense of remoteness gives the area a unique character. The outlying western hills send steep heathery slopes into the basin of Loch Choire; to the north-east, the main ridge drops unexpectedly in a series of steep walls enclosing five fine corries. The north-west ridge of Ben Armine rises gradually from Loch Choire Lodge for fifteen kilometres over five tops: Meall Ard (634m), Creag na h-Iolaire (694m), Meall nan Aighean (695m), Creag a'Choire Ghlais (705m) and Creag Mhor(713m) the highest point in the area. From there the ridge slopes southwards towards Ben Armine Lodge, one of the three habitations to be found in an area covering almost 400 square kilometres.

Ben Armine and Loch Choire are primarily deer forests, and the comprehensive network of tracks is well maintained. Undoubtedly this is an area for the walker, by virtue of the distance of the hills from motorable roads and the limitations of the

Morven from Corrichoich bothy

estate vehicle tracks serving the shooting lodges. The foot tracks are found to interconnect, thereby opening several interesting possibilities for long cross-country walking expeditions.

Morven (*big hill*) (706m)
Scaraben (*divided hill*) (626m)
Maiden Pap (*maiden breast*) (484m)

These splendid little hills tend to be neglected by virtue of their peculiar location tucked into the south-east corner of Caithness between the head-waters of the Rivers Berriedale and Langwell. They have exceptional character. Morven is the highest point in Caithness, a regular cone of Old Red Sandstone which is a prominent landmark from all directions. Scaraben is a different type of hill. It consists of three smoothly-rounded tops of quartzite of the Moine series which form a ridge stretching for almost four kilometres to fill the entire area between the two rivers. Maiden Pap forms the third point of the triangle – it is a miniature version of Morven with delightful scrambling to its summit on rough sandstone conglomerate. Three kilometres equidistant from all three is an additional bonus in the form of the Smean, a weird sandstone outcrop reminiscent of Dartmoor.

The whole group is best approached from the north side. Leave the main trunk road (A9) at Dunbeath at the junction on the south side of the village (grid reference 155 300). A good single track road is followed westwards for nine kilometres to Braemore. Park at the telephone kiosk beside the bridge over the River Berriedale. A good track passes Braemore Lodge and takes to the open moors through a gate past the stalker's cottage. Maiden Pap rises two kilometres along the track, but it is best to continue for a further two kilometres to the estate bothy at Corrichoich, where the track finishes. Morven lies two kilometres further west across flat moorland and the ascent can be tackled anywhere; the slopes are uniformly steep heather with a final 100 metres of delightful scrambling to the summit. From there the remainder of the tops described can be climbed in any order selected. If the complete circuit is tackled, it makes for a long strenuous day, but one to be recommended.

Beinn Dhorain (*hill of the otter*) (628m)

This rounded hill of Old Red sandstone is the highest point along the sides of Glen Loth, ten kilometres to the west of Helmsdale. It can be reached by the rough track which leaves the A9 road eight kilometres north of Brora and winds its way over Glen Loth to Kildonan Lodge at the mouth of Strath Kildonan. Its main interest is in winter when the glen normally has good snow-holding potential.

Ben Griam Mor (*big dark hill*) (592m)
Ben Griam Beg (*small dark hill*) (580m)

These twin cones of Old Red Sandstone are conspicuous landmarks in the central

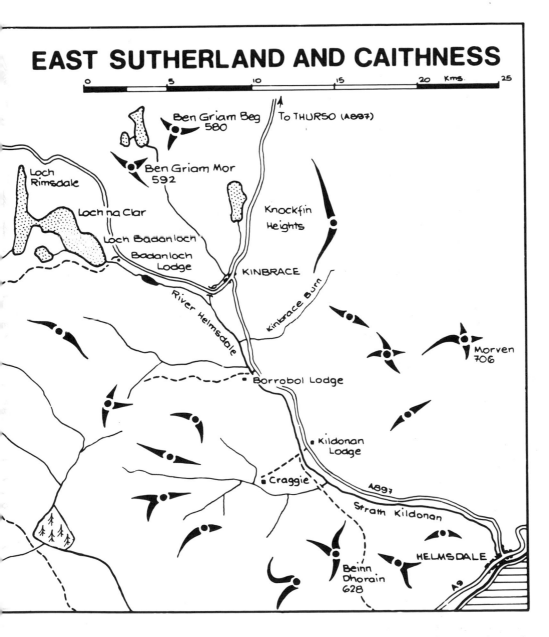

EAST SUTHERLAND AND CAITHNESS

part of this area. They lie between Strath Halladale and Strath Naver and can be reached from Forsinard or from Garvault, on the Kinbrace/Syre road. From either direction the distance is six kilometres.

Ben Griam Beg is important as an archaeological site. It has on its summit the remains of the highest hill fort in Scotland.

PATHS AND WALKS

As has been already suggested, the whole of the Ben Armine/Loch Choire area lends itself to exploration on foot. A well-kept system of tracks encircles the Ben Armine ridge, connecting Ben Armine Lodge in the south-east with Loch Choire Lodge in the north-east. These in turn connect with tracks leading westwards towards the Lairg road (A836) opening up a variety of combinations for pleasant cross-country walking expeditions of 25 kilometres and more if need be. Three possible approach routes to the area can be suggested: further permutations are left to individual choice.

1. From Sciberscross (grid reference 775 101) 20 kilometres inland along Strath Brora from Brora on the A9 trunk road. An estate road leaves from the keeper's house on the west side of the main road and winds 13 kilometres inland over the open moorland to Ben Armine Lodge. The gate on the main road is seldom locked, but the track is entirely unsuitable for anything except landrover or similar vehicles.

2. By way of Strath Kildonan or Strath Naver. Leave the Syre/Kinbrace road at Loch Badanloch. If the gate there is locked enquire at the stalker's house at Badanloch Lodge. An estate road similar in condition to the Sciberscross road reaches Loch Choire Lodge across 18 kilometres of moorlands.

3. From the Lairg/Crask road (A836) an estate road branches eastwards at a bridge eight kilometres north of Lairg (grid reference 575 140). Dalnessie Lodge (usually occupied by a shepherd) is reached after seven kilometres; the track continues for another two kilometres across the River Brora. It now links with a shooting path which follows the east bank of the river for almost three kilometres and then swings away to meet one of the Ben Armine tracks at Green Face.

4. The approach from Crask to Loch Choire has been noted previously.

CLIMBING

The mountains described have given little in the way of climbing routes to date. The north-west face of Ben Hope has a wide gully flanked by two rocky ridges as a main feature. This attracted the earliest explorers and most of the activity which followed. Climbs of up to 240m are recorded varying in difficulty from Moderate to Difficult. The gullies there may produce some good winter routes however.

Climbing on Ben Loyal has been more prolific. A gully climb on the north prow of Sgor Chaonasaid gives 150m of mixed climbing – Very Difficult. There are routes on the twin tors of Sgor a'Bhatain; one Mild Severe and one Very Severe. The best possibilities would seem to be on Sgor a'Chleirich. There have been two routes climbed there of over 250m, both Very Severe.

Climbing on Ben Klibreck is limited to the crags below the main summit, *Eyrie Buttress*; routes are of 150m ranging in difficulty from Moderate to Difficult. It must be recorded that the earliest routes here were made by local egg collectors in adverse conditions.

On Morven, looking towards Maiden Pap

The coastline offers countless possibilities for climbing and there has been an increasing amount of exploration. On the north coast, the headlands of Holborn and Dunnet enclose Thurso Bay, and further to the east beyond Clardon Head, Dunnet Bay with its six kilometres of golden sands. Dunnet Head reaches a height of over 120m above the sea, the most northerly point on the mainland of Scotland. The Clett Rock, a 50m high stack which stands off Holborn Head, has been climbed, the standard is Severe. The stack is separated from the mainland by a 24 metre wide channel with dangerous currents. Expert local advice is advocated. On the north side of Dunnet Bay, Dwarwick Head is reputed to give the best sea-cliff climbing in Caithness and has been intensively investigated. Climbing is also recorded on Creag an Dherne (grid reference 540 470), Strathy Point (grid reference 820 690), Holborn Head (grid reference 109 716) and Duncansby Stacks (grid reference 400 719). The headland of Duncansby lies three kilometres east of John o'Groat's House, the north-east tip of mainland Scotland.

A GLOSSARY OF SOME GAELIC WORDS WHICH OCCUR
COMMONLY AS PART OF PLACE NAMES

aber	*river mouth, confluence*
abhainn, amhainn	*stream, river*
achadh	*field, plain, meadow*
aird, ard	*high point, promontory*
airidh, airigh	*shieling*
allt, ault	*burn, stream*
an	*the*
aonach	*ridge, height*
ath	*ford*
ba	*cattle*
bac	*bank*
ban, bhan	*white*
baile, bhaile	*town, township*
barr	*top, summit*
bealach, bhealach	*pass, col*
beg, beag, bheag	*small*
beith, beithe	*birch tree*
beinn, bheinn	*hill, mountain, peak*
breac, bhreac	*speckled*
bidean, bidein	*peak*
binnean, binnein	*peak*
bo	*cow*
bodach	*old man*
bothan	*hut, bothy*
braigh, bhraigh	*brae, high place*
buachaille	*herdsman*
buidhe, bhuidhe	*yellow*
buiridh, bhuiridh	*bellowing (of stags)*
cailleach	*old woman*
caisteal	*castle*
camas, camus	*bay, channel, creek*
caol, caolas	*narrows, strait*
caor (pl. caoran)	*rowan*
caora (pl. caorach)	*sheep*
capull	*horse*
carn	*cairn, hill, pile of stones*
ceann	*head*
coinneach	*mossy place*
cioch (gen. ciche)	*breast, pap*
ciste	*chest, coffin*
clach	*stone, stony*
clachan	*village*
cleit	*cliff, crag, reef*
cnap, cnoc	*hillock*
coille	*wood, forest*
coire	*corrie, high mountain valley*
corran	*low pointed promontory*
creachan	*rock*
creag	*cliff, crag*

crois	*cross*
croit	*croft*
cruach	*hill, heap*
cul	*back*
curra	*bog, marsh*
da	*two*
dail	*dale, field, plain*
damh	*stag*
darach	*oak, oakwood*
dearg	*red*
deas	*south*
diollaid	*saddle*
donn	*brown*
dorus	*door, gate, strait*
drochaid	*bridge*
drum, druim	*ridge*
dubh, duibh	*black*
dun	*fort*
each	*horse*
eag (eagach)	*notch (notched place)*
ear	*east*
eas	*waterfall*
eighe	*file, notched*
eilean	*island*
eun (gen. eoin)	*bird*
fada (gen. fhada)	*long*
faochag	*whelk*
fearn	*alder tree*
fiadh	*deer*
fionn	*white*
fraoch	*heather*
frith (gen. frithe)	*deer forest*
fuar	*cold*
fuaran	*well*
gabhar	*goat*
gaoth	*wind*
garbh	*rough*
geal	*white*
gearr	*short*
gille	*young man, boy*
glac, glaic	*hollow, trough*
glas, ghlas	*green, grey*
gleann	*glen*
gorm	*blue*
iar	*west*
iasgair	*fisherman*
inbhir, inver	*rivermouth, confluence*

inch, innis	*island, meadow*	rath	*fort*
iolaire	*eagle*	righ	*king*
		ron	*seal*
ken, kin (from ceann)	*head*	ruadh	*red*
knock (from cnoc)	*hillock*	rubha, rudha	*point, promontory*
kyle (from caol)	*narrows, strait*	ruigh	*shieling*
ladhar	*hoof, fork*	sail	*heel*
lag, lagan	*hollow*	scuir	*rocky peak*
lairig	*pass*	seann	*old*
laogh	*calf*	sgeir	*reef*
laroch	*dwelling place*	sgiath	*wing*
leac	*slab, stone*	sgor, sgorr, sgurr	*rocky peak*
leathad	*slope*	sith (sithean)	*fairy (fairy hill)*
leitir	*slope*	slochd	*deep hollow, pit*
liath	*grey*	sneachd	*snow*
lochan	*small loch*	spidean	*peak*
		srath	*strath, wide level glen*
maighdean	*maiden*	sron	*nose*
(mhaighdean)		stac	*steep rock, sea-stack*
meirg	*rust-coloured*	stob	*peak*
mam	*rounded hill*	stuc	*peak, steep rock*
maol	*headland, bare hill*	suidhe	*seat*
meadhon	*middle*		
meall	*hill*	teallach	*forge, hearth*
moin, mhoin, moine	*bog, moss*	tigh	*house*
monadh	*hill range*	tioram	*island dry at low tide*
mor, mhor	*big*	tir	*land*
muc (gen. muic)	*pig*	tobar	*well*
muileann	*mill*	toll, tholl	*hole*
(gen. mhuilinn)		tom	*hill*
mullach	*top, summit*	torr	*small hill*
		tuath	*north*
na, nan	*of, of the*		
		uaine	*green*
odhar	*dun-coloured*	uamh	*cave*
		uig	*bay*
poite	*pot*	uisge	*water*

INDEX OF PLACE NAMES